Books for You

 Bibliography Series

Books for You

An Annotated Booklist for Senior High

Fourteenth Edition

Kylene Beers and Teri S. Lesesne, Editors,

and the Committee on the Senior High School Booklist
of the National Council of Teachers of English

With a Foreword by

Michael Cart

NCTE Bibliography Series

National Council of Teachers of English
1111 W. Kenyon Road, Urbana, Illinois 61801-1096

Prepress Services: Precision Graphics

Production Editor: Bonny Graham

Interior Design: Doug Burnett

Cover Design: Precision Graphics

Series Cover Design: R. Maul

Cover Illustration: From *To Every Thing There Is a Season,* illustrations by Leo & Diane Dillon. Published by The Blue Sky Press, an imprint of Scholastic, Inc. Illustrations copyright ©1998 by Leo & Diane Dillon. Reprinted by permission.

NCTE Stock Number: 03723-3050

About the Cover

This beautiful art, created by Leo and Diane Dillon, is from the front cover of the picture book *To Every Thing There Is a Season,* published by The Blue Sky Press, an imprint of Scholastic, Inc. The Dillons have used multiple media to illustrate the timeless Bible passage that begins "To every thing there is a season, and time to every purpose under the heaven; A time to be born, and a time to die . . . A time to weep, and a time to laugh . . . A time to get, and a time to lose. . . ." Drawing on artistic techniques from cultures around the world, these award-winning artists celebrate on many levels the diversity of our culture as they illustrate the passage of our lives. We chose this image for the cover of *Books for You* not only because it reflects the diversity of the books within this volume and the readers who we hope will enjoy it, but also because as we move from one millennium to the next, as we watch our high school students move from grade to grade, as we ourselves progress through life, we each must learn that, indeed, to everything there is a season. We are most grateful to Leo and Diane Dillon and Blue Sky Press/Scholastic, Inc. for allowing us to reprint this art on our cover.

ISBN 0-8141-0372-3

ISSN 1051-4740

This edition of Books for You *is dedicated*
to the memory of Robert Cormier—
a writer and friend who
dared to disturb the universe . . .
1925–2000

Contents

About the NCTE Bibliography Series

The National Council of Teachers of English is proud to be part of a tradition that we want to share with you. In our bibliography series are four different booklists, each focused on a particular audience, and each updated regularly. These booklists are *Adventuring with Books* (pre-K through grade 6), *Kaleidoscope* (multicultural literature, grades K through 8), *Your Reading* (middle school/junior high), and *Books for You* (senior high). Together, these volumes list thousands of recent children's and young adult trade books. Although the works included cover a wide range of topics, they all have one thing in common: they're good books that students and teachers alike enjoy.

How are these volumes put together? The process begins when an educator who knows literature and its importance in the lives of students and teachers is chosen by the NCTE Executive Committee to serve as booklist editor. That editor then works with teachers and librarians who review, select, and annotate hundreds of new trade books sent to them by publishers. It's a complicated process that can last three or four years. But because of their dedication and strong belief in the need to let others know about the good literature that's available, these professionals volunteer their time and serve as an inspiration to all of us. The members of the committee that compiled this volume are listed in the front of the book, and we are truly grateful for their hard work.

As educators know, no single book is right for every reader or every purpose, so inclusion in this booklist is not necessarily an endorsement from NCTE. But it does indicate that the professionals on the booklist committee feel that the works listed here are worthy of teachers' and students' attention, whether for their informative or aesthetic qualities. Similarly, exclusion from an NCTE booklist is not necessarily a judgment on the quality of a given book or publisher. Many factors—space, time, availability of certain books, publisher participation—may influence the final shape of the list.

We hope that you'll find this booklist a useful resource for discovering new titles and authors, and we hope that it will encourage you to consult the other booklists in the series. Our mission is to help improve the teaching and learning of English and the language arts, and we hope you'll agree that the quality of our booklists contributes substantially toward that goal.

Zarina M. Hock
Senior Editor

Acknowledgments

This edition of *Books for You* represents the hard work of many people. Committee members read books, discussed books, traded books, and annotated books. Together, this group—composed of authors, high school and middle school teachers and librarians, university professors, and graduate students—reviewed over twenty-five hundred books. These folks not only read the books we sent them, but many committee members, on their own, sought out titles to find "just the right book" for a particular category. These dedicated professionals agreed to serve on this committee with full understanding of the time commitment required. "I'll do it," Peggy Hill told us, "because I want to help create something that connects kids to books." Time and time again we heard that comment. Without the efforts of this committee, this book would be but a wish.

We must also thank the publishers whose generosity provided the books for this booklist. Their willingness to send review copies not only for this edition but also for all the previous editions underscores their ongoing commitment to helping teachers, librarians, and students to find just the right book. Without the support of publishers, this booklist would not exist.

In addition to publishers and committee members, we must give a special thanks to Alexis Schadel, Meredith Beers, and Cali Wright, who opened book shipments, cataloged books, created databases, and carried box after box after box of books to the post office. Many thanks to them for always smiling when we asked them to do yet one more thing or run one more errand.

The NCTE staff, especially Pete Feely, Bonny Graham, and Cheri Cameron, have supported us throughout this project. Many thanks for their willingness to answer questions and offer guidance.

Finally, we must offer heartfelt thanks to our husbands, Brad Beers and Henry Lesesne. We would not have begun this project without their support; we could not have finished it without their encouragement. Throughout the making of this book, they drove carpool, ran errands, fixed dinners, rubbed shoulders, carted boxes of books, carted more boxes of books, and listened with patience to unending talk about young adult literature and the trials and tribulations of creating this booklist. More thanks to our children and grandchildren, who fill our lives with laughter, joy, and continual talk of the books they love.

Kylene Beers and Teri Lesesne

Foreword: A Brief History of Young Adult Literature

[**Editors' note:** *As we leave the twentieth century, we thought it only appropriate that this edition of* Books for You *pay homage to the history of young adult literature. To provide this retrospective, we could think of no better person than Michael Cart, former president of the Young Adult Library Services Association of the American Library Association and author of* From Romance to Realism: Fifty Years of Growth and Change in Young Adult Literature.]

Future literary historians, I'm convinced, will view the 1990s as one of the most significant and breathtakingly dramatic decades in the history of young adult literature. A ten-year period of turbulence and change, the decade began in a miasma of gloom and doom, as many leading experts could be heard arguing that the genre was, if not dead, at least dangerously near the grave. Alleen Pace Nilsen, co-author of *Literature for Today's Young Adults,* noted, for example, that assessing the "health of the genre" was not unlike "gathering at the bedside of an ailing loved one" (1994, 30). Connie Epstein, former editor-in-chief of Morrow Junior Books, agreed, saying, "Some editors, marketing directors, and subsidiary rights directors have been wondering whether the young adult novel was ready for burial" (1990, 237). One of these editors was Linda Zuckerman of Harcourt Brace who, at an American Library Association conference in 1994, categorically declared, "I think young adult literature is dying" (quoted in Cart, 1996, 161).

And yet, by the end of the decade the "patient" had not only recovered, but was also in the most robust good health imaginable. In fact, young adult literature had entered a new golden age, as evidenced by the amazing quality of the books then being published (many of which you will find in the annotated lists that follow). Even more evidence could be found in the 1999 establishment of the Michael L. Printz Award, which will be presented annually by the Young Adult Library Services Association (YALSA) to the author of the best young adult book of the year, with "best" being defined solely in terms of literary merit. Young adult literature, long regarded as "the B-team of literature"—as novelist Chris Lynch memorably put it (1994, 37–38)—is now the first team, having finally come of age as a viable body of literature.

If young adult literature didn't end in the 1990s, it didn't begin then either, although exactly when the genre first appeared is open to argument. Pioneering young adult librarian Margaret A. Edwards once said that it was with the 1936 publication of Helen Boylston's novel *Sue Barton, Student Nurse* that "the dawn of the modern teen age story came up like thunder" (1954, 88). Others have called Maureen Daly's 1942 book *Seventeenth Summer* the first young adult novel. Still others declare it was S. E. Hinton's *The Outsiders,* although that didn't appear until 1967.

Specific titles aside, it is inarguably true that there could not be a literature for young adults until there were readers called "young adults." Not until, that is, society recognized adolescence as a separate, distinct period of life, just like childhood and adulthood. And that didn't occur until the 1930s. Before then, young people moved directly from childhood to adulthood, a passage that took place on the day they started their first job. Why did this change in the 1930s? The answer is simple: It was then that the Great Depression forced many teenagers out of work and into high school. Although only 6 percent of Americans graduated from high school in 1900, by 1939, 75 percent of teenagers were enrolled in high schools, which became a kind of de facto social laboratory for the development of this new period of transition that came to be called "adolescence."

Publishers were quick to recognize the commercial potential of this new audience of adolescent readers, and cautiously began issuing titles targeted at them. I've already noted the publication of *Sue Barton* in 1936. This was followed two years later by another important early title, John R. Tunis's first sports novel, *The Iron Duke.*

Despite these bellwethers, it was not until the 1940s that teenagers became firmly enough entrenched as a social phenomenon that a literature published for them could become viable. Enter *Seventeenth Summer,* which, as previously noted, was published in 1942. Although technically published for adults, it was quickly discovered by teenaged readers, who embraced it as their own. Indeed, if the novel were to be published today, it would almost certainly be as a young adult novel (as would another important adult novel, J. D. Salinger's 1951 *The Catcher in the Rye*).

Two years after Daly's novel was published, *Seventeen* magazine debuted. Four years later, the first issue of *Hot Rod* was published, and by the end of the decade, a market researcher named Eugene Gilbert was acknowledging that "our salient discovery is that within the past decade teenagers have become a separate and distinct group in our society" (quoted in Palladino, 1996, 110).

The success of *Seventeenth Summer* inspired countless other novels of teenage love by such one-time household names as Betty Cavanna, Janet Lambert, Anne Emery, Rosamund DuJardin, and James L. Summers. So many of these titles appeared that the 1940s are remembered principally as the decade of romance fiction, although by the end of the decade, books about cars were also appearing. The first classic in this genre was Henry Gregor Felsen's *Street Rod*, published in 1950.

Another new genre, science fiction, also became a factor in the young adult lists of the late forties, beginning with the 1948 publication of Robert A. Heinlein's first novel for teens, *Farmer in the Sky*. Andre Norton followed in 1952 with *Star Man's Son, 2250 A.D.*

Animal, sports, action-adventure, and career stories were also staples of the 1940s and 1950s, decades in which genre fiction clearly ruled. Walter Farley's still-popular Black Stallion series debuted in 1941 and straddled the border between children's and teenage literature. John R. Tunis continued to rule as king of sports fiction in the forties and fifties. And as for action-adventure, Howard Pease, who had begun writing in the 1920s, enjoyed enormous popularity through the 1950s, as did Robb White, whose first novel, *The Nub*, had appeared in 1935. White's remarkable career spanned half a century, with his most popular novel, *Deathwatch*, appearing in 1972, and his final book, *Two on the Isle*, being published in 1985.

Arguably the most popular kind of career fiction remained the nurse story. Boylston wrote six more Sue Barton books (as well as four about a girl actor named Carol Page), while the twenty-volume Cherry Ames series by Helen Wells rivaled Sue Barton for reader popularity throughout most of this period.

Romances that were set in idealized small towns, and that focused on first dates, true love, and the junior prom, obviously had a place in the *Saturday Evening Post* era of the 1940s and 1950s. But by the 1960s, the United States was changing, and so were the lives of teenagers. It was time for a new kind of book to be born: the novel of realism, which reflected—with refreshing candor—the real lives of real teenagers. It was time, in short, for a Tulsa, Oklahoma, teenager named S. E. Hinton to write *The Outsiders*, her mean streets account of social warfare between the lower-class kids she called "greasers" and their upper-class counterparts, the "socs" (short for "socials"). There is no question that this novel—with its first-person voice, its contemporary urban setting, and its exploration of cutting edge social issues—revolutionized the field of young adult literature, introducing the kind of fiction to which we now refer when we routinely employ that phrase "young adult literature." Nevertheless, it should be remembered that a second writer of realism, Robert Lipsyte, was also present at the creation. His first novel, *The Contender,* was published in that same landmark year, 1967, and endures as a modern classic.

It should also be acknowledged that these novels—important as they are—did not appear out of nowhere. Earlier in the 1960s, writers like Frank Bonham, Nat Hentoff, and even Jeanette Eyerly (who in the 1970s became queen of the problem novel) were also experimenting with realistic fiction, but it is Hinton and Lipsyte who were the first to give us fully realized, enduring works of realism, the popularity of which opened the floodgates to this new kind of young adult novel and, in the process, said good-bye to innocence. And high time, too, because teenagers themselves were eager for books that were more relevant to the realities of their daily lives. Hinton spoke for her whole generation (she was only seventeen when *The Outsiders* was published) when she wrote,

> The world is changing, yet the authors of books for teenagers are still fifteen years behind the times. In the fiction they write romance is still the most popular theme, with a horse-and-the-girl-who-loved-it coming in a close second. Nowhere is the drive-in social jungle mentioned. In short, where is the reality? (1967, 26)

Obviously the reality was now to be found in the pages of *The Outsiders, The Contender,* and, within a year, in Paul Zindel's first novel, *The Pigman,* and, a year after that, in John Donovan's first novel, *I'll Get There, It Better Be Worth the Trip,* the first novel to explore the theme of homosexuality. The times they were indeed a-changin', as Bob Dylan sang. So were the books that depicted them, and never more vigorously or momentously than in 1974, when Robert Cormier's first novel, *The Chocolate War,* was published. Not only was it one of the first works of literary fiction for young adults, but it was also arguably the first that dared suggest not all endings in teenage fiction—or in teenage lives, for that matter—would be happy ones. Cormier's theme of determinism versus free will has proven to be an enduringly powerful one, and that—along with his skill as a stylist, his mastery of characterization, and his prowess as a plotter—have reinforced his stature as the single most important writer in the history of young adult literature.

The Chocolate War and Cormier's other 1970s novels *I Am the Cheese* and *After the First Death* would, in themselves, have been enough to mark the decade of the seventies as the first golden age of young adult literature, but Cormier did not write in splendid isolation. Hinton, Lipsyte, Zindel, and Donovan continued to produce significant fiction, and were joined by a host of remarkable new talent, writers whose names today have come to constitute a veritable who's who of young adult authors, including Richard Peck, Lois Duncan, M. E. Kerr, Walter Dean Myers, Judy Blume, Robin McKinley, William Sleator, Felice Holman, Robert Newton Peck, Sandra Scoppettone, Barbara Wersba, Sue Ellen Bridgers, Terry Davis, Harry Mazer, Norma Fox Mazer, Zibby Oneal, and Ouida Sebestyan. What an amazing roster of writers, all of whom published for the first time in the 1970s. Thanks to strides in racial equality, which resulted from the civil rights struggle of the 1960s, the 1970s also saw the appearance of African American faces in young adult literature for the first time, in books by Rosa Guy, Walter Dean Myers, Julius Lester, Alice Childress, Virginia Hamilton, Mildred Taylor, and others.

Unfortunately, not all was golden in the seventies. A less salutary trend was the rise of the so-called problem novel. These ripped-from-the-headlines works of social realism were offshoots of the trend toward realistic fiction, but without the redeeming literary quality of the works by Cormier, Hinton, Lipsyste, and others. Typically these problem novels were populated with one-dimensional characters, written in a pedestrian style and focused thematically on what came, jokingly, to be called "the problem of the week"—for example, parental divorce, teenage pregnancy, abortion, or drug and alcohol abuse. Because it was the problem that drove the narrative—not the characters—these were didactic works of near nonfiction masquerading as novels. Their treatment of problems became increasingly shrill and sensationalistic as the decade drew to a close.

Perhaps as a result, readers began rejecting realism and clamored instead for a return to the happy days of the 1940s and 1950s and an attendant revival of romance. Publishers were only too happy to oblige, and in short order, the problem of the week had been reduced to nothing more significant than finding a date for the junior prom. In other words, the same subject and the same scenarios that had been hallmarks of teen fiction forty years earlier became prominent once again. There was one difference, however. Formerly readers had looked for the new novel by their favorite author. Now they looked for the new novel in their favorite series, whether it was called Wildfire or Sweet Valley High, Caprice or Sweet Dreams, First Love or Wishing Star.

Which brings us to another hallmark of the 1980s: it was *the* decade of the young adult paperback book, especially the original paperback series like the romances cited above. It was also the decade when teenagers themselves became the marketing target of publishers. This was an important new trend because traditionally the market for hardcover young adult books had not been teens (who didn't buy books for themselves) but libraries and schools. As institutional budgets took a nosedive in the 1980s, however, publishers began searching for a new consumer, and discovered that teens themselves would buy books if the format, price, and subject were right. The smaller, more affordable, more portable (and more easily hidden, if you were a teen who didn't want to be caught reading) paperback fit the bill in every respect. Publishers found the perfect outlet for these books: the chain bookstores that had become fixtures of shopping malls, which had become a home away from home for U.S. teens in the 1970s.

Although publishers did well, economically, by focusing on paperback series, the literature did not. This is one reason why, by the end of the decade, many observers were pronouncing the form near death. Another reason was the dip in the teenage demographic. Beginning in 1977 and continuing throughout the eighties, the number of young people entering their teenage years declined dramatically. Happily, it was not all bad news in the 1980s. A number of important new writers emerged, including Bruce Brooks, Francesca Lia Block, Brock Cole, Chris Crutcher, Cynthia Voigt, Ron Koertge, and Virginia Euwer Wolff, among others.

Nevertheless, the number of novels being published continued to decline, as did the age of fictional protagonists, who were growing ever younger. Indeed, as the 1980s drew to a close, young adult literature was fast becoming middle-school literature, targeted at readers as young as eleven. Why? In part it was due to the new middle-school movement in the United States, but also in part to the increasing market importance of super bookstores (Barnes & Noble, Borders, Crown, and others), whose buyers focused their attention on young adult books that came dangerously close to being children's books. No wonder that, by 1994, editor Marc Aronson was referring to teens in high school, the traditional young adult audience, as "this strange no-person zone" (Cart, 1996, 162).

As if all this weren't enough, the rampant popularity of horror, another new genre series that burst on the publishing scene at the very end of the decade, seemed to sound the death knell for serious young adult literature. And yet, by the second half of the 1990s, young adult literature had not only revived, it was flourishing. What happened? The answer involves a number of factors, but perhaps most significant was a turnaround in teenage demographics. Beginning in 1992, teenagers became one of the fastest-growing segments of the U.S. population. Also significant was a turnaround in institutional budgets, which began recovering. In addition, a number of venturesome and gifted young editors started working in young adult literature, including people like Marc Aronson at Henry Holt and David Gale at Simon & Schuster. And in an effort to expand the market, publishers began experimenting with what has come to be called the crossover book, whose potential audience can be as old as twenty-five. The targeting of this new, older audience by publishers made it possible for writers to produce more adventuresome, risk-taking, and literary fiction.

The result of all this activity was the emergence around 1997 of what I have already dubbed a new golden age of young adult literature. Interestingly, it is not confined to the United States, although young adult literature—like jazz and the Broadway musical—is a distinctively American gift to world culture. This renaissance is now a global phenomenon. Consider the emergence of writers like Margaret Mahy and Maurice Gee in New Zealand; John Marsden and Sonya Harnett in Australia; Tim Wynne-Jones, Martha Brooks, and Diana Wieler in Canada; Emma Donoghue in Ireland; and Melvin Burgess and Diana Wynne Jones in England.

Nor is the golden age confined to fiction. Nonfiction is also flourishing, although for many years it had functioned only as a kind of utilitarian adjunct to the curriculum. James Cross Giblin and Russell Freedman changed all that when they began producing literary-narrative nonfiction in the 1980s; Giblin's *Chimney Sweeps* won the American Book Award in 1983, while Freedman's *Lincoln: A Photobiography* captured the 1987 Newbery Medal. As Hinton and Lipsyte had done with fiction, so Giblin and Freedman did with nonfiction: they opened the floodgates to a new kind of expository prose, a narrative art form from which readers can derive the same kind of aesthetic pleasure and entertainment they find in fiction. The design and illustration of nonfiction is also blossoming, thanks in large part to the pioneering graphic efforts of the British publisher Dorling Kindersley. Today's nonfiction is a feast not only for the mind, but for the eye as well.

It is also a wonderful period for poetry. The new, nearly universal fascination with this form has resulted in the creation of a National Poetry Month (April); the establishment of the position of poet laureate at the Library of Congress; and the embrace of poetry as performance, resulting in a spate of open microphone nights at coffeehouses, library poetry readings, poetry slams, and a plethora of PBS programming. Particularly noteworthy in the field of young adult poetry is the rise of the novel in verse, a form pioneered by Mel Glenn. More recently, we have seen similar work by Virginia Euwer Wolff *(Make Lemonade)* and Karen Hesse *(Out of the Dust),* while Sonya Sones's *Stop Pretending* was a finalist for the 2000 *Los Angeles Times* Book Prize. Even the grandmaster of young adult fiction, Robert Cormier, has written a novel in verse *(Frenchtown Summer),* which won the 2000 *Los Angeles Times* Book Prize.

It is also a golden age for the short story, a renaissance that first appeared in adult literature in the early 1980s, but is now a fixture of young adult literature as well. As evidence, consider the new theme-driven collections of original commissioned stories (my own collection, *Tomorrowland: Ten Stories about the Future,* is an example) that have become increasingly popular and are giving writers latitude to experiment and be innovative. Newer writers like Ellen Wittlinger *(What's in a Name?)* and E. R. Frank *(Life Is Funny),* as well as established pros like Walter Dean Myers *(145th Street)* and Chris Lynch *(Whitechurch),* are also writing volumes of short stories that, linked by common characters and themes, are blurring the lines between the novel and the short-story collection.

Graphic and visual elements are becoming increasingly important as well, as reflected in the rise of graphic (or adult picture) novels like Art Spigelman's *Maus.* Related to this phenomenon is the burgeoning field of the young adult picture book, pioneered by Lane Smith and John Scieszka in such titles as *The True Story of the Three Little Pigs* and *The Stinky Cheese Man,* with the latter being both a Caldecott Honor Book and an ALA Best Book for Young Adults in 1993.

Clearly, for young adult literature, the decade of the 1990s was a nearly unrivaled period of growth, change, and innovation. Happily, because the increase in the teenage population is projected to continue through the year 2011, we can presume that the new decade that dawned with the turn of the century will be a similarly expansive period.

Although the decades of the 1970s and 1990s are particularly notable for the evolution of young adult literature as art, every decade since the 1930s has given readers the gift of books that are distinguished by their literary excellence or their groundbreakingly innovative aspects. Because this is a book whose purpose is the formulation of lists of outstanding books for young adults, it might be appropriate to conclude this introduction with my own list of titles that I think are particularly significant. Here it is, with entries arranged by decade of publication.

— Michael Cart

Significant Titles Sorted by Decade

1930s	Author	Title
	John R. Tunis	*The Iron Duke*

1940s	Author	Title
	Maureen Daly	*Seventeenth Summer*

1950s	Author	Title
	Henry Gregor Felsen	*Two and the Town*
	J. D. Salinger	*The Catcher in the Rye*

1960s	Author	Title
	John Donovan	*I'll Get There, It Better Be Worth the Trip*
	Ann Head	*Mr. and Mrs. Bo Jo Jones*
	S. E. Hinton	*The Outsiders*
	Robert Lipsyte	*The Contender*
	Paul Zindel	*The Pigman*

1970s	Author	Title
	Anonymous (Beatrice Sparks and Linda Glovach)	*Go Ask Alice*
	Judy Blume	*Forever*
	Robert Cormier	*After the First Death*
	Robert Cormier	*I Am the Cheese*
	Robert Cormier	*The Chocolate War*
	Terry Davis	*Vision Quest*
	Lois Duncan	*Killing Mr. Griffin*
	Rosa Guy	*The Friends*
	Virginia Hamilton	*The Planet of Junior Brown*
	M. E. Kerr	*Gentlehands*
	Robert Lipsyte	*One Fat Summer*
	Anne McCaffrey	*Dragonsinger*
	Robb White	*Deathwatch*

1980s	Author	Title
	Francesca Lia Block	*Weetzie Bat*
	Bruce Brooks	*The Moves Make the Man*
	Brock Cole	*The Goats*
	Chris Crutcher	*Stotan!*
	Nancy Garden	*Annie on my Mind*
	Diana Wynne Jones	*Knight's Moving Castle*

1980s	Author	Title
	M. E. Kerr	*Night Kites*
	Ron Koertge	*The Arizona Kid*
	Margaret Mahy	*Memory*
	Margaret Mahy	*The Changeover: A Supernatural Romance*
	Walter Dean Myers	*Fallen Angels*
	Walter Dean Myers	*Scorpions*
	Gary Paulsen	*Hatchet*
	Richard Peck	*Remembering the Good Times*
	Cynthia Voigt	*Izzy Willy-Nilly*
1990s	**Author**	**Title**
	Laurie Halse Anderson	*Speak*
	Avi	*Nothing but the Truth*
	Francesca Lia Block	*Baby Bebop*
	Bruce Brooks	*What Hearts*
	Brock Cole	*The Facts Speak for Themselves*
	Robert Cormier	*We All Fall Down*
	Paul Fleischman	*Whirligig*
	Annette Curtis Klause	*Blood and Chocolate*
	Lois Lowry	*The Giver*
	Chris Lynch	*Gypsy Davy*
	Victor Martinez	*Parrot in the Oven: Mi Vida*
	Kyoko Mori	*Shizuko's Daughter*
	Walter Dean Myers	*Monster*
	Louis Sachar	*Holes*
	Ellen Wittlinger	*Hard Love*

Works Cited

Cart, Michael. 1996. *From Romance to Realism.* New York: HarperCollins.

Edwards, Margaret A. 1954. "The Rise of Teen-age Reading." *Saturday Review* 37 (November 13): 88–89, 95.

Epstein, Connie. 1990. "A Publisher's Perspective." *Horn Book* 66 (March/April): 237–41.

Hinton, S. E. 1967. "Teenagers Are for Real." *New York Times Book Review* (August 27): 26–29.

Lynch, Chris. 1994. "Today's YA Writers: Pulling No Punches." *School Library Journal* 40 (1): 37–38.

Nilsen, Aileen Pace. 1994. "That Was Then, This Is Now." *School Library Journal* 40 (April): 30–33.

Palladino, Grace. 1996. *Teenagers: An American History.* New York: Basic Books.

Introduction

As an English teacher, chances—good chances—are that you like to read, and perhaps even love to read. You know which book you want to read next, and which author you are waiting to learn has published another book. You know whether it is mysteries or histories, poems or short stories, realistic fiction or science fiction that sends you in search of a comfortable chair, a rainy day, and nothing to do but get lost in the world that awaits you between the covers of a book. You know exactly which books are for you. But often that's not true for our students. They aren't sure which books are the books they want.

Books for You—an annotated list of books high school students might enjoy reading—is created with students in mind. Arranged by topic (animals, adventure and survival) and genre (short stories, realistic fiction, poetry), this annotated volume gives students a chance to discover which book is for them.

Using This Book—A Word to Students

Books for You was written with you, a high school student, in mind. That means several things.

First, if the end of the plot is important to the enjoyment of the book, the summary doesn't give away the ending. If you look in the mystery section, you'll find summaries that set the stage and explain the nature of the mystery, but none tell you whodunit.

Second, if you are looking for a certain type of book—mystery, historical fiction, romance—check the table of contents and see if there's an entire chapter devoted to that topic. If so, you can turn to that section and begin scanning for a title or summary that catches your interest. If you don't find your topic there, don't give up. Turn instead to the end of the book. There you'll find three indexes: an author index, a title index, and a subject index. If you've got a favorite author—such as Joan Lowery Nixon, Walter Dean Myers, or Naomi Shihab Nye—then look to the author index to see if we've included books by that author in this edition. If you don't have an author or title in mind, look to the subject index. There you'll find a list of the many topics that are considered in the books we have listed here, everything from adoption, alcohol, and anorexia to zines, zoology, and the zodiac. In addition, if you want or need to read an award-winning book, appendix A includes a list of books that have won awards since 1997.

Third, while you certainly should use this book to help you find books you want to read on your own, don't forget that this is also a great resource to use for class assignments. Whether it's a book for your English class or a book to help you with a history report, *Books for You* lists one thousand fiction and nonfiction titles.

Fourth, once you find a book you think looks interesting, what do you do? Many of these books will be in your school library. If they are not there, ask your librarian if your district has an interlibrary loan program that would allow you to obtain the book from another school's library. If that's not possible, try your city or county library. If those two options don't work, try a local or online bookstore.

Fifth, you might be wondering how we decided which books to include and which not to include. To begin with, you must keep in mind that this edition of *Books for You* considered only books published in 1997, 1998, or 1999. So, if your favorite book was published in 1996, chances are it won't be listed here. You might check the previous edition of *Books for You* to see if it appeared in that edition. Our criteria for inclusion in *Books for You* was fairly simple and straightforward: We asked ourselves, "Does this seem to be a book that a high school student would enjoy reading?" That's a difficult question when you consider the diversity of high school students. Some of you love horror books; others think they are horrible. Some of you enjoy light, humorous books; others prefer more difficult, serious texts. Some of you are first-year students in high school, barely fourteen years old; others of you are going on nineteen. You have a broad range of interests, experiences, and expectations. Consequently, some of you look for very realistic or gritty language and actions from the characters you encounter in books, while others might be offended by certain language or behavior. The committee who chose the books included here tried to keep a wide range of tastes in mind, while constantly asking ourselves, "Is there something redeeming in this book?" If we included a book with graphic language, violence, or behavior, we also included a comment in the annotation to make you aware of these features of the book. As always, you are the best judge of what offends you. If the language a character uses or the choices a character makes bother you, stop reading the book. The books in *Books for You* are included so that all students can find the books that work for them. Please don't expect all books to be appropriate for all readers. Keep looking through this book until you find the ones that are right for you.

One last word on what helped us decide whether or not to include a particular book. We only reviewed books that were sent to us by publishers. Some publishers sent us many books; others sent only a few. Some even sent books generally read by adults—such as books by John Grisham or Danielle Steele—but often enjoyed by teenagers. If we had a chance to see the book, we considered it for inclusion. If a book didn't come to us, however, we didn't know it existed, and consequently couldn't review it. Many thanks to those publishers who, for three years, sent us thousands of books to review.

A Word to Teachers

This edition of *Books for You* includes over one thousand books published in the past three years that this committee believes will interest or be of help to today's high school students, or to you as you plan units of study. We've included fiction and nonfiction, easy and difficult texts, classics and contemporary novels. This edition, like previous editions, includes books with characters who are African American, Latino, Asian American, Native American, European American, Hindu, Muslim, Jewish, Christian, agnostic, and atheist. There are gay and lesbian characters, straight characters, and characters whose parents are divorced, separated, and married happily. There are books with characters facing a range of situations: moving, finding friends, facing first loves, alienation, fear, and loss. It's a multicultural book in the broadest sense. Are there books included here that will offend some readers? Most certainly. No one book will work or be appropriate for all readers. We've tried to tell readers enough about the book in the annotation to give them a general sense of the nature of the book they are about to read. However, we encourage you to look carefully at any book you're considering using in the classroom. Inclusion in this booklist does not constitute an endorsement of a book by NCTE. It simply means it is a book that another adult has found merit in, and has recommended for inclusion in this booklist for high school students.

The readers who made these recommendations were school librarians, university professors, middle-school and high-school English teachers, book review columnists, and authors. Several of the readers for this edition of *Books for You* have served on previous booklist committees, reviewed young adult literature for review journals, or served on the board of the Adolescent Literature Assembly of the National Council of Teachers of English (ALAN). Many thanks to each of those folks who diligently read books and wrote annotations.

It's our hope that this book not only will help you connect your students to reading, but also will help you with curriculum planning as you look for books to complement a unit of study. We hope you enjoy scanning the chapters. As you do, we're sure you'll find a book that's right for you and, more important, right for your students.

Kylene Beers and Teri S. Lesesne

1 Adventure and Survival

"Life is either a daring adventure or nothing."
Helen Keller

1.1 Armstrong, Jennifer. **Shipwreck at the Bottom of the World: The Extraordinary True Story of Shackleton and the *Endurance*.** Crown, 1998. 134 pp. ISBN 0517800136. Nonfiction.

This thrilling real-life adventure tells the story of Ernest Shackleton and twenty-seven men who were stranded in the Antarctic for nineteen months between January 1915 and August 1916. These men sailed from England in August 1914 hoping to become the first team of explorers to cross the frigid continent. Five months later, their ship, the *Endurance*, became trapped in ice. They lived that first winter on the ship. After an iceberg crushed the ship, they camped on an ice floe for five months. Using the provisions they got off the ship, including three lifeboats, they eventually made their way to an uninhabited and inhospitable island named Elephant Island, located six hundred miles from Cape Horn. From there, Shackleton led a smaller group of men across eight hundred miles of treacherous glacier-filled seas to reach South Georgia Island, where they eventually found help for the others still stranded on Elephant Island. This story of courage, daring, and raw survival shows Shackleton's commitment to getting every one of his men home alive.

1.2 Bauer, Joan. **Backwater.** Putnam, 1999. 185 pp. ISBN 0399231412. Fiction.

Preferring the study of history, sixteen-year-old Ivy Breedlove's dislike of her family's tradition of pursuing careers as lawyers and judges results in her family's disapproval. When she takes over the compilation of the family history, she learns that her father's sister has also shunned family tradition and may be living a secluded life as a hermit in the Adirondack Mountains. Ivy's determination to find the missing woman and reunite her family results in her surviving storms, a collapsed cabin, and a shifting ice lake—that shifts while she's on it!

1.3 Brown, Sandra. **Unspeakable.** Warner, 1998. 439 pp. ISBN 0446519790. Fiction.

George longs to be a cowboy. When he gets the opportunity, he doesn't hesitate to leave his home in Texas to go on a cattle drive. The drive isn't exactly what he expects it to be. Instead of riding herd over the cattle, he is assigned to stay with the cook's wagon, chop wood, and do anything else that the cook needs done. Finally George gets his chance when the job of rounding up the horses in the morning and bedding them down at night are added to his chores. Things would almost be perfect if it weren't for Charlie, who doesn't want an African American around. Before long, Charlie challenges George and a fight ensues. The boss quickly puts an end to the fight, but the tension of the moment doesn't disappear.

1.4   Buettner, Dan. **Africatrek: A Journey by Bicycle through Africa.** Lerner, 1997. 105 pp. ISBN 0822529513. Nonfiction.

Can you imagine bicycling 11,855 miles across the continent of Africa, from Tunisia in the north to South Africa in the south? Author Dan Buettner, his brother, and two other men took 262 days to cross fourteen African countries on their bike trek. Along the way, they crossed the Sahara Desert, encountered rain forests, were offered grasshoppers and centipedes to eat, and fought tsetse flies, malaria, dysentery, and guerrilla soldiers. The photographs of their adventures help make the trip come alive for readers.

1.5   Burks, Brian. **Wrango.** Harcourt Brace, 1999. 118 pp. ISBN 0152018158. Fiction.

Carl Herbold escapes from prison with only one thing on his mind: revenge against his stepfather, Delray Corbett, whose testimony was crucial in his conviction. He heads to Texas, letting nothing and nobody get in his way, even if it means killing. Carl enjoys violence. Corbett lives on a remote farm with his grandson and widowed daughter-in-law Anna. Fearing for her safety because Anna is both deaf and mute, Corbett seeks help from a mysterious drifter.

1.6   Carter, Alden R. **Between a Rock and a Hard Place.** Scholastic, 1999. 224 pp. ISBN 0590374869. Fiction.

Mark doesn't want to take the wilderness canoe trip, but he doesn't have much choice because his father sees it as a rite of passage that Mark must go through. Reluctantly, Mark and his diabetic cousin Randy head off on the ten-day trip. Though not good friends, the boys decide to make the best of their situation. For a while they have a good time until a bear destroys the food pack that contains Randy's insulin. Now with no supplies and Randy in trouble, Mark must figure out how to ensure their survival.

1.7 Clifford, Hal. **Falling Season: Inside the Life and Death Drama of Aspen's Mountain Rescue Team.** Mountaineer, 1999. 272 pp. ISBN 0898866332. Nonfiction.

Hal Clifford is a member of Mountain Rescue–Aspen, a group of volunteers dedicated to helping those who are lost or injured in the Aspen mountains. In this book, he provides first-hand knowledge of real life emergencies that he's been a part of. He writes, "I keep climbing, up toward a pile of rocks that is the 12,430-foot summit. I look up again and see a body, 50 yards ahead. It is lying head downhill, face turned up to the sky." This book will keep you wanting to read page after page to find out if he makes the rescue or not. It's a great read that also gives information on what it takes to rescue someone in danger.

1.8 Coleman, Michael. **Weirdo's War.** Orchard, 1998. 184 pp. ISBN 0531301036. Fiction.

Daniel, a brilliant student, has been a loner all through school, and is constantly the object of fellow student Tozur's mean practical jokes and Coach Axelmann's taunts. Daniel's father decides that it would be good for him to spend a week on a school trip in the wilderness. This trip is even worse than Daniel anticipates. Who is there? His two worst tormentors, of course. Although his boots are thrown in the lake and he is led into thorny bushes, he does not let his humiliation show. During one activity he is partnered with Tozur. The two must find their way back to camp with only a map and a compass. They arrive late, and Axelmann, jeering as usual, finds them. When it begins to rain, they all take refuge in an abandoned mine. Almost as soon as they enter the mine, the floor collapses and the three are trapped in a deep, dark pit. Axelmann is unconscious and Tozur is terrified. It is up to Daniel to try to find a way out or they will die; they must work together in order to survive.

1.9   Cook, Robin. **Vector.** Putnam, 1999. 400 pp. ISBN 03991447144. Fiction.

A Russian scientist and immigrant who has become disenchanted with his life as a taxi driver in the United States decides to return to his homeland. Before leaving, he intends to release a large dose of anthrax into Central Park in New York City. He hopes to kill millions in retaliation for wrongs he believes he faced while in the United States. However, his plans meet stumbling blocks as Dr. Jack Stapleton and Dr. Laurie Montgomery realize that a deadly disease is infecting people. Can the two doctors prevent the deaths of thousands of innocent victims? To do so means tracking down a wily killer.

1.10   Durbin, William. **The Broken Blade.** Delacorte, 1997. 163 pp. ISBN 0385322240. Fiction.

Pierre hears his father chopping wood one Saturday morning; he knows he should get up, since it is his job, but the bed feels so good that he falls back asleep. That decision changes his life. The next thing Pierre hears is his father's scream. His father has severed his thumb. Although he is still in school, Pierre knows his family will starve if his father does not fulfill the pledge he made when he signed on as a voyager. But that job requires that he be able to paddle the twenty-four hundred miles necessary to trade fur. Pierre, although only thirteen, feels compelled to sign on to take his father's place. He is much too young, but thankfully is big for his age. In the beginning he counts each stroke he takes with the paddles. By the end of the first day the blisters on his hands are bleeding. When he stops for the day he discovers that he cannot unbend his hands. The older men call him "puppy," and play tricks on him, but in time he shows that he is as brave and strong as the best of them.

1.11   Durbin, William. **Wintering.** Delacorte, 1999. 191 pp. ISBN 0385325983. Fiction.

In this companion book to *The Broken Blade*, the adventure continues for fourteen-year-old Pierre La Page, a *voyageur* in the French Canadian wilderness. Traveling with a diverse crew from the North West Company, Pierre and his companions trade goods for furs and learn how to live in a land of beauty and danger. Soft-spoken Commander McHenry shares his love of books with

Pierre. Bowman Jean-Baptiste Beloit teases Pierre unmercifully and disgusts him with his crude ways. Young Louie, seeking refuge and peace from his home life, looks to Pierre to lead the way. When they stop to stay the winter, the Ojibwe befriend the traders. Pierre and Red Loon forge a friendship as they explore the wilderness. The destinies of all these individuals are entwined as they confront wild bears, forest fires, gut-wrenching cold, and near-starvation in their effort to survive the winter.

1.12   Dygard, Thomas, J. **River Danger.** Morrow Junior Books, 1998. 151 pp. ISBN 0688148522. Fiction.

When eleven-year-old Robbie Douglas's father is injured and unable to take their planned canoe trip down the Buffalo River in Arkansas, his brother Eric, who just graduated from high school, reluctantly accompanies him. On the second day of their trip, Robbie wanders off, winding up at an old barn used by a car theft ring, where he is captured by the criminals. Eric now must find his way through the woods to find help and plan a way to rescue Robbie.

1.13   Easley, Maryann. **I Am the Ice Worm.** Yearling, 1998. 128 pp. ISBN 044041444X. Fiction.

Fourteen-year-old Allison is flying from California to Alaska to visit her mom when the small plane she's in crashes. She is the only survivor and wonders just how long she'll live in this frozen land until a hunter comes along and takes her to a small, remote Inupiat village. There, Allison must learn a new way of life that doesn't involve microwaves, CDs, and shopping malls.

1.14   George, Jean Craighead. **Julie's Wolf Pack.** HarperCollins, 1997. 208 pp. ISBN 0060274077. Fiction.

You probably read *Julie of the Wolves* and then read *Julie,* the sequel. Now you can continue to follow the lives of the wolves that saved Julie when she was that young child those many years ago. In this third book, told from the point of view of the members of the wolf pack, you'll meet Kapu, Sweet Fur Amy, Ice Blink, and Willow Pup Julie. The lives of the wolves are explained in detail, and George's meticulous description of what life in a wolf pack is like makes this as valuable a book on studying wolves as it is an adventure book about the dangers the wild wolves face.

1.15 Gerstein, Mordicai. **Victor: A Novel Based on the Life of the Savage of Aveyron.** Farrar, Straus and Giroux, 1998. 258 pp. ISBN 0374381429. Nonfiction.

Based on the true story of a feral child captured in the forests of Aveyron, France, at the end of the French Revolution, this book describes the attempts of Dr. Jean-Marc-Gaspard Itard to civilize the "savage" boy. Although others believed the boy to be retarded and uneducable, Itard spent years trying to prove the opposite.

1.16 Herman, John. **Deep Waters.** Philomel, 1998. 198 pp. ISBN 0399232354. Fiction.

From his older brother, thirteen-year-old Andrew hears all about Camp Winasaukee and is thrilled to be there, making new friends, excelling in swimming, and meeting his first girlfriend. However, he comes under the influence of the clever, manipulative, rule-breaking Julian, who constantly fuels the rivalry between two male counselors over an attractive female counselor named Marsha. When the death of one of the rivals occurs, Andrew must examine his role in the tragedy, which still haunts him two years later.

1.17 Hill, David. **Take it Easy.** Dutton. 1997. 163 pp. ISBN 0525457631. Fiction.

Rob is on a hiking expedition with five other teenagers and a guide who is taking them through the thick bush country in New Zealand. Everything is going fine until their guide dies sometime during the second night. When the teens become lost in the bush and one of them becomes critically injured, Rob and another boy leave to try and find help. Soon his companion is injured, and Rob must go on himself. Will he get help in time?

1.18 Hite, Sid. **The Distance of Hope.** Henry Holt, 1998. 198 pp. ISBN 080505054X. Fiction.

Fifteen-year-old Yeshe Anjur is the heir to the throne of Padma. During the past two years, he has mysteriously begun to lose his eyesight. There is no medical explanation for this loss. His parents send him on a journey, along with three bodyguards, to find the legendary White Bean Lama, who may be able to restore his sight. There are many perils along the way; only Yeshe and one bodyguard finally reach the Lama, where the secret of Yeshe's ailment is revealed.

1.19   Hobbs, Will. **Far North.** Morrow Junior Books, 1996. 226 pp. ISBN 0688141927. Fiction.

When Clint, their bush pilot, promised them a sightseeing tour they would never forget, fifteen-year-old Gabe Rogers and Raymond Providence had no idea that it was going to include a five-month struggle to survive in Canada's Northwest Territories. After the destruction of their plane and Clint's death, Gabe and Raymond learn to survive in the wilderness with the help of Raymond's elderly and dying great-uncle, Johnny Raven, a Native American.

1.20   Hobbs, Will. **Ghost Canoe.** Morrow Junior Books, 1997. 185 pp. ISBN 0688141935. Fiction.

Fourteen-year-old Nathan lives on the lighthouse island with his parents and helps to keep the light going. During a particularly bad storm, a ship crashes and everyone is believed dead, but mysterious footprints in the sand, the robbery of the local trading store, and the stories about a "hairy man" and hidden treasure raise suspicions about the shipwreck. When Nathan moves to town with his mother, he has an opportunity to investigate. With the help of his Makah friend, Nathan soon becomes involved in a dangerous hunt to find answers. What he doesn't realize is that he has only a short time to catch a killer before he becomes the next victim.

1.21   Hobbs, Will. **Jason's Gold.** Morrow Junior Books, 1999. 221 pp. ISBN 0688150934. Fiction.

Upon learning that gold has been discovered in the Klondike, fifteen-year-old Jason Hawthorn finds his way home, where he hopes to borrow a portion of his brothers' inheritance so he can head to the Klondike. However, when he reaches Seattle, Jason discovers his brothers have themselves already left for Canada and the Klondike. As he races to catch up with them, Jason meets an adventurous girl, an unknown author named Jack London, as well as the brutal perils of the wilderness.

1.22 Hobbs, Will. **The Maze.** Morrow Junior Books, 1998. 200 pp. ISBN 0688150926. Fiction.

Fourteen-year-old Rick Walker, who has bounced from one foster family to another, is sentenced to a juvenile detention center for a petty offense. After reporting corruption at the facility, he is forced to flee for his life, ending up in a remote part of Utah's canyon country called the Maze. Befriended by bird biologist Lon Peregrino, Rick not only extricates himself from his personal maze, but helps bring to justice two antigovernment criminals who are hiding a cache of weapons.

1.23 Hobbs, Will. **River Thunder.** Delacorte, 1997. 201 pp. ISBN 0385323166. Fiction.

This companion novel to *Downriver* brings back those rebellious adolescents, the self-proclaimed "Hoods in the Woods," one year later as they attempt to conquer the mighty Colorado River . . . legally, this time. Believing that Al, their previous guide, invited them, they return only to discover that their invitations were sent by the troublemaking Troy, who is still interested in Jessie. They are game for the experience, but record rainfall and runoff make the already dangerous trip even more demanding and treacherous.

1.24 Holcomb, Jerry Kimble. **The Chinquapin Tree.** Marshall Cavendish, 1998. 189 pp. ISBN 0761450289. Fiction.

Jessie and her younger half-siblings don't want to leave the foster family they're living with. They particularly don't want to leave if that means going home to their abusive mother. When they hear that that's exactly what's going to happen, they run away from their foster home, escaping through a tunnel and going around a cliff to take up residence in a huge, centuries-old tree. There, these kids show that they know what it takes to survive—not fairy god-mothers and wishes, but hard work and courage.

1.25 Junger, Sebastian. **The Perfect Storm: A True Story of Men against the Sea.** Harper Mass Market Paperback, 1998. 301 pp. ISBN 006101351X. Nonfiction.

Weathermen called it "the storm of the century." People caught in it called it "hell." Here's the story of fishermen caught at sea when this terrifying storm hit the United States eastern seaboard in

October 1991. Six members of the swordfish boat the *Andrea Gail* were lost five hundred miles from home in hundred-foot waves. The last moments of those fishermen as well as others caught in the storm is recreated with radio dialogue, eyewitness accounts, and other published material about the storm.

1.26 Kaniut, Larry. **Danger Stalks the Land: Alaskan Tales of Death and Survival.** Griffin, 1999. 320 pp. ISBN 0312241208. Nonfiction.

Think of Alaska and you think of glaciers, ice floes, fishing, hunting, frigid temperatures, stunning sunsets, polar bears, kayaking, avalanches, and long months filled with dark days and even darker nights. Listen to stories about Alaska and you'll hear stories of fearless (and sometimes not-so-fearless) explorers who have been stranded on icy cliffs, faced wild bears, been dunked in freezing water, or been caught in an avalanche. Read their true stories in this book that not only shows you how people survive in the toughest of conditions, but also shows you the natural beauty of this rugged state.

1.27 Kehret, Peg. **I'm Not Who You Think I Am.** New York: Dutton, 1999. 153 pp. ISBN 0525461531. Fiction.

While celebrating her thirteenth birthday, Ginger notices someone staring at her. Her mother reassures her, saying that the woman is probably lonely and is just sharing her celebration from afar. Several days later, after realizing that the woman is following her, Ginger decides to confront her. The strange woman insists that she is Ginger's real mother, but there are many inconsistencies in her story. Soon Ginger realizes that this woman will stop at nothing, including kidnapping her.

1.28 King, Stephen. **The Girl Who Loved Tom Gordon.** Scribner, 1999. ISBN 0684867621. Fiction.

Nine-year-old Trisha McFarland is hiking in the Maine woods with her mother and older brother. Tired of listening to the two of them bicker, Trisha slips off the path for a moment, seeking a private place to relieve herself. When she comes back to the path, she can no longer see or hear her mother and brother. Determined to retrace her steps, Trisha moves slowly, carefully calculating her next move. Eventually, she must admit that she is hopelessly lost. Plagued by eerie noises, hungry mosquitoes, and a growing sense of dread, Trisha has only one source of comfort: the Walkman radio over which she can still receive the play-by-play for the Boston Red Sox team. Her favorite pitcher, Tom Gordon, becomes an imaginary traveler as Trisha determinedly tries to find her way back to civilization.

1.29 King, Stephen. **Hearts in Atlantis.** Scribner, 1999. 523 pp. ISBN 0684853515. Fiction.

This collection of stories takes readers on a journey from the 1960s to the 1990s, from a summer of innocence for a band of eleven-year-old friends, through the burgeoning war in Vietnam during their college years, to their troubled adult lives in the present. In "Low Men in Yellow Coats," eleven-year-old Bobby Garfield's summer focus changes from the new Schwinn bike he covets to his fear for his new friend Ted's life. The title story, "Hearts in Atlantis," picks up the story of Bobby's childhood girlfriend, Carol, and her experiences in the new antiwar protest movement, experiences that lead her to trust the wrong people. The final story in the collection has Bobby and Carol reunited for the funeral of their old chum Sully John. Through these stories we learn the history of a very turbulent time in America and in the lives of King's main characters.

1.30 Krakauer, Jon. **Into Thin Air: A Personal Account of the Mt. Everest Disaster.** Villard, 1997. 291 pp. ISBN 0679457526. Nonfiction.

One out of every four persons who attempts to climb Mt. Everest, the highest summit on earth, dies in the quest. But as author Krakauer says, "Any person who would seriously consider it is almost by definition beyond the sway of reasoned argument." On May 10, 1996, accomplished climber and guide Rob Hall, Krakauer, seven of Hall's clients, three guides, and four Sherpas set out to attack the summit. Traffic jams, inadequate oxygen, and a raging storm confirm the unpredictability of events at twenty-nine thousand feet.

1.31 LaHaye, Tim, and Jerry B. Jenkins. **Nicolae: The Rise of Antichrist.** Tyndale, 1997. 420 pp. ISBN 0842329145. Fiction.

This is the third book in the popular Left Behind series, which began with *Left Behind* and continued with *Tribulation Force.* In the first book, millions of people were left behind after the Rapture, the moment when Christians are swept away, leaving unbelievers on Earth. In the second book, Rayford Steele, his daughter Chloe, her husband Buck, Rayford's new wife Amanda, and their pastor Bruce Barnes have all become believers, and they suspect they know the identity of the prophecized antichrist. In this third book, the saga continues as those characters attempt to convert unbelievers, while facing death at every corner.

1.32 Lawrence, Iain. **The Smugglers.** Delacorte, 1999. 178 pp. ISBN 0385326637. Fiction.

Traveling in a coach to Dover, sixteen-year-old John Spencer and his father receive an ominous warning from a fellow passenger that the schooner they intend to buy has been "christened with blood." There is death in store, they are told, for all who touch the *Dragon*, a smuggler's ship. Ignoring the warning, John and his father purchase the *Dragon* and hire the mysterious Captain Crowe to pilot the schooner on its journey to London. Just before she sails, John's father is called away and John must voyage alone with Captain Crowe, dashing Tommy Dusker, and a few good men. Shortly after they leave the dock, John spots a body floating in the water. Days later, he receives a whispered warning that someone on the ship is plotting to kill him and throw him to the seas. Trusting no one, John battles the smugglers and the seas, wondering if he will live to see his father.

1.33 Marsden, John. **The Dead of Night.** Houghton Mifflin, 1997. 278 pp. ISBN 0395837340. Fiction.

This sequel to *Tomorrow, When the War Began*, begins with Ellie recapping how she and six friends returned from a campout to discover their homes empty and their families imprisoned by an enemy. Now the kids continue the fight as they look for friends, search for a guerrilla group, and come to grips with a tragic death. Their choice to fight this enemy means they live undercover and on the run, and must learn to trust no one except themselves.

1.34 Marsden, John. **A Killing Frost.** Houghton Mifflin, 1998. 275 pp. ISBN 0395837359. Fiction.

Continuing the drama begun in *Tomorrow, When the War Began* and *The Dead of Night*, Ellie and her friends are still fighting the enemy that has taken over their Australian community. These five teens, hiding in a place called Hell—"a wild basin of rock and bush"— keep up the resistance against the enemy by blowing up bridges and finally freeing the sixth member of their group, Kevin. Ellie and Homer face a critical moment when they stow away on a ship in order to blow it up. The bomb detonates and suddenly the two teens are swimming for their lives as guns fire all around them.

1.35   McCaughrean, Geraldine. **The Pirate's Son.** Scholastic, 1998. 294 pp. ISBN 0590203444. Fiction.

When pirate's son Tamo White leaves the confining life of an eighteenth-century English private school, he takes the orphan siblings Nathan and Maud Gull with him. Their adventures on Tamo's native Madagascar force them to examine their personal and religious beliefs as they encounter deceitful pirates and exotic natives. Nathan's prudish upbringing clashes with native beliefs, and he desires nothing more than to return to England. The once-timid Maud savors the Malagasy way of life. Tamo's much-anticipated meeting with his mother is not what he expects, but she does prove her love for her son. This coming-of-age story elaborately portrays three young people searching and finding their place in the world.

1.36   McManners, Hugh. **101 Essential Tips: Hiking.** Dorling Kindersley, 1998. 72 pp. ISBN 0789427761. Nonfiction.

Learn to cook outdoor meals, tie knots, or use a compass with this book of helpful tips for safe and enjoyable hiking and camping. For would-be campers who aren't sure what weather signs to watch for, need help in building a campfire from scratch, want a refresher course on first aid, or are interested in some valuable information about the environment, this book is the one to have. Diagrams, pictures, and brief explanations make this resource easy to access.

1.37   Myers, Edward. **Climb or Die.** Hyperion, 1997. 180 pp. ISBN 078682350X. Fiction.

Fourteen-year-old Danielle and her thirteen-year-old brother Jake are riding with their parents on a Rocky Mountain road in a blinding snowstorm. When the car skids off the road and both parents are injured, Danielle and Jake wait for a while and then realize that help isn't coming. Jake knows that there's a weather look-out up on Mt. Remington and Danielle believes she knows enough about mountain climbing to get them there safely. So with no other choices and the temperature dropping, the two set off on a climb that tests their courage and will to live.

1.38 O'Reilly, James, Larry Habegger, and Sean O'Reilly, editors. **Danger: True Stories of Trouble and Survival.** Travelers' Tales Guides, 1999. 309 pp. ISBN 1885211325. Nonfiction.

This anthology of twenty-eight stories provides readers with non-stop adventure. From "Hyena" ("No sterilization? Who cares? I was alive.") to "Chimney Rock" ("My left arm hung at a bizarre angle. My left leg was twisted outward and throbbing."), you'll find yourself turning pages quickly as you encounter glaciers and ghettos, mountains and deserts, and men and women who know what kind of courage it takes to survive.

1.39 Paulsen, Gary. **Brian's Return.** Delacorte, 1999. 115 pp. ISBN 0385325002. Fiction.

This conclusion to the story that began with the Newbery Honor book *Hatchet* takes sixteen-year-old Brian back to the wilderness he loves. Two years have gone by since Brian returned from his adventure. He has come to realize that he is now more at home and at peace away from the fast-paced world. After a vicious fight with a classmate, Brian is sent to a counselor who sees the need for Brian to return to the wilderness. Once in the wilderness, Brian discovers there is much more to be learned from nature and much more to discover about himself.

1.40 Pfetzer, Mark, and Jack Galvin. **Within Reach: My Everest Story.** Dutton, 1998. 222 pp. ISBN 0525460896. Nonfiction.

In May 1996, experienced mountaineer Mark Pfetzer was set to begin the last stage of a climb that would take him to the summit of Mt. Everest. However, as he camped on the mountain with his assault team, a fierce storm with seventy-knot winds enveloped the mountain, sending temperatures to one hundred degrees below zero. Mark and his team spent the day of their ascent not climbing, but hunting for climbers who had not returned to camp the previous day. By the end of a day that should have seen Mark standing on top of the world, the world was learning of the great tragedy on Mt. Everest as the bodies of climbers were found. Mark's passion for climbing—a passion that emerged when he was fifteen and continued as he became a world record climber of many peaks—was challenged as he fought to overcome the physical and emotional damage from that tragic night on Everest.

1.41 Platt, Richard. **Disaster!** Illustrated by Richard Bonson. Dorling Kindersley, 1997. 32 pp. ISBN 0789420341. Nonfiction.

Although published for a younger audience, *Disaster* is sure to be a winner with anyone who wants to know more about the great disasters that have shaken this world. Because catastrophes are overwhelming, the book designers rightly chose to describe the twelve calamities in an oversized book. Using double-page spreads, detailed pictures, a timeline, captions, and sidebars, events such as the 79 C.E. eruption of Mt. Vesuvius that left the city of Pompeii a tomb of muck and dust and the 1912 sinking of the "unsinkable" *Titanic* in the freezing waters of the Atlantic are described.

1.42 Preston, Richard. **The Cobra Event: A Novel.** Random House, 1997. 394 pp. ISBN 0679457143. Fiction.

A New York teenager has symptoms of a cold, then dies a violent death. When similar deaths occur elsewhere, Alice Austen, a pathologist from the Epidemic Intelligence Service, is sent to observe the autopsy of one of the victims. One day later, FBI agents Will Hopkins and Mark Littleberry raid an Iraqi mobile biological weapons laboratory where Littleberry glimpses trays of flat crystals—crystals similar to ones that had shown up in the autopsy Austen observed. Soon, Austen, Hopkins, and Littleberry realize they are fighting a biological war against a mysterious virus known as Cobra. Now they must stop this virus before it strikes again.

1.43 Shahan, Sherry. **Frozen Stiff.** Delacorte, 1998. 151 pp. ISBN 0385323034. Fiction.

Cody and her cousin Derek sneak the kayaks out in the Alaskan waters for a quick weekend of camping while their mothers are gone. With very few provisions, the inexperienced kayakers find themselves trapped when the Hubbard Glacier "surges" and blocks their return. With their few supplies washed away in Cody's kayak, they are wet, cold, hungry, and exhausted. Cody suffers from snow blindness and just when it seems that things can't get worse, Derek seems to have been kidnapped. Will the pair survive their harrowing journey?

1.44 Stedham, Glen. **Bush Basics: A Common Sense Guide to Backwoods Adventure.** Orca, 1998. 224 pp. ISBN 1551430983. Nonfiction.

If you plan to go on a backwoods adventure (or perhaps are even just thinking of a long hike on a wilderness trail), then you probably want to look at this book. With easy-to-understand explanations of topics such as compass declination and distance calculations, great advice on how to avoid hypothermia and dehydration, and practical suggestions on packing a backpack and figuring out how to use the toilet while in the forest, this book is sure to answer all your questions.

1.45 Strasser, Todd. **Buzzard's Feast: Against the Odds.** Minstrel, 1999. 128 pp. ISBN 067102311X. Fiction.

In this book, part of the Against the Odds series, nineteen-year-old Luke volunteers to drive Henry and his little brother Paul from Los Angeles, where they live with their mother, to Las Vegas, where they'll visit their father. Amber, Luke's sister and Henry's school friend, decides to go along on the ride. Luke is a bit of a show-off while driving, and gets them into real trouble when he drives the van off the road and crashes it. Now all four kids are stuck in the Mojave Desert with little food or water and lots of poisonous snakes, brutal temperatures, and scorching sand. Other books in this series include *Grizzly Attack*, *Gator Prey*, and *Shark Bite*.

1.46 Taylor, Michael R. **Cave Passages: Roaming the Underground Wilderness.** Vintage / Random House, 1997. 285 pp. ISBN 0679781250. Nonfiction.

Slide through thin passages. Explore water-filled caverns. Rappel into the bowels of Earth. Reading this book is like taking an actual guided adventure through the deepest and most challenging caves in the world. But some of the best and the most skilled cave explorers have died. Taylor captures the tragic death of an experienced caver in the beginning chapters of this book. Then he celebrates the heroic skills of those still exploring the uncharted underworld of Earth. Join the caving adventure!

1.47 Taylor, Theodore. **Rogue Wave and Other Red-Blooded Sea Stories.** Harcourt Brace, 1997. 184 pp. ISBN 015201408X. Fiction.

Using his own naval experience and interest in the sea, Theodore Taylor presents eight adventure-filled stories, five of them previously published between 1952 and 1967. Among the best stories are the newly written ones. In "The Butcher," nineteen-year-old Michael attempts to avenge his father's death in the jaws of a great white shark; and in "Rogue Wave," a teenage girl is trapped inside the cabin of an overturned sailboat. Lots of action and information about the sea can be found in this collection.

1.48 Tessendorf, K. C. **Over the Edge: Flying with the Arctic Heroes.** Atheneum Books for Young Readers, 1998. 116 pp. ISBN 0689318049. Nonfiction.

Most Americans name Admiral Richard Byrd as the first person to circle the North Pole. But was he? Norwegians claim the Amundsen/Ellsworth team carries that honor. In *Over the Edge,* you get not only an up-close examination of historical and scientific data about who really was first, but you also read about other arctic exploration by air from balloonists, pilots, and dirigiblists. From the first fateful Swedish balloon expedition in 1897 to the comic series of events in 1930 with the Nobile/Amundsen dirigible, you learn of the many trials these early explorers faced as they searched for that elusive North Pole.

1.49 Thomas, Rob. **Green Thumb.** Simon & Schuster, 1999. 192 pp. ISBN 0689817800. Fiction.

Grady Jacobs is a genius. He has won the science fair at his school every year, and has just been selected to spend the summer assisting the renowned Dr. Phillip Carter in his rain forest reforestation attempt. Dr. Carter has managed to genetically engineer a tree whose growth is so rapid, it can ease the effects of the clear-cutting of the old wood in the rain forest. What Grady soon discovers, though, is that this miracle of modern science is not all Dr. Carter says it is. The genetically engineered tree poisons the plants and other wildlife of the forest. Dr. Carter will not admit his mistake, and who would ever believe a mere thirteen-year-old?

1.50 Vanasse, Deb. **Out of the Wilderness.** Clarion, 1999. 176 pp. ISBN 0395914213. Fiction.

Fifteen-year-old Josh wants to live near girls and hockey games and hamburger stands, but instead he lives in the Alaskan wilderness with his father and his half-brother Nathan, who is determined to live in the wild. When Josh kills a bear that is attacking them, Nathan believes they can no longer live together because Josh is someone who would kill a wild animal and Nathan is someone who identifies with bears. Nathan decides to move out of the cabin and puts the entire family in jeopardy.

1.51 Willis, Clint, editor. **Climb: Stories of Survival from Rock, Snow, and Ice.** Thunder's Mouth, 1999. 360 pp. ISBN 1560252502. Nonfiction.

Mountain climbing takes a special kind of courage, a special kind of skill, and a special kind of person who wants to hang over cliffs, grab on to two-inch ledges, scramble up near-vertical inclines, sleep in frigid temperatures, and gasp for oxygen on summits where humans usually never go. When you find such people, they generally have intriguing stories to tell of their adventures. Willis found these people and has recounted their stories in this adventure book. You'll read about people who have climbed the peaks of mountains from Alaska to the Himalayas. You'll gasp at some of the near-death experiences and laugh at some of the funnier ones (How do you get a llama to stop running?).

2 Animals, Pets, and the Natural World

"Animals are such agreeable friends—
they ask no questions, they pass no criticisms."

George Eliot

2.1   Alderton, David. **101 Essential Tips: Caring for Your Bird.** Dorling Kindersley, 1996. 72 pp. ISBN 078941077X. Nonfiction.

Listen to the sweet chirping of a bird in even the most crowded high-rise, and you'll be transported to a wilder, less crowded place within your imagination. Having birds in your home can be a rich experience if you provide proper care and a suitable habitat. This book will help you learn how to select, care for, and carefully handle a bird. It even discusses ways to create a closer bond with your bird, and how to teach a bird to talk. Colorful photographs depict the many bird species that are suitable for living within the close confines of a home. Of particular note is the section on the health, feeding, and breeding of birds in captivity. If treated and cared for properly, birds can bring years of enjoyment and beauty into your home.

2.2   Behler, John L. **National Audubon Society First Field Guide: Reptiles.** Scholastic, 1999. 160 pp. ISBN 0590054678. Nonfiction.

Want to learn about the reptiles around your home or school? This is the book for you! Learn to differentiate among the various species of turtles, salamanders, lizards, snakes, frogs, toads, and even alligators, and to distinguish the harmful from the harmless. Sections within the book describe reptile habitats, habits, life cycles, defense mechanisms, geographic distribution, and specific characteristics of species and subspecies. Additional information, including keys to identification, is provided through 450 color photographs, illustrations, and diagrams. This is a valuable reference for the home, and a useful field guide to take along on outings.

2.3   Carson, Rachel. **The Edge of the Sea.** Mariner, 1998. 304 pp. ISBN 0395924690. Nonfiction.

Stand still at that place where the shore meets the sea and you stand between two worlds. Look closely enough and you'll discover an ecosystem that survives daily by literally "going with the tides." With this book, you'll learn to identify what you're seeing in that seashore world and learn about environmental and conservation efforts to protect this delicate ecosystem.

2.4   Coleman, Loren, and Jerome Clark. **Cryptozoology A to Z: The Encyclopedia of Loch Monsters, Sasquatch, Chupacabras, and Other Authentic Mysteries of Nature.** Fireside, 1999. 272 pp. ISBN 0686856026. Nonfiction.

You've heard about them—the Loch Ness Monster, Bigfoot, the Abominable Snowman—but what do you really know about them? Are they real? Are they myth? To understand these creatures and the legends that surround them, Loren Coleman, a cryptozoologist (one who studies hidden animals), did the research and wrote this book. Eyewitness accounts and never-before-seen drawings and photographs will help you decide if these animals of legend are real or not.

2.5   Davis, Jim. **20 Years and Still Kicking! Garfield's Twentieth Anniversary Collection.** Ballantine, 1998. 187 pp. ISBN 0345421264. Nonfiction.

Every Garfield fan will enjoy this collection of Garfield comic strips, which includes a special section called "Jim's Top 20: The Pick of the Litter." Jim Davis, creator of this famous feline, relates his life story with the same humor that he uses in the daily escapades of Garfield. Laugh along with Garfield and the gang in this tribute to the world's feistiest—and funniest—feline!

2.6   Draper, Judith, Debby Sly, and Sarah Muir. **The Ultimate Book of the Horse and Rider.** Barnes & Noble, 1999. 511 pp. ISBN 0760717419. Nonfiction.

Over five hundred pages of illustrations, photographs, and text give you all the information you need about horses and riding. Learn about horse breeds, grooming, dressage, horse competitions, and all the necessary equipment you need to make you and your horse comfortable. If you want to be a polo player, have decided to jump fences, want to show your horse in the arena, expect to enter races, or just want to learn how to groom your own Mr. Ed, this book is the book for you.

2.7   Dunn, Jon L. **National Geographic Field Guide to the Birds of North America: Revised and Updated.** National Geographic, 1999. 480 pp. ISBN 0792274512. Nonfiction.

With descriptions of over eight hundred different bird species found in North America, this book is the amateur bird-watcher's favorite guide. Photos will help you identify the bird you are seeing, and descriptions of behavior, habitat, and song help you understand it. In this guidebook, you'll also find maps and birding techniques. Dust off the binoculars and take this book out with you to the park!

2.8   Fogle, Bruce. **Dachshund.** Dorling Kindersley, 1997. 80 pp. ISBN 0789416131. Nonfiction.

A favorite pet of Queen Victoria and Prince Albert, dachshunds continue to be popular pets today. With their short legs and long bodies, they have a distinctive look. Their loyal nature makes them excellent watch dogs, and their aggressive personalities make them excellent hunting dogs. Learn about the different types of dachshunds, how to train them, what types of problems to look out for, and how to keep them healthy. This book is part of the Dog Breed Handbook series from Dorling Kindersley.

2.9   Fogle, Bruce. **101 Essential Tips: Puppy Care.** Dorling Kindersley, 1997. 72 pp. ISBN 0789414635. Nonfiction.

Dr. Fogle, a well-known veterinarian, brings his expertise to puppy care in this outstanding book for first-time and experienced puppy owners. Fogle writes about choosing the right puppy (so read this book before you choose one!), as well as caring for and training the puppy. Although Fogle discusses the care puppies require and deserve, he also stresses the importance of consistent and careful training. This is a very complete resource guide for the entire family. Color photographs clearly illustrate both the care and training of puppies.

2.10   Fogle, Bruce. **Training Your Dog.** Dorling Kindersley, 1997. 72 pp. ISBN 0789414600. Nonfiction.

Fido won't fetch? Lassie won't come home? Rover won't sit, stay, or stop barking? If those descriptions fit your canine, then *Training Your Dog* is probably the book you want. The book contains 101 easy-to-understand tips that give expert advice in a nutshell. From deciding which dog is right for you to basic and advanced training tactics, this handy, concise guide provides quick answers to all your pet related questions.

2.11 Grassy, John, and Chuck Keene. **National Audubon Society First Field Guide: Mammals.** Scholastic, 1998. 160 pp. ISBN 0590054716. Nonfiction.

This reference guide to the mammals of North America includes both terrestrial and aquatic animals, along with a reference card for quick mammal identification. Learn to identify the unique characteristics and habits of mammals, as well as their benefits, niches, and links within the food chain. Readers will marvel at the adaptability of various species to hot deserts and cold arctic habitats. Over 450 color photographs, illustrations, and charts help the reader spot species quickly and learn the important characteristics of each mammal. This is a useful home reference.

2.12 Lanting, Frans. **Penguin.** Taschen America, 1999. 168 pp. ISBN 3822865192. Nonfiction.

Photographer Frans Lanting traveled to the Antarctic to photograph these flightless, tuxedoed birds. He caught them playing, eating, mating, and simply standing majestically. With photos of newly-hatched chicks, teasing teenagers, and sedate adults, this book will entertain you as you look into the world of the frozen south and those birds that call it home.

2.13 Lembke, Janet. **Despicable Species: On Cowbirds, Kudzu, Hornworms, and Other Scourges.** Illustrated by Joe Nutt. Lyons, 1999. 208 pp. ISBN 1558216359. Nonfiction.

From cowbirds (who lay their eggs and then head off, leaving new hatchlings to fend for themselves) to fruit flies (who can live for several days without their heads) to the microbe *Pfiestreria piscicida* (which is deadly to humans and fish), Lembke explains just why you should be kind to some of the creatures that most often cause us to shudder.

2.14   Lessem, Don. **Dinosaurs to Dodos: An Encyclopedia of Extinct Animals.** Illustrated by Jan Sovak. Scholastic Reference, 1999. 112 pp. ISBN 0590316842. Nonfiction.

From one-celled sea creatures and the thirty-foot armored fish *Dunkleosteus* to eight-foot wide spiders and the one-hundred-ton plant eater *Argentinosaurus,* this book has it all. Here you'll read about extinct animals, as well as the modern discoveries that are helping paleontologists piece together how they might have lived and what might have caused their extinction. Organized by eras, periods, and epochs, this book shows how the end of each time period has been marked by the extinction of many animals. These mass extinctions have often resulted in fossil galleries that now help scientists think through the mysteries of the past.

2.15   Levin, Betty. **Look Back, Moss.** Greenwillow, 1998. 152 pp. ISBN 0688156967. Fiction.

Jody can't believe what his mom is doing: stealing. His mom can't believe Jody doesn't understand that she's not stealing, but rather rescuing mistreated animals from undeserving owners. Finally, Jody begins to understand his mother's commitment to protecting animals when he finds an abused collie that desperately needs his help. Together Jody and his mom rehabilitate the dog, and together they face the conflicts that arise when confronted with the knowledge that returning the dog to its owner means more abuse for the dog and perhaps trouble for the two of them.

2.16   McDougall, Len. **The Complete Tracker: The Tracks, Signs, and Habits of North American Wildlife.** MJF Books, 1997. 273 pp. ISBN 1567313264. Nonfiction.

Ever seen a squirrel in your neighborhood and wondered where it lives? Planning a hike through a national forest and trying to figure out how you'll identify those tracks you're sure to come across? Pick up a copy of this book to find the answer to these questions and dozens of others about deer, boars, javelinas, bears, wolves, foxes, wild cats, weasels, raccoons, beavers, porcupines, rabbits, and squirrels. Throughout the book you'll find information on wildlife that ranges from how to recognize tracks and what food each one likes to mating habits, vocalizations, and habitats. Printed in a handy size so you can tuck it into your backpack, and filled with photographs and illustrations, this book is a must for anyone who wants to identify the wildlife they'll encounter on the nature trail.

2.17   Mills, Dick. **101 Essential Tips: Aquarium Fish.** Dorling Kindersley, 1996. 72 pp. ISBN 0789410746. Nonfiction.

Learn to build a freshwater, tropical, or cold water marine aquarium with this handy guide. To help the novice aquarium owner, Mills has included numerous photographs of fish, the necessary equipment, and the process for building and maintaining an aquarium. Helpful hints on everything from hardy stock and the right size for buying fish to understanding the temperament of various species of fish will help you to stock or maintain your aquarium. Finally, there are numerous suggestions for feeding fish and maintaining a balanced, healthy aquarium.

3 Arts and Architecture

*"Fiction is art and art is the triumph over chaos . . .
to celebrate a world that lies spread out around us like
a bewildering and stupendous dream."*

John Cheever

3.1 Albert, Fred. **Barkitecture.** Abbeville, 1999. 96 pp. ISBN 0789203731. Nonfiction.

Looking for ideas for Fido's new digs? Check out some of the coolest canine homes around in this slim collection. From the standard doghouse to the more lush creations featuring all of the modern conveniences like air conditioning, you will marvel at how some pooches have all the luck.

3.2 Bernard, Bruce, editor. **Century: One Hundred Years of Human Progress, Regression, and Hope.** Phaidon, 1999. 1120 pp. ISBN 0714838489. Nonfiction.

This photographic history of the past century gives you a look at the world's best and worst moments. Divided into eras—1899–1914, 1914–1933, 1933–1945, 1945–1965, 1965–1985, and 1985–1999—the book presents about ten photos for each year. You'll see a photograph of Monet watering his daylily gardens next to a photo of children starving at the end of World War I. You'll see images of rock stars next to images of political prisoners. You'll see American GIs next to prisoners at Auschwitz. It's a look at the past century that captures the glory and the pain of the people who lived that century.

3.3 Bottomer, Paul. **Let's Dance: Learn to Swing, Jitterbug, Rumba, Tango, Lambada, Cha-Cha, Waltz, Two-Step, Fox Trot and Salsa with Style, Grace and Ease.** Black Dog / Leventhal, 1998. 258 pp. ISBN 1579120466. Nonfiction.

The subtitle says it all. If you are interested in learning the moves of some of the most popular ballroom dances, this book provides step-by-step illustrations and directions. If you have two left feet, here is the book to help you transform yourself from klutz to cool.

3.4 Burian, Peter K., and Robert Caputo. **National Geographic Photography Field Guide: Secrets to Making Great Pictures.** National Geographic Society, 1999. 352 pp. ISBN 0792274989. Nonfiction.

Here's all the advice you need for taking great photographs of nature. Learn about selecting the right film, filter, camera, lens, and background. Learn how to use light correctly. Get some travel tips, learn where to go to take the best shots, and get some secret techniques that we can't tell you about here or they wouldn't be secret!

3.5 Cruz, Barbara C. **Jose Clemente Orozco: Mexican Artist.** Enslow, 1998. 128 pp. ISBN 0766010414. Nonfiction.

Despite a childhood accident that resulted in the amputation of his left hand, Jose Clemente Orozco went on to become one of the leading mural painters of the nineteenth century. Orozco did more than paint beautiful murals, however. Much of his work was influential in the Mexican political arena. The artist believed that it was important to comment on the controversial issues of his time, and that art could affect society in more than one way. His concern for humanity is mirrored in his paintings.

3.6 Cumming, Robert. **Great Artists.** Dorling Kindersley, 1998. 112 pp. ISBN 078942391X. Nonfiction.

This oversized art book begins with a discussion of what makes an artist great: "most artists reflect their own times but no more, whereas the outstanding artist has the ability to capture the imagination of future generations and say something of direct relevance to them." It then proceeds to a look at the life and works of fifty artists. The biographical profiles highlight the important events in each artist's life, and explain each artist's style and technique. The oversized pages give ample room for reproducing noted works. Arranged chronologically, this book not only gives insight into particular artists, but also into specific schools and movements such as post-impressionism and cubism.

3.7 Greenfield, Lois. **Airborne: The New Dance Photography of Lois Greenfield.** Chronicle, 1998. 112 pp. ISBN 0811821552. Nonfiction.

Noted choreographer and photographer Greenfield combines her two talents in one powerful book. Stark black-and-white illustrations capture dancers in mid leap or at the moment a ballet dancer's toes touch the ground. The dancers seem to be traveling on air; gravity has no effect on their graceful maneuvers. Anyone interested in the fine points of taking action pictures would do well to turn the pages of this book.

3.8   Hennessey, Maureen Hart, and Anne Knutson, editors. **Norman Rockwell: Pictures for the American People.** Abrams, 1999. 196 pp. ISBN 0810963922. Nonfiction.

This collection of 133 of Rockwell's paintings is a delight to experience. Complementing the art are essays by art historians such as Thomas Hoving, the former Metropolitan Museum of Art director. The book includes Rockwell's great works, such as *The Four Freedoms, The Gossips,* and *Rosie the Riveter.* The book is the companion to the traveling exhibition of Rockwell's work.

3.9   Hoving, Thomas. **Art for Dummies.** IDG Books Worldwide, 1999. 382 pp. ISBN 0764551043. Nonfiction.

Thomas Hoving, the former director of the Metropolitan Museum of Art, takes you on a tour of the art world. Even if you wouldn't know cubism from representationalism, you'll find yourself nodding in understanding and agreement and seeking out your nearest art museum. With tidbits throughout the book on everything from how to visit a museum to a how to begin your own collection, you'll discover that this book is not for dummies, but for anyone with any level of art knowledge and an interest in learning more about the subject.

3.10   Partridge, Elizabeth. **Restless Spirit: The Life and Work of Dorothea Lange.** Viking, 1998. 122 pp. ISBN 067087888X. Nonfiction.

Dorothea Lange has given the American public poignant and haunting black-and-white photographs of American life. At a time in American history when women were expected to stay home and take care of families, Lange's passion was being out among the nation's people, photographing them to capture their agonies and ecstasies. This beautiful book not only reproduces many of her photos, but also chronicles her life as a child and adult. From photos of children picking crops in California and families escaping the Dust Bowl storms in Oklahoma to Japanese

American families awaiting evacuation during World War II, this book shows Lange's evolution from a photographer who captured people in the midst of harsh events to one who wanted to capture people's relationships with one another, to show "things you have to look very hard to see."

3.11 Schama, Simon. **Rembrandt's Eyes.** Knopf, 1999. 750 pp. ISBN 067940256X. Nonfiction.

Seventeenth-century Dutch artist Rembrandt left the world not only great art, but great self-portraits from most periods of his life. He also left us with many questions about his life. This epic biography attempts to bring some clarity to the life of this man who has remained a puzzle for centuries. The story that Schama tells is more than a biography; it's a history of the time and a comparison of Rembrandt to another great artist, Peter Paul Rubens. It is also a wonderful book to own because of the art reproduced in it.

3.12 Seidner, David. **Artists at Work: Inside the Studios of Today's Most Celebrated Artists.** Rizzoli Bookstore, 1999. 216 pp. ISBN 0847822370. Nonfiction.

Twenty of the most famous contemporary artists are the focus of the photographic essays in this collection. Jasper Johns, Chuck Close, Roy Lichtenstein, and a host of others share those private spaces where they create the fantastic images we see in art galleries. Here is an up-close look at the media and tools artists use in their creative endeavors, as well as the spaces in which they work.

3.13 Siliotti, Alberto. **Guide to the Valley of the Kings.** Barnes & Noble, 1997. 168 pp. ISBN 076070483X. Nonfiction.

Alberto Siliotti, a scientific journalist and photographer, is the only photographer who has been granted full access to the Egyptian Valley of the Kings for the past decade. This guide provides some never-before-seen works of art and architecture, allowing armchair travelers to experience the tombs of the nobles and the Valley of the Kings in a most dramatic way. Part art book and part history book, this volume covers everything from the building of a royal tomb and the tombs of the eighteenth, nineteenth, and twentieth dynasties to the tombs of Rameses III's sons and the private tombs.

3.14   Smith, Ray. **Watercolor Color.** Dorling Kindersley, 1998. 72 pp. ISBN 0789432927. Nonfiction.

This paperback volume, part of the DK Art School series and written in association with the Royal Academy of Arts, focuses on the role of color in painting. Beginning with the history of pigments in different types of paints, this beautifully illustrated book demonstrates how different artists in various periods used color to convey mood, symbol, or message. It includes step-by-step instructions for projects that teach how to use watercolors in different styles of painting.

3.15   Stolley, Richard B., and Tony Chiu, editors. **Life: Our Century in Pictures.** Bullfinch, 1999. 423 pp. ISBN 0821226330. Nonfiction.

More than 740 photographs chronicle the events of the twentieth century. History, politics, and popular culture are combined to present a visual history of the past one hundred years. From the horrific shots of John F. Kennedy's assassination to the lighter moments of celebrity high jinks, each chapter provides you with information about the people and events that were important. What events from the 1980s and 1990s did the editors select to showcase the high and low points of your lifetime?

3.16   Tambini, Michael. **The Look of the Century.** Dorling Kindersley, 1996. 288 pp. ISBN 078940950X. Nonfiction.

Look around. What do you see? Chairs, couches, tables, candlesticks, washing machines, dryers, refrigerators, toilets, sinks, hair dryers, cars, wallpaper, watches, hats, cameras, bicycles, jewelry, swimsuits, dresses, toasters, suits, toothbrushes—well, you get the idea. You see thousands of things, and all of those things were, at some point, designed. But who were the designers, and how did their visions help create the look of this century? This comprehensive look at the designs and designers of the twentieth century gives you a panoramic view of art nouveau, art deco, modernism, and postmodernism.

3.17   Weitzman, Jacqueline Preiss. **You Can't Take a Balloon into the Metropolitan Museum.** Illustrated by Robin Preiss Glasser. Dial Books for Young Readers, 1998. Unpaged. ISBN 0803723016. Fiction.

This textless picture book gives art fans an exciting romp through the Metropolitan Museum. A balloon that's being held for a young Met patron by a kindly guard gets away and floats throughout the museum while the girl visits exhibits. With two story lines to follow—that of the escaped balloon and the girl's visit in the museum—your eyes will never lack for things to view. Placed throughout the text are reproductions of eighteen works of art the girl sees on her trip. These masterpieces include Fragonard's *Portrait of a Lady with a Dog*, Degas's *Grand Arabesque, Third Time*, Monet's *Bridge over a Pool of Water Lilies*, and Cassatt's *Lady at the Tea Table*.

3.18 Wilkinson, Philip. **Super Structures.** Dorling Kindersley, 1996. 44 pp. ISBN 0789410117. Nonfiction.

How does a tidal barrier hold back the surges of the ocean? What type of reinforcement is needed to run a tunnel under a body of water? Explore these questions and others in this book as you discover the secrets behind the structures you see every day. From the roller coaster at your favorite amusement park to the inner structure of an airport, this book peels back the facade and shows what lies underneath. Other titles in the DK Inside Guides series include *Animal Homes, Incredible Earth*, and *Amazing Bugs*.

3.19 Wright, Michael. **An Introduction to Pastels.** Dorling Kindersley, 1998. 72 pp. ISBN 0789432900. Nonfiction.

The DK Art School series, in association with the Royal Academy of Arts, presents this volume about using pastels. Pastels are ideal for beginning artists because they are relatively easy to use and have a wide range of color possibilities. Starting with examples by Degas, Cassatt, and Picasso, Wright discusses types of paper to use with pastels, composition, sketching, blending, and other techniques as he introduces a variety of projects to help students understand how to use the medium.

4 Autobiography and Biography

"When you put down the good things you ought to have done, and leave out the bad ones you did do—well, that's Memoirs."

Will Rogers

4.1 Bober, Natalie S. **Abigail Adams: Witness to a Revolution.** Aladdin, 1998. 248 pp. ISBN 0689819161. Nonfiction.

Abigail Adams holds a distinctive place in history for being one president's wife and another president's mother. Learn more about this remarkable woman in this biography, which reveals a strong and loving marriage between Abigail and John Adams, even while mourning the loss of an infant daughter or separated for long periods of time by his work. In an unusual relationship for the time, John Adams considered his wife his intellectual equal and often sought her opinion on difficult matters he faced. And Abigail understood the man she married was driven to serve his country, even when that meant leaving his family for months or years at a time. Rich with letters she wrote as well as letters written to her, this award-winning biography helps us understand why Abigail Adams was called the "guiding planet around which all revolved."

4.2 Bober, Natalie S. **Thomas Jefferson: Man on a Mountain.** Aladdin, 1998. 274 pp. ISBN 0689815239. Nonfiction.

The life of Thomas Jefferson continues to intrigue historians, scholars, and students. This biography offers a complete look at a very human man whose accomplishments seem superhuman. Jefferson considered himself a perpetual student; he was always eager to learn more. This thirst for knowledge led to his involvement in the government of the newly free United States of America. Jefferson drafted the Declaration of Independence, served two terms as president, and lived long enough to see the fiftieth birthday of the nation.

4.3 Bolden, Tonya. **And Not Afraid to Dare: The Stories of Ten African-American Women.** Scholastic, 1998. 216 pp. ISBN 0590480804. Nonfiction.

These are the stories of African American women who not only lived through adversity, but triumphed over racism and sexism to reach their goals. Clara "Mother" Hale dedicated her life to caring for babies stricken with AIDS. Ellen Craft, disguised as a man, escaped from slavery to help others do the same. Ida Wells wrote poignantly against lynchings at great risk to her own life. The women whose stories are told in this book represent the strength and courage many women have shown when they became "determined to be free, to be heard, to succeed."

4.4 Bridges, Ruby. **Through My Eyes.** Scholastic, 1999. 64 pp. ISBN 0590189239. Nonfiction.

The date: November 14, 1960. The place: William Frantz Public School in New Orleans, Louisiana. The people: six-year-old Ruby, her first-grade teacher Barbara Henry, and a nation in protest. The problem: Ruby, an African American, now sits in a first-grade classroom once reserved only for white children. The outcome: a school year in which Ruby attends school alone as white parents refuse to let their children attend an integrated classroom. And, of course, the larger outcome: a lifetime of segregation in one school in one city that ends as Ruby climbs the stairs to her classroom every day. This compelling autobiography, filled with Ruby's memories, photographs that document that year, and quotes from people such as her mother, her teacher, and national newspapers, help us all understand not only what happened that year to one little girl, but also what happened to a nation as it faced integration.

4.5 Cox, Clinton. **Fiery Vision: The Life and Death of John Brown.** Scholastic, 1997. 230 pp. ISBN 0590475746. Nonfiction.

Although he was executed more than 140 years ago, John Brown remains one of the most controversial figures of his time. He believed that all men were created equal, and he fought to see an end to slavery in the nineteenth century. Brown and a band of followers captured the fort at Harper's Ferry, Virginia, in 1859. Was John Brown an abolitionist hero, or simply a madman set on insurrection?

4.6   Doherty, Kieran. **William Bradford: Rock of Plymouth.** Twenty-first Century, 1999. 192 pp. ISBN 0761313044. Nonfiction.

William Bradford was the governor of Plymouth Colony after John Carver's death, and he kept that position for most of the rest of his life. He surrounded himself with people we know well from history books—such as Miles Standish, John Alden, Squanto, and Samoset—and he listened to their counsel. But who was this Pilgrim who died believing himself to be a failure, when those around him saw him "as a common blessing and a father to them all"? His "scribbled writings" left us the book we know today as *Of Plymouth Plantation,* one of the greatest books of colonial history ever written, and the colony he governed had a tremendous impact on the formation of the United States we know today. This powerful biography, complete with paintings and engravings, brings William Bradford to life, and dispels many of the myths that surround Pilgrims.

4.7   Ford, Barbara. **Paul Revere: Rider for the Revolution.** Enslow, 1997. 128 pp. ISBN 0894907794. Nonfiction.

On the eighteenth of April in 1875, Paul Revere set off on an historic ride to warn the people of Massachusetts of the advance of British troops. Revere's involvement with the events of the American Revolution did not end on that fateful night. He continued to work for American independence, and he made many contributions to the United States throughout his life. Revere was also a gifted silversmith whose work is exhibited in museums today. This book is a part of the Historical American Biographies series. Other subjects include Susan B. Anthony, Robert E. Lee, and Clara Barton.

4.8   Freedman, Russell. **Babe Didrikson Zaharias: The Making of a Champion.** Clarion, 1999. ISBN 0395633672. Nonfiction.

Babe Didrikson Zaharias, called the greatest woman athlete the world has ever seen, loved sports all her life. As a second grader she won her school's marbles championship, and the championships just kept coming. Christened Mildred Ella, but always called Babe, she grew up in Beaumont, Texas, during a time when little girls were supposed to play with dolls, not balls. But as this excellent biography points out, Babe's attraction to sports was too strong for her to ignore. Babe was an All-American basketball player, an Olympic gold medalist in track and field, a championship golfer, a tennis player, a baseball player, a diver, and a bowler. This book helps us all to understand this extraordinary woman's contribution to the world of sports.

4.9 Gelernter, David. **Drawing Life: Surviving the Unabomber.** Free Press, 1997. 159 pp. ISBN 0684839121. Nonfiction.

"One morning in June 1993 I was almost killed by a mail bomb." Thus begins the compelling account of David Gelernter's life from the moment he opened a package from the Unabomber that contained a bomb—a bomb that exploded, blowing off most of his right hand and damaging his hearing and eyesight. Gelernter not only tells how this event impacted both his and his family's life, but he also raises questions about good and evil, giving up and going on, and retribution and compassion.

4.10 Giovanni, Nikki, editor. **Grand Fathers: Reminiscences, Poems, Recipes, and Photos of the Keepers of Our Traditions.** Henry Holt, 1999. 230 pp. ISBN 0805054847. Nonfiction.

Grandfathers are the keepers of our traditions, and the forty-seven multicultural and intergenerational pieces in this book reflect the diversity of grandfathers and our relationships with them. From Victor Emmanuel, or Poppa, whose life "bridged the gap between slavery and African-American determination to move from backseats," to Leo Kamell, who supplied fruit to twenty-six grocery stores in Westchester County and "the lost souls in Sing Sing prison," these grandfathers represent our past and our future. Renowned poet Nikki Giovanni is the editor of this collection, which includes stories, poems, recipes, and a piece of music—all about grandfathers who stand tall in our memories. She encourages young people who read this book to continue the tradition, to "solve some of their families' mysteries . . . [to] ask questions and listen to answers spoken and unspoken."

4.11 Goodnough, David. **Simon Bolivar: South American Liberator.** Enslow, 1998. 128 pp. ISBN 0766010449. Nonfiction.

At one time, Spain owned South America. At the tender age of twenty-three, Simon Bolivar began to lead the people of South America in a revolt against their Spanish rulers. Bolivar led an army that defeated the Spanish in Venezuela, Colombia, and Peru.

To demonstrate their gratitude, those countries elected him president. Bolivar's commitment to freedom continued until his death in 1830. This brief biography follows Bolivar from his privileged childhood to his death, and is part of a series of Hispanic/Latino biographies that cover the lives of activist Cesar Chavez, actor Raul Julia, singer Gloria Estefan, and teacher Jaime Escalante.

4.12   Hansen, Joyce. **Women of Hope: African Americans Who Made a Difference.** Scholastic, 1998. 32 pp. ISBN 0590939734. Nonfiction.

This stunningly beautiful book profiles the lives of twelve African American women who have made a difference through their words and actions. The black-and-white portrait photographs that accompany each biographical sketch were chosen from a series of posters honoring "Women of Hope." Read about such women as Ida B. Wells-Barnett, Marian Wright Edelman, Alice Walker, Alexa Canady, Mae C. Jemison, and Ruby Dee. In this book, you will encounter Maya Angelou's stirring words, "You may write me down in history with your bitter, twisted lies, you may trod me in the very dirt but still like dust, I'll rise," and Toni Morrison's exclamation, "My world did not shrink because I was a black female writer. It just got bigger." This book reminds young people, especially young African American women, that "greatness looks like them."

4.13   Hightower, Paul. **Galileo: Astronomer and Physicist.** Enslow, 1997. 128 pp. ISBN 0894907875. Nonfiction.

Galileo, one of the greatest scientists of all time, helped prove that Earth and the other planets in our solar system revolve around the sun. Additionally, Galileo's work led to other discoveries. He was able to fashion his own telescope. Through it, he found four of Jupiter's moons. Galileo used experiments to prove the law of the pendulum and the law of freely moving bodies. Despite his many accomplishments, Galileo's life was plagued by controversy. His discoveries about the universe put him in opposition to the teachings of the church of his time, and Galileo was arrested for his outspoken pronouncements. This book is part of the Great Minds of Science series, which includes books about Madame Curie, Albert Einstein, Isaac Newton, and other famous scientists.

4.14 Hurley, Joanna. **Mother Teresa, 1910–1997: A Pictorial Biography.** Courage Books / Running Press, 1997. 120 pp. ISBN 0762402148. Nonfiction.

One of the most beloved figures of the twentieth century is Mother Teresa, the lone nun who founded the Missionaries of Charity, which ministers to thousands of the poor throughout the world. This moving pictorial biography shows this Nobel laureate at work among the poor, praying with the dying, and feeding the starving. With simple prose, her life is recounted from childhood until her death, and breathtaking black-and-white photographs capture her deeds for all to appreciate.

4.15 Jeffrey, Laura S. **Barbara Jordan: Congresswoman, Lawyer, Educator.** Enslow, 1997. 112 pp. ISBN 0894906925. Nonfiction.

As this book, part of the African-American Biography Series, demonstrates, Barbara Jordan was a woman of many firsts. She was the first African American elected to the Texas state senate (1972), and the first African American woman from the South ever elected to the United States Congress. Even after her retirement from politics, Jordan continued to prove her leadership skills. She became a professor, delivered powerful speeches, and continued to work for the good of her community. She was awarded the Presidential Medal of Freedom shortly before her death in 1996. The biographer, Laura Jeffrey, writes a compelling account of Jordan's life complete with photographs, timelines, and quotations that not only give us historical insight but offer us personal glimpses of this remarkable woman.

4.16 Jiang, Ji-Li. **Red Scarf Girl: A Memoir of the Cultural Revolution.** HarperCollins, 1997. 285 pp. ISBN 0060275855. Nonfiction.

Ji-Li Jiang is what her name means in Chinese: lucky and beautiful. An exemplary and well-respected student, Ji-Li has a bright future in Chairman Mao's new China. When the Cultural Revolution begins in 1966, Ji-Li aspires to become a member of the Red Guard and to destroy the "Four Olds"—old ideas, old culture, old customs, and old habits—that interfere with the creation of the new socialist society. But Ji-Li discovers that the status of her wealthy family marks her as an enemy of Communism. Former friends and classmates viciously malign Ji-Li and her family, who live in constant fear of arrest. When Ji-Li's father is "detained," she is given a choice: She can renounce her father and look toward a better future, or she can refuse, and seal her fate as a counterrevolutionary.

4.17   Judson, Karen. **Ronald Reagan.** Enslow, 1997. 112 pp. ISBN 0894908359. Nonfiction.

Part of the United States Presidents series, this slim biography recounts the life of the fortieth president of the United States. Ronald Reagan began his career as an actor. Later he ran for governor of California. He was elected to two terms as president, and survived an assassination attempt in 1981. During his tenure as president, Reagan helped bring about an end to the Cold War, establishing a more open and friendly relationship with the Soviet Union. In 1994, the public learned that the former president is suffering from Alzheimer's Disease. Included in this accessible biography are excerpts from speeches such as his first inaugural address and his final address to the nation.

4.18   Keenan, Sheila. **Scholastic Encyclopedia of Women in the United States.** Scholastic, 1996. 199 pp. ISBN 0-590-22792-0. Nonfiction.

Filling a gap in our knowledge of U.S. history, this reference work includes brief biographies of 217 women and mention of forty-three more. Divided into six periods of history from the 1500s to the 1990s, the entries balance accounts of the lives of famous women with those of unknown women who represent the spirit of their times. The women listed are indexed by career, making it possible to look for women who were poets, painters, ambassadors, or Olympic sports figures. In addition, text in the margins of the book contains quotations by and about women, anecdotes about the roles of women in society, and short entries about other women who are not the subject of complete biographies.

4.19   Kent, Zachary. **Andrew Carnegie: Steel King and Friend to Libraries.** Enslow, 1999. 128 pp. ISBN 0766012123. Nonfiction.

Andrew Carnegie (1835–1919) spent his childhood in Scotland, where hardship was what he knew best. By the time of his death, however, he had given away over 300 million dollars—nearly ninety percent of his earnings. This volume tells the story of this unparalleled philanthropist, who emigrated to the United States with his family in 1848, and worked as a telegraph operator, railroad superintendent, and investor on his way to becoming a railroad magnate and steel tycoon. Part of the well-designed Historical American Biographies series, this book offers an up-close look at the life of a businessman who believed the best business to be in was the "business of giving." Photographs, maps, a glossary, an index, and a list of further readings make this biography especially helpful. Other books in this series include *George Armstrong Custer: Civil War and Western Legend* and *William Seward: The Mastermind of the Alaskan Purchase.*

4.20   Kort, Michael G. **Yitzhak Rabin: Israel's Soldier Statesman.** Millbrook, 1996. 191 pp. ISBN 0761301003. Nonfiction.

Rabin began as a foot soldier in the Israeli army. Later, he served as Israel's ambassador to the United States. He rose through the political ranks to eventually become prime minister of Israel. Sadly, an assassin's bullet ended the brilliant political career of a man who continued to fight for liberty long after his career as a soldier had ended. This comprehensive biography carefully guides readers not only through Rabin's life, but through Israel's struggles. Photographs and maps supplement the detailed text.

4.21   Krakauer, Jon. **Into Thin Air: A Personal Account of the Mt. Everest Disaster.** Villard Books, 1997. 291 pp. ISBN 0679457526. Nonfiction.

One out of every four persons who attempts to climb Mt. Everest, the highest summit on earth, dies during the quest. But as the author of this book says, "Any person who would seriously consider it is almost by definition beyond the sway of reasoned argument." On May 10, 1996, accomplished climber and guide Rob Hall, the author Jon Krakauer, seven of Hall's clients, three guides, and four Sherpas set out to attack the summit. Too many people on too tight a trail, an inadequate oxygen supply, and a raging storm combined to make this trek a deadly one.

4.22   Krull, Kathleen. **They Saw the Future: Oracles, Psychics, Scientists, Great Thinkers, and Pretty Good Guessers.** Illustrated by Kyrsten Brooker. Atheneum Books for Young Readers / An Anne Schwartz Book, 1999. 108 pp. ISBN 0689812957. Nonfiction.

Is it possible to predict the future? Some claim it is. This book looks at the lives and prophecies of twelve individuals who predicted the future, including the Delphic Oracle (who always answered questions in riddles), the Sibyls (who suggested that "a tree that sank into the ground, with only a few branches showing, was a warning about forthcoming human slaughter"), Leonardo da Vinci (who drew designs for hundreds of mechanical devices—including air conditioners, parachutes, contact lenses, and helicopters—centuries before they were invented), and Edgar Cayce ("the most documented psychic of the twentieth century").

4.23 Litwin, Laura Baskes. **Benjamin Banneker: Astronomer and Mathematician.** Enslow, 1999. 128 pp. ISBN 0766012085. Nonfiction.

For the first forty years of his adult life, Benjamin Banneker, an African American, was a tobacco farmer. Then he developed an intense interest in astronomy, and found himself trading tobacco leaves for star charts. About the same time, he publicly challenged Secretary of State Thomas Jefferson about his racist views. This informative book details Banneker's life, and includes black-and-white photos and a bibliography of other books and Web sites about Banneker for those interested in additional information.

4.24 Macy, Sue. **Winning Ways: A Photobiography of American Women in Sports.** Henry Holt, 1996. 207 pp. ISBN 0805041478. Nonfiction.

It is said that a picture is worth a thousand words. In the case of women athletes, one picture can tell us quite a bit about the history of the time in which the photo was taken. This collective photobiography shows American female athletes engaged in sports as diverse as baseball, boxing, tennis, and trap shooting. Other snapshots show historic moments, including Martina Navratilova watching as her banner is raised to the ceiling of Madison Square Garden and Althea Gibson winning her first title at Wimbledon. This book is proof positive that girls and women can be successful athletes, despite some of the barriers placed in their way.

4.25 Mah, Adeline Yen. **Chinese Cinderella: The True Story of an Unwanted Daughter.** Delacorte, 1999. 205 pp. ISBN 0385327072. Nonfiction.

This is the autobiography of a "fifth daughter." Shortly after Wu Mei's birth, her mother dies. When her father remarries, Wu Mei finds herself an unwanted child, the youngest of five siblings.

Despite bringing home perfect report cards, she is treated with contempt and neglect by her family. Her only salvation is the books she reads. There she can escape the harsh cruelties of her life and dream of the victories she will have if she can only find a way out of China. When she wins a writing contest in high school, Wu Mei's father finally agrees to allow her to attend college in England. There she pursues her dreams and becomes a doctor. Included in the book is a complete glossary with historical information about Chinese society and politics during the 1940s and 1950s.

4.26 Monceaux, Morgan, and Ruth Katcher. **My Heroes, My People: African Americans and Native Americans in the West.** Portraits by Morgan Monceaux. Farrar, Straus and Giroux, 1999. 64 pp. ISBN 0374307709. Nonfiction.

Here are portraits and biographical sketches of African Americans and Native Americans who helped settle the west. Some famous, some not so famous, but all a part of history, these men and women include mail-order brides, soldiers in the Ninth Cavalry, robbers, stagecoach drivers, lawyers, and tribal chiefs. From Sitting Bull to Toussaint L'Ouverture, this book is filled with people who were legends in their own times.

4.27 Muller, Melissa. **Anne Frank: The Biography.** Translated by Rita and Robert Kimber. Henry Holt, 1998. 330 pp. ISBN 0805059970. Nonfiction.

Anne Frank was not yet sixteen years old when she died, a victim of the Holocaust. People throughout the world know her story from her famous diaries. But who was the person behind those haunting words? In this book, you will discover more about the girl who hid in the secret annex of a home in Amsterdam, and wrote in her now-famous diary. Muller interviewed over twenty of Anne's childhood friends, as well as many family members and friends of the Frank family, to develop this portrait. Anne was rambunctious, obstinate, and demanding. She was seen as a leader among her friends, although her chattering often got her in trouble. Muller follows Anne and her sister Margot to Westerbork and on to Auschwitz. An epilogue traces the Holocaust experiences of many of Anne's friends and family members.

4.28 Murphy, Tom. **Jack and Bobby.** Metro, 1998. 120 pp. ISBN 1567995918. Nonfiction.

If you've read about John F. (Jack) Kennedy and Robert F. (Bobby) Kennedy but still aren't sure you understand what these two brothers really had to offer this country, take a look at this photographic tribute. With more than 150 photographs—including many rare photos pulled from archives—you'll see the two brothers at work for the nation and at home with their families. Family photos of both men with their wives and children and behind-the-scenes shots of them at work offer a look at how these men balanced home and work. The book progresses from childhood photos, through Jack's presidency and assassination, to Bobby's political rise and tragic assassination. Reading this book will give you a look at not only the men whose lives it chronicles, but also the country they loved.

4.29 Myers, Walter Dean. **At Her Majesty's Request: An African Princess in Victorian England.** Scholastic, 1999. 143 pp. ISBN 0590486691. Nonfiction.

In 1848, Dahomian raiders slaughtered hundreds of Egbadoes and surrounded the Egbado village of Okeadan in Africa. One of the few who were spared so they could later be sold as slaves or sacrificed in rituals was a little five-year-old girl who had the carvings of a princess on her cheeks. Two years later, when Gezo, King of Dahomey, was about to sacrifice the now seven-year-old girl, a British commander named Forbes intervened and convinced the African leader to offer the girl as a gift to Queen Victoria. Gezo agreed, and the girl, called Sarah Forbes Bonetta, left Africa with Commander Forbes and headed for a life among English royalty. This biography follows Sarah as she grows up with the Queen's children, is educated at the best of schools, and eventually marries and has a child to whom Queen Victoria herself is godmother.

4.30 O'Grady, Scott, with Michael French. **Basher Five-Two: The True Story of F-16 Fighter Pilot Captain Scott O'Grady.** Doubleday, 1997. 133 pp. ISBN 038532300X. Nonfiction.

On June 2, 1995, Captain Scott O'Grady sat in his F-16 and prepared to take off from his base in northeastern Italy to fly over Bosnia on a peacekeeping mission. While on this mission, his plane was shot down. O'Grady ejected from the plane and parachuted five miles to the ground. For the next several days he was trapped behind enemy lines with little water and no food. This autobiography gives us the thrilling account of one pilot's determination to stay alive.

4.31 O'Mara, Michael. **Diana, the Princess of Wales: A Tribute in Photographs.** St. Martin's, 1997. 160 pp. ISBN 0312184239. Nonfiction.

This book shows the world of Diana up close through family photos when she was a toddler, a youngster, and a teen; royal photos when she was Princess of Wales; and tragic journalists' photographs of her funeral. See her life through the eyes of the camera, which caught her at work with the charities she so ardently supported, at home, and at play with her beloved sons.

4.32 Pfetzer, Mark, and Jack Galvin. **Within Reach: My Everest Story.** Dutton, 1998. 222 pp. ISBN 0525460896. Nonfiction.

In May 1996, experienced mountaineer Mark Pfetzer was set to begin the last stage of a climb that would take him to the summit of Mt. Everest. However, as he camped on the mountain with his assault team, a fierce storm with seventy-knot winds enveloped the mountain, sending temperatures to one hundred degrees below zero. Mark and his team spent the day of their ascent not climbing, but hunting for climbers who had not returned to camp the previous day. By the end of a day that should have seen Mark standing on top of the world, the world was learning of the great tragedy on Mt. Everest as the bodies of climbers were found. Mark's passion for climbing—a passion that emerged when he was fifteen and continued as he became a world record climber of many peaks—was challenged as he fought to overcome the physical and emotional damage from that tragic night on Everest.

4.33 Severance, John B. **Einstein: Visionary Scientist.** Clarion, 1999. 144 pp. ISBN 0395931002. Nonfiction.

Albert Einstein, a man whose very name is synonymous with genius, was thought to be retarded when he was a baby. As he grew older, he was slow to talk, slow in school, and did not enjoy playing with children. His elementary school principal once remarked that he probably wouldn't amount to much. But by adulthood, his genius had emerged. When Einstein was twenty-six, he published four related papers, one of which earned him a Ph.D., another that eventually led to the 1921 Nobel Prize in physics, and a third that changed our understanding of the universe. That paper, titled "On the Electrodynamics of Moving Bodies," came to be known as the special theory of relativity. This biography, filled with photographs and details, helps readers understand why *Time* magazine in 1999 named Einstein the Person of the Millennium.

4.34 Severance, John B. **Thomas Jefferson: Architect of Democracy.** Clarion, 1998. 192 pp. ISBN 0395845130. Nonfiction.

Although many people know that Jefferson was one of the primary forces behind the United States' struggle for independence, and know that the famous words of the Declaration of Independence are his, most don't know the specifics of his life—a life that included a talent for architecture, a love of books, and a great interest in philosophy. This biography takes readers on a tour of Monticello, Jefferson's home, and explores the scandal that surrounded his relationship with Sally Hemings and his confusing contradictory stance on slavery. Stunning black-and-white prints and many quotes from Jefferson help this biography not only provide information but offer enjoyment to readers.

4.35 Smith, Dean, with John Kilgo and Sally Jenkins. **A Coach's Life.** Random House, 1999. 350 pp. ISBN 037550270X. Nonfiction.

Dean Smith, retired basketball coach of the University of North Carolina, is known as one of the most successful college basketball coaches in the history of the game. His career included seventeen Atlantic Coast Conference titles, thirteen Conference championships, two national championships, and an Olympic gold medal. But Coach Smith is more than a game-winning coach. His ability to inspire and instill in his players discipline, respect, and a spirit of camaraderie makes Dean Smith a truly inspirational teacher, mentor, and friend. In this memoir, Smith tells an engaging story about the memorable games, the personalities, his philosophy, and his many basketball innovations. He also discusses the issues facing college basketball, both during his career and today. *A Coach's Life* is more than a story about the game of basketball; it is a story about life.

4.36 Todras, Ellen H. **Angelina Grimke: Voice of Abolition.** Linnet, 1999. 178 pp. ISBN 0208024859. Nonfiction.

"As a Southerner I feel it is my duty to stand up here tonight and bear testimony against slavery . . . I have seen it! I know it has horrors that can never be described." That a woman spoke these words in public in 1838 is extraordinary. That the woman was a southerner from a distinguished slave-owning family is beyond belief. The speaker, Angelina Grimke, along with her sister Sarah, traveled through the North speaking against slavery, often facing ridicule and physical danger from proslavery mobs. The first woman to publicly address a U.S. political body and defend her right to do so, Angelina not only advanced the antislavery movement in the United States, but she also paved the way for the women's rights movement. Based on her diaries, letters, and other primary sources, this biography traces Angelina's life from her childhood on a southern plantation, through her activist career.

4.37 Turner, Glennette Tilley. **Follow in Their Footsteps: Biographies of Ten Outstanding African Americans with Skits about Each One to Act Out.** Dutton, 1997. 182 pp. ISBN 0525651918. Nonfiction.

Imagine stepping into the shoes of Thurgood Marshall and adjudicating cases on the Supreme Court of the United States, or spending one day as Malcolm X, Alex Haley, Charlemae Rollins, or one of the other extraordinary African Americans whose lives are documented in this book. From sculptress Edmonia Lewis to entrepreneur A. G. Gaston, you will learn about the important contributions each of these individuals made. Short skits follow each biographical entry for those who want to take that extra step in someone else's shoes.

5 Colleges

"The function of the university is not simply to teach bread-winning, or to furnish teachers for the public schools or to be a center of polite society; it is, above all, to be the organ of that fine adjustment between real life and the growing knowledge of life, an adjustment which forms the secret of civilization."

W. E. B. Du Bois

"Educational progress is a national concern; education is a private one."

Nikki Giovanni

5.1 Adler, Joanne. **100 Colleges Where Average Students Can Excel.** IDG Books Worldwide, 1997. 121 pp. ISBN 002861044X. Nonfiction.

If college seems intimidating, something only for the really smart kids, then you might want to check out this book. This guide will help you find a college that's willing to help the average student get a great higher-level education. With small classes, creative professors, lots of academic support, and interesting classes to take, you'll find all the things you need to be successful in college.

5.2 **Barron's Profiles of American Colleges.** Barron's, 1997. 1591 pp. ISBN 0764171348. Nonfiction.

This reference book profiles more than 1650 four-year colleges. For each college listed, you'll get information about its size, tuition, number of faculty, types of degrees offered, admission procedures, required SAT or ACT scores, student life, programs of study, and financial aid. Additionally, in the blue pages you'll find valuable tips for choosing a college, getting through the admissions procedure, applying for financial aid, and managing your first year. An enclosed CD helps you prepare application forms and write letters of application.

5.3 Edwards, Stephen. **101 Things a College Guy Should Know.** Andrews McMeel, 1998. 64 pp. ISBN 0836252934. Nonfiction.

Leaving high school and moving on to college can be more than exciting—it can be a little unnerving and a little frightening. Get over some of those fears and set aside some of the butterflies with this easy-to-read guide that explains everything from choosing a major, a meal in the dining hall, or courses to joining a fraternity, doing laundry, and dealing with professors. A companion book, *101 Things a College Girl Should Know,* is just as helpful for girls.

5.4 **Peterson's Guide to College Visits.** Peterson's, 1999. 540 pp. ISBN 0768904005. Nonfiction.

Choosing the right college is easier when visiting the campus is a part of the selection process. Hearing about a place or reading about it just isn't the same as really going there. This guide book will help you plan your visit. It not only offers tips on scheduling and organizing trips, making appointments, and assessing what you see, but gives you valuable information for more than six hundred colleges and universities. For each college or university listed you'll learn who to contact to arrange a visit, tuition amounts, enrollment, where to stay, calendars, and when you can or can't visit. You'll also find information about campus facilities and local attractions. Arranged alphabetically by state and packaged with a CD that helps you plan your trips, this guide is a big help for those high school students who want to preview college campuses either before or after making a selection.

5.5 **Scholarship Handbook 2000.** The College Board, 1999. 590 pp. ISBN 0874476275. Nonfiction.

If a college education is your goal, don't let financial constraints keep you from reaching that dream. This handbook gives you the information you need to apply for a scholarship, and to understand how disabilities, gender, ethnic background, religious affiliation, minority status, choice of career, connection to the military, or connection to an employer affect your scholarship choices and chances. The book lists thousands of scholarship choices, and provides information on when to apply, how much money you could expect, what the requirements are for receiving money, and who to contact to apply. This is an invaluable aid as you begin thinking about those college years.

5.6 Wilson, Erlene B. **The 100 Best Colleges for African-American Students.** Plume, 1998. 352 pp. ISBN 0452279542. Nonfiction.

If you're an African American with questions about college life that other sources don't seem to answer, you might want to look at this book. Based on interviews with students and recent graduates, this book gives insight into the social and academic life of one hundred U.S. colleges. It discusses the racial composition of the student body and faculty, African American fraternities and sororities you can join, the amount of security on campus, the availability of childcare services, the accessibility of computers and online services, tuition, SAT requirements, and the number of scholarships available.

6 Computers and Technology

*"Is it a fact—or have I dreamt it—that, by means of electricity,
the world of matter has become a great nerve, vibrating
thousands of miles in a breathless point of time?"*

Nathaniel Hawthorne

6.1 Campbell-Kelly, Martin, and William Aspray. **Computer: A History of the Information Machine.** Basic, 1997. 352 pp. ISBN 0465029906. Nonfiction.

If you think—like most people do—that Steve Jobs (the personal computer guru), John von Neumann (the father of scientific computing), and Alan Turing (the Word War II cryptologist) are the grandfathers of computers, you might want to pause and read this book. This riveting history takes us back to the beginnings of computers and pioneers such as William Mauchley (who was intent on making a machine that would allow racetracks to post wins faster) and Jay Forrester (who worked hard to build a flight simulator that in turn impacted the development of the first real-time computer). This book reminds us of the earliest computers—groups of people who worked in factories and sat hundreds to a room working on individual projects that all contributed to a whole product—and in doing so reveals a history that is rich with anecdotes and filled with unsung heroes who deserve our appreciation.

6.2 Collier, Bruce, and James H. MacLachlan. **Charles Babbage and the Engines of Perfection.** Oxford University, 1998. 144 pp. ISBN 0195089979. Nonfiction.

A book from the Portraits in Science series, *Charles Babbage and the Engines of Perfection* gives us an up-close look at one a computer pioneer. This nineteenth century mathematician studied mathematics at Trinity College, Oxford, and then married quite young. He created the difference engine as he pondered how to get out of dull classroom computations. Next he invented a small mechanical calculating machine. Then he turned to the analytical engine, which had many of the elements that appeared with electronic brains, such as a CPU and memory banks. This fairly technical book also manages to capture this man's interesting personality. Includes black-and-white photographs.

6.3   Dickinson, Joan D. **Bill Gates: Billionaire Computer Genius.** Enslow, 1997. 104 pp. ISBN 0894908243. Nonfiction.

Harvard dropout Bill Gates is now a billionaire. What happened between 1977 when Gates left Harvard and 1996 when his wealth was estimated at $18 billion? This biography, part of the People to Know series, gives you a quick look at the man who created the Microsoft empire, and explains his impact on the computer world. See pictures of his $50 million home, and read about his new wife and child.

6.4   Greenia, Mark W. **History of Computing: An Encyclopedia of the People and Machines That Made Computer History.** Lexicon Services, 1998. 1100 pp. ISBN 0944601782. Nonfiction.

This book is available only on CD-ROM. It's worth its less-than-$20.00 price, as it covers everything you might ever want to know about the history of computing. Beginning with the earliest ways people kept track of numbers, moving through mechanical adding machines and calculators, and ending with the early computers of the 1940s and 1950s and today's microcomputers, this CD is full of information. Graphics and illustrations, over one thousand pages of text, discussions of early programming languages and robotics, and a full glossary make this a computer history buff's dream. As a bonus, several additional titles are included on the CD: *Computer Security and Privacy, SuperGlossary, Science, Law, Medicine, Sports, Broadcasting, Financial Planning and More,* and *Internet Access Guide for Beginners.*

6.5   Hahn, Harley. **Harley Hahn Teaches the Internet.** Que, 1999. 501 pp. ISBN 0789720930. Nonfiction.

This book provides lots of information needed for accessing the information superhighway. Hahn begins with an introduction to the Internet, and then explains everything from working with search engines, using e-mail, using plug-in applets, downloading programs, subscribing to mail groups, and ensuring your safety and security when on the Internet. Hahn explains computer and Internet language, options like Web TV and DSL, conducting online research, and selecting and using domain names. He concludes with a discussion of creating Web pages, and offers an extensive glossary and a sample directory of Web sites.

6.6   Hahn, Harley. **Harley Hahn's Internet and Web Yellow Pages,** Millennium Edition. Osborne, 1999. 909 pp. ISBN 007212170X. Nonfiction.

Hahn's latest edition of his best-selling Internet and Web yellow pages begins by continuing the introduction that was started five editions ago. These yellow pages include categories such as art, computers, environment, literature, movies, music, sports, and world cultures, and list thousands of sites that will both educate and entertain. The fun part of the book, however, comes from the inclusion of stranger topics: UFOs and aliens, intrigue, and cool but useless devices. Along with all the Web addresses, Hahn includes "ads" in the style of phone book yellow pages and offers tidbits of information from newsgroups and FAQs (frequently asked question lists). It's not only a very useful book, but a fun book as well.

6.7   Healy, Jane M. **Failure to Connect: How Computers Affect Our Children's Minds—for Better and Worse.** Simon & Schuster, 1998. 350 pp. ISBN 0684831368. Nonfiction.

Although written for adults, anyone interested in how computers impact today's youth—including today's youth—will find this book thought-provoking. In a time of technology frenzy, Healy questions the use of computers for children at school and at home. She explores the impact computers have on children's creativity, brain development, and emotional growth. With comments from individuals ranging from pediatricians and brain researchers to principals, parents, and students themselves, Healy uncovers another aspect of the digital divide—the folks who are for children's connection to technology and the folks who are against it.

6.8   Hellman, Hal. **Beyond Your Senses: The New World of Sensors.** Lodestar, 1997. 87 pp. ISBN 0525675337. Nonfiction.

The senses—vision, touch, hearing, taste, smell—have long been the property of humans. But now, in this world of technology, machines are able to mimic human senses. Optical scanners read printed text. Supermarket doors open when a sensor commands them. Smoke detectors know when to go off. Robug II—a four-legged, spider-like device used for cleaning tall chimneys—encounters obstacles while climbing up chimneys and navigates around them. Scientists are working on a glucose sensor that would help diabetics monitor glucose levels. Scentinel takes "smell prints" unique to each person for security purposes. Everywhere sensors are used to help machines work more like humans—only better.

6.9 Kennedy, Angus J. **The Internet: The Rough Guide 2000.** Rough Guides, 1999. 501 pp. ISBN 1858284422. Nonfiction.

This outstanding, concise guide to the Internet tells you in plain English how to get connected and what you can do once you're online. Learn how to find anything, how to send e-mail, how to play free music samples, how to download software, and how to create your own Web page. Read a history of the Internet and take a look at over two thousand sites to visit on the World Wide Web. This small, hand-size book eliminates geek-speak and focuses on getting you the information you need fast.

6.10 Lampton, Christopher. **Home Page: An Introduction to Web Page Design.** Franklin Watts, 1997. 63 pp. ISBN 0531158543. Nonfiction.

If you want to learn to design your own Web pages but find the how-to books too intimidating, try this easy-to-follow book. If your computer has a text editor (such as Notepad) and an Internet browser (such as Netscape Navigator), you're ready to get started. With this book in hand, you'll learn Hypertext Markup Language (HTML) and discover how to make a Web page template. Although the really sophisticated elements of sound and animation aren't covered in this beginner's book, you will learn how to illustrate your Web page and create links to other pages.

6.11 Leebow, Ken. **300 Incredible Things for Golfers on the Internet.** Illustrated by Marty Bucella. 300Incredible.com, 1999. 128 pp. ISBN 0965866831. Nonfiction.

From golf jokes to golf tips to golfing destinations you won't want to miss, this Leebow book gives golf enthusiasts a winning shot. Through the sites listed in this book, you'll learn about golf pros, find classes via the Internet that will improve your swing, and discover new places to play the game.

6.12 Leebow, Ken. **300 Incredible Things for Kids on the Internet,** 7th edition. 300Incredible.com, 1999. 128 pp. ISBN 0965866807. Nonfiction.

This reference work provides Web addresses for everything from general reference sites that contain dictionaries and almanacs to specialized sites that show you how to build a science project. Although many of the sites listed are geared toward the younger crowd, others will appeal to kids of all ages.

6.13 Leebow, Ken. **300 Incredible Things for Sports Fans on the Internet.** Illustrated by Marty Bucella. 300Incredible.com, 1999. 128 pp. ISBN 0965866823. Nonfiction.

Do you like to play golf and want to see what some of the world's greatest courses look like without flying around the world to take a look? Want to check out the Web page of your favorite football team? Interested in having a live conversation with some of your favorite sports stars? If you answered yes to any of these questions, then you'll probably be interested in this great book that connects our culture's passion for sports with our newest hobby: surfing the Internet. With this book you can find the sites that will make your favorite sport even more enjoyable.

6.14 Lindsay, Dave, and Bruce Lindsay. **Dave's Quick 'n' Easy Web Pages.** Erin, 1999. 128 pp. ISBN 0969060971. Nonfiction.

Dave, the fourteen-year-old Webmaster for the Redwall Abbey homepage (one of the most visited sites in children's and young adult literature), gives information for creating a Web page in this practical, easy-to-follow book. With a little editorial help from his dad Bruce, Dave explains how to use Hypertext Markup Language (HTML). He shows how to add sound, images, backgrounds, and the animations that make a site enjoyable. With inserts labeled "Dave's Advice," he helps novice Webmasters avoid problems he encountered. The book is filled with examples from his own site. Although it has a low-budget format, it has a high interest appeal.

6.15 McCormick, Anita Louise. **The Internet: Surfing the Issues.** Enslow, 1998. 128 pp. ISBN 0894909568. Nonfiction.

Hackers. The Digital Divide. Viruses. Web TV. Censorship. Pornography. Encryption. These important and controversial topics must be considered when looking at computers and technology, and McCormick's book does just that. She offers readers information about computer usage, and isn't afraid to tackle the tough issues. Furthermore, she explains the history of the development of the Internet, speculates on its future uses, and provides a list of additional readings and organizations to contact.

6.16   Murray, Charles J. **The Supermen: The Story of Seymour Cray and the Technical Wizards behind the Supercomputer.** Wiley, 1997. 220 pp. ISBN 0471048852. Nonfiction.

Seymour Cray is a legendary name in the computer industry. He not only built some of the earliest supercomputers, he also set some of the cultural standards we associate with the computer workplace such as informal dress codes and small, cooperative, stand-alone teams. Cray and his work team pushed back the limits of science and strained the boundaries of bureaucracy. This history shows us what happened when a group of highly creative and highly motivated men worked under one of the true computer geniuses. Called "the Albert Einstein," "the Thomas Edison," and "the Evel Knievel" of supercomputing, Cray and his maverick engineers beat out the huge IBM corporation to become the computer industry's leader.

6.17   Northrup, Mary. **American Computer Pioneers.** Enslow, 1998. 112 pp. ISBN 0766010538. Nonfiction.

Part of the Collective Biographies series, this book provides a look at the major players in the development of computers and technology. Northrup not only details the contribution of folks such as An Wang, Herman Hollerith, Grace Hopper, Bill Gates, Steve Jobs, and Marc Andreessen, but also provides a historical look at the evolution of computers, from punch cards to Netscape and the Internet. She shows that creativity and the willingness to take risks are qualities worth cultivating.

6.18   Pedersen, Ted, and Francis Moss. **Internet for Kids! A Beginner's Guide to Surfing the Net.** Price Stern Sloan, 1997. 220 pp. ISBN 0843179376. Nonfiction.

This beginners guide isn't just for kids; it is for anyone who's a beginner when it comes to surfing the Internet. Topics include learning how to log on, connecting to e-mail, downloading files, and using search engines and Web browsers. A long list of recommended sites is included, plus a great glossary that defines everything from ASCII, cookies, and handshakes to kludges, threads, and zaibatsu. You can visit the authors online to keep up with the newest information.

6.19 Pedersen, Ted, and Francis Moss. **Make Your Own Web Page! A Guide for Kids.** Illustrated by Nate Evans. Price Stern Sloan, 1998. 64 pp. ISBN 0843174595. Nonfiction.

Although simple in format, this book is no fluff. You'll learn Hypertext Markup Language (HTML), step-by-step guidelines for basic planning in Web design, and how to add hypertext links and graphics. You'll also learn how to publicize your Website, and read some important tips about safety on the Internet and e-mail usage. If your PC or Apple computer has a plain text editor and a Web browser, you're ready to learn to make your own Web page!

6.20 Polly, Jean Armour. **The Internet Kids and Family Yellow Pages,** 1999 Edition. Osborne McGraw-Hill, 1999. 784 pp. ISBN 0072118490. Nonfiction.

This comprehensive guide lists thousands of Internet sites worth visiting. Some educational and some entertaining, this book lists sites for everyone from baby brother and sister to mom and dad. This third edition includes a Web site (netmom.com) to visit to find the latest updates on Web sites listed in the book. You also get a CD-ROM that contains a clickable version of all the Web site addresses listed in the book.

7 Environment and Ecology

"It had been startling and disappointing to me to find out that story books had been written by people, that books were not natural wonders, coming up of themselves like grass."

Eudora Welty

7.1 Archer, Jules. **To Save the Earth: The American Environmental Movement.** Viking, 1998. 198 pp. ISBN 0670871214. Nonfiction.

Read about four extraordinary environmentalists who devoted their lives to making our world a better one. This book describes John Muir's passion for creating a national park system; Rachel Carson's determination to free lakes, rivers, and oceans of pollution; David McTaggart's initiatives to save marine mammals; and Dave Foreman's hand-on tactics to save the forests. The culminating chapter discusses the 1990s, the impact of recent environmental legislation and mandates, and how we in the twenty-first century can continue the crusades of these four courageous leaders.

7.2 Brooks, Bruce. **The Red Wasteland.** Henry Holt, 1998. 143 pp. ISBN 0805044957. Nonfiction.

Science and words are Brooks' two great passions, and in his rich collection of science poems and essays by twenty well-known authors, Brooks focuses the reader's attention upon the beauty of words and the power of science. For example, Brooks reads "Elixirs of Death" by Rachel Carson as a reminder of the importance of being tuned into nature. Edward Abbey's "Desert Solitaire" describes in words the magical beauty and power of nature and shouts the message, "Leave Nature Alone!" This connection of poetry with science provides a powerful model for how to combine two seemingly different human endeavors.

7.3 Brown, Lester R. **State of the World 1999: The Millennium Edition.** Norton, 1999. 259 pp. ISBN 039331815X. Nonfiction.

This book provides national leaders and interested citizens with a detailed look at environmental issues facing Earth at the turn of the millennium. Assembled by the Worldwatch Institute, the book provides a look at dangerous environmental trends and suggests possible solutions to those problems. This comprehensive look at what has changed in the environment in the past one hundred years gives you an idea of what might happen in the next one hundred years if some radical environmental measures aren't taken.

7.4   Cassie, Brian. **National Audubon Society First Field Guide: Trees.** Scholastic, 1999. 160 pp. ISBN 0590054724. Nonfiction.

In this field guide about trees, you will learn how trees convert carbon dioxide into oxygen, and how they are connected to seasonal and climatic changes. Furthermore, you'll read about the unique characteristics of specific species, their life cycles, and their habitats. As a final plus, you'll read about how they provide food and protection for birds, mammals, insects, fungi, and algae. With over 450 photographs, charts, and graphs, this reference book is a valuable resource for outdoor adventurers as well as homeowners. Naturalist activities are also included in this book.

7.5   Conner, Susan, and Lloyd A. Freeman. **Drinking Water Quality— Taking Responsibility.** Waterworks, 1998. 62 pp. ISBN 0966252098. Nonfiction.

What happens to water that we pollute? It eventually becomes part of the water cycle, which means it gets returned to earth to be used again—polluted or not—and polluted water means ill people. What do we do to clean up the water that we drink? What are the ultimate consequences of water pollution? For a quick overview of the issues surrounding a clean drinking water supply, take a look at this book. It will make you thirsty for a clear glass of water.

7.6   Daley, Michael J. **Nuclear Power: Promise or Peril.** Lerner, 1997. 144 pp. ISBN 0822526115. Nonfiction.

Careful documentation, a useful glossary, and lists of resources for further information help achieve this book's purpose, which is to provide accurate information both pro and con in order to allow readers to make informed decisions about nuclear power. The proponents of nuclear power argue that power plants provide plentiful electricity that is safe, clean, reliable, and inexpensive. Opponents argue that the risks are too great, using the Russian Chernobyl nuclear plant meltdown and the resulting environmental and health effects as an example of what is likely to happen if we become more dependent on nuclear power. If you find out tomorrow that a nuclear plant is being planned for your community, what will your stance be?

7.7   Dolan, Edward F. **Our Poisoned Waters.** Cobblehill, 1997. 121 pp. ISBN 0525652205.

Earth's water sources are poisoned and vanishing! From sewage spills and depletion of wetlands to population growth and simple carelessness, there are many causes of the destruction of plant, animal, and human water resources. So how can we ensure quality water for generations to come? This book explains the many misconceptions about water pollution, how our waters became polluted, and how we as individuals and groups can join with public and private organizations to remedy this critical problem.

7.8   Doyle, Kevin. **Environmental Careers in the 21st Century.** Island, 1998. 280 pp. ISBN 155963586X.

If you are thinking about pursuing a job that connects you to the environment, then you will want to look at this book. Read about jobs in fishery management, parks and outdoor recreation, air and water quality management, hazardous waste management, land and water conservation, solid waste management, or forestry management. In each area, learn about salaries, educational requirements, and how to conduct a job search. This book is an excellent resource as you prepare to leave high school to begin college or pursue a career.

7.9   Gallant, Roy A., and Christopher J. Schuberth. **Earth: The Making of a Planet.** Marshall Cavendish, 1998. 160 pp. ISBN 0761450122. Nonfiction.

Ever wonder how galaxies are born or how our changing planet might look in a century? This narrative explains through diagrams, pictures, and descriptions the ever-changing Earth within the context of the solar system. The chapter titled "A Planet under Stress" examines the health of our planet and explains how global warming and pollution create changes that will impact all populations on Earth. A complete glossary is included.

7.10 **Global Resources.** Opposing Viewpoints Series. Greenhaven, 1998. 189 pp. ISBN 1565106725. Nonfiction.

Can bicycles become viable alternatives for transportation? What are the pros and cons of this mode of transportation? This wonderful resource provides opposing views and specific information about environmental, economic, land use, and natural resource issues. Written by experts, the information in this book can be used as the foundation for reports, position papers, or debates. Find out how long our oil reserves will last, or whether the world's rain forests have suffered irreparable damage that will impact our planet.

7.11 Hertsgaard, Mark. **Earth Odyssey: Around the World in Search of Our Environmental Future.** Broadway, 1998. 352 pp. ISBN 0767900588. Nonfiction.

In 1991, Mark Hertsgaard took off on a trip around the world asking people what they thought were the major environmental problems. This book is his report of what he found after interviewing people in nineteen different countries. In an effort to discover how people are coping with famine, air and water pollution, deforestation, and drought, Hertsgaard talked with everyone from taxi drivers to farmers and politicians. Interviews with Jacques Cousteau and Vaclav Havel help explain the global calamity we face if pollution continues unchecked.

7.12 Lanting, Frans, Galen Rowell, and David Doubilet. **Living Planet: Preserving Edens of the Earth.** Crown, 1999. 256 pp. ISBN 060960466X. Nonfiction.

The World Wildlife Fund, together with the Living Planet campaign, plans to preserve a portion of every major type of ecosystem on the planet. The introduction to this book explains the project's goals: "By conserving the broadest variety of the world's habitats, we can conserve the broadest variety of the world's species and most endangered wildlife." This book is a historical record of all that happened as this goal was attempted. Stunning photographs capture the beauty of animals, birds, insects, and fish trying to survive in precarious places.

7.13 Larson, Gary. **There's a Hair in My Dirt! A Worm's Story.** Harper-Collins, 1998. 64 pp. ISBN 006019104X. Nonfiction.

A young earthworm is disgusted when he finds a hair in his dinnertime serving of dirt. His father explains how the hair ended up in his dirt, telling his son of a beautiful but stupid young woman named Harriet who thought all of nature was cute and cuddly. Harriet never quite figured out that nature is to be understood and respected, perhaps even feared. This tongue-in-cheek look at the way some people interact with nature is brought to you by the man who created "The Far Side." If zany humor is your interest, this picture book is perfect.

7.14   Maclean, John N. **Fire on the Mountain: The True Story of the South Canyon Fire.** Morrow, 1999. 275 pp. ISBN 0688144772. Nonfiction.

The 1994 catastrophic South Canyon fire in Colorado burned for ten days. It took the lives of fourteen firefighters and cost over $4.5 million to contain. What made this fire so expensive—both in human lives and dollars? Maclean reconstructs the bureaucratic bunglings and internal fighting that kept attention off the blazes and on personalities during the war against the fire.

7.15   McKibben, Bill. **Hope, Human and Wild: True Stories of Living Lightly on the Earth.** Hungry Mind, 1997. 227 pp. ISBN 1886913137. Nonfiction.

After you've read McKibben's best seller *The End of Nature,* you'll want to pick up this book, which focuses on the environmental recovery of nature. In this series of essays, McKibben shows what some communities are doing to reverse environmental damage. He scouts his area of the Adirondack Mountains and goes as far away as Brazil and India to find models of what's working.

7.16   Pandell, Karen. **Journey through the Northern Rainforest.** Photographs by Art Wolfe. Dutton Children's Books, 1999. Unpaged. ISBN 0525458042. Nonfiction.

Travel along the western coast of the United States, up through British Columbia, and into Alaska as you take a tour of the coastal northern rain forests. Stunning color photographs offer images of trees, wildlife, waterfalls, and plant life. Read about the migration of salmon, the effects of the logging industry, and the ecosystem of this disappearing land.

7.17 Powledge, Fred. **Pharmacy in the Forest: How Medicines Are Found in the Natural World.** Atheneum Books for Young Readers, 1998. 50 pp. ISBN 06889808631. Nonfiction.

In the United States each year, 500 million prescriptions are written for drugs—25 percent of which are from plants! Most of these plants come from the world's rain forests. However, within vacant lots and our own backyards, there are many plants that can help heal us. For example, in this text you'll discover that the common periwinkle is responsible for helping diabetics as well as lowering the white cell count in leukemia patients. *Pharmacy in the Forest* combines history and biology to describe how we have learned from shamans and other native medicine people to use plants to cure illness.

7.18 Roulac, John. **Backyard Composting: Your Complete Guide to Recycling Yard Clippings.** Chelsea Green, 1997. 96 pp. ISBN 0962976830. Nonfiction.

See all those leaves in your backyard? See those grass clippings? See those fallen branches and that kicked-aside dirt? Well stop raking and bagging, and start piling and saving! Turn your backyard waste into a compost pile that will help your garden grow greener and stronger.

7.19 Strasser, Susan. **Waste and Want: A Social History of Trash.** Metropolitan, 1999. 355 pp. ISBN 0805048308. Nonfiction.

This fascinating book chronicles what we throw away daily, why we throw it away, and what it means to live in a throw-away society. Going back to the nineteenth century, Strasser shows how "disposability was promoted for its ability to make people feel rich: with throwaway products, they could obtain levels of cleanliness and convenience once available to people with many servants." But this attitude has resulted in landfills that are full, and pollution that's destroying nature.

7.20 Wilcove, David. **The Condor's Shadow: The Loss and Recovery of Wildlife in America.** Freeman, 1999. 288 pp. ISBN 0716731150. Nonfiction.

Environmental Defense Fund ecologist David Wilcove believes that as much as sixteen percent of all U.S. flora and fauna are in danger. He suggests that in this country we tend to "ignore a problem until it becomes a crisis," and he believes that pattern is certainly playing itself out in the wilderness areas that are being destroyed daily. He writes, "More than 85 percent of the virgin forests of the United States have been logged, 90 percent of the tallgrass prairies have been plowed or paved, and 98 percent of the rivers and streams have been dammed, diverted, or developed." With statistics like that, many might think all is lost. But Wilcove also sees wonderful conservation efforts trying to undo the damage. This book discusses both the damaging practices and the recovery efforts underway now.

7.21   Wilson, Christina. **National Audubon Society First Field Guide: Insects.** Scholastic, 1998. 159 pp. ISBN 059005483X. Nonfiction.

Ever wonder how old insects are or what purposes they serve us? This new field guide is rich with photographs and descriptions of common insects. In addition, it also offers broad categories of information about insect groups, insect structures, habitats, and life cycle differences. In addition, there is a section that helps the reader understand differences between insects and spiders, butterflies and moths, and the many different kinds of beetles. This is a perfect book for insect identification and information. Also included in the First Field Guide series are *Rocks and Minerals* by Edward Ricciuti and Margaret W. Carruthers, *Wildflowers* by Susan Hood, and *Birds* by Scott Weidensaul.

8 Family Relationships

"There are books which rank in our life with parents and lovers and passionate experiences, so medicinal, so stringent, so revolutionary, so authoritative."

Ralph Waldo Emerson

8.1   Abelove, Joan. **Saying It Out Loud.** DK Ink, 1999. 136 pp. ISBN 0789426099. Fiction.

Mindy's life is one of dull predictability. All of that changes when her mother is diagnosed with a malignant brain tumor. Although her father will not admit the truth out loud, and pretends that their lives are perfectly normal, Mindy knows that her mother's life is in danger. She visits her mother in the hospital, but is frightened by the shell of a person her mother has become. Mindy understands that she must be able to voice her concerns and fears if she is to find someone to help her. It is now that she will discover who her real friends are.

8.2   Aker, Don. **Stranger at Bay.** Stoddart Kids, 1997. 246 pp. ISBN 0773674683. Fiction.

Randy Forsythe feels betrayed. The pharmaceutical company his father works for has downsized. As a result, Randy's father has been relocated from Ontario to Nova Scotia. Randy is forced to leave his school and friends behind. Now living in a tiny apartment with his father and stepmother, Randy manages to adapt to his new school. When he meets the beautiful Natalie McCormick, though, Randy begins running with a new crowd, one that seems a bit too interested in the fact that his father works for a drug company. Randy ends up in real trouble, and only his stepmother can help him escape.

8.3   Anderson, Janet S. **The Monkey Tree.** Dutton Children's Books, 1998. 152 pp. ISBN 0525460322. Fiction.

Fourteen-year-old Susanna wonders just how she'll do what her grandma did—look after her great-uncle, who hasn't left his bedroom for twenty years. Susanna dreads the job, is fearful that Uncle Louis is crazy, and doubts her ability to take care of him. After a painful encounter with her best friend and some very hurtful comments from a teacher, Susanna also doubts who she is as a person and what her real talent is as an artist. Then Susanna finds a sanctuary in the most unusual of all places—Uncle Louis's bedroom. She discovers that he, too, is an artist, and finds that he has turned his room into a haven where creating art is all that matters. Susanna discovers how safe it feels to be in one place, and must face the reality that if she doesn't leave the room, she'll become a recluse like her uncle.

8.4   Atkins, Catherine. **When Jeff Comes Home.** Putnam, 1999. 231 pp. ISBN 0399233660. Fiction.

Thirteen-year-old Jeff is kidnapped when his family stops at a roadside rest area. He is returned to his family two and a half years later. Jeff's family is relieved to have him home, but cannot understand his reluctance to discuss what happened during his absence. Jeff refuses to talk to his family, his friends, and even to the FBI, who are looking for Ray, the man who kidnapped him. Jeff's long road to recovery begins when his captor is apprehended, and he must come to terms with what he was forced to do to survive life with Ray.

8.5   Bell, William. **Zack.** Simon & Schuster. 1999. 192 pp. ISBN 0689822480. Fiction.

It is bad enough growing up with a Jewish father and an African American mother, but then Zack's parents move to the country during his senior year. His grades suffer terribly, and he is on the brink of failing history, when his teacher offers him the option of doing a research paper. His mother has always refused to talk about her parents, but a slave collar he finds while gardening gives him the perfect subject: A history of who owned their land previously, and how these Civil War artifacts ended up on their property. Perhaps at the same time he can discover his own history.

8.6   Bloor, Edward. **Crusader.** Harcourt Brace, 1999. 390 pp. ISBN 0152019448. Fiction.

Fifteen-year-old Roberta Ritter doesn't like her looks, doesn't like her home life, doesn't like her dad's newest girlfriend, doesn't much like her job at the family arcade, and doesn't care too much for the friends her cousins constantly bring around. After a new virtual reality game arrives at the arcade—one filled with graphic violence—things begin to change. Skinheads begin to patronize the arcade, the mall where Roberta works may close, she moves out of her home and away from her father, and she stumbles across evidence that leads her to her mother's murderer—a discovery that she almost wishes she had never made. Roberta discovers that she, like the characters in the virtual reality game, is a crusader—she just isn't sure if she wants to be a part of this crusade.

8.7 Brooks, Bruce. **Vanishing.** HarperCollins, 1999. 160 pp. ISBN 0060282363. Fiction.

Eleven-year-old Alice has seen more than her share of hardship in life. When her parents divorce, Alice elects to live with her father. Although he seems to lack direction, anything is preferable to living with her alcoholic mother. However, circumstances force Alice to return to her mother. A severe case of bronchitis lands her in the hospital where, for a time, Alice feels safely in charge of her own life. In the hospital, she meets Rex, a terminally ill boy who has deemed himself the King of Remissions. Their friendship grows, despite the fact that Alice has decided to go on a hunger strike. If she cannot get well, the doctors cannot send her home to her mother, right? Even death seems a better option, until Rex falls seriously ill.

8.8 Bunting, Eve. **Blackwater.** HarperCollins, 1999. 146 pp. ISBN 0060278382. Fiction.

The arrival of his cousin Alex ruins all of Brodie's plans for the summer. Maybe he can salvage some fun by teaching Alex to swim. The Blackwater River can be quite dangerous, but Brodie plans to take his cousin to the swimming hole where he, too, learned to swim. Alex and Brodie set out early one morning, and their actions lead to a tragic accident, one that will change the lives of many families who live near the river.

8.9 Cadnum, Michael. **Rundown.** Viking, 1999. 168 pp. ISBN 0670883778. Fiction.

Jennifer is weary of all the attention being paid to her older sister, Cassandra. After all, what is the big deal about a wedding? Can't her parents think of anything else besides dresses, flowers, and food? Jennifer plots a way to shift the focus to herself by faking a failed attack by a serial rapist thought to be in the area. Her plan backfires, though, when the police begin to find holes in Jennifer's version of the events.

8.10   Carter, Alden R. **Crescent Moon.** Holiday House, 1999. 153 pp. ISBN 08234151X. Fiction.

Jeremy plans to spend the summer with his friends doing all kinds of fun things. When his plans change and Jeremy finds himself with spare time on his hands, he begins to spend several hours a day working with his Uncle Mac, a carver, who in Jeremy's mind is out of touch with the modern world. His Uncle Mac is planning to make a carving out of a pine log taken from the last log drive on the Chippewa River. Jeremy is given the arduous task of sanding the log by hand. They begin preparing the new log, which Uncle Mac says he will make into a statue of a Native American maiden. While he helps, Jeremy learns about Native Americans in the area, his uncle, and himself.

8.11   Caseley, Judith. **Losing Louisa.** Farrar, Straus and Giroux, 1999. 236 pp. ISBN 0374346658. Fiction.

Lacey Monroe Levine could have been named Louisa after Louisa May Alcott. But she wasn't. She could have lived a life like that portrayed in *Little Women.* But she didn't. Instead, Lacey watches as her father leaves the family to start a new life with his secretary, her mother seeks her youth in a relationship with a bodybuilder, and her nearly perfect sister almost loses herself in a relationship with an all-consuming boyfriend. As Lacey confronts the changes in her family, she looks for a love of her own. Encounters with Charles and his onion, sausage, and cream soda breath, and with David and his roaming hands and drunken protestations of love, lead Lacey to wonder if she should become a spinster.

8.12   Chbosky, Stephen. **The Perks of Being a Wallflower.** Pocket, 1999. 213 pp. ISBN 0671027344. Fiction.

In a series of letters addressed simply "Dear Friend," Charlie talks about his first year of high school. Although he is not one of the geeks, Charlie is also not part of the in crowd. He is, by his own description, a wallflower, a young man who is shy, especially in social situations. As we read his letters, we get to know more about Charlie's talent for writing, a talent nurtured by his English teacher. We watch as Charlie makes friends and suffers through his first crush on a girl. There are other obstacles for Charlie to navigate as well, particularly family problems. Charlie faithfully records all of the pain and joy of life as a ninth grader.

8.13 Conly, Jane Leslie. **Trout Summer.** Henry Holt, 1998. 234 pp. ISBN 0805039333. Fiction.

Following your dreams seems like a good idea, but unfortunately for thirteen-year-old Shana Martin, her father's dream is to travel around the world, leaving his family behind. A divorce moves Shana, her mother, and her brother Cody to Laglade, Maryland, which is very different from their smaller hometown. Although Shana adjusts well, Cody hates their new setting, much preferring their summer cabin on the river. When summer arrives, Cody and Shana convince their mom to let them live alone in the cabin. Things seem peaceful enough until they realize they aren't alone.

8.14 Conrad, Pam. **Holding Me Here.** Harper Trophy / HarperCollins, 1997. 184 pp. ISBN 0064471667. Fiction.

Fourteen-year-old Robin is still upset about her parents' divorce, when her mother decides to take in a boarder named Mary to make ends meet. Sensing sadness in the boarder, Robin begins to snoop and read Mary's diary. When she finds that Mary has two children and a husband in another city, she decides to intervene so they can all be reunited. How can she know that she will make the situation worse, and put both Mary and herself in danger?

8.15 Cooney, Caroline B. **Tune in Anytime.** Delacorte, 1999. 186 pp. ISBN 0385326491. Fiction.

Sixteen-year-old Sophie Olivette is living a dream life. Her older sister, Marley, has gone off to college, and Sophie has her room to herself. In addition, she's just aced a history exam, given a speech without throwing up, and has an incredible set of fingernails! But when Sophie's father announces that he is leaving her mother to marry Marley's gorgeous college roommate, Sophie's life turns into a soap opera that Sophie doesn't want to be in.

8.16 Cooney, Caroline B. **What Child Is This? A Christmas Story.** Delacorte, 1997. 147 pp. ISBN 0385323174. Fiction.

"How do you get what you want for Christmas?" High school English teacher Mrs. Wrenn asks her students to write a paper answering this question. Liz Kitchell, whose parents have a themed Christmas tree in every room at home, wonders about the true meaning of Christmas. Tack Knight works after school for his father, who runs the local inn. For him, Christmas means granting the wishes of others. Matt Morden, a foster child shuffled from one home to another, has never had a real Christmas. Katie, aged eight, has a mother in prison, and wants a family for her Christmas present. In the season of miracles, the lives of these people connect, and it seems almost anything is possible.

8.17   Cormier, Robert. **Frenchtown Summer.** Delacorte, 1999. 113 pp. ISBN 0385327048. Fiction.

A young boy's summer in the French-Canadian town of Monument is presented in blank verse. Although only thirteen, Eugene sees events with the wisdom of someone much older than he is. Perhaps because he is largely unnoticed by his family, he is better able to observe the world around him. Eugene desperately wants love and approval from his father. He struggles to keep a terrible secret for another member of his family. As he travels the streets on his paper route, Eugene learns much about life and death.

8.18   Couloumbis, Audrey. **Getting Near to Baby.** Putnam, 1999. 211 pp. ISBN 039923389X. Fiction.

"When I got into bed, there was a sick feeling in my stomach that stayed with me through my sleep. I came out there to breathe deep of the fresh air but that sick feeling has not yet gone away." So begins Willa Jo's story as she sits on the roof of her Aunt Patty's house and thinks about what happens to people confronted by tragedy. Willa Jo contemplates all she's really lost since Baby suddenly died, and finally comes to realize what it will take to get her nearer to Baby.

8.19   Danticat, Edwidge. **Krik? Krak!** Vintage Contemporaries, 1996. 227 pp. ISBN 067976657X. Fiction.

In nine beautifully written but challenging stories, Edwidge Danticat vividly portrays both the pain and the beauty of the lives of contemporary Haitian people, especially the strong women who endure unimaginable horrors in the strife-torn country they love. The Haitian tradition of passing of stories from mother to daughter, generation to generation, is sustained in this collection of stories that takes its title from a Haitian saying, "They ask Krik? We say Krak!"

8.20 Dessen, Sarah. **Keeping the Moon.** Viking, 1999. 224 pp. ISBN 0670885495. Fiction.

It is bad enough having Kiki Sparks, noted weight loss guru, for a mother. Now Colie Sparks learns that her mother intends to dump her for the summer at her Aunt Mira's house in North Carolina. Although Colie has managed to shed quite a few pounds at her mother's insistence, she is still the insecure, sullen person she was before the weight loss. The prospect of a summer with an eccentric aunt is dismal. But Colie soon makes friends with two waitresses who work with her at the Last Chance Café. There may also be romance in her future once Colie meets Norman, a gifted young artist. Perhaps the summer won't be quite as bad as she dreaded.

8.21 Dominic, Andie. **Needles.** Scribner, 1998. 224 pp. ISBN 0684842327. Fiction.

Needles have been a part of Andie's life for as long as she can recall. Her older sister Denise, who has diabetes, uses needles daily to inject herself with insulin. Andie, who is fascinated by the syringes and needles, creates elaborate childhood games about needles and diabetes. The games become frightfully real when, at age nine, Andie is herself diagnosed with juvenile onset diabetes. As she watches her older sister lead a reckless lifestyle that causes her death at age thirty-three, Andie fears that the same fate awaits her.

8.22 Draper, Sharon M. **Forged by Fire.** Aladdin, 1998. 156 pp. ISBN 0689818513. Fiction.

Gerald Nickleby, one of the characters from *Tears of a Tiger,* loses his best friend in a drunk driving accident. Gerald has more than his share of burdens to shoulder as his mother, imprisoned for several years for neglecting him as a child, has returned to take him home. Now Gerald has a stepsister and a stepfather. When Gerald discovers that his stepfather is abusing his new sister, he must find the courage to defend her, even if it puts his own life in danger.

8.23   Garland, Sherry. **The Last Rainmaker.** Harcourt Brace, 1997. 324 pp. ISBN 0152006494. Fiction.

After her beloved grandmother's death, Caroline leaves her embittered Great Aunt Oriona to find out the truth about her mysterious mother, who died at Caroline's birth. She eventually joins the Wild West show in which her mother was a star. Caroline's journey to find out the truth about her mother brings her face-to-face with her own prejudiced feelings about the Native Americans she meets in the show, but it also brings her a grandfather she didn't know existed.

8.24   Gilbert, Barbara Snow. **Stone Water.** Front Street, 1998. 168 pp. ISBN 1886910111. Fiction.

Fifteen-year-old Grant can't believe what his grandfather wants him to do. Furthermore, he doesn't know what it means will happen to him if he obeys his grandfather. He listens carefully to his grandfather's request: to help him die if his disease becomes terminal and he's put on life-support systems. Grant wonders if doing this deed will make him a murderer and make his father hate him more than Grant already believes he does, or if obeying his grandfather is the right thing to do.

8.25   Grisham, John. **The Testament.** Doubleday, 1999. 435 pp. ISBN 0385493800. Fiction.

Troy Phelan, an eccentric billionaire, commits suicide and leaves his vast fortune to an illegitimate daughter, Rachel Lane, instead of to his other six grown children, who have greedily spent what they think they will soon inherit. Rachel, on the other hand, knows nothing of the wealth that is now hers because she lives in Brazil as a missionary. Phelan's children band together to contest the will, and soon Nate O'Riley, attorney for the Phelan estate, finds himself on a mosquito-infested river hunting for a woman who is now worth billions. Once he finds her, he is shocked at her reaction to the money, and overwhelmed by his reaction to her.

8.26   Haddix, Margaret Peterson. **Don't You Dare Read This, Mrs. Dunphrey.** Aladdin Paperbacks, 1997. 125 pp. ISBN 0689815433. Fiction.

Sixteen-year-old Tish Bonner has a new best friend—the journal she keeps for Mrs. Dunphrey's English class. Unlike Mrs. Dunphrey, who has promised not to read entries marked "Do not read," we can read every word. Tish writes frankly about school, her teachers, her friends, working at the Burger Barn, and the problems she and her younger brother Matt face when their parents' lives fall apart. Tish tries to keep her family together, but Matt's problems, her mother's breakdown, and her father's desertion become too much for Tish.

8.27 Holeman, Linda. **Mercy's Birds.** Tundra, 1998. 198 pp. ISBN 0887764630. Fiction.

Mercy cut off her blonde hair and dyed it black. She has also taken to wearing all black clothes. Although Mercy is trying to keep up the outward appearances of a normal home life, it is quite difficult when your family consists of a mother who is clinically depressed and an aunt who is an alcoholic. Sixteen-year-old Mercy is the "adult" in the family, often bringing home the only paycheck from her after-school job at the florist shop. It is here that she gets the love and attention she needs from the owner, Vince, and his mother, Mama Gio. Because of their emotional support, Mercy has enough courage to stand up to Barry, her Aunt Moo's boyfriend, who has threatened to hurt her if she tells anyone about his sexual advances.

8.28 Holt, Kimberly Willis. **When Zachary Beaver Came to Town.** Henry Holt, 1999. 192 pp. ISBN 0805061169. Fiction.

Nothing much seems to happen in Antler, Texas. About all Toby Wilson has to look forward to is the annual release of ladybugs at his friend's farm. Toby's mother has left to seek her fame and fortune as a singer in Nashville, leaving Toby feeling a little abandoned. Enter Zachary Beaver, billed as the world's fattest boy at six hundred pounds. Toby becomes fascinated with this boy, who lives his entire life behind a Plexiglas shield in a traveling road show trailer. As Toby learns to listen to and care about this unusual boy, he also learns how to cope with his absent mother, and all of the other problems the summer has brought into his life.

8.29 Howe, James. **The Watcher.** Atheneum Books for Young Readers, 1997. 173 pp. ISBN 0689801866. Fiction.

Thirteen-year-old Margaret sits atop the stairs to the beach watching the beach goers, wishing she were part of fourteen-year-old

Evan's family. She thinks Evan's family is perfect, but appearances are deceptive. She views Chris, the lifeguard, as a guardian angel, but Chris is dealing with the effects the death of a brother has on his relationship with his father. By alternating the perspective among Margaret, Evan, Evan's little sister Callie, and Chris, Howe enables the reader to compare each character's perspective and to see how their lives will intersect. Evan and Chris' discovery of Margaret's physical abuse help Margaret garner the strength she needs to speak out and put an end to her father's reign of terror.

8.30   Ingold, Jeanette. **Airfield.** Harcourt Brace, 1999. 148 pp. ISBN 0152020535. Fiction.

Beatty is staying with her Aunt Clo for the summer, and finds herself spending time at the Muddy Springs Airport where her uncle works. Beatty is there so much she is offered a job—without pay, since not many paying jobs are available in 1933. The more she is around planes, the more fascinating they become. She hopes to take a ride one day, but her father—who is a pilot—won't discuss it. Another thing he won't discuss is Beatty's mother. She longs to find out anything about her mother, who died when she was one. When she finally does learn something, the information shocks her.

8.31   Jenkins, A. E. **Breaking Boxes.** Delacorte, 1997. 182 pp. ISBN 0385325134. Fiction.

Charlie Calmont is a loner. His father abandoned him, and his mother is dead. Now he lives with his older brother, Trent. Charlie keeps his anger and despair boxed inside him, and presents a cool exterior to the outside world. When Charlie's anger finally explodes, he gets into a fistfight with Brandon Chase. On the surface, it appears that Brandon lives a charmed life, but Charlie comes to understand that surface appearances can be deceiving.

8.32   Johnson, Angela. **Heaven.** Simon & Schuster, 1998. 138 pp. ISBN 0689822294. Fiction.

Life for fourteen-year-old Marley in the small town of Heaven, Ohio, is heavenly—until she discovers Momma and Pops aren't her real parents, but rather her aunt and uncle. Her biological father is mysterious Uncle Jack, who writes her letters. She learns he is now coming to Heaven to tell Marley about her mother, who died many years before in a car accident, and to share with her stories about the mother she never knew. With the help of her family, Marley works through her feelings of betrayal, and comes to understand that she does love her father, and that her close African American family is still there—only their titles have changed.

8.33 Jukes, Mavis. **Cinderella 2000.** Delacorte, 1999. 160 pp. ISBN 0385327110. Fiction.

Ashley Ella Toral has been invited to the most exclusive New Year's Eve party of the millennium. Her stepmother has other plans for Ashley, however—plans that involve taking care of her two stepsisters instead of dancing with Trevor at the country club. Maybe Grammie's arrival will change Ashley's miserable existence. Could Grammie be the fairy godmother who can get Ashley to the dance?

8.34 Kehret, Peg. **I'm Not Who You Think I Am.** Dutton, 1999. 153 pp. ISBN 0525461531. Fiction.

While celebrating her thirteenth birthday, Ginger notices someone staring at her. Her mother reassures her, saying that the woman is probably lonely and is just sharing her celebration from afar. Several days later, after realizing that the woman is following her, Ginger decides to confront her. The strange woman insists that she is Ginger's real mother, but there are many inconsistencies in her story. Soon Ginger realizes that this woman will stop at nothing, including kidnapping her.

8.35 Krisher, Trudy. **Kinship.** Delacorte, 1997. 300 pp. ISBN 0385322720. Fiction.

Fifteen-year-old Pert Wilson should be happy. Her father, long absent from the family, has returned. Suddenly the family has the money it needs, and he surprises Pert and her mother with presents. Daddy even has a plan for saving the trailer park, which Pert has called home, from a group of politicians who consider it a blight on the landscape. But Pert has a funny feeling that all is not as perfect as it seems. When her father disappears without explanation, Pert realizes there is a huge difference between kin and family.

8.36 Larson, Rodger. **What I Know Now.** Henry Holt, 1997. 262 pp. ISBN 0805048693. Fiction.

"We'd best look ahead to who we are becoming," warns Dave Ryan's mother in the summer of 1957. The two are loading their belongings into the car as they prepare to leave Dave's father and brother, and return to Dave's mother's childhood home. Dave reflects on his relationship with his distant and sometimes violent father. He also muses about his older brother and his best friend, both left behind in the move. Dave and his mother are soon settled in their new home. The arrival of Gene Tole, a gardener who comes to help landscape the grounds, marks a change in Dave's life as he ponders his own emerging sexuality.

8.37 Letts, Billie. **Where the Heart Is.** Warner, 1998. 376 pp. ISBN 0446672211. Fiction.

Seventeen-year-old Novalee Nation finds herself abandoned by her boyfriend outside of a Wal-Mart store in a small Oklahoma town. Seven months pregnant and penniless, Novalee does not know where to turn for help. She decides to take up residence inside the Wal-Mart store, a plan that works well until she goes into labor one night. Novalee soon discovers that there are plenty of people in the world who will care for her and her new baby daughter. Even Sam Walton, owner of the Wal-Mart chain, comes to her aid with a job offer. She learns that home is most definitely where the heart is.

8.38 Lyon, George Ella. **With a Hammer for My Heart.** Dorling Kindersley, 1997. 213 pp. ISBN 0789424606. Fiction.

While selling magazine subscriptions to earn money to go to college, fifteen-year-old Lawanda Ingle meets and becomes friends with Garland, an alcoholic veteran who lives in two old school buses, one of which is filled with books. After one of Garland's buses is broken into, his journal, which contains incriminating descriptions of the innocent Lawanda, is recovered by the sheriff. As Lawanda attempts to rectify the situation, she becomes the unintended victim of a fire caused by her outraged father.

8.39 Marchetta, Melina. **Looking for Alibrandi.** Orchard, 1999. 250 pp. ISBN 0531301427. Fiction.

Josephine, an Italian-Australian high school senior, lives in Sydney, Australia, with her mom, Christina. Josephine's father left Sydney when Christina was an unwed pregnant teenager. All of her life, it had just been Josephine and her mother. Things begin to change when her father returns to Sydney and decides to become involved in Josephine's life. Confusing matters more, Josephine finds herself having to choose between two boyfriends: John, who is intelligent, rich, and headed for law school, and Jacob, a good-looking, working-class guy who wants to become a mechanic. As Josephine struggles in her relationships with family and friends, she discovers deep family secrets that help her untangle her own identity and bring her to a better understanding of herself and others in her life.

8.40   Marino, Jan. **Searching for Atticus.** Simon & Schuster, 1997. 182 pp. ISBN 0689800665. Fiction.

Sixteen-year-old Tessa has always longed for a closer relationship with her father. When she was younger, her father was a surgeon with a demanding practice. Then he volunteered to go to Vietnam to serve in the war. Now that he has returned home after receiving a medical discharge, Tessa hopes they can build their relationship. As Tessa travels to a new job with her father, however, he begins having horrible dreams. He wakes up screaming, and often sits up all night smoking. Tessa takes charge and brings them to her aunt's house in a small town. Will she ever be able to have a normal relationship with her father?

8.41   Mazer, Norma Fox. **When She Was Good.** Levine / Scholastic, 1997. 228 pp. ISBN 0590135066. Fiction.

Em's life has been filled with emotional and physical pain caused primarily by her older sister, Pamela, who suffers from mental illness. After their mother dies, their abusive father remarries. His new wife dislikes the two daughters, and the girls give up living at home and move to the city where they share an apartment. Pamela's severe emotional problems keep her from working, so fourteen-year-old Em is forced to support them. When Pamela suddenly dies, Em finds herself alone, but still affected by the abusive relationship she had with her sister. Finally Em's inner strength enables her to triumph.

8.42 McNamee, Graham. **Hate You.** Delacorte, 1999. 119 pp. ISBN 0385325932. Fiction.

"Locked in a cell with my imaginary friends, / In a dungeon where the night never ends." Filled with hatred for her father, Alice Silvers writes songs of pain and despair—songs she believes she will never sing. She only hears them in her head, the way she would have sung them before her voice was destroyed one night when her father choked her. Although she and her mother now live a life without the man who brought them terror and pain, Alice continually holds onto the hate she feels for her father. Then Alice's boyfriend, Eric, introduces her to his cousin, Rachel, a lonely girl with the voice of an angel. Just as Alice begins to reach out to others to make friends she never thought she would have, her father re-enters her life.

8.43 McVeity, Jen. **On Different Shores.** Orchard, 1998. 167 pp. ISBN 053130115X. Fiction.

Tess lives with two families. Her biological mother wants her to live with her permanently. But her younger half sister Laura, and her stepmother Kate, want Tess to stay with them. Tess's dad, a member of the Australian parliament, is too busy with his career to care, or so Tess believes. Once a top student and a champion swimmer, Tess now puts her energy into leading a young group of environmentalists called the Green Guerrillas. The group campaigns against air pollution, cosmetic testing on animals, and the killing of baby seals. Tess, the Green Guerrillas, and her two families face one of the biggest challenges of their lives in Whale Bay. Working side by side during a time of crisis brings them together in an exciting climax.

8.44 Nolan, Han. **Dancing on the Edge.** Harcourt Brace, 1997. 244 pp. ISBN 0152016481. Fiction.

According to Gigi, her clairvoyant spiritualist grandmother, Miracle McCloy is special. After all, she was "born from the body of a dead woman." Or so goes the story her grandmother constantly tells her. Miracle's mother died after being run over by an ambulance, and Miracle was rescued from her dead mother's womb. Ever since her father, an eccentric and moody writer, disappeared, Miracle has become afraid of that story, and now she begins to question her very existence. In desperation, she sets herself afire.

In the hospital, she meets Dr. DeAngelis, a young psychiatrist who helps Miracle face the buried truths of her life.

8.45 Nolan, Han. **A Face in Every Window.** Harcourt Brace, 1999. 264 pp. ISBN 0152019154. Fiction.

Fifteen-year-old JP O'Brien's world has always revolved happily around his Grandma Mary, who keeps his small family together. Her sudden death sets everything into a slow-motion fall: JP's mentally disabled father can't cope with the loss, and his mother—who never had to do anything since Grandma did it all—is suddenly faced with adult responsibilities. When his mother wins a farmhouse in a contest, decides that they'll move there, and takes in the neighborhood outcasts, JP and his dad believe they're being replaced. Little by little, JP's anger separates him from his family until, at a critical moment, he realizes that if he loses his family, he loses everything.

8.46 Peck, Robert Newton. **Cowboy Ghost.** HarperCollins, 1999. 199pp. ISBN 0060282118. Fiction.

When Titus is born, his mother dies. For a long time after her death, Titus believes his father looks upon him with disdain. At sixteen, he is scrawny and nothing like his older brother, Micah, who boxes, rides, ropes, and is at home with their ranch life. In an effort to gain his brother's respect, Titus goes along on a cattle drive. On the trail, they encounter a severe thunder storm, and Micah is mortally wounded when a tree falls on him. Now everything is up to the inexperienced Titus, who has suddenly become the trail boss. Should he turn the cattle around and return home, or should he ride out the storm and keep going?

8.47 Pennebaker, Ruth. **Conditions of Love.** Henry Holt, 1999. 256 pp. ISBN 0805061045. Fiction.

Sarah still grieves for her dead father. His unconditional love gave her strength to face all the obstacles life seemed to hurl in her way. Now that he is gone, Sarah feels like a complete misfit. Her only friend at school, the person Sarah could count on and confide in, has problems of her own. Sarah is left to deal with unpleasant facts that begin to surface about the man who loved her most of all. If Sarah was wrong about her father, how can she ever be sure about loving anyone?

8.48   Pennebaker, Ruth. **Don't Think Twice.** Henry Holt, 1996. 196 pp. ISBN 0805044078. Fiction.

Anne, aged eighteen, made the mistake of trusting that her boyfriend would be there to help her. Now she finds herself pregnant and alone. Her parents send her off to a home for unwed teen mothers. There Anne can have her baby, put it up for adoption, and then move ahead with her plans for the future. Being an unwed mother, and being among others her age in similar circumstances, is a challenging experience for Anne, who is expected to be an adult and a child at the same time.

8.49   Pohl, Peter, and Kinna Gieth. **I Miss You, I Miss You!** R & S, 1999. 249 pp. ISBN 9129639352. Fiction.

On the day before their fourteenth birthday, twins Cilla and Tina race out the door of their home on their way to school, excited about all that is before them. Within minutes, however, everything changes as they cross the road and Cilla is hit by a car. Tina, who is unhurt, now faces a life she never imagined—a life without her beloved identical twin. With her parents too stunned by grief to support her, Tina is left alone to sort through the guilt she feels at not being killed, the anger she feels at the driver who killed her sister, and the loss she feels over Cilla's tragic death. It's not until Tina reaches the depths of despair that she learns she does indeed have a life that is worth living.

8.50   Powell, Randy. **Tribute to Another Dead Rock Star.** New York: Farrar, Straus and Giroux, 1999. 215 pp. ISBN 0374377480. Fiction.

Grady is asked to participate in a tribute in Seattle to his mother, a famous rock singer who suffered an untimely death. The timing and the location could not be better. Grady has been living with his grandmother, but that arrangement is no longer possible. He hopes that when he is in Seattle, he will be able to move in with his half brother, Louie, who has a mental disability. There is just one problem: Louie's stepmother, Vickie, doesn't want Grady around. Grady is determined to prove that he can be responsible around Louie, but his decision to take Louie to the concert to participate in the tribute to their mother proves disastrous. Is there anything Grady can do now to prove that he can be responsible around Louie?

8.51 Reynolds, Marjorie. **The Starlite Drive-In.** Berkley, 1998. 292 pp. ISBN 0425165728. Fiction.

The day Charlie Memphis arrives to help Callie Ann's father run the Starlite Drive-In, things begin to change. Callie Ann's mother, long hurt by her husband's callous and cruel treatment, begins to smile again as this stranger treats her gently. Callie Ann watches the two of them slowly fall in love, while her father seems to only see the movies that play on the huge screen each night. Callie falls in love, too, with a boy who thinks she's beautiful and brave. When her mother finally summons the courage to leave her broken marriage and travel with Charlie Memphis, Callie's father decides he'll do anything to keep that from happening. As events unfold, Callie Ann learns that loving is sometimes hurtful, sometimes gentle, but always powerful.

8.52 Ritter, John. **Choosing Up Sides.** Philomel, 1998. 166 pp. ISBN 0399231854. Fiction.

Luke's father has told him repeatedly that being left-handed is surely the sign of the devil. Luke, therefore, has had to train himself to perform everyday tasks with his right hand. Occasionally, when he is certain his father will not see him, Luke reverts to using his left hand. It definitely is the stronger hand for pitching a baseball, Luke discovers. But what good will it do him to perfect a pitch when his father will never allow him to play baseball? Luke wants to please his father but cannot deny the thrill he feels when his pitching is on target. As Luke decides what to do, he discovers that making choices means accepting the consequences.

8.53 Sachs, Marilyn. **Another Day.** Dutton Children's Books, 1997. 180 pp. ISBN 0525457879. Fiction.

Divorce hurts, and fourteen-year-old Karin believes neither of her parents cares about her anymore. She can't even count on her wonderful but recently widowed grandmother, who has withdrawn into silence in her grief. Karen's misery eases when she overcomes her fear of dogs to give an ignored little poodle a better life.

8.54 Salisbury, Graham. **Shark Bait.** Delacorte, 1997. 151 pp. ISBN 0385322372. Fiction.

Fourteen-year-old Eric, ironically nicknamed Mokes (tough guy), is befriended by Booley, one of the local toughs. Being the son of the new Chinese chief of police of Kailua and half *haole* (white), Eric would have been "shark bait" for the other Hawaiian locals without seventeen-year-old Booley's intervention. Disobeying his father's order to stay out of town while a Navy ship is in port, Mokes is there when Booley's attempt to seek revenge for his mother's desertion with a sailor goes awry. Salisbury, a descendent of early missionary families in Hawaii, effectively integrates the modern Hawaiian dialect—often referred to as Pidgin—into the story, as well as references to old Hawaiian beliefs that still exist within the local culture.

8.55   Sneddon, Pamela Shires. **Brothers and Sisters, Born to Bicker?** Enslow, 1996. 98 pp. ISBN 0894909142. Fiction.

Brothers and sisters come in all shapes, sizes, and ages, and can be a mixed blessing. Sneddon examines several brother-sister relationships, and explains the seemingly inevitable conflict that results from them. Interesting graphics, role-playing suggestions, and multiple choice quizzes present different approaches to understanding such relationships. Topics covered include sibling rivalry, childhood/teenage years, and creating positive relationships. Using personal interviews and questionnaires, the author conducted her research for the book with high school teens.

8.56   Springer, Nancy. **I Am Mordred: A Tale from Camelot.** Philomel, 1998. 184 pp. ISBN 0399231439. Fiction.

This is the tale of King Arthur as told by Mordred, his illegitimate son. Mordred wants nothing more than a father who will acknowledge him and love him. So Mordred sets off on a quest to break the prophecy, which predicts that he will murder his own father. On the quest, he meets many magical people, and finally encounters Merlin himself. Ultimately Mordred learns he cannot escape his destiny.

8.57   Springer, Nancy. **Secret Star.** Philomel, 1997. 144 pp. ISBN 0399230289. Fiction.

Tess does not remember anything that happened to her before her tenth birthday, but that really doesn't bother her. She lives with her dad, who is in a wheelchair, in a cement block house on the outskirts of town. She knows he's not her birth father, but he's always been a real father to her. Things are getting bad for Tess and her dad, though, without electricity or running water. Now that their food is running out, Tess wants to quit school and get a job, but her father won't let her. One day when she is walking home from school, Tess is stopped by a young man named Kamo, who believes he is Tess' half brother, since they share the same unusual last name. Tess doesn't believe it and wants nothing to do with this tough-looking stranger. Gradually, however, Kamo becomes a part of their household. Soon they become friends and Tess begins to unravel the stories that surround her life as she hunts for the truth.

8.58 Stanley, Diane. **A Time Apart.** Morrow Junior Books, 1999. 144 pp. ISBN 068816997X. Fiction.

Ginny's mother is battling cancer and must undergo treatments that will render her weak. Ginny longs to remain at her mother's side during this summer of uncertainty. Her mother, however, has other plans for her. Ginny is to go live with her father in England while her mother is in the hospital. Once Ginny arrives in England, she is dismayed to learn that her father is spending his summer as part of an Iron Age community reenactment. Ginny is expected to accompany him, and to become part of this community where electricity and running water are not yet invented. The camp is primitive, but Ginny learns how to cook meals and perform other tasks without the benefits of modern conveniences. Her time apart, she realizes, is a time for her to grow and become strong. She will need all of the strength she can muster to help her mother combat cancer.

8.59 Stevens, Diane. **Liza's Wishing Star.** Greenwillow, 1997. 183 pp. ISBN 0688153100. Fiction.

Liza's little sister Holly has drowned, and nothing in her life will ever be the same. Liza and her mother move to Rockport for the summer to take care of Mama Lacy. Liza wishes she could return quickly to San Antonio to be with her father and her boyfriend. However, Liza makes new friends in Rockport and discovers that time and distance can separate even the best of friends. As she and her family deal with the changes in their lives, Liza learns that friends are important, but family is where the heart is.

8.60 Sweeney, Joyce. **The Spirit Window.** Delacorte, 1998. 243 pp. ISBN 038532510X. Fiction.

Fifteen-year-old Miranda doesn't remember her mother at all, and doesn't know what to expect when Miranda, her father, and her stepmother travel to Florida to visit a grandmother she barely knows. She doesn't understand the rift between her grandmother and father, but she knows it's kept them from talking to one another for the past ten years. Arriving in Florida, Miranda discovers she loves the wetlands, adores her grandmother, and likes eighteen-year-old Adam a lot. Then disaster strikes and Miranda has to wonder if what she believed about Adam, her grandmother, her father, and even herself is true.

8.61 Thesman, Jean. **The Moonstones.** Viking, 1998. 166 pp. ISBN 0670879592. Fiction.

Jane would rather do anything than go with her mother to Royal Bay and clean out her grandmother's house. It is a small town, and Jane is sure it will be boring. When her Aunt Norma and her cousin Ricki arrive, though, things radically change. Ricki is not only obnoxious but adventurous. She convinces Jane to sneak out of the house when their mothers go to sleep. The two girls go to the amusement park, the only interesting place in town. Once there, they meet some boys. For Jane, it is love at first sight when she gazes into Carey's eyes. But Ricki becomes wilder and more hateful because she, too, has her eye on Carey.

8.62 Thesman, Jean. **The Other Ones.** Viking, 1999. 181 pp. ISBN 0670885940. Fiction.

Fifteen-year-old Bridget works very hard to navigate the obstacles of high school life without resorting to her special abilities. She has known since she was quite young that she possesses powers few others do. When one of her neighbors falls ill, Bridget is torn between keeping up the appearance of being a "normal" teen and helping her friend.

8.63 Tolan, Stephanie. **Ordinary Miracles.** Morrow Junior Books, 1999. 221 pp. ISBN 068816269X. Fiction.

Mark and Matthew Filkins are identical twins. If Mark is hurt, Matthew feels the pain, too. Because Matthew is the "older" of the twins, he has been the dominant one. But Mark is weary of always following along, and yearns for his own identity. He is given the chance to become more independent when a Nobel laureate scientist named Dr. Hendrick returns to Mark's hometown to live, and asks Mark to be his assistant. When Dr. Hendrick becomes seriously ill, the strength of Mark's belief in God and the power of miracles is put to the test.

8.64 Tomey, Ingrid. **Nobody Else Has to Know.** Delacorte, 1999. 224 pp. ISBN 0385326246. Fiction.

Webber is thrilled when he makes the high school's cross country team, and even more pleased when his grandfather proposes a trip to the mall for some new, expensive running shoes. His grandfather even allows Webber to drive the car, despite the fact that Webber does not yet have his learner's permit. The drive is exhilarating, until the fateful moment when Webber takes his eyes off the road for a split second. When he awakens in the hospital, Webber realizes his dreams have been shattered. One of his legs is badly broken. Webber is not the only victim of the accident; a young girl hovers between life and death. Even worse, Webber learns that his grandfather told the police that he was driving the car in which his grandson was injured. Webber's grandfather wants to accept responsibility for the accident, and tells Webber that nobody else has to know who was really driving.

8.65 Weaver, Will. **Hard Ball.** HarperCollins, 1998. 240 pp. ISBN 006447208. Fiction.

Billy Baggs is a gifted baseball player who has suffered more than his share of hardship in life. *Striking Out* and *Farm Team,* two previous novels by Weaver, explored Billy's introduction to the sport he loves: baseball. In this third book featuring Billy, he must finally face up to his longtime nemesis, Archer Kingwood. The confrontation turns violent, and Billy and Archer are told by their coach that in order to remain on the team, the two of them must learn how to get along. Coach Anderson's plan is for the two rivals to spend a week living together twenty-four hours a day. Billy is certain that this plan will be disastrous, and Archer agrees. But what each boy learns about the other may just change their relationship from one of rivalry to one of cooperation.

8.66   Williams, Laura. **The Ghost Stallion.** Henry Holt , 1999. 104 pp. ISBN 0805061932. Fiction.

With her long black hair, Mary Elizabeth looks different from her father and sister. Ever since her mother ran off, her gruff father barely pays any attention to her. When her father calls her it is always "girl"; he never uses her real name, yet he calls her younger sister his princess. Meanwhile, there is a "ghost" stallion, which no one has ever seen, stealing mares from her father's stock. One day, when the stallion has once again visited, a stranger appears and accepts their offer of a one hundred dollar reward to find and kill the stallion. Mary Elizabeth wants to go along on the search for the stallion both because she thinks the dark-haired stranger may be her real father, and because she wants to save the stallion's life. Her father orders her to stay home, but she ignores him. The hunt for the stallion is long and hard, and when they finally find him, Mary Elizabeth inadvertently falls into a raging river. Who will come to her rescue?

8.67   Wilson, Budge. **Sharla.** Stoddart Kids, 1997. 163 pp. ISBN 0773674675. Fiction.

Because her father lost his high-paying job in Ottawa, fifteen-year-old Sharla Dunfield and her family have been forced to move to Churchill, Manitoba, a small, isolated community in the subarctic. Both Sharla and her parents are unhappy about the change. Sharla has to adjust to a new school, new friends, her parents' new circumstances, a harsh new environment, and a town famous for the polar bears that invade it annually.

8.68   Yolen, Jane, and Bruce Coville. **Armageddon Summer.** Harcourt Brace, 1998. 266 pp. ISBN 0152017674. Fiction.

"Staring directly into my eyes, Dad said, 'On July twenty-seventh the world as we know it is going to end.'" Jed's dad is a believer. So is Marina's mom. That's why they've come to the mountaintop, following charismatic Reverend Beelson and preparing themselves for the New World. But Jed and Marina aren't sure what they believe in, aside from each other. As the day of judgment approaches, Marina and Jed try to come to terms with their feelings for each other and the beliefs of their parents. When gunshots ring out during the last church service before the day of judgment, Jed and Marina's lives and everything they believe in are changed forever.

9 Fantasy

"The only imaginative works we ought to grow out of are those which it would have been better not have read at all."

C. S. Lewis

9.1 Alexander, Lloyd. **The Iron Ring.** Dutton, 1997. 283 pp. ISBN 0525455973. Fiction.

After losing a bet with a visiting king, young King Tamar is bound by honor to undertake a journey to the land of Mahapura. On his journey, he befriends many talking animals, wins a priceless ruby, and meets a young girl named Mirri. Many of his new friends join him on his journey. When they reach Mahapura, they become entangled in a battle of good versus evil.

9.2 Almond, David. **Skellig.** Delacorte, 1999. 176 pp. ISBN 038532633X. Fiction.

Michael and his family have moved into a new house. He and his father are hard at work making improvements to the house, eager to remove all of the trash and debris left by the former occupants. When Michael explores the garage, he finds something more than trash, however; he discovers Skellig. Exactly who—or perhaps the right word is WHAT—is Skellig? Michael comes to believe that Skellig may just have some magic in him. Is the magic enough to save the life of Michael's newborn sister?

9.3 Avi. **Midnight Magic.** Scholastic, 1999. 256 pp. ISBN 0590360353. Fiction.

Fabrizio is apprenticed to Mangus, a magician who has been forced to renounce magic in order to save his life. Late one night, Mangus is summoned to the court of King Claudio. Accompanied by Fabrizio, Mangus is brought before the king and queen. They seek the aid of the magician in a matter of great importance: An apparition has visited Princess Teresina and demanded that Teresina go with him to the underworld. If Mangus cannot assist the court in ridding the castle of this ghost, he will forfeit his life. And then what will become of Fabrizio?

9.4   Avi. **Perloo the Bold.** Scholastic, 1998. 240 pp. ISBN 0590110020. Fiction.

Perloo, a mild mannered member of the Montmer tribe, is ill-prepared for the myriad changes he is about to experience. He is chosen to become the new leader of his tribe, a surprise even to Perloo. His selection does not sit well with some of the others who have been leading the tribe. Perloo finds himself facing opposition from within his own tribe, as well as a challenge from the sworn enemies of the Montmers.

9.5   Barron, T. A. **The Fires of Merlin: Book Three of the Lost Years of Merlin.** Philomel, 1998. 264 pp. ISBN 0399230203. Fiction.

Urnalda, ruler of the dwarves, calls for Merlin to save her people and pay the debt he owes them from a previous adventure. Valdearg, the dragon, has awakened from his enchanted slumber, a sleep forced upon him by Merlin's now deceased grandfather, Tuatha. Merlin's only hope is to go on a quest to find the Galator, an object of great power once used by Tuatha in his battle against Valdearg.

9.6   Barron, T. A. **The Mirror of Merlin: Book Four of the Lost Years of Merlin.** Philomel, 1999. 245 pp. ISBN 0399234551. Fiction.

A swamp in the remote region of Fincayra seems to be emanating evil. In order to protect his beloved homeland, young Merlin must travel to this swamp. He is accompanied by his friend, Hallia. Hallia possesses the ability to change from a young woman into a deer, and she teaches Merlin how to join her in this transformation. The fleet hooves of the deer may help Merlin and Hallia escape from the awful malevolence that awaits them on their journeys. When Merlin discovers a magical mirror, what he sees in the reflection is the person he least expected to see.

9.7   Block, Francesca Lia. **I Was a Teenage Fairy.** HarperCollins, 1998. 186 pp. ISBN 0060277475. Fiction.

Once upon a time in California, there was a young woman named Barbie. Like the doll after which she was named, Barbie was beautiful. Her modeling career was taking off, but Barbie would have been happier if she had just been left alone. Her mother was a typical stage mother, however, constantly pushing Barbie to do more. Barbie desperately needed a friend to protect her from her mother and a predatory photographer. That's when Mab the fairy appeared, and everything changed.

9.8 Brooke, William J. **A Is for AARRGH!** Joanna Cotler / Harper-Collins, 1999. 249 pp. ISBN 0060233931. Fiction.

Travel back to prehistoric times, when conversation consisted of grunts and gestures, and misunderstandings were cleared up with a club to the head. When young Mog begins to teach his tribe the words for *sun* and *rock,* their lives are transformed. With language, the tribe can now plan for a hunt, think of the future, and, in Mog's case, express love for another in words. Mog grows frustrated and angry when he is not given credit for his invention of language. He leaves the tribe, and joins the girl he loves in the wilderness outside of the tribal lands. When Mog returns to visit the tribe, he finds that language has spawned further developments. Turtle shells are being exchanged for goods and services, and those with the most shells have the most power. Some of the tribe, including Mog's own parents, have lost everything they possess in a quest for turtle shells. Others have used their skill with language itself to gain control over other members of the tribe. How can Mog tame the effects of the language he has brought to his tribe?

9.9 Butler, Charles. **The Darkling.** Margaret McElderry, 1998. 164 pp. ISBN 0689817967. Fiction.

Fifteen-year-old Petra has a strange encounter with Mr. Century, an eccentric old recluse, when she makes a delivery to his house. When Mr. Century dies, strange events continue to connect Petra to him. After a spirit possesses her father, Petra must find a way to sever her connection with Mr. Century if she is to save her father and herself.

9.10 Card, Orson Scott. **Enchantment.** Random House, 1999. 390 pp. ISBN 0345416872. Fiction.

Remember the fairy tale of Sleeping Beauty? Card has given this classic love story a new story line that begins with Ivan, who one day finds a clearing in the dense Carpathian forest. There, on a pedestal encircled by fallen leaves, he sees the stunningly beautiful Princess Katerina, lying as still as death. But ten-year-old Ivan senses something evil from beneath the leaves, and runs for the safety of his cousin Marek's farm. Now, years later, Ivan is an American graduate student engaged to be married—and still haunted by the memory of the beautiful woman in the clearing. So he leaves America and returns to his native land, and once again finds the clearing and the sleeping woman—just as he left them. But this time he does not run. This time he awakens the woman with a kiss. And with that kiss he steps back into a kingdom of a thousand years ago, and an adventure that is the stuff of fairy tales.

9.11 Carroll, Lewis. **Alice's Adventures in Wonderland.** Photographs by Abelardo Morell. Dutton Children's Books, 1998. 115 pp. ISBN 0525460942. Fiction.

As Leonard Marcus's excellent introduction to this book explains, Lewis Carroll was much more than the author of one of the world's best-known books, *Alice's Adventures in Wonderland.* Carroll, whose real name was Charles Dodgson, was a lecturer of mathematics at Oxford University and a well-known photographer. His connection to photography makes this particular volume special, as photographer Abelardo Morell combines Sir John Tenniel's classic original drawings with his own photographs, giving them a three-dimensional quality. So enjoy the adventures of a girl named Alice as she meets strange creatures in a stranger land, and marvel at the artwork that blends today's techniques with yesterday's charm.

9.12 Dalkey, Kara. **The Heavenward Path.** Harcourt Brace, 1998. 224 pp. ISBN 015201652X. Fiction.

In this sequel to *Little Sister,* a spirit haunts Mitsuko for not keeping her pledge to him. To pay her debt, Mitsuko is given a series of seemingly impossible tasks that force her to seek assistance from the shape-shifter Goranu and the dragon Kasi-Lung. She must also figure out a way to avoid the sentence of death handed down to her by the Lord of the Dead, Emma-Oonce.

9.13 Dickinson, Peter. **The Lion Tamer's Daughter and Other Stories.** Delacorte Press, 1997. 298 pp. ISBN 0385323271. Fiction.

The British characters in these four lengthy stories move between present and past in supernatural ways. For example, in "The Spring," Derek finds a boy much like himself in the depths of a hidden spring, and in "Touch and Go," an adult man describes how as a young man, he met a girl from an earlier time who lived in the same place.

9.14 Duane, Diane. **A Wizard Abroad.** Harcourt Brace, 1997. 342 pp. ISBN 0152012095. Fiction.

Nita's parents have sent her off to visit her aunt in Ireland. They wish to separate Nita from Kit, her wizardry partner. Nita soon finds herself called to active wizard duty as she assists the wizards of Ireland, who are battling an evil being that threatens to destroy all of Ireland.

9.15 Galloway, Priscilla. **Snake Dreamer.** Delacorte, 1998. 240 pp. ISBN 038532264X. Fiction.

Snakes haunt the dreams of sixteen-year-old Dusa. In fact, her dreams have become increasingly terrifying over the past few months. She thrashes in her sleep, and is a danger to herself and her mother. The doctors are all puzzled; they can find nothing wrong with Dusa. One night, as Dusa and her mother watch a documentary on television, they learn about the Gordon sisters, two psychologists from Greece who have had success treating Dusa's ailment. Reluctantly, Dusa's mother allows her to travel to Greece with the doctors. Once there, Dusa begins to understand that the Gordons are not what they appear to be, and they have sinister plans for her.

9.16 Hamilton, Virginia. **Dustland.** Scholastic, 1998. 214 pp. ISBN 0590362178. Fiction.

The second book in the Justice and Her Brothers series continues the story of Justice, her twin brothers Levi and Thomas, and their friend Dorian. All four possess extrasensory perception, a gift that brings them together in a race to save future inhabitants of Earth. When his jealousy of Justice's power grows out of control, however, Thomas breaks from the group, taking Levi along with him. This separation endangers all four as they travel through time, and imperils Earth as well.

9.17 Hamilton, Virginia. **The Gathering.** Scholastic, 1998. 214 pp. ISBN 059032626X. Fiction.

This is the third installment in the Justice and Her Brothers series. In this adventure, Justice, her brothers, and Dorian are reunited. The four must use their incredible powers of extrasensory perception to protect future inhabitants of Earth from an evil force. The force, known as Mal, seems impossible to defeat, but Justice, Levi, Thomas, and Dorian must try, or place the future inhabitants of Earth in grave danger.

9.18 Hamilton, Virginia. **Justice and Her Brothers.** Scholastic, 1998. 282 pp. ISBN 0590362143. Fiction.

More than just their familial relationship links Justice Douglas and her identical twin brothers, Levi and Thomas, to one another. The three are able to communicate telepathically. Justice soon learns that this remarkable ability must be put to careful use. Moreover, she and her brothers must learn how to operate as a team, a feat made difficult when Thomas threatens to break from their unit and go off on his own.

9.19 Hite, Sid. **The Distance of Hope.** Henry Holt, 1998. 198 pp. ISBN 080505054X. Fiction.

Fifteen-year-old Yeshe Anjur is the heir to the throne of Padma. During the past two years, he has mysteriously begun to lose his eyesight. There is no medical explanation for this loss. His parents send him and three bodyguards on a journey to find the legendary White Bean Lama, who may be able to restore his sight. There are may perils along the way; only Yeshe and one bodyguard finally reach the Lama, where the secret of Yeshe's ailment is revealed.

9.20 Hughes, Monica, editor. **What If . . . ? Amazing Stories.** Tundra, 1998. 199 pp. ISBN 0887764584. Fiction.

What if you were given only one wish? What if you found a magic scepter and did the wrong thing with it? What if origami paper animals could come to life? What if Frosty the Snowman wasn't really jolly at all? These are some of the fantastic situations explored in the fourteen thought-provoking stories and two poems by Canadian writers that have been assembled in this book by science fiction writer Monica Hughes. These stories will amaze and delight you.

9.21 Jacques, Brian. **Pearls of Lutra.** Philomel, 1996. 408 pp. ISBN 0399229469. Fiction.

When the soldiers of the evil marten, Mad Eyes, kidnap Abbot Durral and demand pearls as ransom, the residents of Redwall Abbey discover that there is indeed a treasure trove of pearls within the abbey walls. However, the pearls are not accessible to the inhabitants of Redwall. There is a mystery which must be solved before the pearls can be retrieved. Martin the Warrior and his friends attempt to rescue the abbot, as he is taken far across the sea to Mad Eyes' island castle. Meanwhile, Transy, Cracklyn, and Rollo must solve the six riddles that will ultimately lead them to the pearls they need to buy the abbot's safe return.

9.22 Jennings, Patrick. **Faith and the Rocket Cat.** Scholastic, 1998. 232 pp. ISBN 0590110047. Fiction.

Faith's family moves back to San Francisco, where Faith tries to prove to her disbelieving classmate Alex that she can fly. Her rocket is powered by pig fat of all things. Alex and Faith plan a trip; they decide Edison, Faith's dog, will go along for the ride too. However, Faith's mother accidentally ends up aboard the rocket during its launch. The entire group is stranded in the desert until they discover Veevy, Faith's long lost cat, who leads them to a spare rocket. Using their remaining fuel, they return home and become famous—once Edison's ability to write and speak in multiple languages is discovered by the media.

9.23 Klause, Annette Curtis. **Blood and Chocolate.** Bantam, 1997. 264 pp. ISBN 0385323050. Fiction.

Vivian is a beautiful young woman, although she is usually a bit of a loner at her high school. Vivian has a secret side, one she has been unwilling to unveil to her peers. Then she meets and falls in love with Aiden, a handsome young man. Vivian is certain that Aiden can handle the truth about her secret side. He seems sensitive and understanding. However, even Aiden is not prepared to learn that Vivian is a werewolf.

9.24 Lally, Soinbee. **A Hive for the Honeybee.** Levine / Scholastic, 1999. 224 pp. ISBN 059051038X. Fiction.

Thora is a worker bee who begins to question why her life and the life of the other worker bees is limited solely to toiling away in the hive so that others may have enough food to eat. Belle, Mo, and Alfred join her in her complaints. All wish to see changes in how the hive is operated. But change never comes quickly, and the four bees' lives are placed in grave peril. This allegory is reminiscent of *Animal Farm.*

9.25 Levine, Gail Carson. **Ella Enchanted.** HarperCollins, 1997. 232 pp. ISBN 0060275103. Fiction.

What if you always had to do what you were told? Not just some of the time, or when you agreed with what you were being told to do, but all of the time? This is the curse Lucinda the fairy placed on Ella of Frell. Because this curse means others can control her, Ella tries to keep the curse a secret. But when her new step-mother's daughters learn just why Ella is so obedient, they begin to make life difficult for her. As Ella struggles to free herself of the curse, she turns to a magical book given to her by her beloved cook, Mandy. Now, as she battles ogres in the flesh and the ogres in her mind, she has Prince Charmont at her side. As Ella grows more independent, so her love for Prince Charmont grows. But will their relationship be permitted? In this new tale based on the old Cinderella tale, Levine provides a fun and thought-provoking look at what might have been.

9.26 Levitin, Sonia. **The Cure.** Silver Whistle / Harcourt Brace, 1999. 192 pp. ISBN 0152018271. Fiction.

The year is 2407. In this distant place, all children are born as fraternal twins, emotions are kept carefully under control, and music in any form is not permitted. Gemm, one half of a pair of twins, cannot seem to conform to the rules of this future society. For some reason, he hears music in his head. Music also seems to play a key role in his dreams. The doctors have done all they can to change Gemm's behavior, but to no avail. He is finally given a choice: opt to be recycled, or undertake the cure. Gemm wants to continue with his life, and so selects the cure. Soon, Gemm finds himself traveling back in time to the Middle Ages. It is there he will learn a cruel lesson about the power of music.

9.27 Matas, Carol, and Perry Nodelman. **Out of Their Minds.** Simon & Schuster, 1998. 183 pp. ISBN 0689819463. Fiction.

This is the third book in the Minds series. In this book, Leonora and Coren finally plan their wedding at the court of Andilla, Coren's homeland. Unfortunately, the Andillans have lost the power of imagination, which is critical for maintaining the sacred Balance. Leonora and Coren embark on a journey to find the source of the problem. Along the way, they discover the Skwoes, a people who have absolutely no imagination. As Leonora and Coren attempt to solve the problems plaguing Coren's people, they must overcome the Skwoes and battle the evil Hevak.

9.28 Napoli, Donna Jo. **Crazy Jack.** Delacorte, 1999. 135 pp. ISBN 0385326270. Fiction.

How would you react if the young man you have known and loved since you were both children suddenly started doing crazy things? Things like planting magic seeds and then claiming he could climb the stalks of his giant plants and enter a magical kingdom? Flora, a young woman who has been promised to Jack since childhood, begins to fear the young man she once loved. Who could possibly believe the incredible tales of treasure and danger Jack spins? Perhaps Flora should find someone else to marry. This retelling of the traditional story of "Jack and the Beanstalk" provides an interesting alternative to the story from childhood that we all know and love.

9.29 Napoli, Donna Jo, and Richard Tchen. **Spinners.** Dutton, 1999. 197 pp. ISBN 0525460659. Fiction.

Long ago, two spinners lived in the same village. They fell in love, and planned to be married. In an effort to prove his worth to his fiancée's father, one spinner makes a fatal error that causes him to be crippled. He is abandoned by the one he loves, as well as by the rest of the people in the community, who find his deformity repulsive. He flees his village and searches for acceptance across the kingdom. When he comes to the rescue of a young woman trapped in a room full of straw, the old spinner believes his search for happiness may be over. This retelling of the childhood tale of Rumplestiltskin is full of romance and magic.

9.30 Naylor, Phyllis Reynolds. **Sang Spell.** Atheneum Books for Young Readers, 1998. 192 pp. ISBN 0689820070. Fiction.

In this story, which combines healthy doses of realistic mystery and eerie fantasy, a young man hitchhikes to Dallas from his home in Boston. Josh has just lost his mother in a car accident, and is traveling cross country to live with his aunt. Along the way, he is mugged and abandoned on a remote stretch of road. A kindly woman comes to Josh's aid. She takes him by horse and cart back to her village of Canara in the Appalachian foothills. The town seems to be untouched by time; there is no electricity, and few of the other niceties of modern life. Josh soon learns that there is no way out of Canara. The roads all seem to lead back to the heart of the village, a village with an entrance but no exit.

9.31 Oppel, Kenneth. **Silverwing.** Candlewick, 1997. 237 pp. ISBN 0763603449. Fiction.

Shade, a young silverwing bat, is separated from his colony by a storm as the bats fly south for the winter. As Shade struggles to become reunited with his colony, Marina, a brightwing bat who has been ostracized from her colony because the humans have banded her, befriends him. Together, Marina and Shade undertake a journey that will put many obstacles in their path. Owls, rats, vampire bats, and other creatures try to prevent Shade and Marina from finding their home.

9.32 Pattou, Edith. **Fire Arrow: The Second Song of Eirren.** Harcourt Brace, 1998. 320 pp. ISBN 015201635X. Fiction.

The second book in the Song of Eirren series tells of the archer Breo-Saight, who is called home to the deathbed of her old nursemaid. Before the nurse dies, she gives Breo-Saight directions to a golden arrow, part of Breo-Saight's birthright. Breo-Saight soon learns that the person who has caused the death of her beloved nursemaid is the same person responsible for the death of her father. She begins to track him across the realms. Her travels lead her to a strange country, where she encounters an evil, one-eyed sorcerer who wishes to use Breo-Saight's magic arrow to conquer the land and its peoples.

9.33 Pierce, Meredith Ann. **The Pearl of the Soul of the World.** Magic Carpet / Harcourt, 1999. 301 pp. ISBN 015201800X. Fiction.

One pearl contains all of the world's wisdom and magic. Care for this valuable gem is left to Ariel. In the third book of The Darkangel Trilogy, Ariel must help her people defeat the White Witch once and for all. Can the redeemed darkangel, Irrylath, be trusted to assist Ariel? If Ariel can unlock the mystery of the pearl, there is hope.

9.34 Pierce, Tamora. **Briar's Book.** Scholastic, 1999. 272 pp. ISBN 0590553593. Fiction.

In this conclusion to the Circle of Magic series, Briar, a former street urchin now living at Winding Circle Temple, is learning from Rosethorn all he can about the healing power and magic of plants. When one of Briar's former street pals becomes ill, he takes her to Rosethorn, certain she can cure the illness. Even Rosethorn's considerable powers are no match for the sickness that seems to be spreading quickly through Summersea. Daja, Tris, and Sandry must all join forces if they are to discover the source of this plague and find a way to fight against it.

9.35 Pierce, Tamora. **Daja's Book.** Scholastic, 1998. 240 pp. ISBN 0590553585. Fiction.

While traveling in the mountains, Daja and her fellow mages discover that their individual magic is jumping from one mage to the other. This third book in the Circle of Magic series tells how the friends attempt to solve this problem.

9.36 Pierce, Tamora. **Emperor Mage.** Random House, 1997. 294 pp. ISBN 0679882901. Fiction.

The third book of the Immortals series takes Daine on a voyage to Carthak as part of a peace treaty delegation from Tortall. While in Carthak, Daine discovers that the gods are angry with the Emperor Mage, and plan to use Daine to channel their powers into the mortal realm to punish the mage. Daine must control her wild magic, as well as the new magic from the gods, as she punishes the emperor for his evil deeds.

9.37 Pierce, Tamora. **The Realms of the Gods.** Atheneum Books for Young Readers, 1997. 209 pp. ISBN 0689319908. Fiction.

In the final book of the Immortals series, Daine and her teacher, Numair, are taken to the realms of the gods to recover from their battle with the flesh-eating Skinners. Soon they realize that they must return to the mortal realm to defeat Ozorne, a powerful stormwing, and Uusoae, Queen of Chaos. Their journey will take them across dangerous realms, and require that they enlist the aid of the dragons in order to save their native land.

9.38   Pierce, Tamora. **Sandry's Book.** Scholastic, 1997. 252 pp. ISBN 0590553569. Fiction.

Sandry is one of four young people with magical powers that the wizard Niklaren Goldeye discovers and brings to the Winding Circle, a magical community. The four form a bond of friendship that will soon be tested as all of their lives are placed in peril.

9.39   Pierce, Tamora. **Tris's Book.** Scholastic, 1998. 251 pp. ISBN 0590553577. Fiction.

The second book of the Circle of Magic series takes place in the magical community of Winding Circle as it is recovering from an earthquake. The quake has weakened the magical defenses of the community, leaving it vulnerable to attack. An evil wizard and a fleet of pirate ships attack Winding Circle. Tris and her three companions must risk enslavement if they are to destroy the wizard and defend their home.

9.40   Pierce, Tamora. **Wild Magic.** Random House, 1997. 299 pp. ISBN 067988288X. Fiction.

After the death of her mother, Daine runs away to find work in the King's stables. On the way, her wild magic is discovered by the mage Numair. Daine becomes his apprentice. When the Castle of Pirates Swoop is attacked and the Queen and heirs are demanded as hostages, Daine and the other mages must call on their powers to defeat the attackers and the evil Immortals who fight with them. This is the first book in the Immortals series.

9.41   Pierce, Tamora. **Wolf-Speaker.** Random House, 1997. 281 pp. ISBN 0679882898. Fiction.

In this second installment in the Immortals series, Daine is called upon by her wolf pack to stop the people who are harming the environment of the valley in which they live. Once there, she finds ambitious mortals and magical immortals that she and the animals must defeat, for the good of the valley and for the entire kingdom.

9.42 Pullman, Philip. **Clockwork.** Levine / Scholastic, 1998. 128 pp. ISBN 0590129996. Fiction.

Karl, the village clockmaker's apprentice, finds himself in trouble. As the year of his apprenticeship comes to a close, he is expected to design and build a new addition to the village's renowned clockwork. Unfortunately, Karl has no idea what to make, and time is running out quickly. Then, one dark night, a sinister stranger enters the tavern where Karl is bemoaning his fate, and offers his assistance in the form of a fabulous figure—an intricate knight—that Karl can take and claim to have carved. Karl is willing to pay any price for help, but little does he realize that when he accepts the gift, he sets into motion a series of events that, like clockwork, keep moving toward a seemingly unstoppable conclusion.

9.43 Pullman, Philip. **The Subtle Knife.** Knopf, 1997. 357 pp. ISBN 0679879250. Fiction.

In this sequel to *The Golden Compass,* Lyra Silvertongue continues her quest to find her long lost father, Lord Asriel. Asriel has somehow managed to create a bridge between two alternate universes. Lyra finds herself in Cittagazze, the alternate universe, where children are in charge. There she encounters a stranger named Will who is from Oxford, Lyra's home. However, when Will leads Lyra back to Oxford, she is shocked to see that Will's Oxford is yet another alternate universe, an Oxford of fast food and fast cars, far removed from the Oxford familiar to Lyra. Armed with the subtle knife, a weapon that can cut through anything (including the veil between worlds), and the alethiometer Lyra uses when she needs to make important decisions, the two youngsters must defeat some incredible foes.

9.44 Rowling, J. K. **Harry Potter and the Chamber of Secrets.** Illustrated by Mary GrandPré. Levine / Scholastic, 1999. 341 pp. ISBN 0439064864. Fiction.

Harry Potter returns to Hogwarts School for Witchcraft and Wizardry for his second year of learning and adventures. Soon he's learning more and having more adventures than he ever wanted. When a hidden chamber of secrets appears to have been found and opened, and mysterious things begin happening to his friends, Harry seems to be the culprit. A house-elf named Dobby, a spirit named Moaning Myrtle, a new professor named Lock-heart, a mysterious boy from Hogwarts' past named Tom Riddle, and a diary that not only holds the past but predicts the future too, are all part of the adventure Harry lives through as he tries to prove his innocence and save his friends.

9.45   Rowling, J. K. **Harry Potter and the Prisoner of Azkaban.** Illustrated by Mary GrandPré. Levine / Scholastic, 1999. 435 pp. ISBN 0439136350. Fiction.

Sirius Black, convicted of killing thirteen people with a single curse, is the heir apparent to the Dark Lord, Voldemort. Imprisoned in the walls of Azkaban, everyone thinks he has been locked away for good. But after twelve long years, Black has made his escape, and now he seems to be heading to Hogwarts School of Witchcraft and Wizardry to find Harry Potter. As Harry prepares for Black's attack, he discovers that a traitor is inside the school and watching his every move.

9.46   Rowling, J. K. **Harry Potter and the Sorcerer's Stone.** Illustrated by Mary GrandPré. Levine / Scholastic, 1998. 309 pp. ISBN 0590353403. Fiction.

Harry Potter thought he was a Muggle (a person with not one drop of magical blood in him) just like everyone else—until his eleventh birthday. Then he receives an invitation to attend the Hogwarts School of Witchcraft and Wizardry. At first his Muggle aunt and uncle say no, but soon, with a little magical help, they happily send him off. There Harry learns not only that he is a wizard, but also that his parents were killed by a wicked wizard while something wonderful protected him. That something wonderful stays with Harry his first year at Hogwarts as he makes friends, learns to ride a broom, becomes great at playing Quidditch, learns about the powerful Voldemort, and discovers the secret of the sorcerer's stone.

9.47   Rubinstein, Gillian. **Under the Cat's Eye: A Tale of Morph and Mystery.** Simon & Schuster, 1998. 204 pp. ISBN 0689818009. Fiction.

Jai is sent off to a boarding school where all the students seem to behave strangely. His two newest friends, Hugo and Seal, confide in Jai, telling him that the new headmaster of the school is stealing the souls of his classmates. As the three begin to investigate this mystery, Jai finds he must join forces with a cat and a dog from a parallel world in order to stop the headmaster, and send him back to the evil world from which he came.

9.48 Schaeffer, Susan Fromberg. **The Autobiography of Foudini M. Cat.** Knopf, 1997. 166 pp. ISBN 0697454748. Fiction.

The wise Foudini M. (Mouser) Cat tells his life's story to Grace, the younger, less experienced cat in the household. He explains how he came to live with his assigned persons, Warm and Pest, in the Cold House and the Mouse House, and tells of his adventures with his dog Sam, the new "puppy child" in the home. Finally, he shares with her his dreams of ghostly cats, such as the cats of Freud and Cleopatra. This unusual autobiography is in a category of its own!

9.49 Sleator, William. **Rewind.** Dutton, 1999. 120 pp. ISBN 0525461302. Fiction.

Angry with his parents, Peter dashes out of his house and directly into the path of an oncoming car. He floats away from his body into a great white light. In the afterlife, he is told that he will be given the chance to return to any moment in his former life to try to prevent his death. If he fails, his life is permanently over. But if he succeeds, his life will continue as it had in the past. Peter has to determine exactly what led to his untimely death if he wishes to hang onto his life.

9.50 Smith, Sherwood. **Crown Duel.** Jane Yolen Books / Harcourt Brace, 1997. 214 pp. ISBN 0152016082. Fiction.

In this first book of the Crown and Court Duet series, Countess Meliara and her brother Branaric swear to their dying father that they will defend the people of the land from the King's greed. As they battle to protect the land and its people, they are caught up in a revolution that may result in death for both of them.

9.51 Somotow, S. P. **The Vampire's Beautiful Daughter.** Atheneum Books for Young Readers, 1997. 116 pp. ISBN 0689319681. Fiction.

Fifteen-year-old Johnny Raitt moves from an Indian reservation to Los Angeles to live with his mother, who is a best-selling author. Once there, Johnny begins having identity problems. Then he meets Rebecca Teppish. The only problem is that Rebecca is half-vampire. On her sixteenth birthday, Rebecca will have to choose whether to remain human, or enter fully into the vampire world. She wants Johnny to join her in eternal life, but Johnny hopes to convince her to remain human.

9.52   Springer, Nancy. **I Am Mordred: A Tale from Camelot.** Philomel, 1998. 184 pp. ISBN 0399231439. Fiction.

This is the tale of King Arthur as told by Mordred, his illegitimate son. Mordred wants nothing more than a father who will acknowledge him and love him. So Mordred sets off on a quest to break the prophecy that predicts that he will murder his own father. On the quest, he meets many magical people, and finally encounters Merlin himself. Mordred learns he cannot escape his destiny.

9.53   Yolen, Jane. **Twelve Impossible Things before Breakfast: Stories.** Harcourt Brace, 1997. 175 pp. ISBN 0152015248. Fiction.

Exercise your imagination with these twelve creative stories by author Jane Yolen. Read about a girl's efforts to keep her mother's blood-sucking ghost in her grave. Follow a girl into Neverland, where she meets Peter Pan and the girls he keeps in virtual slavery. Listen to the complaints of a bridge that longs for the return of a troll who used to keep the goats from clomping all over him. And spend the evening with a babysitter in a haunted house.

10 Friendships, Choices, and Transitions

"When others fail him, the wise man looks
To the sure companionship of books."

Andrew Lang

10.1   Abelove, Joan. **Go and Come Back.** DK Ink, 1998. 176 pp. ISBN 0789424762. Fiction.

Two female anthropologists come to the remote reaches of the Amazon jungle to observe an ancient Peruvian culture. Their plans are to spend a year studying the day-to-day life of the culture, before returning to their own world. One of the native girls, Alicia, does some observing of her own. She is surprised to see how "stupid" these ladies are and makes it her job to educate them in the ways of her people. Through the process, everyone begins to learn what it means to respect another's culture, and how to be a friend.

10.2   Abelove, Joan. **Saying It Out Loud.** DK Ink, 1999. 136 pp. ISBN 0789426099. Fiction.

Mindy's life is one of dull predictability. All of that changes when her mother is diagnosed with a malignant brain tumor. Although her father will not admit the truth, and pretends that their lives are perfectly normal, Mindy knows that her mother's life is in danger. She visits her mother in the hospital, but is frightened by the shell of a person her mother has become. Mindy understands that she must be able to voice her concerns and fears if she is to find someone to help her. It is now that she will discover who her real friends are.

10.3   Bauer, Joan. **Rules of the Road.** Putnam, 1998. 201 pp. ISBN 0300231404. Fiction.

Sixteen-year-old Jenna works for a shoe store chain. In order to get away from her recently returned alcoholic father, she accepts the job of driving the seventy-three-year-old owner of the chain to a major board meeting in Texas. Little does she know what adventures are in store for her, and how her pride in and knowledge about selling shoes will work in her favor.

10.4   Bennett, Cherie. **Life in the Fat Lane.** Delacorte, 1998. 180 pp. ISBN 0385322747. Fiction.

After Lara becomes Homecoming Queen, she hopes the rest of her junior year will be as wonderful. The trouble starts when she begins to gain weight, and nothing she does seems to help. Her parents nag her, put her on diets, and encourage her to work out. Lara is horrified at her ballooning body, and when she gains almost one hundred pounds, she wonders if anyone will still be her friend. More importantly, she wonders if she will be able to accept the person she has become.

10.5   Block, Francesca Lia. **Baby Be-Bop.** HarperTrophy / Harper-Collins, 1997. 106 pp. ISBN 0064471764. Fiction.

Sixteen-year-old Dirk McDonald has always known he's different. He's decided to be strong and brave and daring so no one will notice or pick on him. He's also afraid of losing the love of his wonderful grandmother, who has raised him. When he is beat up and lies unconscious in the hospital, apparitions appear to tell him stories about his great-grandmother, grandmother, and father that help him understand the importance of being himself.

10.6   Block, Francesca Lia. **I Was a Teenage Fairy.** HarperCollins, 1998. 186 pp. ISBN 0060277475. Fiction.

Once upon a time in California, there was a young woman named Barbie. Like the doll after which she was named, Barbie was beautiful. Her modeling career was taking off, but Barbie would have been happier if she had just been left alone. Her mother was a typical stage mother, however, constantly pushing Barbie to do more. Barbie desperately needed a friend to protect her from her mother and a predatory photographer. That's when Mab the fairy appeared, and everything changed.

10.7   Block, Francesca Lia. **Violet and Claire.** HarperCollins, 1999. 128 pp. ISBN 0060277491. Fiction.

Violet and Claire are about as opposite as two friends can be. Violet dresses all in black; she is intensely dark. Claire, on the other hand, is light and whimsical, given to wearing Tinkerbell wings.

Both girls are outcasts at their school, and they seek comfort in one another's acceptance. When Violet's career as a screenwriter begins to take off, Claire worries about the people who only want to hang around Violet for her connections to Hollywood. Violet, in turn, is concerned about some of Claire's acquaintances. The two alternate telling the story of their relationship, and how they both manage to survive others who preyed on them. With graphic language and situations, this book describes what can happen when living on the edge becomes the norm.

10.8 Brooks, Bruce. **Vanishing.** HarperCollins, 1999. 160 pp. ISBN 0060282363. Fiction.

Although only eleven years old, Alice has seen more than her share of hardship in life. When her parents divorce, Alice elects to live with her father. He seems to lack direction, but anything is preferable to living with her alcoholic mother. However, circumstances force Alice to return to her mother. A severe case of bronchitis lands her in the hospital where, for a time, Alice feels safely in charge of her own life. In the hospital, she meets Rex, a terminally ill boy who has deemed himself the King of Remissions. Their friendship grows despite the fact that Alice has decided to go on a hunger strike. If she cannot get well, the doctors cannot send her home to her mother, right? Even death seems a better option until Rex falls seriously ill.

10.9 Bunting, Eve. **Blackwater.** HarperCollins, 1999. 146 pp. ISBN 0060278382. Fiction.

The arrival of his cousin Alex ruins all of Brodie's plans for the summer. Maybe he can salvage some fun by teaching Alex to swim. The Blackwater River can be quite dangerous, but Brodie plans to take his cousin to the swimming hole where he, too, learned to swim. Alex and Brodie set out early one morning, and their actions lead to a tragic accident, one that will change the lives of many families who live near the river.

10.10 Burgess, Melvin. **Smack.** Henry Holt, 1996. 321 pp. ISBN 080505801X. Fiction.

Fourteen-year-old Tar runs away from an abusive father and alcoholic mother. When he finds a place to live in an abandoned building, he is joined by his girlfriend, Gemma. Their new life starts out with parties and drinking, and quickly descends to heroin use with their new friends who also live on the streets. This story shows the ecstasies and horrors of heroin use, and its affect on the lives of these teens.

10.11 Cadnum, Michael. **Taking It.** Puffin, 1997. 135 pp. ISBN 0140375708. Fiction.

Seventeen-year-old Anna Charles, daughter of a Really Important Person, finds herself confused and desperate when her just-for-kicks habit of shoplifting takes a sinister turn: she discovers she has no memory of taking the things that now turn up in her pockets. Anna sees shoplifting as an art, a skill to be honed, and something she controls. Unlike her home life where she has absolutely no control, shoplifting is something she's in charge of. Or is she? Anna feels confused and then desperate, as she discovers she not only can't control what she takes, but also doesn't know when she's taking something and when she isn't.

10.12 Chbosky, Stephen. **The Perks of Being a Wallflower.** Pocket, 1999. 213 pp. ISBN 0671027344. Fiction.

In a series of letters addressed simply "Dear Friend," Charlie talks about his freshman year of high school. Although not one of the geeks, Charlie is also not one of the in-crowd. He is, by his own description, a wallflower, a young man who is shy, especially in social situations. As we read his letters, we get to know more about Charlie's talent for writing, a talent nurtured by his English teacher. We watch as Charlie makes friends, and suffers through his first crush on a girl. There are other obstacles for Charlie to navigate as well, particularly problems with family. Charlie faithfully records all of the pain and joy of life as a ninth grader.

10.13 Cooney, Caroline B. **Burning Up.** Delacorte, 1999. 230 pp. ISBN 0385323182. Fiction.

From marshmallows to relationships, everything is burning up in and around Shell Road, a small, elite beachside community in Connecticut. Fifteen-year-old Macey Clare meets with resistance from friends, family, and the citizens of the community when she decides to research the history of a barn that burned in the town in 1959. Macey's unwilling research partner, Austin, finds himself drawn to Macey like a moth to a flame as they try to open up a past that everyone wants to keep closed. Together they search the Internet, and the memories of those who will talk to them, as they piece together the story of the fire and the hatred that ignited it.

10.14 Cooney, Caroline B. **The Voice on the Radio.** Laurel Leaf, 1998. 183 pp. ISBN 0440219779. Fiction.

In this third book in the series that began with *The Face on the Milk Carton* and continued in *Whatever Happened to Janie?*, Janie must once again open the wounds of her decision to leave her birth family in order to return to the family that raised her after she was kidnapped. Now a senior in high school, Janie had been at relative peace with her decision—that is until her boyfriend, Reeve, decides to share the story of how Janie saw her face on the milk carton with his radio audience. Reeve knows he shouldn't share this very personal story, but his audience is hooked, and they want more. Soon Reeve has a huge nightly audience that listens as he shares more tidbits about Janie's kidnapping, reunion with her birth family, and eventual return to the only family she's known. He rationalizes his decision to air her story by assuring himself that Janie will never find out. But she does.

10.15 Cormier, Robert. **Tenderness.** Delacorte, 1997. 240 pp. ISBN 0385322860. Fiction.

The killings began small. When he was young, Eric would kill stray animals and neighborhood pets. He enjoyed feeling their vulnerable surrender to his tender touch. Now eighteen, Eric Poole is soon to be released from the juvenile detention center. He has served his sentence, and there is insufficient evidence to prove he may be a menace to society if he is set free. Lori, a fifteen-year-old runaway, becomes obsessed with meeting Eric. Little does she know how dangerous the meeting is. Eric is a sociopath, and is willing to do whatever he must to get what he wants.

10.16 Dessen, Sarah. **Keeping the Moon.** Viking, 1999. 228 pp. ISBN 0670885495. Fiction.

Colie Sparks is sure this summer is going to be the worst of her life. And there have been a lot of "worsts" in her life. Her mother, aerobics guru Kiki Sparks, is off touring Europe, and Colie is stuck in dreary Colby, North Carolina, with her rather eccentric aunt Mira, who makes a living as a condolence card artist. But

Colie soon changes her mind when she lands a job as a waitress at the Last Chance Bar and Grille. There she meets Isabel and Morgan, two world-wise waitresses in their twenties, and Norman, an interesting, if somewhat odd, artist who cooks at the Last Chance. With the help of her aunt and her newfound friends, Colie learns to look at herself in a different way, and discovers that believing in herself will make her stronger than she ever imagined.

10.17 Doyon, Stephanie. **On the Road #1: Leaving Home.** Aladdin, 1999. 235 pp. ISBN 0689821077. Fiction.

In this book, the first in a series of four, Miranda and her friend Kirsten decide to delay college for a year. Instead, the two plan to travel together across the United States with no particular destination or itinerary. It sounds crazy, and that is what appeals most to Miranda, who has always been dependable and predictable. The trip will change her life in many ways. Other titles in the series include *Buying Time, Taking Chances,* and *Making Waves.*

10.18 Fleischman, Paul. **Mind's Eye.** Henry Holt, 1999. 144 pp. ISBN 08050631145. Fiction.

Courtney, age sixteen, and Elva, age eighty-eight, find themselves roommates in a nursing home where Courtney's been left after a severed spinal cord injury leaves her unable to ever walk again. Her parents are dead, and she feels alone, with nothing but her anger and grief as companions. Elva is sustained by her memories, and feels anything but lonely. She tries to engage Courtney by proposing that they take an imaginary trip with the help her of 1910 Baedeker's Italy guide, but Courtney balks. Little by little, however, Courtney is drawn into the trip, and the lines between fantasy and reality blur as she finds herself living a life she thought had passed her by. Written completely in dialogue, this compelling book is dramatic and disturbing, uplifting and sorrowful.

10.19 Fleischman, Paul. **Seedfolks.** HarperCollins, 1997. 69 pp. ISBN 0060274719. Fiction.

This is the story of the growth of a garden and a community. The seedfolks are thirteen individuals who are instrumental in transforming a vacant lot in a Cleveland neighborhood from a dumping ground into a place where hope flowers and neighbors come to know and respect one another. The story begins with the voice of Kim, who plants the first seed because she wants to show her father, a farmer from Vietnam, that she too can help things grow. Ana and Wendell, who have lost their faith in youth, regain that faith as they watch and help Kim in the garden. Gonzalo's uncle, Tio Juan, misses the farm and friends he left behind in Guatemala, until he joins the gardeners. Virgil and his Haitian father plant lettuce and dream of riches, and Curtis rekindles his romance with Lateesha while he concentrates on growing the tomatoes she adores. These stories and others show us how a garden, like a community, requires attention and love.

10.20 Fleischman, Paul. **Whirligig.** Henry Holt, 1998. 160 pp. ISBN 0805055827. Fiction.

Sixteen-year-old Brent Bishop is used to having to fit in. He has moved often, and he knows how to assess a new town and school and blend in. When he makes a foolish mistake at a party, he is so distraught that he decides to kill himself. He takes his hands off the steering wheel of his car and points it toward a roadway barrier. Instead of ending his own life, though, Brent ends the life of a fifteen-year-old girl. His court sentence requires that he make restitution for what he has done. The mother of the victim has an unusual request. In trying to fulfill that request, Brent learns about himself and about the world in which he must now live. More importantly, he discovers what is truly important in life.

10.21 Garden, Nancy. **The Year They Burned the Books.** Farrar, Straus and Giroux, 1999. 247 pp. ISBN 0374386676. Fiction.

Jamie Crawford is having a rough senior year at Wilson High School. As the editor of the *Wilson High Telegraph,* she's at the center of the battle between advocates of free speech and a conservative Christian group called the Families for Traditional Values (FTV). Furthermore, Jamie thinks she might be gay. When the FTV begins burning books that deal with homosexuality and sex education, a battle erupts, and things will never be the same in the little town of Wilson. This is a powerful book that examines tough issues such as censorship and sex education in schools. The book contains explicit language, but will pull readers into the story with its carefully drawn characters and sensitive examination of issues facing today's teenagers.

10.22 Grant, Cynthia D. **The White Horse.** Atheneum Books for Young Readers, 1998. 160 pp. ISBN 068921271. Fiction.

Ms. Johnson's class is comprised of all of the students who have not succeeded in a traditional school. Her biggest concern is sixteen-year-old Raina. Raina is pregnant and homeless. She tells Ms. Johnson that she has to stay away from her home because her mother is a heroin addict. Raina's journal entries for Ms. Johnson's class, along with Ms. Johnson's own observations, tell the story of a young woman desperate to make a better life for the child she will soon give birth to. How can Raina deal with a child when she is a child herself?

10.23 Grove, Vicki. **The Starplace.** New York: Putnam, 1999. 214 pp. ISBN 0399232079. Fiction.

It's the year 1961, and Frannie lives in the perfect little town of Quiver, Oklahoma. She is planning a party with her friends to launch their eighth grade school year. Then, Celeste, an African American girl, moves to town. Frannie is drawn to Celeste, but she is afraid to make friends with her because Celeste is the only African American student in the school. As time goes by, however, they become close friends. Through their friendship, Frannie learns some history that was not taught in her school. She discovers prejudice, and Celeste and her father teach her about the horror of the Ku Klux Klan, which killed Celeste's great-great-grandfather. Frannie struggles with this new knowledge.

10.24 Haddix, Margaret Peterson. **Leaving Fishers.** Simon & Schuster Books for Young Readers, 1997. 211 pp. ISBN 068981125X. Fiction.

Sometimes it's better to have no friends at all than to have the wrong friends. Dorry Stevens and her family have moved to Indianapolis. Her efforts to make new friends at Crestwood High School are ignored, and she spends her days alone, wishing she could return to her life in the small town of Bryden. When Angela asks her to sit with her at lunch, Dorry is ecstatic. Finally, she has a friend. Then Angela introduces Dorry to the Fishers of Men and to their leader, Pastor Jim. Soon Dorry realizes that if she wants to keep her new friends, she'll need to be saved and become a Fisherman. Pressured to confess her sins, pray rather than study, and recruit new members for the Fishers, Dorry's life begins to spin out of control. As her grades plummet and her family and friends from Bryden begin to look upon her as a stranger, Dorry starts to wonder what the Fishers are really fishing for.

10.25 Hautman, Pete. **Stone Cold.** Simon & Schuster, 1998. 163 pp. ISBN 0689817592. Fiction.

Everything is going well for Denn. The landscaping business he started after his father deserted his family is flourishing, he's saving money for the future, and he has a girlfriend. All that changes when his friends invite him to a poker game. Not only does he win, he loves it. He discovers he has a real talent for the game. He takes his savings out of the bank and acquires a fake ID so that he can get into a local casino. He quickly learns the strategies he needs to win, and with his success comes addiction. He begins to think he can't lose, but there are other things at stake besides money. Soon he loses his business, his family, and his girlfriend. Can he stop this addiction, or is it too late?

10.26 Henry, Chad. **DogBreath Victorious.** Holiday House, 1999. 188 pp. ISBN 0823414582. Fiction.

Tim Threlfall's life has fallen apart. His father has recently died; his band, called DogBreath, has no bookings and is disintegrating; his grades are dropping lower than the basement; and his mother is broke and barely functioning. Winning the Rad Band Contest at Lewd Fingers Dirt Club may be his only hope, but his school counselor has threatened expulsion if he continues to play in the band. While Tim's mother is gone every night practicing a new Mary Kay skit with her friends, Tim and his friends begin to develop some new numbers for the competition. Can they win?

10.27 Hesser, Terry Spencer. **Kissing Doorknobs.** Delacorte, 1998. 149 pp. ISBN 0385323298. Fiction.

Tara was always a worrier. By age thirteen, her quirks included counting every crack in the sidewalk on the way to school. To calm herself, she performs rituals over and over again. But when she develops the new ritual of leaving the house only after she has kissed the doorknob a prescribed number of times, her parents reach their limit. Little do they understand that Tara has reached her limit, too. She's tired of not understanding why she must perform these rituals, she's humiliated while performing them, and she's exhausted from trying to cover up all that she's going through. This warmly humorous story looks at obsessive-compulsive behavior, and the devastating effects it has on Tara's life.

10.28 Hite, Sid. **Cecil in Space.** Henry Holt, 1999. 160 pp. ISBN 0805050558. Fiction.

Cecil's aunt thinks he has been off in space as an astronaut. But then, everyone in town knows she is a bit crazy. How else can you explain the fact that she took a gun and fired at Cecil and his mother when he was just a baby? Cecil's problems extend well beyond an aunt in a mental hospital, however. There is the small matter of an act of vandalism that may have been caused by his close friend. There is even more trouble with the young women in his life. Cecil wonders if it is possible to remain friends with a girl once he has kissed her. The summer will be one of disappointment and discovery, trauma and triumph.

10.29 Hoban, Julia. **Acting Normal.** HarperCollins, 1998. 206 pp. ISBN 0060235195. Fiction.

At eighteen, Stephanie Holt has everything going for her: she is a star in numerous television commercials, is an aspiring acting student, and has successful parents. But this glamorous life comes tumbling down around her when she begins to study the sense memory method of acting. After a mental breakdown, Stephanie must start her life over. Angry and openly hostile toward her parents, who have been acting strange ever since she "got messed up," and disillusioned with a string of ineffective psychiatrists, Stephanie doesn't think that she will ever be "normal" again. Then she meets Dahlia and a new psychiatrist, Dr. Steinhart. With their caring friendship and help, Stephanie begins to face the dark and disturbing childhood memory that continually haunts her. Julia Hoban presents a realistic view of the everyday problems encountered by adolescents, as well as a serious portrayal of a teenager who struggles with suppressed memories of child abuse.

10.30 Holmes, Barbara Ware. **Letters to Julia.** HarperCollins, 1997. 229 pp. ISBN 0060273429. Fiction.

Liz's English teacher thinks Liz is such a good writer that she should send her work to a New York editor the teacher knows. Imagine Liz's surprise when the editor not only responds to her work, but also establishes a relationship with her through their letters. Liz writes of her eccentric, divided family, and Julia the editor shares much about herself and her life. Unexpected events occur when the two finally meet.

10.31 Howe, James. **The Watcher.** Atheneum Books for Young Readers, 1997. 173 pp. ISBN 0689801866. Fiction.

Thirteen-year-old Margaret sits atop the stairs to the beach watching the beach goers, wishing she were part of fourteen-year-old Evan's family. She thinks Evan's family is perfect, but appearances are deceptive. She views Chris, the lifeguard, as a guardian angel, but Chris is dealing with the affects the death of a brother has on his relationship with his father. By alternating the perspective among Margaret, Evan, his little sister Callie, and Chris, Howe enables the reader to compare each character's perspective and to see how their lives will intersect. Evan's and Chris' discovery of Margaret's physical abuse help Margaret garner the strength she needs to speak out and put an end to her father's reign of terror.

10.32 Ingold, Jeanette. **Airfield.** Harcourt Brace, 1999. 148 pp. ISBN 0152020535. Fiction.

Beatty is staying with her Aunt Clo for the summer, and finds herself spending time at the Muddy Springs Airport where her uncle works. Beatty is there so much she is offered a job—without pay, since not many paying jobs are available in 1933. The more she is around planes, the more fascinating they become. She hopes to take a ride one day, but her father, who is a pilot, won't discuss it. Another thing he won't discuss is Beatty's mother. She longs to find out anything about her mother, who died when Beatty was one year old, but when she finally does, the information shocks her.

10.33 Jenkins, A. E. **Breaking Boxes.** Delacorte, 1997. 182 pp. ISBN 0385325134. Fiction.

Charlie Calmont is a loner. His father abandoned him, and his mother is dead. Now he lives with his older brother, Trent. Charlie keeps his anger and despair boxed inside him, and presents a cool exterior to the world outside. When Charlie's anger finally explodes, he gets into a fistfight with Brandon Chase. On the surface it appears that Brandon lives a charmed life, but Charlie comes to understand that surface appearances can be deceiving.

10.34 Klass, David. **Screen Test.** Scholastic, 1997. 256 pp. ISBN 059048592X. Fiction.

High school sophomore Liz is offered the chance of a lifetime. After starring in a student-made film, Liz receives an offer to go to Hollywood and appear in a feature film. The lure of the silver screen has never really interested Liz before, but how can she refuse a role starring opposite a gorgeous guy? Liz heads off to Hollywood, where she is wined and dined. It is not long before she realizes that making decisions about her career requires that she look beneath the glitzy surface of the people who say they are there to help her.

10.35 Koller, Jackie French. **The Falcon.** Atheneum Books for Young Readers, 1998. 181 pp. ISBN 0689812949. Fiction.

Luke is annoyed when his eleventh grade English teacher requires the class to keep a journal. To his surprise, he soon finds himself recording all his thoughts about his life. He knows that his supportive parents worry about his seemingly reckless behavior, but when his unplanned mountain climbing adventure results in his hospitalization and the possible loss of his sight, he worries about himself, too. Will Dr. Jim be able to help him figure out why he acts so self-destructively?

10.36 Kropp, Paul. **Moonkid and Prometheus.** Stoddart Kids, 1997. 294 pp. ISBN 0773674659. Fiction.

Whiz kid Ian McNaughton (a.k.a. Moonkid) cannot seem to get along with anyone at his high school. When the vice-principal assigns him to tutor Prometheus, a seventh grader, during his free period, Moonkid learns how to break down the art of reading in order to fully explain it. Unfortunately, a teacher disagrees with Moonkid's teaching methods and ends his sessions with Prometheus. The two meet and devise a plan that will allow them to continue their meetings. Soon, Moonkid and Prometheus form a warm friendship.

10.37 Lynch, Chris. **Political Timber.** HarperTrophy, 1996. 166 pp. ISBN 0060273607. Fiction.

Gordon is excited when his grandfather (the ex-mayor, who is now in prison) gives him his spectacular 1963 convertible, in which Gordon dreams of sailing through his senior year. He soon finds out that everything carries a price tag, and the price of the convertible is Gordon's willingness to run for mayor. Politics blends with school life, and Gordon learns a lot about himself and the way politics works.

10.38 Lynch, Chris. **Whitechurch.** HarperCollins, 1999. 192 pp. ISBN 0060283300. Fiction.

The stories of Lilly, Pauly, and Oakley are entwined in this novel about change and how different people deal with the possibilities that change brings. Lilly is determined to leave the small town of Whitechurch after high school graduation. Pauly fears change of any kind. Oakley seems to go along with each of them in turn, afraid to enrage the already unbalanced Pauly and unwilling to part with Lilly, a girl he has known and loved for years. The mix of poetry and prose provides readers glimpses into the complex relationships that exist among friends on the brink of challenges. Its gritty realism, a hallmark of Lynch's work, is brutally honest.

10.39 Mahy, Margaret. **Memory.** Aladdin, 1999. 278 pp. ISBN 0689829116. Fiction.

Nineteen-year-old Jonny Dart, ridden with feelings of guilt after his sister's accidental death, searches for those who could help him unravel the events of the accident. One night, while drunk and wandering through an empty parking lot, he meets Sophie, a senile woman. She thinks he is part of her romantic past, and befriends Jonny. By helping Sophie with her own personal care, Jonny is able to unravel the pieces in his own life that help him understand himself and his sister's death. Jonny's gentle compassion toward Sophie also helps him achieve a sense of himself as he confronts those who had once bullied him.

10.40 Matas, Carol, and Perry Nodelman. **Out of Their Minds.** Simon & Schuster, 1998. 183 pp. ISBN 0689819466. Fiction.

This is the third book in the Minds series. In this book, Leonora and Coren finally plan their wedding day at the court of Andilla, Coren's homeland. Unfortunately, the Andillans have lost the power of imagination, which is critical for maintaining the sacred

Balance. Leonora and Coren embark on a journey to find the source of the problem. Along the way, they discover the Skwoes, a people who have absolutely no imagination. As Leonora and Coren attempt to solve the problems plaguing Coren's people, they must overcome the Skwoes and battle the evil Hevak.

10.41 McDaniel, Lurlene. **Until Angels Close My Eyes.** Bantam, 1998. 242 pp. ISBN 055357115X. Fiction.

Leah, a cancer survivor, discovers that Neil, her loving stepfather, has been in remission from cancer, but is ill again. Angry and seeking comfort, Leah turns to Ethan, an Amish boy she met the previous summer. She convinces Ethan to leave his family and move into her home. Skeptical at first, Leah's mom and stepdad come to depend on Ethan's support, especially as Neil's illness worsens. But can Ethan ultimately abandon his Amish ways?

10.42 McDonald, Joyce. **Swallowing Stones.** Bantam, 1997. 256 pp. ISBN 0385323093. Fiction.

For his seventeenth birthday, Michael receives an extraordinary present: a beautiful rifle. Michael's father cautions him about using the rifle before he takes a gun safety class, but the allure is too great to resist. Michael and his best friend, Joe, take the rifle into the woods and fire off a shot. The next morning, Michael is shocked to hear that a man fixing his roof a mile away from Michael's neighborhood was struck by a stray bullet and killed. Michael cannot believe that his single shot could have killed someone. Surely there is another explanation? Michael comes to the sad realization that he is responsible for the man's death. What should he do?

10.43 McGuigan, Mary Ann. **Where You Belong.** Aladdin, 1998. 171 pp. ISBN 0689823185. Fiction.

Just like the eviction notice said, the marshal and the movers arrive at 8:00 A.M. Fiona's mother decided to leave her alcoholic father "after one more of so many rages," and to start over in the small apartment that they are now forced to leave. Without telling her mother, Fiona decides to go back to her father. The same night she returns, her father flies into one of his drunken rages. Frightened, Fiona runs away. After spending the night on a park bench, she meets Yolanda Baker, a friend from her old school, who tells

Fiona she can stay with her for a while. Maybe this is the place Fiona belongs. But, in the Bronx of the 1960s, what are the chances that a friendship between a Black girl and a White girl can endure?

10.44 McNeal, Laura, and Tom McNeal. **Crooked.** Knopf, 1999. 224 pp. ISBN 0679893008. Fiction.

Clara and Amos are both wrestling with difficult changes in their lives. Clara's parents have recently divorced, and Clara is living with her father. The trouble is, he is frequently out of town for business. Amos has lost his father to stomach cancer. His family is still reeling from the loss. Somehow the two manage to begin a friendship that just might blossom into romance. Unfortunately, a local tough guy also has his sights set on Clara. When Eddie Tripp begins to stalk Clara, the situation spins quickly out of control.

10.45 Myers, Walter Dean. **Monster.** HarperCollins, 1999. 240 pp. ISBN 0060280778. Fiction.

Sixteen-year-old Steve Harmon sits in the courtroom every day, and in his jail cell every night, wondering whether he is the monster the prosecuting attorney makes him out to be. Steve is on trial for murder, accused of being the lookout for a convenience store robbery that resulted in the slaying of the owner. Several other participants have fingered Steve as the lookout, even though he maintains that he is innocent. Unable to deal with the fear and pain that is his life, Steve decides to keep a record of all that is happening. An aspiring filmmaker, Steve opts to tell about his life in the form of a script for a movie. As the film plays out, you will have to decide whether Steve is guilty or innocent.

10.46 Naidoo, Beverly. **No Turning Back: A Novel of South Africa.** HarperCollins, 1995. 189 pp. ISBN 0060275065. Fiction.

Sipho loves his Ma, but he just can't take the beating from his stepfather anymore. Thinking that anything would be better than this life of fear and brutality, Sipho runs away from his home in a South African township to live on the streets of Jo'burg. Here Sipho meets other *malunde* (people living on the streets), and learns how to live a day-to-day existence, parking cars, pushing grocery carts, sweeping up for small change to buy something to eat. At night, Sipho and his friends sleep an uneasy sleep in the bitter cold, always fearful that the plainclothes police will find their *pozzie* (hideout), and haul them off in the *gumba-gumba* (large police van). Based on real-life stories of Black South African street children, this powerful novel paints a realistic picture of personal and societal struggles in a country at a turning point in history.

10.47 Neenan, Colin. **Live a Little.** Harcourt Brace, 1996. 252 pp. ISBN 0152012427. Fiction.

In this sequel to *In Your Dreams,* we rejoin Hale O'Reilly during the final days of his senior year. Hale is stuck in the middle between his two best friends. Sonny is bemoaning his recent breakup with his girlfriend. Zoe, on the other hand, seems to be making moves on Sonny. Hale learns some valuable lessons about being a friend. The bottom line is that it is a lot tougher than it looks.

10.48 Pattou, Edith. **Fire Arrow: The Second Song of Eirren.** Harcourt Brace, 1998. 320 pp. ISBN 015201635X. Fiction.

The second book in the Song of Eirren series tells of the archer Breo-Saight, who is called home to the deathbed of her old nurse-maid. Before the nurse dies, she gives Breo-Saight directions to a golden arrow, part of Breo-Saight's birthright. Breo-Saight soon learns that the person who has caused the death of her beloved nursemaid is the same person responsible for the death of her father. She begins to track him across the realms. Her travels lead her to a strange country where she encounters an evil, one-eyed sorcerer who wishes to use Breo-Saight's magic arrow to conquer the land and its peoples.

10.49 Philbrick, Rodman. **Max the Mighty.** Blue Sky / Scholastic, 1998. 166 pp. ISBN 0590188925. Fiction.

Maxwell Kane doesn't mean to get into trouble. It's just that he met eleven-year-old red-haired Worm when he protected her from bullies, and now she's in real danger, so what's he to do? He makes a snap decision to take her away from her trouble, and is pursued by the police and a man called Undertaker. Together, Worm and Max flee across the country, dodging in and out of adventures and staying ahead of the law—until Worm believes that she is safe.

10.50 Rapp, Adam. **The Buffalo Tree.** HarperCollins, 1997. 188 pp. ISBN 006440711X. Fiction.

Sura is a young man shipped off to Hamstock, a juvenile detention facility where violence is the norm. The business of trying to reform kids has somehow been forgotten. Sura and his roommate Coly Jo try to get by, and to survive the sadistic games of the other inmates and the guards. After Coly Jo is badly beaten, Sura begins to plan an escape. Can he pull it off?

10.51 **Real Teens: Diary of a Junior Year.** Scholastic, 1999. 201 pp. ISBN 0439084083. Nonfiction.

Follow the lives of eight teens in this diary, as they live through the ups and downs of their junior year in high school. Marybeth writes about the pain she feels as Greg tells her that it's over between them; Kevin writes about how his parents "don't know how bad I still feel about my sister's getting killed and how angry that makes me"; Katie writes about feeling so lonely that all she can do is cry on her bathroom floor. Sad times, funny times, confusing times, and worrisome times are all described in this nonfiction account of what real teens live through during one school year. Part of the Real Teen series.

10.52 Roberts, Laura Peyton. **Ghost of a Chance.** Delacorte, 1997. 183 pp. ISBN 0385325088. Fiction.

Sixteen-year-old Melissa Soul is having a few problems. Her parents are getting a divorce, her younger brother is a royal pain, and there is a "For Sale" sign in front of the house she calls home. The only positive thing in her life seems to be her best friend, Chloe, and their upcoming summer vacation. When Melissa meets James—a funny, gorgeous, older guy—she thinks her life just may be on the upswing. However, the situation gets sticky when Melissa realizes that Chloe likes the same guy. What happens when two best friends fall for the same guy—a guy who is, by the way, a ghost?

10.53 Salisbury, Graham. **Shark Bait.** Delacorte, 1997. 151 pp. ISBN 0385322372. Fiction.

Seventeen-year-old Booley, one of the local toughs, befriends fourteen-year-old Eric, who is ironically nicknamed Mokes (tough guy). Being half *haole* (white) and the son of the new Chinese chief of police of Kailua, Eric would have been "shark bait" for the other Hawaiian locals without Booley's intervention. Disobeying his father's order to stay out of town while a Navy ship is in port, Eric is there when Booley's attempt to seek revenge for his mother's desertion with a sailor goes awry. Salisbury, a descendant of early missionary families in Hawaii, effectively integrates into the story both the modern Hawaiian dialect and references to old Hawaiian beliefs that still exist within the local culture.

10.54 Seago, Kate. **Matthew Unstrung.** Dial, 1998. 236 pp. ISBN 0803722303. Fiction.

It's 1910, and Matthew Hobson is a student at Priory Bible College. He is preparing to follow his father, a fire-and-brimstone preacher, into the church ministry. But Matthew's grades are failing, and the future he and his father have so carefully planned seems to be evaporating. When Matthew is dismissed from the college, he suffers a complete mental breakdown and is placed in an asylum. His father, convinced that Matthew is only shirking his responsibilities, abandons Matthew to the asylum's harsh and often brutal conditions. All seems lost for Matthew until he is rescued by his older brother, Zack, and taken to Zack's ranch in Colorado. Surrounded by the love he desperately needs, Matthew begins his journey back to sanity.

10.55 Singer, Marilyn, compiler and editor. **Stay True: Short Stories for Strong Girls.** Scholastic, 1998. 204 pp. ISBN 0590360310. Fiction.

Eleven strong women writers, including M. E. Kerr, Rita Williams-Garcia, Norma Fox Mazer, and Andrea Davis Pinkney, tell original stories about young women learning about themselves and about life. They deal with personal independence, integrity, abuse, friendships, generational differences, and gender roles.

10.56 Stevens, Diane. **Liza's Wishing Star.** Greenwillow, 1997. 183 pp. ISBN 0688153100. Fiction.

Liza's little sister Holly has drowned. Nothing in her life will ever be the same. Liza and her mother move to Rockport for the summer to take care of Mama Lacy. Liza wishes she can return to her father and her boyfriend in San Antonio. However, Liza makes new friends in Rockport, and discovers that time and distance can separate even the best of friends. As she and her family deal with the changes in their lives, Liza learns that friends are important, but family is where the heart is.

10.57 Stoehr, Shelly. **Wannabe.** Delacorte, 1997. 215 pp. ISBN 0385322232. Fiction.

Furious with her older brother for getting involved with the local mob, Catherine Tavarelli suffers from the same attraction. Brother Mickey is attracted to the money and potential power, and Catherine falls for Joey, the coolest of the bad. But along with money, power, and love come alcohol, drugs, and bigger troubles. In the style of her earlier books, *Crosses* and *Weird on the Outside*, Shelly Stoehr tells another story of hard-shelled, vulnerable teens trying to live in the fast lane.

10.58 Tashjian, Janet. **Multiple Choice.** Henry Holt, 1999. 208 pp. ISBN 0805060863. Fiction.

Fourteen-year-old Monica worries about everything. She has trouble making decisions due to her obsessive-compulsive nature. In desperation, she devises a plan to make decisions easier. She takes four Scrabble tiles, and whichever tile she selects dictates her choice: a normal choice, an uncharacteristic choice, a charitable choice, or an outrageous choice. When Monica allows this random method of decision making to take control, she makes some decisions that have near tragic consequences. She soon understands that she needs professional help to deal with her obsessive-compulsive behavior.

10.59 Thomas, Rob. **Satellite Down.** Aladdin, 1998. 299 pp. ISBN 0689830521. Fiction.

Good-looking Patrick becomes a student reporter on a teen news show in California. But once he leaves for the glamour of Hollywood, he suddenly finds that he is one of many good looking men with little talent to show for themselves. Through cheating and lying, he loses his girlfriend, best friend, and parents' confidence. On a trip to Ireland to report the news, Patrick becomes disillusioned with the news media, so he abandons his job, and seeks to investigate his own historical roots in southern Ireland. The town befriends him, and he learns much about himself as a person as he establishes new goals for himself and sets about reestablishing broken relationships.

10.60 Walter, Virginia. **Making Up Megaboy.** Illustrated by Katrina Roeckelein. Delacorte, 1999. 64 pp. ISBN 0385326866. Fiction.

This slim graphic novel tells the story of thirteen-year-old Robbie Jones. On his birthday, Robbie takes his father's gun, walks into a neighborhood grocery store, and shoots the owner. Told from the points of view of those who witnessed the shooting or who know Robbie, this novel looks for the reason why a nice young man would do such a horrible thing.

10.61 Wittlinger, Ellen. **Hard Love.** Simon & Schuster Books for Young Readers, 1999. 224 pp. ISBN 0689821344. Fiction.

"How long would it take my parents to notice if I escaped?" Sixteen-year-old John Galardi Jr. pours out his thoughts in poetry, plays, and essays, and publishes them in a homemade magazine or "zine" titled *Bananafish*. Using the pen name Giovanni, John connects with other zine writers: Marisol Guzman, who describes herself as a "Puerto Rican Cuban Yankee Cambridge, Massachusetts, rich spoiled lesbian private-school gifted-and-talented writer virgin looking for love"; and Diana Tree, a guitar-playing singer who wants to protect all those who come close to her. As he writes about his mother who can never touch him, his father who is busy living the life of a swinging bachelor, and his own love for a girl who can never love him back, John comes to terms with himself and his dreams.

10.62 Yamanaka, Lois-Ann. **Name Me Nobody.** Hyperion, 1999. 229 pp. ISBN 0786804521. Fiction.

Abandoned by her mother years ago, fourteen-year-old Emi-Lou Kaya grows up believing she is a nobody. Her only friends are her beloved grandmother and her best pal Yvonne. Yvonne puts Emi-Lou on a strict diet, hoping to change her friend's sense of herself. However, Emi's problems worsen as rumors about Yvonne and Emi begin to surface in town. Emi must overcome quite a bit if she is to be able to forge new relationships with her peers.

10.63 Young, Karen Romano. **Video.** Greenwillow, 1999. 160 pp. ISBN 0688165176. Fiction.

Eric Gooch's life has taken several turns for the worse lately. His leg is badly broken in a skiing accident, his parents are getting a divorce, and he must leave his private boarding school and enroll in the local public school, where he is sure to be an outcast. His luck continues going downhill as his term assignment pairs him with Janine, the bossy girl who lives in his neighborhood. Janine is fascinated with the area's wetlands, and begins to spend more and more of her spare time exploring the deserted area. Eric watches her through the lens of his video camera. He sees what she cannot: danger.

11 Geography and Archeology

*"Touch the earth, love the earth, honour the earth,
her plains, her valleys, her hills, and her seas
rest your spirit in her solitary places."*

Henry Beston

11.1 Aston, Mick, and Tim Taylor. **The Atlas of Archeology.** Dorling Kindersley, 1998. 208 pp. ISBN 0789431890. Nonfiction.

Using fourteen full-color maps that show over 1,200 sites from around the world, Aston and Taylor explain everything from hunter-gatherer societies (see an early skull skeleton from the Zhoukoudian Cave for an "inside" view as to how these early people looked) to pottery found from 3700 B.C.E. to the rituals surrounding a Saxon burial. Filled with photographs, drawings, and maps, this atlas of archeology shows how the signs of the past give us insight into the nature, customs, and beliefs of our ancestors. Unlike many archeology books, this one doesn't just present findings; instead, it shows all the steps from excavation to analysis so that you too might become inspired by the archeologist's world.

11.2 Buettner, Dan. **Africatrek: A Journey by Bicycle through Africa.** Lerner, 1997. 105 pp. ISBN 0822529513. Nonfiction.

Can you imagine bicycling 11,855 miles across the continent of Africa, from Tunisia in the north to South Africa in the south? Author Dan Buettner, his brother, and two other men crossed fourteen African countries on their 262-day bike trek. Along the way, they crossed the Sahara Desert, encountered rain forests, ate grasshoppers and centipedes, and fought tsetse flies, malaria, dysentery, and guerrilla soldiers. The photographs of their adventures help make the trip come alive for readers.

11.3 Haywood, John. **Historical Atlas of the Ancient World: 4,000,000 to 500 B.C.** Barnes & Noble, 1998. Unpaged. ISBN 0760719713. Nonfiction.

This atlas is the first volume of a six-volume set. This volume provides world and regional maps of the ancient world. Timelines at the bottom of each two-page spread chart major events, and brief text highlights four major themes: the origins of humanity, the evolution and spread of humans, the beginnings of agriculture, and the emergence of civilization. Other books in this series include *Historical Atlas of the Classical World, Historical Atlas of the Medieval World, Historical Atlas of the Early Modern World, Historical Atlas of the 19th Century,* and *Historical Atlas of the Modern World.*

11.4 McPhee, John A. **Annals of the Former World.** Farrar, Straus and Giroux, 1998. 696 pp. ISBN 0374105220. Nonfiction.

This ambitious, entertaining, and completely absorbing geological history of North America takes readers on a historical journey of the continent's formation. Moving from the Rockies to the Appalachian Mountains, and covering everything from the shifting sands of surface deserts to the continent's core, this book not only provides information about North America's formation, but also offers a glimpse of geologists of the past.

11.5 Palmer, Douglas. **Atlas of the Prehistoric World.** Discovery, 1999. 224 pp. ISBN 1563318296. Nonfiction.

For four and a half billion years, the planet Earth has gone through dramatic changes. Mountains have risen and fallen. Oceans and rivers have flowed and dried up. Life has had many different forms and faces. This book provides a view of the planet's evolution through geology and paleontology (the scientific study of fossils), offering a "time traveler's version of a typical atlas." The book is divided into three major sections, each of which presents a different perspective on Earth's prehistory. In The Changing Globe, different geological periods are represented through computer-generated maps. Ancient Worlds explores the evolution of life on Earth. The final section, Earth Fact File, offers a geological timeline with vignettes about the scientists who pieced together Earth's geological history based on rocks and fossils. Supplemented by full-color photographs, illustrations, and maps, this atlas is a highly readable and informative source.

11.6   Pandell, Karen. **Journey through the Northern Rainforest.** Photographs by Art Wolfe. Dutton Children's Books, 1999. Unpaged. ISBN 0525458042. Nonfiction.

Travel along the western coast of the United States, up through British Columbia, and into Alaska as you take a close-up look at the coastal northern rain forests. Stunning color photographs offer images of trees, wildlife, waterfalls, and plant life. Read about the migration of salmon, the effects of the logging industry, and the ecosystem of this disappearing land.

11.7   Ruth, Maria Mudd. **The Deserts of the Southwest.** Marshall Cavendish, 1998. 64 pp. ISBN 0761408991. Nonfiction.

Bounded by mountains on one side and the ocean on the other, the deserts of the Southwest seem to support no life. Scorching sun, miles of sand dunes, and frigid nighttime temperatures make this area inhospitable to say the least. But a closer look reveals a unique ecosystem that not only survives but thrives. This book will help you understand what makes the deserts of the Southwest a place so many creatures call home.

11.8   Sayre, April Pulley. **Africa.** Twenty-First Century Books, 1999. 62 pp. ISBN 0761313672. Nonfiction.

As one of the books in the Seven Continents series, *Africa* provides an overview of the landscape, geology, weather, and ecosystems of the continent of Africa. Particular emphasis is placed on the desert landscape of the Sahara and other deserts of Africa. The book introduces some of the environmental challenges to the survival of animals, plants, and human beings on the continent.

11.9   Sobel, Dava. **Longitude: The True Story of a Lone Genius Who Solved the Greatest Scientific Problem of His Time.** Penguin, 1996. 184 pp. ISBN 0140258795. Nonfiction.

John Harrison (1693–1776) spent forty years trying to figure out how people at sea could determine where they were. For centuries, ships found themselves lost at sea because sailors couldn't calculate their east-west position, and astronomers couldn't figure out how to help them. Finally, Harrison, a clockmaker, found the answer.

11.10 World Reference Atlas. Dorling Kindersley, 1998. 731 pp. ISBN 078943251X. Nonfiction.

More than five thousand illustrations, maps, charts, and diagrams will help readers locate and understand the nations of the world today. The book begins with a detailed map of the world and an overview of global history. Each nation is then individually surveyed and mapped. Information is provided about climate, ecology, and recent history for each nation. Also included is a section discussing global issues such as hunger, tourism, conflict, and the environment. An index provides a list of thousands of the world's most important places, with alternate spellings and indications of any recent name changes.

12 Historical Fiction

"As soon as histories are properly told there is no more need of romances."

Walt Whitman

12.1 Ayres, Katherine. **North by Night: A Story of the Underground Railroad.** Delacorte, 1998. 176 pp. ISBN 0385325649. Fiction.

"'Caught!' The word still sends shivers down my spine." The year is 1851. President Fillmore has just signed the Fugitive Slave Act, and the Underground Railroad is flourishing. Sixteen-year-old Lucinda Spencer, feisty and self-reliant, lives with her family in the frontier village of Atwater, Ohio. She secretly fights for others' rights while discovering some unexpected truths about the world in which she lives. *North by Night* is a compelling insight into characters fighting for freedom.

12.2 Baer, Edith. **Walk the Dark Streets.** Farrar, Straus and Giroux, 1998. 280 pp. ISBN 0374382298. Fiction.

The city where Eva Bentheim lives is changing before her eyes. Nazi flags and swastikas on red armbands are everywhere. At school, Eva is not allowed to take a new class called Rassenkunde—race science—because she is not Aryan. Many theaters, restaurants, and shops are off limits to Jews. As the political climate becomes more threatening, "those who don't want to go along with the Nazis get beaten up and packed off to the *Konzentrationslager*"—the concentration camps. One night, during a raid on Jewish homes and synagogues, Eva's father is taken prisoner. With the help of her friend, Arno, Eva's father is released. But this triumph is only temporary, and Eva and her family face many more difficulties as they hopelessly attempt to escape Germany together. A sequel to *A Frost in the Night*, this moving story presents a thought-provoking glimpse at a turning point in history.

12.3 Barrett, Tracy. **Anna of Byzantium.** Delacorte, 1999. 210 pp. ISBN 0385326262. Fiction.

Anna Comnena, the firstborn princess, will someday rule the powerful Byzantine Empire, even though many think her younger male brother should be named successor. When Anna begins lessons with her manipulative grandmother in warfare strategy and diplomacy, she proves a worthy and adept student. As Anna grows into an intelligent and literate young woman, she realizes that her grandmother's ambition is to be the real power when Anna becomes Empress. Anna's arrogance leads her to openly challenge her grandmother and threaten her younger brother, both of which are mistakes. Anna's promise of the throne is taken away, and she is subsequently banished from the palace. This intriguing story of rivalry and treachery is based on the life of Anna Comnena, author of *The Alexiad*, an epic about her father, Alexius I of Byzantium.

12.4 Bartoletti, Susan. **No Man's Land: A Young Soldier's Story.** Blue Sky / Scholastic, 1999. 171 pp. ISBN 059038731X. Fiction.

All his life, fourteen-year-old Thrasher Magee's pap has made him feel like a weakling and a coward. When Thrasher cannot muster the courage to save his father from an alligator attack, he sets out to prove that he has what it takes to become a hero. Thrasher joins up with the Confederate Army's Okefinokee Rifles, a top company from Georgia. Anxious to fight the Yankees alongside the heroic General Stonewall Jackson, Thrasher and his company march to Virginia. Along the journey, they face the gruesome realities of war, and Thrasher discovers courage and an inner strength he never imagined. This realistic and informative story is based on events related to the Twenty-Sixth Regiment Georgia Volunteer Infantry, its company the Okefinokee Rifles, and its participation in the Seven Days' Battle in Virginia's Shenandoah Valley.

12.5 Blackwood, Gary. **The Shakespeare Stealer.** Dutton, 1998. 208 pp. ISBN 0525458638. Fiction.

In Elizabethan England, being an orphan means having to fight for your existence. Fourteen-year-old Widge has been bought by Dr. Bright, and taught how to take down information in a sort of shorthand. This skill is what attracts Simon Bishop to young Widge. Bishop, a playwright, sends Widge off to steal a new play from William Shakespeare. While Widge is in the audience at the Globe Theatre, however, he becomes so involved in *Hamlet* that he is unable to transcribe all of the drama for his new master. Widge is sent back to the Globe, where he soon becomes a member of the acting troupe.

12.6   Booth, Martin. **War Dog.** Margaret McElderry, 1997. 133 pp. ISBN 0689813805. Fiction.

Jet, whose human owner has been arrested for poaching, is remanded to the British Army's Canine Division and renamed Bess—Dog D-67. There she receives intensive military training that complements her natural hunting abilities. In this wartime tale, Bess serves her country with dutiful pride and expertise. She also manages to transform all who know her.

12.7   Bruchac, Joseph. **The Arrow over the Door.** Illustrated by James Watling. Dial, 1998. 89 pp. ISBN 0803720785. Fiction.

Samuel Russell and Stands Straight are young teens caught in a turbulent era that they neither like nor understand. Samuel and his family are Quakers—pacifists who refuse to fight the British or their Indian scouts. Stands Straight hates all white settlers because they killed his mother and brother. But neither of these young men is prepared for the transformation that occurs when they encounter each other, and take time to examine the ways of peace.

12.8   Bunin, Sherry. **Dear Great American Writers School.** Bantam, 1997. 168 pp. ISBN 0440220386. Fiction.

"Writers!!! Turn Stories Into Dollars! Everyone has stories to tell— and SELL! Send TODAY for the complete, reliable 10 Writing Lessons Course!" When Bobby Lee Pomeroy sees that advertisement in a magazine, she knows her problems with writing are over. Desperate to be a writer, Bobby sends away for the ten lessons. Believing that real editors are reading her letters, Bobby continues to write to Susan Buckley at the Great American Writers School for over a year. Through those letters, Bobby shares what life in her small Kentucky town in 1944 is all about. In the end, Bobby discovers a secret about the writing school, and the real secret to good writing.

12.9   Cadnum, Michael. **In a Dark Wood.** Orchard, 1998. 246 pp. ISBN 0531300714. Fiction.

The legend of Robin Hood is familiar to most readers, but this retelling places Geoffry, the Sheriff of Nottingham, at center stage. Geoffry's squire, Hugh, was an orphan rescued by the priests, and he acts as a foil to the evil sheriff. As the story unfolds from Geoffry's point of view, Robin Hood appears to be a clever outlaw who plays a frustrating game of cat and mouse with his counterpart.

12.10 Calvert, Patricia. **Sooner.** Atheneum Books for Young Readers, 1998. 166 pp. ISBN 0689811144. Fiction.

In this powerful sequel to *Bigger*, Tyler Bohanon returns to the family farm in Missouri after a search for his father, Black Jack Bohanon, a Confederate soldier who refuses to acknowledge the end of the Civil War. In the absence of his father, Tyler becomes the head of the family, caring for his mother, his younger brother Lucas, and his sister Rosa Lee. He works alongside Sooner, a rusty-haired pup with one blue eye and one brown, and the son of Bigger, who was shot and killed during Tyler's search for his father. Together they outwit a couple of scalawags who attempt to steal their only rifle and their old mule, Patches. Later, Tyler and Sooner fight for the rights of Isaac Peerce, a former slave and a friend, to go to school. Tyler and Sooner experience both success and failure as they learn what it takes to care for family, friends, and the farm at Sweet Creek.

12.11 Carbone, Elisa. **Stealing Freedom.** Knopf, 1998. 268 pp. ISBN 0679893075. Fiction.

Ann Maria Weems patiently endures her arrogant master and demanding mistress, knowing that one day her father will buy his family's freedom. When the family's dreams remain unfulfilled, they seek the help of vigilantes and the Underground Railroad. Ann is devastated that she cannot be part of this plan, until she finds courage through her new friend, Alfred. Finally, Ann receives the opportunity to escape, with one condition: She may never see her family again.

12.12 Cooper, Susan. **King of Shadows.** Margaret McElderry, 1999. 186 pp. ISBN 0689828179. Fiction.

Although some might say that Nat Field has lived a tragic life, he thinks it couldn't be better. He has just been chosen to perform at London's newly rebuilt Globe Theater with a troupe of actors from the United States. By a quirk of fate, he is thrust backward through time to 1599 and Elizabethan England. Nat's destiny is to perform at the original Globe Theater, opposite William Shakespeare himself.

12.13 Cormier, Robert. **Heroes.** Delacorte. 1998. 144 pp. ISBN 0385325908. Fiction.

Francis Joseph Cassavant returns to Monument without a face, a result of a battle in World War II. He has returned to murder his boyhood idol, Larry LaSalle, whom Monument citizens regard as one of their most courageous war heroes. Only Francis and his childhood love, Nicole Renard, know the truth about Larry. Francis blames his own naiveté and cowardice for what happened to Nicole after the big going-away party before the war. Now revenge is Francis Cassavant's only reason for living.

12.14 Crew, Linda. **Long Time Passing.** Delacorte, 1997. 197 pp. ISBN 0385324960. Fiction.

Kathy begins her sophomore year at Chintimini High during one of the most turbulent years in the United States—1966. Vietnam is a major political issue, and drugs, love-ins, hippies, and Haight-Ashbury are topics of everyday conversation. But for Kathy, the challenge is to break away from the mundane life she's lived in her small Oregon town to become her own person—if only she could determine who that person should be.

12.15 Crook, Connie Brummel. **Nellie's Quest.** Stoddart, 1998. 193 pp. ISBN 0773674691. Fiction.

In this second book in a series on Nellie McClung, Canada's prominent crusader for women's rights, Nellie's thoughts and ideas on women and their rights appear radical when compared with public opinion in the late 1880s. While she is serving as a young schoolteacher, Nellie's views are attacked and criticized by her mother and others in the rural community. Her critics do not realize, however, that Nellie's thoughts are being shaped by a young student with family problems that she is helping, and by her romantic feelings for Wes, a lifelong family friend.

12.16 Curry, Jane Louise. **Dark Shade.** Margaret McElderry, 1998. 168 pp. ISBN 0689818122. Fiction.

Kip Maclean and Maggie Gilmour are neighbors in a small Pennsylvania town. One day, Maggie discovers that Kip's bizarre behavior is not the result of the fire that recently killed his parents. Kip has discovered a secret passageway that leads into a dense forest—and the year 1758. Maggie follows Kip, thus initiating a chain of events that threatens to change her present as well as the history of Pennsylvania and the future of the entire United States.

12.17 Curtis, Christopher Paul. **Bud, Not Buddy.** Delacorte, 1999. 245 pp. ISBN 0385323069. Fiction.

Bud believes deep in his heart that his real father is just across the state, waiting to welcome him home. After all, his mother must have saved those posters of "Herman E. Calloway's Dusky Devastators of the Depression!!!!!!" for a reason. Bud runs away in an attempt to find his father. After train-hopping, hitchhiking, and driving a stolen car, he somehow manages to discover the man in his mother's flyers.

12.18 Dean, Robert Diel. **Echoes of Andersonville.** Southern Heritage, 1999. 176 pp. ISBN 1889332272. Fiction.

Andy Parker, a fifteen-year-old boy from Rhode Island, runs away from home to join the Union army in 1861 and become a regimental drummer. After his older brother's death, he puts down his drumsticks and picks up a rifle to join in the killing of the Rebels. In the 1864 Battle of the Wilderness, he's captured by Rebels and sent to Andersonville, the most notorious Confederate prison camp. This overcrowded, brutal camp is made real through the ordeal Andy and his newfound friend, Joshua, face as they try to survive in a place that doesn't want survivors.

12.19 Degens, T. **Freya on the Wall.** Browndeer / Harcourt Brace, 1997. 281 pp. ISBN 0152002103. Fiction.

Freya Koenig lives in East Germany. Between her and the West lies The Wall, which is guarded by dogs, soldiers with guns, and searchlights that pierce the sky overhead. Freya falls in love with childhood friend Winno Wollgast, and together they listen to Freya's Gran Dulla talk about the end of the Second World War and the events that left them behind The Wall. Freya has undying faith in chaos theory—that every action, even the tiniest of actions, has consequences that reach far beyond what we expect, so that the flutter of butterfly wings in Tibet can cause a change halfway around the world. So when Willo and his family escape to the West, Freya waits and watches The Wall for signs of chaos.

12.20 Denzel, Justin. **Return to the Painted Cave.** Philomel, 1997. 200 pp. ISBN 039923117X. Fiction.

Fourteen-year-old Tao's cave paintings are believed to bring about a good hunt. Because of this talent, he wanders among clans and tribes, including the Mountain People. From them, Tao hears stories about blind Deha, and the crippled children who are forced to live in a cave by Zugor, the evil Neander. When Tao learns that the Great Waters contain the medicine to help Deha and the children, he sets off on the adventure of a lifetime.

12.21 Ellison, Suzanne Pierson. **Best of Enemies.** Rising Moon, 1998. 200 pp. ISBN 0873587146. Fiction.

"The Roadrunner Ranch is Rivera land! My land! No Texan will ever set foot upon it again! I will kill you first! I will kill you all!" These are the angry words of Mundo Rivera, a wealthy New Mexico landowner's teenage son. Caught up in the Civil War invasion of New Mexico by the Texans, Mundo is separated from his father during a skirmish and captured by a roving band of deserters. Private Riley, a Texas soldier, and Tenchi, a Navajo slave girl, have also been captured. Each is the sworn enemy of the other. As they await death at the hands of their captors, they must decide if they can trust one another. Can they put aside the hatred they feel for each other and brave the scorching sun of the desert to regain their freedom? Can the best of enemies become friends?

12.22 English, Karen. **Francie.** Farrar, Straus and Giroux, 1999. 199 pp. ISBN 0374324565. Fiction.

Sixteen-year-old Jesse walked into the one-room schoolhouse and sat down. When the teacher called on him to read, he explained, "I ain't learned to read." The teacher thought for a moment and then said, "Francie's a good reader. Maybe she can help you." Thus begins Francie's job as Jesse's tutor, a position she isn't sure she wants. About the only thing Francie is sure of is that she wants her family to move up north to Chicago, where her father is working as a Pullman porter. When Jesse is later accused of attempting to murder a White man, Francie suddenly finds herself not only his tutor, but also his protector. Racial tensions and family conflicts surround Francie, as she is torn between what she wants to do and what is right.

12.23 Fletcher, Susan. **Shadow Spinner.** Atheneum Books for Young Readers, 1998. 219 pp. ISBN 0689818521. Fiction.

Marjan is a young teen living in ancient Persia. One day, while accompanying her aunt to the women's quarters of the Sultan's harem, Marjan's storytelling finesse catches Shahrazad's attention. Soon she finds herself surrounded by jewels and silks, but far from her loving aunt and the bustling life of the city she knows so well. As the courtly intrigue mounts, Marjan finds her life in danger because of her close association with Shahrazad.

12.24 Forrester, Sandra. **My Home Is over Jordan.** Lodestar / Dutton, 1997. 163 pp. ISBN 052567568X. Fiction.

The Civil War has come to an end and Maddie Henry's life of freedom is just beginning. Maddie, a former slave, travels to North Carolina with her family and Tibby, an abandoned child she cannot leave behind. Together, they use what money they have to buy a piece of land and start a new life. As she struggles to save enough money to take her north to college, Maddie is forced to acknowledge that the end of slavery is not the end of persecution. Townspeople first hurl angry words and then rocks at Maddie and her family. The Black schoolteacher from Ohio is attacked, and Maddie must take her place and teach the colony of former slaves to read. As she confronts the hardships in her own life, and those in the lives of her friends and family, Maddie learns that freedom is worth any price.

12.25 Frazier, Charles. **Cold Mountain.** Vintage / Random House, 1997. 449 pp. ISBN 0375700757. Fiction.

Enthralling adventure and a stirring love story all in one! This odyssey follows two people who were once intertwined, then torn apart by the Civil War. Inman became a Confederate soldier, but was wounded in the fighting at Petersburg. Ada, the woman he loved, remained on Cold Mountain in the Blue Ridge Mountains during the Civil War, where she learned to survive in a world that became radically different from the one of her youth. Both Ada and Inman experience adventures that test their wits and strength as they make their way in a world now threatened by slaves, marauders, bounty hunters, and witches.

12.26 Garden, Nancy. **Dove and Sword: A Novel of Joan of Arc.** Scholastic, 1997. 340 pp. ISBN 0590929496. Fiction.

In Domremy, France, in 1429, a young girl named Jeanne d'Arc (also known as Joan of Arc) hears voices. The voices direct her to lead an army to assure that the dauphin is crowned king, thereby saving France. Her dear friend, Gabrielle, who tells this dramatic story, accompanies Jeanne on her mission, and stays with her as she dresses as a man and marches into battle. Gabrielle follows her friend onto the battlefields, wanting to help the wounded, but is overwhelmed by the pain and suffering she witnesses. Then she follows Jeanne to trial, where Jeanne is accused of heresy and found guilty. Her punishment: to be burned alive at the stake.

12.27 Grove, Vicki. **The Starplace.** Putnam, 1999. 214 pp. ISBN 0399232079. Fiction.

It's the year 1961, and Frannie lives in the "perfect" little town of Quiver, Oklahoma. She is planning a party with her friends to launch their eighth-grade school year. Then Celeste, an African American girl, moves to town. Frannie is drawn to Celeste, but she is afraid to make friends with her because Celeste is the only African American student in the school. As time goes by, however, they become close friends. Through their friendship, Frannie learns some history that was not taught in her school. She discovers prejudice, and Celeste and her father teach her about the horror of the Ku Klux Klan, which killed Celeste's great great-grandfather. Francie struggles with this new knowledge.

12.28 Haas, Jessie. **Westminster West.** Greenwillow, 1997. 168 pp. ISBN 0688143832. Fiction.

Life on a Vermont farm in the late 1800s is especially difficult for Sue. Her sister Clare's delicate health gets her excused from the chores. Clare even gets the opportunity for a vacation with wealthy relatives. Two events change Sue's perception of her life. First, she makes a startling discovery. Then a serious illness makes her examine more closely the people she loves and the family she thinks she knows so well. Sue discovers that appearances can be quite deceiving.

12.29 Hardman, Ric Lynden. **Sunshine Rider: The First Vegetarian Western.** Delacorte, 1998. 352 pp. ISBN 0385325436. Fiction.

Wylie Jackson dreams of being a cowboy. One day, in 1881, his dream comes true. However, he never expected his first cattle drive would include babysitting Roselle, a lovesick cattalo (offspring of a longhorn and a buffalo). After a brief stint in the cook's wagon, Wylie swears off meat, providing abundant joke material for his compadres. Wylie encounters unusual characters on his journey, shares his favorite recipes, and manages to survive the range to face another day.

12.30 Hesse, Karen. **A Light in the Storm: The Civil War Diary of Amelia Martin, Fenwick Island, Delaware, 1861.** Scholastic, 1999. 167 pp. ISBN 0590567330. Fiction.

"We watch through the night, ensuring that the beacon stays lit. And at dawn we extinguish the Light. This is the only way I know to go on." Fifteen-year-old Amelia Martin runs the lighthouse on Fenwick Island, along with her father and Keeper Dunne. Late at night, in the lighthouse tower, Amelia pours out her feelings in her diary as she keeps watch and tends the flame. It is she who stands between the ships and the rocky shoals, and she who stands between her parents as they argue. Amelia writes of her feelings for Daniel, a soldier in the war, and a friend whose presence lights her way. She writes of her concern for Mr. Lincoln, for "It is in his hands to hold a whole country together. . . ." This powerful addition to Scholastic's Dear America series gives us a glimpse into the life of one person affected by the Civil War.

12.31 Hesse, Karen. **Out of the Dust.** Scholastic, 1999. 227 pp. ISBN 0439061261. Fiction.

Playing piano solos at the Palace Theater provides an oasis in the life of fourteen-year-old Billie Jo. The incessant winds that cripple Oklahoma's panhandle in 1934 have driven most of her friends' families from their farms. However, just before Billie Jo's mother gives birth to her baby brother, an accident more horrible than anyone could imagine strips this already downtrodden family of all but the smallest hope. And the community's finger of blame points directly at Billie Jo.

12.32 Hill, Pamela. **A Voice from the Border.** Holiday House, 1998. 244 pp. ISBN 082341356X. Fiction.

Fifteen-year-old Reeves feels overwhelmed by the slavery issues that embroil her family and neighbors in Springfield, Missouri. As an abolitionist, Reeves is enraged by her mother's refusal to free their slaves. When her home is appropriated by Union troops, Reeves suddenly finds herself falling in love with a Yankee officer. The death of her father and her new love turn this young writer's life and world inside out.

12.33 Holm, Jennifer L. **Our Only May Amelia.** HarperCollins, 1999. 253 pp. ISBN 0060278226. Fiction.

May Amelia's family says she is a Real Miracle—except when she's a no-good girl. The Real Miracle part comes from being the only girl ever born on the Nasel River, and the no-good girl part is because of her seven brothers. Papa constantly scolds her for chasing after murders, scaring bears, and hanging around the logging camp. Birth, death, hatred, and love encircle May and her family like the river on which they live.

12.34 Holt, Kimberly Willis. **My Louisiana Sky.** Henry Holt, 1998. 200 pp. ISBN 0805052518. Fiction.

Tiger Ann Parker's world feels much like the aftermath of Hurricane Audrey—everything torn apart and scattered everywhere. Corrina, her mother, is mentally disabled, and her father, Lonnie, cannot read an electric bill. Granny has always cared for her and her parents, but granny is dead, and Tiger Ann must face the most difficult decision of her life: Should she move to Baton Rouge with her aunt, or become her parents' caregiver?

12.35 Hoobler, Dorothy, and Thomas Hoobler. **The Ghost in the Tokaido Inn.** Philomel, 1999. 214 pp. ISBN 039923330X. Fiction.

Seikei, a merchant's son, is asked to assist the famous samurai magistrate Judge Oooka in finding a thief who stole a valuable ring. Seikei must demonstrate all of his skills, and the courage of a samurai, as he joins a traveling group of kabuki actors. The thief may just be a part of this company.

12.36 Houston, Gloria. **Bright Freedom's Song: A Story of the Underground Railroad.** Harcourt Brace, 1998. 136 pp. ISBN 0152018123. Fiction.

"I am Marcus. Go back to the house. Say nothing." These are the first words fourteen-year-old Bright Freedom Cameron hears from the man she discovers hiding in the hog pen of her father's farm. Marcus, a former slave, will become a friend to Bright, as he has been to her father, Charles Cameron. Cameron had been an indentured servant, until Marcus helped him to escape the master who owned them both. Bright will join Marcus, her parents, and many others who live in the Appalachian Mountains as they work to help slaves travel the Underground Railroad on their way to freedom. As she becomes involved with the movement, Bright learns of the dangers faced by those who risk their lives to escape bondage. She herself faces danger as she attempts to shelter, and then to transport, the escaped slaves northward.

12.37 Ingold, Jeanette. **Airfield.** Harcourt Brace, 1999. 148 pp. ISBN 0152020535. Fiction.

"I won't ever fly too close to the sun," promises fifteen-year-old Beatty Donnough. Beatty's mother died when she was barely one year old, and Beatty has spent most of her life being shuffled from one relative to another, waiting for her father, a pilot, to touch down. It is 1933, and Beatty lives with her Aunt Clo and her aunt's husband Grif at the Muddy Springs Hi-Way Tourist Court in Texas. Grif works as the relief station manager at the airport. Beatty and her homeless friend Moss volunteer at the Muddy Springs Airport, where they learn about airlines, passengers, pilots, the dangers posed by violent weather, and malfunctioning machines. It is also where Beatty uncovers some surprising information about her mother.

12.38 Jordan, Sheryl. **The Raging Quiet.** Simon & Schuster, 1999. 266 pp. ISBN 0689821409. Fiction.

Long ago in medieval times, a sixteen-year-old girl reluctantly marries the son of the lord who owns her parents' farm, and travels with him to a distant fishing village. When he is killed thatching the roof of their cottage two days later, Marnie acknowledges her guilt, because she prayed for something like this to happen so he wouldn't want her any more. Only the village priest and the town madman befriend her. She discovers that the young man is deaf, not mad, and she begins to communicate with him using a sort of sign language. As she tames him, the distrustful villagers begin to think she is a witch, and the two outcasts begin to fall in love.

12.39 Katz, Welwyn Wilton. **Out of the Dark.** Margaret McElderry, 1996. 176 pp. ISBN 0689809476. Fiction.

Ben, his father, and his brother move to a remote Newfoundland village after the violent murder of his mother. Ben escapes his memories and feelings of guilt by immersing himself in the Viking lore his mother shared with him, and by building a detailed model of a Viking ship. He takes on the persona of Tor, a Viking shipbuilder, and engages in a battle that obscures the boundaries between a modern and an ancient Viking reality.

12.40 Kimmel, Elizabeth Cody. **In the Stone Circle.** Scholastic, 1998. 225 pp. ISBN 0590213083. Fiction.

Cristyn's father has accepted a research assignment in Wales, where they will share a sixteenth century stone house with another family. Cristyn and Miranda, both fourteen, occupy a room in which strange dreams and disappearing photos direct the girls to a concealed door and a mysterious staircase. Cristyn learns much about the house's hidden past, her deceased mother, and the history of Wales, both from her father and from the resident ghost.

12.41 Klass. Sheila Solomon. **Shooting Star: A Novel about Annie Oakley.** Holiday House, 1996. 173 pp. ISBN 0813412792. Fiction.

As the daughter of Quaker parents on the Ohio frontier, Phoebe Anne Moses shuns violence. But when her father dies, she faces a dilemma: starve, or use her unusual talent for shooting to feed her family. Annie, who hates her given name, discovers that she can earn more as a market hunter than as a seamstress—and can have more fun, too. Because of her stubborn courage, Annie survives and succeeds in a world dominated by bullies, and biased against women.

12.42 LaFaye, A. **Edith Shay.** Viking, 1998. 183 pp. ISBN 0670875988. Fiction.

Katherine Lunden loves newspapers. They take her far from her life in a Wisconsin logging town. On a whim, Katherine buys a ticket to Chicago. With nothing more than her satchel, an abandoned suitcase bearing the name Edith Shay, and ten cents in her pocket (which actually buys some things in 1865), she arrives in the city, and must find a place to stay and a job. For an inexperienced girl like Katherine, glamorous dreams turn into a reality of mending sheets, cooking, and cleaning—until she meets Aeslynn O'Dell, a dressmaker who offers Katherine her friendship and a job. But Katherine is still not satisfied. Torn between her longing to travel, her feelings of loneliness and separation from her family, and her growing fascination with the mysterious owner of the suitcase, Edith Shay, Katherine leaves Chicago determined to return the suitcase to its owner. What Katherine finds at the end of her journey is more rewarding than she ever imagined.

12.43 Laird, Christa. **But Can the Phoenix Sing?** Greenwillow, 1998. ISBN 0688158609. Fiction.

In this sequel to *Shadow of the Wall,* Misha Edelman writes to his stepson, Richard, and describes his experiences in the World War II resistance movement. His experiences include living in forests with bands of partisans, and smuggling Jews and weapons. He is the perfect courier because of his Aryan looks and quick mind, but he suffers from an identity crisis after passing as a non-Jew for so long. What will his answer be to the question, "Can the phoenix sing?"

12.44 Lasky, Kathryn. **Alice Rose and Sam.** Illustrated by Theresa Flavin. Hyperion, 1998. 208 pp. ISBN 0786803363. Fiction.

Alice Rose Tucker is not a happy person. She has just witnessed a murder in the rough-and-tumble mining town of Virginia City, Nevada, where she lives with her father. A young newspaper reporter named Samuel Clemens befriends Alice Rose, and together they try to solve the crime and make sense of their topsy-turvy existence—while searching for truth and beauty in an imperfect world.

12.45 Lawrence, Iain. **The Wreckers.** Delacorte, 1998. 196 pp. ISBN 0385325355. Fiction.

The *Isle of Skye* fights the raging storm for seven days and nights before the lookout detects lights. Within moments, rocks emerge, shattering the ship, and scattering its cargo and crew. John Spencer regains consciousness, and gradually becomes aware that the people whom he believes saved him are totally evil. John learns that his father has also survived, but to rescue him, John must combat a depraved community that lures unsuspecting sailors and their ships to a watery grave.

12.46   Lester, Julius. **Pharaoh's Daughter.** Silver Whistle / Harcourt Brace, 2000. 192 pp. ISBN 0152018263. Fiction.

Defying her father's edict, Meryetamun, daughter of the Egyptian Pharaoh, snatches a boy-child from the river. Almah, the infant's sister, moves to the palace as Meryetamun's companion and royal nursemaid. These two young women are bound by their love of infant Moses, yet separated by personal struggles with their gods and the society into which they have been born. Murder and love create a chasm that inevitably separates and alienates them from their different worlds.

12.47   Lewin, Michael Z. **Cutting Loose.** Henry Holt, 1999. 408 pp. ISBN 0805062254. Fiction.

In the late nineteen century, Jackie Cross lives her life dressed as a boy in order to fulfill her dream of playing professional baseball like her pa. Her best friend, Nance, rode in the Buffalo Bill Wild West Show. When Nance is murdered, Jackie gives up her baseball career and devotes her life to finding Nance's murderer. Jackie never gives up trying to track Nance's murderer, and finally finds herself in London, where she not only solves one mystery, but also finds herself confronting her father's killer.

12.48   Lyons, Mary. E. **The Poison Place.** Aladdin Paperbacks, 1997. 167 pp. ISBN 0689826788. Fiction.

In the gloom of the evening on February 22, 1827, enter the Peale Museum with former slave Moses Williams. Step carefully around the mirrored glass pond, surrounded by stuffed waterfowl. Heed the warning signs against the wall that read: "Do Not Touch the Birds. They Are Covered With Arsenic Poison." Listen along with his daughter, Maggie, as Moses recalls the life he lived as he served Charles Willson Peale, a portrait painter who founded a museum of art and taxidermy in Philadelphia. Moses unburdens himself and lets the secrets within him fly free as he gives to Maggie both his story and the pages he has copied from Peale's diaries. Through Moses' words, Peale is revealed as a powerful man, driven by a desire to create the "Great School of Nature," despite the costs to his own family and those who work for him.

12.49 Matas, Carol. **After the War.** Simon & Schuster, 1996. 133 pp. ISBN 0689807228. Fiction.

After being liberated from one of Hitler's concentration camps, young Ruth returns to her home. There she is saddened to learn that she is the only member of her family to have survived the camps. She joins a group of teenaged Zionists leading a group of young Jewish refugees on a perilous journey to Palestine. This adventure story is based on actual events.

12.50 Matas, Carol. **The Garden.** Simon & Schuster, 1997. 102 pp. ISBN 0689803494. Fiction.

Having survived Buchenwald, Ruth Mendelson hopes that kibbutz life will provide the carefree peace other teens take for granted. But as a leader of the Haganah, Ruth vows to defend her new home. When Palestinian soldiers destroy her garden, Ruth fights back. This fast-paced sequel to *After the War* stands on its own as background to the current Israeli-Palestinian hostilities, and as the touching story of a tenacious young woman.

12.51 Matas, Carol. **Greater than Angels.** Simon & Schuster, 1998. 133 pp. ISBN 0689813538. Fiction.

Anna Hirsch is a performer, a teenage actor who continues her dramatics even in the concentration camps that suck the life from her friends and family. Anna is one of the fortunate young people who escapes to Le Chambon-sur-Lignon from a French refugee camp, and who survives through the efforts of the villagers. On their way to Switzerland and eventual freedom, the young people question people's inhumanity toward one another and God's seeming indifference to the tragedies that surround them.

12.52 Matcheck, Diane. **The Sacrifice.** Farrar, Straus and Giroux, 1998. 198 pp. ISBN 0374363781. Fiction.

According to Apsaalooka tribal beliefs, only one twin can prosper. Consequently, Weak-One-Who-Does-Not-Last should not have survived. Her mother died giving birth, and her father and twin, Born Great, have also died. Weak One sets out to prove that she, not her brother, should be the one destined to lead the tribe to greatness. Her warrior-like beliefs are challenged, however, when she's captured and treated kindly by a band of Pawnee. Gradually, Weak One perceives the horror of her real destiny.

12.53 Mazer, Norma Fox. **Good Night, Maman.** Harcourt Brace, 1999. 185 pp. ISBN 0152014683. Fiction.

In June 1940, the Nazis begin their occupation of Paris. Karin, Marc, and their mother must find someplace where they can be safe from the German invasion. As Jews, they know their lives are in danger. For a while, they find a hiding place in France, but as the situation worsens, they must leave their home. When Maman falls ill, Marc and Karin must leave her behind. Eventually, the two are sent to the United States. But what has become of Maman?

12.54 McLaren, Clemence. **Inside the Walls of Troy: A Novel of the Women Who Lived the Trojan War.** Atheneum Books for Young Readers, 1996. 199 pp. ISBN 0689318200. Fiction.

This is the story of two young women, blessed (or cursed?) by the gods. Helen, the most beautiful woman in the world, is able to disregard her extraordinary loveliness. Cassandra remains trapped in her nightmare-like visions of war and destruction. The two youthful princesses are thrown together as the Trojan War ravages their lives, and destroys the men they love. This account of Cassandra's and Helen's roles in the Trojan War affords an exciting and sensitive alternative to Homer's classic tale.

12.55 Menick, Stephen. **The Muffin Child.** Philomel, 1998. 224 pp. ISBN 0399233032. Fiction.

Tanya, orphaned when her parents drown in a freak flash flood, is unprepared to care for herself. Nonetheless, she refuses help from the scheming, calculating villagers who care more for her homestead than for her well-being. With Gypsies camping in her fields and the villagers asserting that she is a kidnapper and murderess, Tanya's home, barn, and cow are set afire by her neighbors. Miraculously, she survives the fire only to disappear in the smoke.

12.56 Meyer, Caroline. **Mary, Bloody Mary.** Harcourt Brace, 1999. 227 pp. ISBN 015201065. Fiction.

Imagine being born into a world where your father, the King of England, calculates your every move. This is the situation of Mary, the daughter of Henry VIII. In his quest for a son to rule England, Henry is willing to do anything, even divorce his wife and declare Mary an illegitimate child. When Henry's other wives do not provide him with the sons he so desperately wants, blood-shed ensues and Mary's life is turned upside down. History comes to life in this fascinating and frightening story of the life and death struggle Mary faced on her way to becoming Queen of England.

12.57 Miklowitz, Gloria D. **Masada: The Last Fortress.** Eerdmans Books for Young Readers, 1998. 188 pp. ISBN 0802851657. Fiction.

Seventeen-year-old Simon ben Eleazar tells the graphic story of the Jews who struggled to save Masada from Roman Imperialists. Masada, the fortress city, seemed to be invincible. Romans had conquered the rest of Israel, and only Masada remained. Simon was the physician's assistant in the bloodbath that followed, as the Romans tried again and again to conquer the walled city. This is a story of courage, daring, and painful decisions.

12.58 Morpurgo, Michael. **Joan of Arc of Domremy.** Illustrated by Michael Foreman. Harcourt Brace, 1999. 124 pp. ISBN 0152017364. Fiction.

This fictionalized account of Joan of Arc begins when Eloise, a girl of today, learns that she and her family are moving to the ancient French city of Orleans, the city where Joan lifted the siege and drove out the English. While sitting on the banks of a river in Orleans, Eloise begins hearing voices and seeing the events that Joan once faced. Weaving together historical facts and compelling fiction, this account brings Joan of Arc to life nearly six hundred years after her death.

12.59 Murphy, Jim. **The Journal of James Edmond Pease: A Civil War Union Soldier.** Scholastic, 1998. 173 pp. ISBN 059043814X. Fiction.

When sixteen-year-old James Edmond Pease joins the Union Army, he finds himself saddled with the unusual job of journal keeper. Although James does not consider himself the best speller or the smartest in his company, his Lieutenant orders him to keep "an accurate and honest account" of G Company of the

122nd Regiment, New York Volunteers, from Onondaga County. Encouraged to include more details and characterization in his daily entries, James' duty becomes therapeutic as he records his personal reactions to the tragedies of war and a youth passed by. Also included are sketches, reproductions, and maps.

12.60 Namioka, Lensey. **Ties That Bind, Ties That Break.** Delacorte, 1999. 154 pp. ISBN 0385326661. Fiction.

In 1911, young Ailin said no to having her feet bound, even though her mother, grandmother, and sisters all had endured life-long pain to continue the two-thousand-year Chinese tradition of foot binding. But Ailin had seen her older sister's unbound feet; she had seen the bent-back toes. She had watched the women in her family hobble instead of run, shuffle instead of walk. So she said no. In an unusual move, her father honored her wishes. What neither the young Ailin nor her ailing father realized was that her defiant gesture set her aside and left her in disgrace. Eventually shunned by her family, young Ailin is left alone to make her way in a land that judges women by the size of their feet.

12.61 Neufeld, John. **Gaps in Stone Walls.** Aladdin, 1998. 186 pp. ISBN 0689816405. Fiction.

Merry Skiffe lives on Martha's Vineyard in 1880, a time when hereditary deafness afflicts one of every five residents in her community. When the body of Ned Nickerson, the richest landholder in the area, is found battered and bloody, Merry is among the suspects. She is gravely fearful, and rightfully so. Her neighbors and family are willing to admit the possibility that she killed Nickerson—even without knowing what he did to her on the south shore so long ago.

12.62 Newth, Matte. **The Dark Light.** Translated by Faith Ingwersen. Farrar, Straus and Giroux. 1998. 246 pp. ISBN 0374317011. Fiction.

Tora, a Norwegian teenager from an isolated mountain farm, contracts leprosy and is abandoned by her family at the lepers' hospital in Bergen. She is angry, but eventually transforms her anger into determination by befriending the one person at the hospital who can teach her to read. Although her family has listed her name among the dead, Tora continues living and attempting to improve the appalling conditions of her prisonlike hospital.

12.63 Nixon, Joan Lowery. **Circle of Love.** Delacorte, 1997. 167 pp. ISBN 0385322801. Fiction.

Six years after Frances Mary Kelly cut her hair and began to call herself Frankie, she agrees to chaperone a group of Orphan Train riders from New York to Kansas. Frances Mary's visit to her old home town offers no solutions for her romantic problems, but a handsome young preacher she meets on the train provides challenges and surprises on the long trip home. *Circle of Love,* the seventh Orphan Train adventure, is a welcome treat for fans of the earlier books.

12.64 Osborne, Mary Pope. **Standing in the Light: The Captive Diary of Catherine Carey Logan.** Scholastic, 1998. ISBN 0590134620. Fiction.

Catherine Logan is a young Quaker girl growing up in the Delaware Valley of Pennsylvania in the 1760s. Her life is filled with school, Quaker meetings, tending to her younger siblings, and the everyday chores of farming, such as feeding livestock, collecting eggs, and cooking. One morning, on the way to school, Catherine's life changes forever when she and her brother Thomas are taken captive by a group of Lenape. At first Catherine fears for her life, but with the caring help of her adoptive family, and the young hunter "with the eagle painted on his cheek," Catherine comes to realize that the Lenape people are not unlike herself or her family, and she experiences a closeness to them as well as to the earth to which they are attached "by a thousand threads." Another volume in the Dear America series, this diary provides a sensitive portrayal of the Lenape people.

12.65 Patrick, Denise Lewis. **The Longest Ride.** Henry Holt, 1999. 164 pp. ISBN 0805047158. Fiction.

Midnight Son, as escaped slave, has already seen some powerful bad stuff in his short fifteen years. There seems no challenge too great for the young cowboy, until a fierce blizzard interrupts his plans to rescue his folks, who are slaves on a Texas plantation. Lost and injured from a fall, Midnight is saved from certain death by a band of Arapaho. When Midnight is told that his help is needed to carry a message through Union lines to another Arapaho camp, he is faced with a choice. Should he abandon his own rescue plans for his family, and risk his freedom—and even his life—for people who are not his kin? In this companion to *The Adventures of Midnight Son,* Denise Lewis Patrick tells a coming-of-age story about a young man who stands up to adversity with bravery and courage in the final days of the Civil War.

12.66 Paulsen, Gary. **Sarney: A Life Remembered.** Delacorte, 1997. 180 pp. ISBN 0385321953. Fiction.

In this sequel to *Nightjohn,* learn what happened to the young slave girl, Sarney, who learned to read in the dark from a teacher called Nightjohn. Now she is a ninety-four-year-old woman who has lived a full life. Step back in time with Sarney as she recounts all that happened to her, from the moment she fled the plantation where she was a slave during the last days of the Civil War, to her search for the children she lost through slavery and her time with Miss Laura, a woman in New Orleans who changes Sarney's life.

12.67 Paulsen, Gary. **Soldier's Heart.** Delacorte, 1998. 106 pp. ISBN 0385324987. Fiction.

At fifteen years of age, Charlie Goddard was too young to join the Union army legally, so he walked to Ft. Snelling, where they didn't ask any questions or have any uniforms for enlistees. Charlie discovered what a shooting war meant as he participated in battle after battle. He and the other First Minnesota Volunteers were ordered to charge the Rebs as they ran up the hill at Gettysburg. Wounded in body and spirit, Charlie's soldier's heart would never heal.

12.68 Pfitsch, Patricia Curtis. **The Deeper Song.** Simon & Schuster, 1998. 148 pp. ISBN 0689811837. Fiction.

Could a woman have written the first five books of the Bible? Judith, a gifted storyteller and the daughter of a Hebrew priest of King Solomon, is caught between two worlds. In her father's world, women have no power, and "cannot speak to God." But in the temple of the Goddess Asherah, a deity despised by the Hebrew priests, Judith could become a singer, a leader who tells the story of the Goddess. When a young Hebrew priest named Samuel approaches Judith to secretly write down the stories of Yahweh, she must make a choice. Whose story will Judith decide to tell? Based on a theory that a woman authored the oldest part of the Bible, this what-if story blends elements of history, adventure, and romance.

12.69 Rinaldi, Ann. **An Acquaintance with Darkness.** Harcourt Brace, 1997. 294 pp. ISBN 015201294X. Fiction.

At the end of the Civil War, Mary Louise Pigbush dies, leaving fourteen-year-old Emily an orphan in Washington, D.C. Emily is a smart, headstrong teen with concrete ideas about right and wrong. She is forced to confront her beliefs and values when she goes to live with her Uncle Valentine, a doctor suspected of body snatching—and again when her best friend's mother is arrested on suspicion of being involved in the plot to assassinate President Lincoln.

12.70 Rinaldi, Ann. **Amelia's War.** Scholastic, 1999. 259 pp. ISBN 0590117440. Fiction.

Hagerstown, Maryland, is a place of divided loyalties during the Civil War; it is a southern town with Union sympathies. The war starts for Amelia when she watches Dewitt Clinton Rench get shot down in the streets for being a Rebel. Shocked by what she has seen, Amelia rushes to relay the story to Mr. Dechart, the editor of the town paper. Shortly after he prints the story, Mr. Dechart is arrested, the presses of the *Hagerstown Mail* are destroyed, and everyone understands the consequences of speaking out. As the war rages on, there is fighting in the streets, and the residents of Hagerstown are trapped inside their houses. When Confederate soldiers send a note demanding that they pay a huge ransom to save the town from being burned, Amelia knows that she must act.

12.71 Rinaldi, Ann. **The Coffin Quilt.** Harcourt Brace, 1999. 228 pp. ISBN 0152020152. Fiction.

Set in the 1880s along the West Virginia and Kentucky border, this fictional account focuses on the rivalry between the Hatfield and McCoy families. Fanny, the youngest of the fourteen McCoy children, explains that the family feud began with an argument over the ownership of a herd of pigs. Since that dispute, the Hatfields and the McCoys have lived by their own mountain code of revenge. However, when Roseanne, Fanny's favorite older sister, runs away with Johnse Hatfield, a handsome member of the rival family, the hatred between the two families escalates, resulting in senseless raids, killings, and heartbreak. Roseanne's obsession with sewing a coffin quilt serves as a gruesome illustration of the tragedy of the feud as the death toll mounts and one coffin after another is moved from the border of the quilt to the center.

12.72 Rinaldi, Ann. **Mine Eyes Have Seen.** Scholastic, 1998. 271 pp. ISBN 0590543180. Fiction.

"Writing has saved my life on many occasions." These are the words author Louisa May Alcott offers Annie Brown, the daughter of abolitionist John Brown. Alcott tells Annie to "talk the fire out" of her life. Annie writes, revealing the events of the summer of 1859, when she lived on a Maryland farm with her sister-in-law Martha, and the men her father assembled in a plot to raid the U.S. arsenal at Harper's Ferry. Annie's duty was to sit and watch on the porch, warning the others of visitors. Her encounters with her father (who is consumed by his mission to end slavery), Mrs. Huffmaster (a suspicious neighbor whose visits send the men into hiding), Dangerfield Newby (a former slave who hopes to rescue his wife and children), Dauphin (the man she loves and hopes to marry), and the others in her father's provisional army will change Annie's her life forever.

12.73 Rinaldi, Ann. **The Second Bend in the River.** Scholastic, 1997. 277 pp. ISBN 0590742582. Fiction.

It is 1798 in the Ohio wilderness, and seven-year-old Rebecca stands paralyzed, gaping at Tecumseh and his circling red-tailed hawk. Over the next ten years, Rebecca begins to treasure Tecumseh's visits with her family, as she tutors him in English. Tecumseh, in turn, reveals flowers, forests, and nature to her. This is a moving and well-documented glimpse into the human side of a great Shawnee chief, and his seldom-mentioned love for a young white girl.

12.74 Seago, Kate. **Matthew Unstrung.** Putnam, 1998. 236 pp. ISBN 0803722303. Fiction.

It's the year 1910, and Matthew Hobson desperately hopes to please his father by following him into the ministry. But the stress of schooling threatens Matthew's precarious grip on reality. Caught between a rigid and unrelenting father and a life with little joy, Matthew's sanity slips away. It isn't until his older brother spirits him off to a ranch in Colorado and he begins playing music that Matthew regains some interest in life and hope for the future.

12.75 Shakespeare, William. **Macbeth.** Retold by Bruce Coville. Illustrated by Gary Kelley. Dial, 1997. Unpaged. ISBN 0803718993. Fiction.

Although geared toward younger audiences who may be encountering Shakespeare for the first time, this rendition of *Macbeth* is certainly one that any reader will enjoy. The introduction explains that when speaking of the play in theatrical circles, "it is preferred that you call it 'The Scottish play' because it is considered to be cursed, and actors' lore has it that you must never mention the title inside a theater." Coville combines Shakespeare's language with his own dramatic prose to create a wonderful rendition of one of the Bard's most famous plays.

12.76 Skurzynski, Gloria. **Spider's Voice.** Atheneum Books for Young Readers, 1999. 200 pp. ISBN 0689821492. Fiction.

At a time when physically disabled children were considered idiots, Aran's family sells him to a man who displays human freaks as entertainment for the wealthy. Aran escapes his fate when Abelard, the most brilliant man in the world, rescues him. The only thing more brilliant than Abelard's mind is his forbidden love for Hèloïse. This is the poignant love story of two of France's most celebrated lovers, Abelard and Hèloïse.

12.77 Sterman, Betsy. **Saratoga Secret.** Dial Books for Young Readers / Penguin Putnam. 1998. 249 pp. ISBN 0803723326. Fiction.

When Amity's father and many of her neighbors rush off to fight General Burgoyne and keep the Hudson Valley from being captured by the British, he leaves sixteen-year-old Amity, her mother, and baby Jonathan alone to protect their farm. Amity wonders why Cheppa John, the handsome young peddler, is the only man who doesn't join the troops. Is her dream man a spy for the British? In the face of a dangerous attack by the enemy, Amity volunteers to carry secret information across the countryside to reach the Revolutionary generals.

12.78 Sutcliff, Rosemary. **Sword Song.** Farrar, Straus and Giroux, 1998. 272 pp. ISBN 0374373639. Fiction.

The Viking Bjarni Sigurdson, banished for murdering a wandering holy man, hopes to sell his sword-service in the hustling port of Dublin. Instead, High King Halfdan's captain laughingly says, "Go sprout yourself a beard." During the ensuing five years, Bjarni wanders through the British Isles, until he links up with a skillful seafarer who becomes his hero, and the wise Lady Aud, who becomes his love. Bjarni battles enemy tribes on land and sea, protecting his patron while maturing into one of the clan's most trusted and valued swordfighters.

12.79 Talbert, Marc. **Heart of a Jaguar.** Aladdin, 1997. 216 pp. ISBN 0689813325. Fiction.

Balam is a misfit in his ancient Mayan society. At fourteen, he's no longer a child, but he's still not regarded as a man. The village shaman, Balam's godfather, recognizes special qualities in the young teen that are confirmed when Balam confronts a jaguar, a "relative of the rain gods" and the "embodiment of Lord Sun." Now everyone looks to Balam to appease the gods and save their society. Will Balam have the courage to sacrifice himself for his loved ones' safety?

12.80 Turner, Nancy E. **These Is My Words: The Diary of Sarah Agnes Prine, 1881–1901, Arizona Territories.** HarperCollins, 1998. 384 pp. ISBN 0060987510. Fiction.

"I got it in my head to set to paper all these things that have got us thus far on our way. . . ." So begins seventeen-year-old Sarah Prine's diary, which chronicles her family's westward journey to the wild frontier of the Arizona Territories. Besides growing up, marrying, and becoming a mother, Sarah gains confidence and resists temptations to reign in her feisty, undaunted spirit.

12.81 Watts, Irene N. **Good-bye Marianne.** Tundra, 1998. 106 pp. ISBN 0887764452. Fiction.

Pursued by the Gestapo, Marianne Kohn's father has gone into hiding. When she arrives at school one morning, Marianne is shocked to find locked doors and a sign reading, "Jewish students are prohibited from attending German schools." Against her mother's wishes, Marianne befriends Ernest, who has moved into her family's apartment building. Although he is a member of the

Third Reich, Marianne learns a valuable lesson through her friendship with Ernest: not all Germans are the same.

12.82 Westfall, Robert. **Time of Fire.** Scholastic, 1997. 172 pp. ISBN 0590477463. Fiction.

Set in England during World War II, *Time of Fire* takes readers inside the life of Sonny Prudhoe, a young boy fascinated by the war raging around him. Sonny becomes expert at identifying the German planes bombing his hometown of Newcastle. When a German bomb kills Sonny's mother, he uses his skill to identify the plane that dropped the fatal bomb. Overcome with rage and grief, Sonny's father enlists in the Royal Air Force, vowing to avenge his wife's death. When this plan fails, Sonny is forced into action. After the German pilot who killed Sonny's mother is shot down over Newcastle, Sonny must make a life-or-death decision when he confronts the wounded pilot.

12.83 Wharton, William. **A Midnight Clear.** Newmarket, 1997. 242 pp. ISBN 1557042578. Fiction.

Six young American soldiers are sent on reconnaissance on Christmas Eve, 1944. Mistakenly, they believe they are alone in the Ardennes Forest of France, until their equally lonely and confused German counterparts indicate their presence—with presents, games, and other diversions. Fear, homesickness, sexual curiosity, and the insanity of war invade Will Knott's reality, until reality itself is too difficult to face.

12.84 Winter, Kathryn. **Katarina.** Farrar, Straus and Giroux, 1998. 257 pp. ISBN 0374339848. Fiction.

As the Germans move into Czechoslovakia in March 1939, Katarina finds her life turned inside out. Her peaceful world, filled with the love of her aunt and the innocence of youth, slowly begins unraveling as she faces her Jewish heritage. Katarina was born a Jew, but does not believe in her heart that she really is Jewish, because her family never imparted any Jewish traditions or values. Katarina maintains her enthusiasm for life and positive outlook throughout the war.

12.85 Wolff, Virginia Euwer. **Bat 6.** Scholastic, 1998. 230 pp. ISBN 0590897993. Fiction.

If baseball is the all-American sport for boys, then softball is the all-American sport for girls—especially the girls of Barlow and Bear Creek Ridge. For fifty years, the sixth-grade girls from the two neighboring communities have battled it out on the softball diamond. This year, on May 29, 1949, the fiftieth anniversary game will be played. No one could reasonably anticipate the fireworks that erupt when Shazam, center fielder for Barlow, encounters Aki, Bear Creek Ridge's star player.

12.86 Wyeth, Sharon Dennis. **Once on this River.** Knopf, 1998. 150 pp. ISBN 0679983503. Fiction.

In 1760, Monday and her mother, Leslie, venture from their home in Madagascar to the American colonies to free her uncle, Frederick. They are free citizens coming to a world of slavery. Monday tries to comprehend why life is the way it is in the colonies. Leslie proves Frederick should be freed, but Monday comes to a new understanding of the injustice in her world while discovering her true parentage.

13 History

"Good writing is almost the concomitant of good history. Literature and history were joined long since by the powers which shaped the human brain, we cannot put them asunder."

C. V. Wedgwood

13.1 Ashabranner, Brent. **To Seek a Better World.** Photographs by Paul Conklin. Cobblehill / Dutton, 1997. 88 pp. ISBN 0525652191. Nonfiction.

Since 1980, over 200,000 Haitians desperate for a better life have climbed into small and often unsafe boats, and taken to the sea through the Windward Passage in an attempt to reach southern Florida. They arrive hungry, sick, illiterate, tired, and poor. And though the words on the Statue of Liberty say "Give me your tired . . ." many immigrants feel unwelcome. Prior to this influx of illegal immigrants, thousands of Haitians came to the United States legally in the 1950s and 1960s to escape the regime of the dictator Francois Duvalier. These tradespeople and professionals quickly became accepted citizens of their new country. Now, there are approximately 500,000 Haitians in the United States. Problems surrounding illegal immigration and questions about Haitians in the United States continue. This interesting book helps readers understand who these people are.

13.2 Bennett, William J., editor. **Our Country's Founders: A Book of Advice for Young People.** Simon & Schuster Books for Young Readers, 1998. 304 pp. ISBN 0689821069. Nonfiction.

Bennett includes speeches, poems, letters, and articles by the early American patriots as inspiration to young people today. He includes some love letters from John Adams addressed to "Miss Adorable," Abigail Smith, during their courtship. Enjoy letters between George Washington and his son, Ben Franklin's "Advice to a Young Tradesman," and notes from Alexander Hamilton's diary. The book also includes facsimiles of important historical documents, including the Constitution and Declaration of Independence.

13.3 Bock, Judy, and Rachel Kranz. **Scholastic Encyclopedia of the United States.** Scholastic Reference, 1997. 140 pp. ISBN 0590947478. Nonfiction.

This guide to the fifty states presents readers with statistical information (population, area, capital, state bird, state flower, state tree, nicknames, motto, and historical sites), fascinating facts ("It used to be illegal in Pennsylvania to talk loudly at picnics" and "It used to be illegal in South Dakota for an eighty-year-old woman to stop in the street to talk to a young married man"), and a succinct history. Photographs, maps, an extensive bibliography for each state, and an index make this reference book as accessible as it is interesting.

13.4   Burchard, Peter. **Lincoln and Slavery.** Atheneum Books for Young Readers, 1999. 196 pp. ISBN 0689815700. Nonfiction.

In Lincoln's sixth debate against Stephen Douglas, Lincoln made his opposition to slavery clear. What was the origin of Lincoln's absolute intolerance of slavery? How did this self-educated man become the beloved leader of a nation? In this biography of the sixteenth president, readers not only find a history of the Civil War, but also will gain insight into the man who reminded a nation torn asunder that this country was founded under "the proposition that all men are created equal," and who vowed only weeks before his death that Union armies would fight "until every drop of blood drawn with the lash, shall be paid for [by] another drawn with the sword."

13.5   Clarke, Joanne, and Chrisanne Beckner. **100 African Americans Who Shaped American History.** Bluewood, 1997. 112 pp. ISBN 0912517182. Nonfiction.

You know about the important contributions of Martin Luther King Jr., Rosa Parks, Harriet Tubman, and Frederick Douglass, but what other African Americans shaped American history? Who are the scientists, the athletes, the politicians, the poets, and the civil rights advocates who helped this nation become what it is today? In this book readers not only learn about noteworthy African Americans, but also about the social, cultural, political, or religious contributions they made.

13.6   Colbert, David, editor. **Eyewitness to America.** Pantheon / Random House, 1997. 598 pp. ISBN 0679442443. Nonfiction.

This book presents the great moments in history of the last five hundred years in the words of the people who made it happen.

Read the words of Christopher Columbus, Patrick Henry, Jackie Robinson, and Ryan White. Follow along as others recount important battles, give details about epic disasters, and chronicle the events that continue to shape our destiny. This unusual approach to recording the important historical events of the past makes history come to life for the reader.

13.7 De Angelis, Therese. **Native Americans and the Spanish.** Chelsea House, 1997. 128 pp. ISBN 079102654X. Nonfiction.

Native Americans and Spanish explorers clashed as Spanish conquerors tried to overrun Native Americans. Spanish missionaries and explorers eradicated entire Native American cultures in the name of religious and economic principles. As Native Americans resisted the Spanish conquerors, the Spanish became more violent. This look at the early history of European contact with the Americas is both unsettling and difficult, but vitally important.

13.8 Dramer, Kim. **Native Americans and Black Americans.** Chelsea House, 1997. 96 pp. ISBN 0791044629. Nonfiction.

This book is worth reading because it discusses a topic generally overlooked in history books—the relationship between Native Americans and African Americans. It's a little known fact that some Native American tribes owned Black slaves. This book discusses how that practice came about, and what its social, political, and cultural implications were. This book uses a simple approach to offer a basic understanding of a critical issue.

13.9 Dudley, William, editor. **Asian Americans: Opposing Viewpoints.** Greenhaven, 1997. 128 pp. ISBN 1565105249. Nonfiction.

This collection of speeches and articles presents opposing viewpoints about Asian Americans and how they have been treated since their arrival in the United States in the 1800s. Topics discussed include restriction of Chinese immigration, acceptance of Asian Americans in Hawaii, the internment of Japanese Americans during World War II, the assimilation of Japanese people into U.S. culture, and life for Asians in the United States since 1965. Part of the Opposing Viewpoints series, this book provides some much needed primary source information about this growing body of people who live in this country.

13.10 Duncan, Dayton. **People of the West.** Little Brown, 1996. 120 pp. ISBN 0316196274. Nonfiction.

The West: wide open prairie, seemingly never-ending deserts, and majestic mountains. This book chronicles the experiences of the people who struggled to make this land their home. From the "first encounters between native Americans and Europeans . . . from mountain men, missionaries, and Mormons, to prospectors, cowboys, and homesteaders," this photographic history tells us about the people who settled the West.

13.11 Edwards, Judith. **Lewis and Clark's Journey of Discovery.** Enslow, 1999. 128 pp. ISBN 0766011275. Nonfiction.

"The object of your mission is to explore the Missouri River and such principal streams of it, as by its course and communication with the waters of the Pacific Ocean, whether the Columbia, Oregon, or Colorado or any other river may offer the most direct and practicable water communication across the continent for the purposes of commerce." That directive came from President Thomas Jefferson to Meriwether Lewis and William Clark when they agreed to lead the expedition that would explore the land and resources in the newly acquired Louisiana Territory. Setting out in 1804 to gather this information for President Jefferson, Lewis and Clark led a group of men called the Corps of Discovery. This interesting account of their journey explains what they found and what difficulties they encountered. This book is part of the In American History series. Other titles in this series include *The Industrial Revolution, The Lincoln Assassination, McCarthy and the Fear of Communism, The Panama Canal* and *The Watergate Scandal.*

13.12 Finklestein, Norman H. **The Way Things Never Were: The Truth about the "Good Old Days."** Atheneum Books for Young Readers, 1999. 112 pp. ISBN 0689814127. Nonfiction.

Have your parents ever begun a conversation with the phrase, "back when I was a kid"? If so, this book will help you to learn about those good old days of the 1950s and 1960s, as well as why they were not necessarily the best of times. Photos, factoids, and illustrations provide information about the civil rights movement, the McCarthy era, and other often overlooked events of times past.

13.13 Flexner, Stuart Berg, and Anne H. Souknanov. **Speaking Freely: A Guided Tour of American English from Plymouth Rock to Silicon Valley.** Oxford University, 1997. 472 pp. ISBN 019510692X. Nonfiction.

Who today doesn't know the phrase "dot com"? But if you had said that in 1950, listeners would have shaken their heads and wondered what in the world you meant. Each time period in our nation's history had its own unusual words and phrases, and this fascinating book offers a history of the evolution of language in the United States. The book is arranged by topics such as Pop Culture, Cyberspace: I Hear America Clicking, To Your Health, Trash and Garbage, and Outspace Space: The Final Frontier. You'll discover the meaning and origin or such phrases as "The devil made me do it," "Just the facts, ma'am," and "Been there, done that!" and enjoy photographs of many of the people who made these terms and phrases popular.

13.14 Gearhart, Sarah. **The Telephone.** Atheneum Books for Young Readers, 1999. 80 pp. ISBN 0689828152. Nonfiction.

Methods for getting a message from one place to another have come a long way. There's evidence that Stone Age couriers in Asia carried messages by memory from place to place. Later, messages were written down for the courier to carry. Delivering messages began to speed up by the fifth century B.C.E., when people began using horses. This popular mode of transporting messages continued through the days of the Pony Express. In the nineteenth century C.E., the mode of message delivery was basically the same as it had been for hundreds of years. But on March 10, 1876, Alexander Graham Bell made history when he spoke the following words: "Mr. Watson—come here—I want to see you." Those words, spoken into the first telephone, marked the beginning of a way of communicating that changed the world. This book, part of the Turning Point Invention series, explains the invention and the inventor.

13.15 Giblin, James Cross. **When Plague Strikes: The Black Death, Smallpox, AIDS.** HarperTrophy / HarperCollins, 1997. 212 pp. ISBN 0064461955. Nonfiction.

The three deadliest epidemics in human history are the Black Death, smallpox, and AIDS. The Black Death—also known as the bubonic plague—ravaged the human population along the coast of the Black Sea in early 1347. Smallpox was probably a common disease among people early as 1500 B.C.E. AIDS first surfaced in Zaire, Africa, sometime in the mid-1970s. Centuries apart, these diseases had similar social, political, and cultural ramifications. Read about the history of these epidemics in this fascinating book that not only informs you about the diseases, but also teaches you about facing life in the midst of death.

13.16   Haskins, Jim. **The Geography of Hope: Black Exodus from the South after Reconstruction.** Twenty First Century, 1999. 133 pp. ISBN 0761303235. Nonfiction.

After the Civil War, Northerners, especially escaped slaves living in the North, hoped for the equality they presumed freedom would bring. In fact, releasing the slaves from bondage did not release them from the inequality they had faced and would continue to face. Twenty years after the end of war, disillusioned African Americans fled the South in search of a better life in the newly settled frontier. This book details their exodus, the hardships they overcame, and their continual hope of finding the promised land.

13.17   Haskins, Jim. **Separate but Not Equal: The Dream and the Struggle.** Scholastic, 1998. 184 pp. ISBN 0590459104. Nonfiction.

The struggle for equal access to education for African Americans did not begin with the showdown at Central High School in Little Rock, Arkansas, in 1957. However, that event certainly focused national attention on the issue. This book chronicles the fight for integration from colonial times to the present. The book includes a discussion of the landmark court cases, prominent individuals and events, and the general climate of the different time periods during which struggles for integration were most intense. A chronology, index, and bibliography for further reading are included.

13.18   Hurmence, Belinda. **Slavery Time When I Was Chillun.** Putnam, 1997. 98 pp. ISBN 0399230483. Nonfiction.

In 1936, the Library of Congress began a project that would continue through 1939. During those three years, African Americans who were once slaves were interviewed and recorded on audiotape so their history could be preserved. These oral histories gave firsthand insight into the lives of slaves, an insight never before available. Now Hurmence has taken some of the most poignant stories of African American slave children and compiled them in this important book. Retaining the dialect of the speakers, Hurmence has created a volume that shows us firsthand the life slave children lived. The book includes comments such as "I was worth a heap to mares George because I had so many chillun. The more chillun a slave had, the more they was worth. . . . mine was muley strong and healthy." This book is not only an important historical document, but also a compelling read.

13.19 Jones, Charlotte Foltz. **Yukon Gold: The Story of the Klondike Gold Rush.** Holiday House, 1999. 99 pp. ISBN 0823414035. Nonfiction.

Gold fever hit almost as soon as people heard that gold had been discovered in the Canadian Yukon. It was the spring of 1897, and people in the United States and Canada were suffering through an economic depression. The thought that gold nuggets were lying in streambeds just waiting to be found proved too irresistible for thousands of people. Most didn't understand the treacherous paths they would have to travel to get to this territory. For instance, White Pass trail was a "series of loose gravel, marshes and muskeg, shallow streams, and boulders and included about a mile of sand. The trail along a sheer granite cliff called Devil's Hill was barely two feet wide in places . . . and there were places where a misstep would mean a 500-foot fall to death." Read about this trail and others that men, women, and children followed as they searched for the gold at the end of the Yukon rainbow.

13.20 Katz, William Loren. **Black Pioneers: An Untold Story.** Atheneum Books for Young Readers, 1999. 193 pp. ISBN 0689814100. Nonfiction.

When most people think of the history of westward expansion or tales of the frontier, they rarely think of the African Americans who played such a vital role settling the Ohio and Mississippi Valleys. For African Americans, the frontier meant freedom from slavery and oppression, but Southern slave owners wanted to make the West part of the slave states. "Black laws" were passed in the new territories, giving basic rights only to White settlers. To fight against this spread of White domination, African American pioneers fought hard for their freedom. From Ohio to Kansas, they fought against slavery, helped maintain the Underground Railroad, and joined Indian nations. In this history, readers will learn about such influential African American freedom fighters as Sara Jane Woodson, Peter Clark, and Dred Scott.

13.21 Katz, William Loren. **Breaking the Chains: African-American Slave Resistance.** Aladdin, 1998. 194 pp. ISBN 0689314930. Nonfiction.

In the introduction to this powerful book, Katz writes, "When American courage is celebrated, slaves are left out." He explains that slave masters, in order to justify their actions, insisted that slaves "love their master and his family and the attachment is reciprocated." Slave owners went to great lengths to convince others that slaves wanted to be slaves. Katz presents a much different view, however, by showing the powerful resistance slaves mounted against slavery. His book reminds us of the slaves who were heroes as they fought daily for their lives and their liberty.

13.22 Keenan, Sheila. **Scholastic Encyclopedia of Women in the United States.** Scholastic, 1996. 199 pp. ISBN 0590227920. Nonfiction.

Filling a gap in our knowledge of American history, this reference work includes brief biographies of 217 women and mention of forty-three more. Divided into six historical periods from the 1500s to the 1990s, the entries intersperse the lives of famous women with lesser-known women who represent the spirit of their times. The entries are organized by career, making it possible to look for women who were poets, painters, ambassadors, or Olympic sports figures. In addition, side comments in red include words by and about women, anecdotes about the roles of women, and short entries about other women not treated in a full-length entry.

13.23 Koslow, Philip. **Building a New World: Africans in America, 1500–1900.** Chelsea House, 1997. 72 pp. ISBN 0791031446. Nonfiction.

Africans who were brought to America came against their will, leaving their homes, their freedom, and sometimes their family behind. This book discusses the life African Americans led while in Africa, and compares it to the life of slavery they faced in the

United States. Additionally, Koslow discusses the important contribution African American slaves and their descendants made to the United States.

13.24 Krull, Kathleen. **They Saw the Future: Oracles, Psychics, Scientists, Great Thinkers, and Pretty Good Guessers.** Illustrated by Kyrsten Brooker. Atheneum Books for Young Readers, 1999. 108 pp. ISBN 0689812957. Nonfiction.

Is it possible to predict the future? Some claim it is. This book looks at the lives and prophecies of twelve individuals who predicted the future, including the Delphic Oracle (who always answered questions in riddles), the Sibyls (who suggested that "a tree that sank into the ground, with only a few branches showing, was a warning about forthcoming human slaughter"), Leonardo da Vinci (who drew designs for hundreds of mechanical devices including air conditioners, parachutes, contact lenses, and helicopters—centuries before they were invented), and Edgar Cayce ("the most documented physic of the twentieth century").

13.25 Lemesurier, Peter. **Decoding the Great Pyramid.** Barnes & Noble, 1999. 255 pp. ISBN 0760719624. Nonfiction.

For over forty centuries, the Great Pyramid has caused conversation as people have wondered whether it was something other than a royal tomb. This grand structure invites speculation when you consider that it was built over four thousand years ago, with stones weighing over seventy tons and so finely cut and positioned that their joints are less than a fiftieth of an inch thick. Curious coincidences—such as the fact that the Great Pyramid is built exactly aligned with the earth's four cardinal points, and is at the exact center of the geometrical quadrant formed by the Nile Delta—make this great wonder even more mysterious. This book looks at all of the myths and mysteries that surround the Great Pyramid, and provides a close-up look at its structure.

13.26 Lindop, Edmund. **Great Britain and the United States: Rivals and Partners.** Twenty First Century, 1999. 127 pp. ISBN 0761314717. Nonfiction.

Although Great Britain and the United States were once enemies, during the twentieth century, their strong partnership helped to end the Cold War, strengthen global economic prosperity, and promote transatlantic business mergers and cultural exchanges. Through two world wars and numerous conflicts, these countries remained strong allies. Lindop, an author and public school teacher, has written a concise account of the reciprocal relationship between these two great powers that shows how they remain dependent upon each other even today.

13.27 McKissack, Patricia C., and Fredrick L. McKissack. **Black Hands, White Sails: The Story of African-American Whalers.** Scholastic, 1999. 160 pp. ISBN 0590483137. Nonfiction.

Although the United States led the way in the international movement to save the whale, two centuries ago the nation led the whaling industry. This industry began to thrive in the New World not long after Columbus arrived at Hispaniola. Whale ships and slave ships were both a part of the development of the U.S. economy, and became even more connected as escaped slaves found work on whaling ships. This book not only gives information about the whaling industry, but also explains the little known story of African Americans' connection to this industry between 1730 and 1880. Photos and drawings complete this fascinating history.

13.28 Meltzer, Milton. **Witches and Witch-Hunts: A History of Persecution.** Blue Sky / Scholastic, 1999. 128 pp. ISBN 0590485172. Nonfiction.

This historical analysis of witch-hunts and witch trials reveals the true—and ugly—nature of these events. What you'll find when you look closely is that these hunts against not only witches, but also Jews and communists, share a common bond: a strong tie to racism, prejudice, discrimination, and superstition on the part of the hunters. Readers will travel from medieval Europe to the 1940s and witness the persecution some people faced when they were declared different.

13.29 Millennium Year by Year: A Chronicle of World History from A.D. 1000 to the Present Day. Dorling Kindersley, 1999. 894 pp. ISBN 0789446413. Nonfiction.

The millennium that just ended witnessed peace, war, great inventions and discoveries, and horrific events. All of the major events of the millennium are chronicled here, and presented as newspaper stories, complete with headlines, captions, and photos. This volume provides just enough detail about the major events and players of each era to pique the reader's curiosity.

13.30 Miller, Marilyn. **Words That Built a Nation: A Young Person's Collection of Historic American Documents.** Scholastic Reference, 1999. 172 pp. ISBN 059029881X. Nonfiction.

This book is a collection of documents and historical information that might benefit any high school or college student. From the Mayflower Compact to Hillary Rodham Clinton's speech at the United Nations Conference on Women, the book carefully documents the historical and political events surrounding each document, and includes photographs and a copy of the actual document. These documents represent the voices, hopes, and dreams of the American people, and the events that shaped the nation.

13.31 Myers, Walter Dean. **Amistad: A Long Road to Freedom.** Dutton Children's Books, 1998. 99 pp. ISBN 0525459707. Nonfiction.

In 1839, the slave ship *Amistad* set sail from Havana, Cuba, for the Puerto Principe. Along the way, the slaves rebelled, killed the captain, and took control of the ship. The mutineers tried to sail to Africa, but instead landed in the United States. There they were accused of murder and tried. As the case against the slaves unfolded, it was discovered that these people weren't slaves, but instead were kidnapped and sold as slaves. Three years and many trials later, these people were finally allowed to return to their homeland. The *Amistad* case captured the attention of the nation, as abolitionists took up their cause. Read this dramatic history in Myers's account of the men on the *Amistad,* and their journey back to freedom.

13.32 Myers, Walter Dean. **One More River to Cross: An African American Photo Album.** Browndeer / Harcourt Brace, 1999. 166 pp. ISBN 0152020217. Nonfiction.

They say that a picture's worth a thousand words. If that's true, then this book is worth thousands and thousands of words, because it's filled with black-and-white photographs of African Americans from the time of slavery and reconstruction to the civil rights movement of the 1960s and modern events of the 1990s. This portfolio will give inspiration to all who strive for racial, social, and gender equality.

13.33 Nappo, Salvatore. **Pompeii: A Guide to the Ancient City.** Barnes & Noble, 1998. 168 pp. ISBN 0760712352. Nonfiction.

The ancient Roman town of Pompeii was a center of culture and urban development, a vacation destination for the wealthy, and a town of great prosperity. In a mere forty-two hours, all that ended with the sudden and horrific eruption of Mount Vesuvius. Homes, marketplaces, shops, streets, and people were buried completely under twenty-three feet of ash. In the eighteenth century, an accidental discovery led to an excavation of the ancient city. This book brings together photographs of the many artifacts recovered from the excavation site. See what the city looked like as you gaze at photographs of ancient statues, artwork, houses, washing vats, theaters, temples, kitchens, courtyards, playgrounds, bathrooms, sewer systems, musical instruments, and market areas. You'll be amazed at how modern this ancient civilization was.

13.34 Nardo, Don. **The Great Depression.** Greenhaven, 1998. 127 pp. ISBN 156510742X. Nonfiction.

This book from the Opposing Viewpoints series offers insight into the causes and consequences of the Great Depression. Here you'll find arguments surrounding many of the issues related to the Depression. Read about the concerns over President Roosevelt's New Deal, study what economic and political experts had to say about social security, and read what people had to say about how African Americans benefited from the New Deal. A timeline and study questions for each chapter will help you learn about the events during this tumultuous time in history.

13.35 Oliver, Marilyn Tower. **Alcatraz Prison.** Enslow, 1998. 128 pp. ISBN 0894909908. Nonfiction.

The famous criminals Al Capone and Machine Gun Kelly were imprisoned there. Robert Stroud, known as the Birdman, became famous while there for the book he wrote, titled *Stroud's Digest of the Diseases of Birds.* Frank Lee Morris escaped from there and became famous in a movie starring Clint Eastwood. Where were all these men? In Alcatraz Prison, located on a small island in San Francisco Bay. Called "The Rock" because it was on a twelve-acre rocky island, this prison was designed to hold the most dangerous prisoners. It had the most advanced security measures available at the time. So what happened to this prison? Why was it eventually closed? How did some prisoners plan escapes? Was it too tough a prison? This book, part of the In American History series, answers these and many other questions.

13.36 Philip, Neil, editor. **In a Sacred Manner I Live: Native American Wisdom.** Clarion, 1997. 93 pp. ISBN 0395849810. Nonfiction.

Great Native Americans such as Black Elk, Geronimo, and Sitting Bull are represented in this book in their own words. Speeches and philosophical statements by everyone from Chief Powhatan in 1609 to Leonard Crow Dog in 1995, give you insight into the beliefs and traditions of Native American people. These leaders talk about the seasons, education, peace, and betrayal.

13.37 Siliotti, Alberto. **Guide to the Valley of the Kings.** Barnes & Noble, 1997. 168 pp. ISBN 076070483X. Nonfiction.

Alberto Siliotti, a scientific journalist and photographer, is the only photographer who has been granted full access to the Egyptian Valley of the Kings for the past decade. This guide provides some never-before-seen works of art and architecture, allowing armchair travelers to experience the tombs of the nobles and the Valley of the Kings in a most dramatic way. Part art book and part history book, this volume covers everything from the building of a royal tomb and the tombs of the eighteenth, nineteenth, and twentieth dynasties to the tombs of Rameses III's sons and the private tombs.

13.38 Spangenburg, Ray, and Diane K. Moser. **The American Indian Experience.** Facts on File, 1997. 128 pp. ISBN 0816034036. Nonfiction.

This book will help readers learn about Native Americans, their culture, their history, and their current status. Each chapter focuses on a different location, from Alcatraz Island in the San Francisco Bay to the Cahokia Mounds in Illinois. At each place, readers learn about the Native Americans who lived there, and about the significant events that surrounded their lives. Black-and-white photographs and maps help readers understand each nation's culture and movements.

13.39 Stanley, Jerry. **Digger: The Tragic Fate of the California Indians from the Missions to the Gold Rush.** Crown, 1997. 128 pp. ISBN 051770952X. Nonfiction.

This book attempts to tell the story of what happened to Native Americans living in California between 1769 and 1850. It was in 1769 that the first Spanish Mission was founded in California, and it was in 1850 that the Gold Rush reached its height. This book provides some much needed information about events generally overlooked in textbooks, including accounts of how Spanish missionaries brutally treated Native Americans in California as they attempted to Christianize them, and how Native Americans were often kidnapped, murdered, or sold into slavery by white settlers during the Gold Rush. This graphic account provides a sobering look at a time in history often seen as simply adventurous.

13.40 Uys, Erroll Lincoln. **Riding the Rails: Teenagers on the Move during the Great Depression.** TV Books, 1999. 288 pp. ISBN 1575000377. Nonfiction.

During the Great Depression, hundreds of thousands of teens across the country left home, hopped a freight train, and started riding the rails. Some left in search of jobs in order to help keep their families afloat during the financial crisis. Others left in search of adventure, only to find that life riding the rails was dangerous. Uys has collected letters and vintage photographs from thousands of the teens who lived life on the road and rail. Here readers will find tales of people being run over by the wheels of the great locomotives, as well as tales about the kindness of strangers, who would share food, clothes, and whatever else they had. Walker Evans, Dorothea Lange, and others recount the hopes and the hardships of these teens on the move.

14 Math and Science

*"Science is a way of thinking much more
than it is a body of knowledge."*

Carl Sagan

14.1 Gardner, Robert. **Science Projects about Math.** Enslow, 1999. 112
pp. ISBN 0894909509. Nonfiction.

If the science fair is in your future or if you just enjoy seeing how
math and science interact, then this book is for you. Most of these
experiments require only materials easily found around the home.
Through these experiments you'll learn the scientific method and
have the chance to make some interesting discoveries.

14.2 Gerwick-Brodeur, Madeline, and Lisa Lenard. **The Complete
Idiot's Guide to Astrology.** Alpha, 1997. 396 pp. ISBN 002861951X.
Nonfiction.

If you think Pluto is the name of a Disney character, the word
house is a synonym for *home,* or your vital statistics are your name,
height, and weight, then you need to take a look at this guide to
astrology. With this book, you'll not only learn what Pluto and
house mean to an astrologer, but you'll also discover your own
astrological sign and what the signs of the zodiac are all about.
From the first chapter (which explains what astrology is) to the
twenty-seventh chapter (which shows how astrologers use the
stars to predict the future), this complete guide offers fun reading
while explaining a centuries-old science.

14.3 Goodstein, Madeline. **Sports Science Projects: The Physics of Balls
in Motion.** Enslow, 1999. 128 pp. ISBN 0766011747. Nonfiction.

Can't think of a thing to do for your upcoming science fair? Just
toss a baseball in the air a few times, hit a tether ball around the
pole, or lob a tennis ball over the net. As you watch balls spin, fall,
slow down, make arcs, and come to a resting point, you're watching the physics of balls in motion. This book shows you how to
turn those observations into fascinating science projects that let
you combine your love of sports with the laws of science.

14.4 Greene, Brian. **The Elegant Universe: Superstrings, Hidden Dimensions, and the Quest for the Ultimate Theory.** Norton, 1999. 448 pp. ISBN 0393046885. Nonfiction.

If you frequently confuse superstrings with super glue, this book might not be for you. But if you're a science person who wonders how the theory of relativity and quantum mechanics coexist in black holes, then you might want to look at this book, which explains how superstring theory provides an ultimate explanation of the universe. Using everyday examples to explain this complex theory (and managing to avoid math completely), Greene explains how vibrating strands (superstrings) rather than subatomic particles are the fundamental building blocks of the universe.

14.5 Gribbin, John R. **Almost Everyone's Guide to Science: The Universe, Life, and Everything.** Yale University, 1999. 240 pp. ISBN 0300081014. Nonfiction.

If you're the least bit interested in understanding how the world around you works, but fear that you don't have a scientific thought in your brain, then this is the book for you. Chemistry, geology, physics, biology, meteorology—all the sciences are covered here. Gribbin writes about science without writing like a scientist, and once you start reading you'll find yourself absorbed by the world of Einstein and Darwin and contemplating everything from relativity to evolution.

14.6 Gulberg, Jan. **Mathematics: From the Birth of Numbers.** Norton, 1997. 1120 pp. ISBN 039304002X. Nonfiction.

If you think a book about math would be boring, think again. Loaded with anecdotes and cartoons about math and mathematicians, this book is more than a reference book of formulas; it's an entertaining and informative look at everything from simple addition to trigonometry. If you need help understanding algebraic formulas or can't keep straight the difference between sines and cosines, grab a pencil and some paper and sit down with this book.

14.7 Hawking, Stephen. **A Brief History of Time: 10th Anniversary Edition.** Bantam Doubleday Dell, 1998. 212 pp. ISBN 0553380168. Nonfiction.

Hawking, a brilliant scientist, wrote this brief history book for nonscientists in an effort to answer questions like, How did the universe begin? Where did it come from? and What does it mean to say the universe is expanding? Staying clear of technical terms, Hawking discusses gravity, big bang theory, time, dimensions, chaos theory, and black holes. This anniversary edition contains a new chapter on wormholes and time travel, as well as an introduction by Hawking.

14.8 Levy, Matthys, and Mario Salvadori. **Earthquake Games: Earthquakes and Volcanoes Explained by 32 Games and Experiments.** Illustrated by Christina C. Blatt. Simon & Schuster / Margaret McElderry, 1997. 116 pp. ISBN 0689813678. Nonfiction.

Written by two engineering experts, this book explains through brief narratives and graphic examples how earthquakes and volcanoes occur. Simple experiments using rolling pins, cereal boxes, and rulers help explain the earth's volatile nature. You become the engineering expert by learning how structures should be built in an active seismic area, and then constructing your own models.

14.9 Taylor, Barbara. **Earth Explained: A Beginner's Guide to Our Planet.** Henry Holt, 1997. 69 pp. ISBN 0805048731. Nonfiction.

Tornadoes! Earthquakes! Volcanoes! You've heard about each of these natural disasters, but do you know what causes them? Find the answers in this book as you read about the internal and external forces that shape our earth. With the help of outstanding graphics and photographs, see how an ice flow carves out mountains and creates valleys, inspect microscopic ice crystals, and examine glaciers up close.

14.10 Vecchione, Glen. **100 First-Prize Make-It-Yourself Science Fair Projects.** Sterling, 1998. 192 pp. ISBN 0806907037. Nonfiction.

Build rockets. Make pulleys. Design greenhouses. Test temperatures against different colors. With easy-to-follow directions, plenty of illustrations to help you see what you're doing, and suggestions for outstanding displays, this book offers all you need for designing and carrying out your own experiments or science fair projects.

15 Mysteries, Intrigue, Suspense, and Horror

"Many a book is like a key to unknown chambers within the castle of one's own self."

Franz Kafka

15.1 Almond, David. **Skellig.** Delacorte, 1999. 176 pp. ISBN 038532633X. Fiction.

Michael and his family have moved into a new house. He and his father are hard at work making improvements to the house, eager to remove all of the trash and debris left by the former occupants. When Michael explores the garage, he finds something more than trash, however; he discovers Skellig. Exactly who—or perhaps the right word is WHAT—is Skellig? Michael comes to believe that Skellig may just have some magic in him. Is the magic enough to save the life of Michael's newborn sister?

15.2 Avi. **Midnight Magic.** Scholastic, 1999. 249 pp. ISBN 0590360353. Fiction.

Fabrizio, the only servant of Mangus the Magician, doesn't have much to look forward to. Ever since Mangus was forced to stop practicing magic or face execution, Fabrizio's life has been dull and empty. But when Mangus and Fabrizio are summoned to the castle of King Claudio, the young servant finds himself caught up in a world of madness, magic, and murder. The king's son has disappeared on his way to Rome, and Claudio fears that grief is driving Princess Teresina to madness. She claims to be visited by the ghost of her brother, who cries out for Fabrizio to avenge his death. Mangus's job is to discover what Teresina is seeing. The plot thickens as Fabrizio discovers that the dead brother just might not be dead, and the innocent Teresina might be more calculating than anyone ever imagined.

15.3 Bachman, Richard, Jr. **Desperation and The Regulators: A Boxed Set.** Signet, 1997. ISBN 0451935659. Fiction.

These two books are packaged together for two simple reasons: they tell the same story from two very different perspectives, and the author of both books is Stephen King (a.k.a. Richard Bachman). In both novels, an evil being known as Tak hops from body to body, wreaking havoc. Although the settings of the two stories are different, many of the same characters appear in both novels, making this an interesting set to read back-to-back. The horror is nonstop, and the evil Tak seemingly invincible. Is there anything or anyone that can stop Tak from his course of annihilation?

15.4 Baldacci, David. **The Simple Truth.** Warner, 1998. 470 pp. ISBN 0446523321. Fiction.

After serving twenty-five years of a life sentence for a murder he did not commit, Rufus Harms smuggles out an appeal to the U.S. Supreme Court. One of the clerks, Mike, sees the appeal, recognizes the names in it, and hides the appeal with the intention of investigating on his own. But Mike is murdered, and a friend and fellow clerk is determined to find out why. The book contains mature language and situations.

15.5 Brown, Sandra. **Unspeakable.** Warner, 1998. 439 pp. ISBN 0446519790. Fiction.

Carl Herbold escapes from prison with only one thing on his mind: revenge against his stepfather, Delray Corbett, whose testimony was crucial to Carl's conviction. He heads to Texas, letting nothing and no one get in his way, even if it means killing. Corbett lives on a remote farm with his widowed daughter-in-law Anna and his grandson. Fearing for Anna's safety, Corbett seeks help from a mysterious drifter.

15.6 Butler, Charles. **The Darkling.** Simon & Schuster / Margaret McElderry, 1998. 164 pp. ISBN 0689817967. Fiction.

Fifteen-year-old Petra has a strange encounter with Mr. Century, an eccentric old recluse, when she makes a delivery to his house. When Mr. Century dies, strange events continue to connect Petra to him. After a spirit possesses her father, Petra must find a way to sever her connection with Mr. Century if she is to save her father and herself.

15.7 Cargill, Linda. **Pool Party.** Scholastic, 1996. 211 pp. ISBN 059058112. Fiction.

Sharon has moved back home for her senior year so that her mother can refurbish an old Victorian house and open an inn. Sharon's boyfriend, Phil, convinces her to have a pool party, but before she gets the chance to invite anyone, people she does not even know get expensive invitations addressed "To the Best of the Best." Phil tells Sharon not to worry, and assures her that he will do everything he can to make the party a success. On the big day, an expensive caterer arrives with steak and lobster, and a band arrives and plays so loudly that no one can talk or be heard over them. Then, while people are eating, three of the partygoers disappear. What is going on here, and why?

15.8 Clarke, Judith. **The Lost Day.** Henry Holt, 1997. 154 pp. ISBN 0805061525. Fiction.

Melbourne, Australia, has more dance clubs than any other city in the world. On most Saturday nights, you can find Vinny, Josh, Jasper, and their friends roaming from club to club. After one evening of clubbing, Vinny disappears. One minute he is standing with the rest of his group on a street corner, and the next moment he has vanished. Vinny is officially classified a missing person, and the lives of his friends are turned upside down by his disappearance.

15.9 Clark, Mary Higgins. **All around the Town.** EconoClad, 1999. 341 pp. ISBN 0785100099. Fiction.

Laurie Kenyon was kidnapped at the tender age of four, and subjected to physical and emotional abuse by her two captors. Now she is twenty-one and enrolled in college, and she is working hard to put the past behind her. Unfortunately, the trauma of her childhood has caused Laurie to develop four alternate personalities: Leona, Kay, Debbie, and a young boy. Laurie's tentative hold on her sanity comes to a shattering end when she is discovered standing over the bloody body of one of her professors. How can she prove her innocence?

15.10 Clark, Mary Higgins. **All through the Night: A Suspense Story.** Simon & Schuster, 1998. 170 pp. ISBN 0684856603. Fiction.

An eighteen-year-old woman leaves her newborn child at the doorstep of a local church. Little does she know that inside the church, a burglar is stealing a precious gold chalice. The thief takes off with the baby stroller as a cover for his crime, and raises the child as his own. Years later the mother, wishing to locate her abandoned child, turns to the church for help. Lucky for her, Alvirah and Willy, the amateur sleuths who hit it big in a previous Clark novel, *The Lottery Winner,* are there to help. The trail leading to the lost child is twisted, but Alvirah and Willy are up to the challenge.

15.11 Clark, Mary Higgins. **We'll Meet Again.** Simon & Schuster, 1999. 314 pp. ISBN 0684835975. Fiction.

Molly Lasch, a socialite, is incarcerated for killing her husband, Gary. When she is finally released from prison, she is the subject of a TV news feature presented by her old classmate, Fran Simmons, who doesn't believe Molly is guilty. As Fran investigates the circumstances of Gary's death, she discovers information about her own father's suicide. Soon Fran finds herself caught in a tangled web of murders, and in danger from those who would kill anyone to keep themselves safe.

15.12 Cook, Robin. **Vector.** Putnam, 1999. 400 pp. ISBN 0399144714. Fiction.

A Russian immigrant, who has become disenchanted with his life in the United States as a taxi driver, decides to return to his homeland. Before leaving the United States, he intends to release a large dose of anthrax into Central Park, New York. His plan is to kill millions as revenge for the many slights he was subjected to. Complications arise when a militia organization catches wind of the plot, and wants to join forces in order to make a political statement. It is up to Dr. Jack Stapleton and Dr. Laurie Montgomery to stop them before the deadly anthrax is released.

15.13 Cormier, Robert. **In the Middle of the Night.** Bantam, 1997. 182 pp. ISBN 0440226864. Fiction.

The phone calls come in the middle of the night, and for years Denny has been forbidden to answer the phone when it rings. His parents finally explain to Denny why people call, especially around Halloween. Twenty-five years ago, Denny's father was an usher in a movie theater where tragedy struck one Halloween evening. Children were killed and injured, and many people still blame Denny's father for the events. While he is home alone one day, Denny answers the phone. The voice at the other end of the line does not seem menacing, but Denny's naiveté may lead to danger.

15.14 Cornwell, Patricia. **Black Notice.** Putnam, 1999. 415 pp. ISBN 0399145087. Fiction.

Medical examiner and master sleuth Kay Scarpetta is back to help solve another baffling mystery. A man has been found dead inside a cargo container. There are few clues to his identity, and all Kay is able to find are some strange looking animal-like hairs and a mysterious tattoo. When another puzzling death occurs soon afterward, Kay finds the same hairs. Her attempt to identify the victims and get clues about their killers leads Kay on an international search. There are plenty of red herrings to keep you guessing about the mysterious person responsible for these deaths.

15.15 Cornwell, Patricia. **Point of Origin.** Putnam, 1998. 356 pp. ISBN 0399143947. Fiction.

The intrepid coroner Kay Scarpetta faces one of the greatest medical mysteries of her career. Someone has been setting fires that have resulted in deaths. Could the recent rash of arsons be tied to Carrie Grethen, a psychotic killer recently escaped from prison? If Carrie is the killer, then the lives of Kay Scarpetta and her family and friends are in jeopardy. Kay is responsible for putting Carrie behind bars, and even in prison, Carrie continued to send threats to Kay. She will not stop until she has exacted her revenge.

15.16 Cray, Jordan. **Danger.com@1//Gemini7/.** Aladdin, 1997. ISBN 0689814321. Fiction.

Life is great for Jonah. Milleridge High is about to let out for the summer, and he's got a steady girlfriend named Jen, a best friend named Matt, and two fairly understanding "parentals." Then, as Jonah says, "One day I took a ride with the top down . . . on the Net." Jonah enters a chat room, and soon he's connecting with six girls. Despite what Matt says, Jonah doesn't think he is cheating on Jen, until one of the girls—Nicole—shows up on his doorstep. Nicole will stop at nothing to see that she and Jonah are together forever. Mysterious events begin to occur, such as Jonah passing a trig final without studying, and his father getting a promotion after his competition for the position is fired. When Jonah, Jen, and others narrowly escape death and destruction, it occurs to Jonah that what began as a harmless online flirtation with Nicole may now spell danger.com. This book is part of a series devoted to mysterious complications that arise from the Internet. Other titles in the series include *danger.com@2//Firestorm/, danger.com@3// Shadow Man/, danger.com@6//Bad Intent/,* and *danger.com@7//Most Wanted/.*

15.17 Cross, Gillian. **Tightrope.** Holiday House, 1999. 216 pp. ISBN 0823415120. Fiction.

Fourteen-year-old Ashley goes to school, hangs out with her friends, frightens them sometimes with her constant walks across high and narrow places, and begrudgingly takes care of her disabled mother. Then her life takes a turn when she realizes that someone who has been leaving her mysterious letters is actually stalking her. At first she thinks this new twist in her life is somewhat exciting. When excitement gives way to nuisance, she believes that ignoring the messages will solve the problem. Her feelings turn to fear after the stalker's messages become threatening. Then Ashley knows she needs help. She soon finds herself on a tightrope that seems to lead to disaster.

15.18 Dettman, Joy. **Mallawindy.** Pan Macmillan Australia, 1998. 524 pp. ISBN 0330361333. Fiction.

Ann Burton was born on the banks of a river the night her drunken father tried to burn their house down. Her brother, Johnny, breathed life into her lungs, and helped her breathe her first breath. At age six, she witnesses the murder of her seven-year-old sister, Liza. The brutality of that murder blocks her memory and robs her of speech. For the next six years, she retreats into her own mind and lives to read and create poetry. Through the help of a loving teacher, Ann regains her speech, escapes the bondage of her family, and creates a successful career. Still plagued with guilt and dark thoughts, she finally confronts her fears as the mystery of Liza's murder is unraveled.

15.19   Dolan, Robert W. **Serial Murder.** Chelsea House, 1997. 81 pp. ISBN 0791042758. Nonfiction.

Drawing on in-depth case studies of serial murder, former New York City police officer Robert Dolan provides an inside look at the motives and methods of serial killers. Readers learn about the history of serial murder, possible causes for violent behavior, the patterns or rituals of such killers, and how criminal profiling and nationwide information sharing have aided law enforcement officials in the investigation and arrest of criminals involved in serial murders. Other books in this series include *Capital Punishment; Classic Cons and Swindles; Detectives, Private Eyes and Bounty Hunters; The FBI's Most Wanted; Hate Crimes;* and *Infamous Trials.*

15.20   Duncan, Lois. **Gallow's Hill.** Laurel-Leaf, 1999. 229 pp. ISBN 0440227259. Fiction.

What begins as a Halloween hoax soon leads to tragedy for Sarah Zoltanne. Sarah, anxious to fit in at her new school, agrees to play a fortune-teller at the annual Halloween Carnival. At first, Eric Garret, one of her classmates, feeds her inside information on her clients so that it will seem that Sarah's talents are real. Soon, Sarah makes predictions of her own, predictions that horrifyingly come true. Now Sarah is haunted by dreams of the Salem witch trials. Has she unwittingly set into motion a tragic series of events?

15.21   Duncan, Lois, editor. **Night Terrors: Stories of Shadow and Substance.** Aladdin Paperbacks, 1997. 192 pp. ISBN 0689807244. Fiction.

Here are eleven selections that are "not exactly bedtime stories," written especially for this collection by some of the top writers in the business. Among them are Joan Aiken, Annette Curtis Klause, Joan Lowery Nixon, Theodore Taylor, and Patricia Windsor. From mysterious visitors and a snake-shaped bracelet that moves to the Bogey Man in the basement, these horror stories were designed to be "more terrifying than nightmares."

15.22   Gee, Maurice. **The Fat Man.** Simon & Schuster, 1997. 182 pp. ISBN 0689811829. Fiction.

"Say your prayers, kid," Herbert Muskie, the fat man, said to Colin, a skinny kid, when he caught Colin stealing a chocolate bar from his rucksack. Herbert only laughed when Colin said he was sorry, said he'd give it back, and asked if he could go. But Herbert

Muskie didn't believe in forgiveness or forgetting. He knew that he had found the kid he needed to help him with his next burglary job, and there was no way he was going to let him go. Little did Colin realize that Herbert was about to terrorize Colin and his family—and that was only the beginning.

15.23 Genberg, Ira. **Reckless Homicide.** St. Martin's, 1998. 296 pp. ISBN 031217974X. Fiction.

Still grieving the loss of his daughter and his failing marriage, Charlie Ashmore, a pilot for Brandon Airlines, is fired after testing positive for taking the drug Seconal. Michael, Charlie's brother and corporate counsel for the airline, hides another failed drug test, orders a new one, and convinces the airline to rehire his brother. Later, Charlie's plane crashes, leaving no survivors, and Charlie is found to have another drug, Phenobarbital, in his system. Michael now finds himself the scapegoat in an elaborate cover-up, and goes to trial for reckless homicide.

15.24 Gerritsen, Tess. **Bloodstream.** Pocket, 1998. 324 pp. ISBN 0671001675X. Fiction.

Dr. Claire Elliot moved to a small town with her son, Noah, to protect him from the evils of the city. Everything seemed perfect until the violence started in school, and continued to escalate until one student brutally attacked Noah's family. Noah was taken to the hospital for observation, where he was handcuffed to the railing and heavily sedated. During the night, he chewed his wrist and hand until he was able to slip out of his restraints and escape. Little did he know that this incident was just the beginning of the horror.

15.25 Glenn, Mel. **Foreign Exchange: A Mystery in Poems.** Morrow Junior Books, 1999. 159 pp. ISBN 0688164722. Fiction.

Some of the students from Tower High School are participating in a unique exchange program. They will spend a week living with the families of teens who reside in a rural part of the state. Each group of teens has preconceived notions of what to expect from the other. The city kids believe their country counterparts will be hicks; the country kids assume the city kids will be gangsters. What neither group suspects is that one among them may be a killer. When beautiful Kristen is found dead, suspicions turn immediately to Kwame, the last person seen with her.

15.26 Grafton, Sue. **O is for Outlaw.** Henry Holt, 1999. 318 pp. ISBN 0805059355. Fiction.

Kinsey Millhone, the private investigator from Grafton's series of alphabet mysteries (*A is for Alibi, N is for Noose,* etc.), is back to solve a case that becomes quite personal. It all begins with a storage space scavenger, someone who buys the contents of abandoned storage spaces in an attempt to find hidden treasure. Kinsey receives a phone call from someone who has a box of stuff with her name on it. The box, it turns out, was stored with the possessions of Kinsey's ex-husband, Mickey. In the box Kinsey discovers evidence about a long-closed case, the case that ended her marriage to Mickey and ended his career as a cop. When Mickey suddenly ends up shot under mysterious circumstances, Kinsey must delve into his past.

15.27 Grisham, John. **The Partner.** Doubleday, 1997. 366 pp. ISBN 038547295. Fiction.

Danilo Silva once lived a different life. He was once a partner in a prestigious law firm, and went by the name Patrick Lanigan. Now Danilo lives the life of an unhurried man in Brazil, but is always looking over his shoulder. That's because he embezzled millions of dollars from his former firm, staged his own death, and then fled with his money to start a new life. The only problem is, he's been found out. Now he faces new challenges as he wheels and deals his way through the court system, trying to keep the money hidden and himself out of jail.

15.28 Hoobler, Dorothy, and Thomas Hoobler. **The Ghost in the Tokaido Inn.** Philomel, 1999. 214 pp. ISBN 039923330X. Fiction.

Seikei, a merchant's son, is asked to assist the famous samurai magistrate, Judge Oooka, in finding a thief who stole a valuable ring. Seikei must demonstrate all of his skills, and the courage of a samurai, as he joins a traveling group of kabuki actors. The thief may just be a part of the company.

15.29 Kellerman, Jonathan. **Billy Straight.** Random House, 1999. 467 pp. ISBN 0679459596. Fiction.

Late one night, Billy, a twelve-year-old boy, witnesses a particularly brutal murder. The police need his help, but he is able to avoid them by using the knowledge he has gained living in the streets. He knows he should come forward, but if he does, he will be sent back to the abusive home that he ran away from, so he keeps running. Who will find him first, the killer or the police?

15.30 King, Stephen. **Bag of Bones.** Scribner, 1998. 529 pp. ISBN 0684853507. Fiction.

Mike Noonan, still reeling from the unexpected death of his pregnant wife, returns to their beloved summerhouse to seek asylum and perhaps to heal. Shortly after his arrival, he rescues three-year-old Kyra and, in the process, befriends her mother, Mattie. Mattie and Kyra have their own demons with which to contend, and Dark Score Lake seems to be the place where the fates of Mike, Mattie, and Kyra will be decided. This blend of real-life evil and the relentless threat of ghosts seeking revenge for past deeds is sure to please fans of King and the horror genre.

15.31 King, Stephen. **The Girl Who Loved Tom Gordon.** Scribner, 1999. ISBN 0684867621. Fiction.

Nine-year-old Trisha McFarland is hiking in the Maine woods with her mother and older brother. Tired of listening to the two of them bicker, Trisha slips off the path for a moment to rest. When she comes back to the path, she can no longer see or hear her mother and brother. Although she carefully attempts to retrace her steps, eventually she must admit that she is hopelessly lost. Plagued by eerie noises, hungry mosquitoes, and a growing sense of dread, Trisha has only one source of comfort: the Walkman radio over which she can still receive the play-by-play for the Boston Red Sox game. Her favorite pitcher, Tom Gordon, becomes an imaginary traveler, as Trisha desperately tries to find her way back to civilization.

15.32 King, Stephen. **Hearts in Atlantis.** Scribner, 1999. 523 pp. ISBN 0684853515. Fiction.

This collection of stories takes readers on a journey from the 1960s to the 1990s. Follow the characters from a summer of innocence as eleven-year-old friends, through their college years and the war in Vietnam, to their troubled adult lives. In "Low Men in Yellow

Coats," the focus of eleven-year-old Bobby Garfield's summer changes from the new Schwinn bike he covets to his fear for his new friend Ted's life. The title story, "Hearts in Atlantis," picks up the story of Bobby's childhood girlfriend, Carol, and her experiences in the new antiwar protest movement, experiences that lead her to trust the wrong people. The final story in the collection sees Bobby and Carol reunited for the funeral of their old chum, Sully John. Throughout these stories, readers encounter the history of a very turbulent time in the United States and in the lives of the main characters of all of King's stories.

15.33 Koontz, Dean. **Seize the Night.** Bantam, 1999. 401 pp. ISBN 0553106651. Fiction.

When children start disappearing in Moonlight Bay, Christopher Snow (a character first seen in *Fear Nothing*) knows it is up to him to find out what is happening, because the police can't be trusted. With his intelligent dog, Christopher follows the tracks of the latest victim, and ends up at a supposedly deserted army base on the outskirts of town. Christopher keeps going even after his trusty dog disappears, but soon realizes that he can't do it alone.

15.34 Lee, Marie. **Night of the Chupacabras.** Avon, 1999. 120 pp. ISBN 0380797739. Fiction.

Mi-Sun is invited to spend the summer in Mexico with her friend Lupe. Her parents give her permission to go, but only if she takes her little brother, Ju-Won. Reluctantly, she agrees. When they arrive in Mexico, their adventure begins. An old man warns them to beware the *chupacabra*, a beast from Mexican folklore believed to suck the blood from its victims. A few days later, a mother goat disappears and is later found with fang marks on her neck. Next, vegetables appear in the kitchen with fang marks and all the juice sucked out. Are the chupacabras really causing the damage, or is it something else? They must find out before the *chupacabras* find them!

15.35 Levitin, Sonia. **Evil Encounter.** Aladdin Paperbacks, 1997. 277 pp. ISBN 0689806019. Fiction.

Michelle and her mother, Sandra, have just moved to Los Angeles from Philadelphia, after her parents' recent divorce. Coping with the new separation seems difficult for Michelle, so with urging from her mother, Michelle joins a therapy group. The group proves to be nothing like what Michelle expected. They sing and dance. They confess their deepest emotions through role-playing. Luke, the group's unconventional leader, is so caring and charismatic, that everyone in the group, including Michelle, practically worships him as if he were a saint. However, as Michelle becomes more involved with Luke, cracks begin to appear in his image. Then one fateful night, at a weekend therapy retreat, the whole facade is shattered. Luke is found dead, and Michelle's mother is charged with his murder. In order to help her mother, Michelle conducts her own detective work to unravel the truth.

15.36 Levitin, Sonia. **Yesterday's Child.** Simon & Schuster, 1997. 245 pp. ISBN 0689808100. Fiction.

When Laura's mother, Jasmine, dies suddenly, Laura feels guilty about not having had a close relationship with her, even though Jasmine's secretive and mysterious ways always seemed to push them apart. Seeking to reconcile her feelings, Laura goes through her mother's things and finds a letter to a woman named Megan, written the day before her mother died. The letter reveals that Jasmine and Megan were childhood friends who had lost touch with each other, and also mentions "forgiveness." On a class trip to Washington, D.C., Laura visits her mother's hometown, just outside the city, and makes some disturbing discoveries about her mother's past. Laura's obsession with uncovering the shocking truth about her mother finally leads her to Megan, and puts Laura in extreme danger.

15.37 Lewin, Michael Z. **Cutting Loose.** Henry Holt, 1999. 520 pp. ISBN 0805062254. Fiction.

In the late nineteen-century, Jackie Cross lives her life dressed as a boy in order to fulfill her dream of playing professional baseball like her pa. Her best friend, Nance, rode in the Buffalo Bill Wild West Show. When Nance is murdered, Jackie gives up her baseball career and devotes her life to finding Nance's murderer. She finally finds herself in London, where she not only solves the mystery of Nance's murder, but also finds herself confronting her father's killer.

15.38 Lynch, Patrick. **The Policy.** Signet, 1999. 400 pp. ISBN 0451193261. Fiction.

What could be safer than being an actuary for an insurance company and working with numbers all day? That is what Alex thinks, until a company executive is found dead. Her boyfriend is promoted to fill the executive's position, and he inexplicably turns nasty. Alex doesn't understand what is happening, or why. One day, she inadvertently discovers an unusual coincidence in the numbers of people dying from heart attacks, and from that moment on, her life is in danger.

15.39 Mahy, Margaret. **The Tricksters.** Aladdin Paperbacks, 1999. 266 pp. ISBN 0689829108. Fiction.

Haunting and intriguing, this supernatural fantasy combines universal truths with family intrigue. Seventeen-year-old Harry is obsessed with the romantically fanciful novel that she is writing. When three tricksters suddenly drop in on the family's Christmas vacation, everything changes. The supernatural and reality collide as the tricksters, through Harry's writing, force confessions of family secrets. Friendships and relationships change as a result.

15.40 Naylor, Phyllis Reynolds. **Sang Spell.** Atheneum Books for Young Readers, 1998. 192 pp. ISBN 0689820070. Fiction.

In this story that combines healthy doses of realistic mystery and eerie fantasy, a young man hitchhikes to Dallas from his home in Boston. Josh has just lost his mother in a car accident, and is traveling cross-country to live with his aunt. Along the way, he is mugged and abandoned on a remote stretch of road. A kindly woman comes to Josh's aid. She takes him by horse and cart back to her village of Canara in the Appalachian foothills. The town seems untouched by time; there is no electricity, and few of the other niceties of modern life. Josh soon learns that there is no way out of Canara. The roads all lead back to the heart of the village, a village none of the inhabitants want to leave.

15.41 Nixon, Joan Lowery. **The Haunting.** Delacorte, 1998. 184 pp. ISBN 038532247X. Fiction.

Graymoss has been a part of Lia's family for generations. Now possession of the old house has fallen to Lia's mother. She is determined to ignore the old rumors of malicious spirits, and plans to convert the mansion into a group home for neglected and abused children. Lia believes the house does have an evil presence, a feeling confirmed when she visits Graymoss. How can she convince her mother to abandon her plans? Is there a way to rid the house of the evil that possesses it?

15.42 Nixon, Joan Lowery. **Who Are You?** Delacorte, 1999. 192 pp. ISBN 0385325665. Fiction.

When wealthy recluse Douglas Merson is found shot in his Houston mansion, the police find a folder of information about Kristi Evans. Kristi is a gifted artist, one whose work has garnered attention beyond her high school. But why would Douglas Merson be interested in Kristi? As Kristi begins to ask questions, she finds out a secret her parents have kept from her for many years. That secret will change forever the way Kristi views herself and her family.

15.43 Patterson, James. **When the Wind Blows.** Little Brown, 1998. 416 pp. ISBN 0316693324. Fiction.

Frannie O'Neill, a veterinarian, lives a quiet life as she tries to come to grips with her husband's murder. Quiet, that is, until she meets eleven-year-old Max, who puts her life in turmoil and in danger. Max has been part of a diabolical experiment that has given her unusual powers, including the ability to fly.

15.44 Penzler, Otto, editor. **50 Greatest Mysteries of All Time.** Newstar, 1998. 567 pp. ISBN 0787109630. Fiction.

From the incredible Sherlock Holmes and Dr. Watson to super sleuth Kinsey Milhone, the great detectives and their creators offer us a sumptuous feast of suspense. Match wits with the best minds and see if you can figure out whodunit before they do. Stories by contemporary authors such as Stephen King join classic detective and mystery stories by writers like P. D. James. All of the stories presented here offer up tasty mysteries loaded with clues for those with quick wits.

15.45 Pullman, Philip. **Clockwork.** Levine / Scholastic, 1998. 128 pp. ISBN 0590129996. Fiction.

Karl is apprenticed to the village clockmaker. As the year of his apprenticeship comes to a close, he is expected to design and build a new addition to the village's renowned clockworks. Unfortunately, Karl has no idea what to build, and time is running out quickly. A stranger enters the tavern where Karl is bemoaning his fate, and offers his assistance. Karl is willing to pay any price for help, but does not realize his own life may be in jeopardy from the stranger.

15.46 Qualey, Marsha. **Close to a Killer.** Delacorte, 1999. 224 pp. ISBN 0385325975. Fiction.

Barrie's mother and her business partners are all ex-cons. They own and operate Killer Cuts, the hottest new beauty salon in town. Barrie works in the shop after school and on weekends. She and her mother are just beginning to forge a new relationship when tragedy strikes. First, one client of the salon is found murdered. Then a second ends up dead under suspicious circumstances. Barrie has also noticed someone hanging around the shop at night. Barrie is uncertain how close the killer is, but she is starting to suspect it is too close for comfort and for safety.

15.47 Rhodes, Amelia Atwater. **In the Forests of the Night.** Delacorte, 1999. 147 pp. ISBN 0385326742. Fiction.

In 1684, Rachel lived a fairly normal life. One night changes her life, however, as she is turned into a vampire by someone whom she believes has also murdered her beloved brother. For three hundred years, Rachel, now known as Risica, has sought her revenge. The time may be drawing near. Risica has become one of the most powerful vampires. She does not fear holy water, crosses, or the other traditional means of destroying a vampire. There is only one thing to fear: Ather, the vampire who turned her. Her confrontation with Ather must lead to one of their deaths. Who will be the one to survive?

15.48 Roberts, Willo Davis. **Pawns.** Atheneum Books for Young Readers, 1998. 154 pp. ISBN 0689816685. Fiction.

Is Dora really who she says she is? That is what Teddi, a teenage orphan living with her next-door neighbor, Mamie, is determined to find out. Mamie's younger son Ricky has recently died in a plane crash. When Dora shows up on Mamie's doorstep pregnant, homeless, and claiming to be Ricky's wife, Teddi feels threatened by her presence. But some things about Dora just do not add up. Why didn't Ricky tell his mother about his wife and expected baby? And why did Ricky name Mamie as beneficiary on the travel insurance policy, and not Dora? An exciting conclusion brings answers to Teddi's questions.

15.49 Roberts, Willo Davis. **Twisted Summer.** Aladdin, 1998. 189 pp. ISBN 0689804598. Fiction.

Fourteen-year-old Cici is excited to be returning to her grandparents' beach house for the summer. She hopes Jack will now consider her old enough to pay attention to. Once there, she is shocked to find out a murder has been committed, and Jack's brother is in jail for the crime. She's sure a mistake has been made, and begins to investigate, but she is horrified when it appears that someone close to her may have been involved in the crime.

15.50 Ryan, Mary Elizabeth. **Alias.** Aladdin Paperbacks, 1998. 214 pp. ISBN 0689822642. Fiction.

Toby and his mom, Annie Chase, are always moving. The pattern is always the same: new town, new name, new identify. When Toby comes home from school and finds his mom wearing a new hairstyle and stuffing all her belongings into garbage bags, he knows they are leaving Los Angeles. But Toby learned early on not to ask his mom any questions. This time, their destination is the small, rural town of Donner, Idaho. Things go pretty well at first. Jenny Parker, as Toby's mom now calls herself, has a job at a greenhouse, and they both live in a cabin on the grounds. But when Toby discovers old news clippings while doing research for a history project about the Vietnam War, all hopes for a normal life seem to be destroyed.

15.51 Sachar, Louis. **Holes.** Farrar, Straus and Giroux, 1998. 233 pp. ISBN 0374332657. Fiction.

Stanley Yelnats, whose name is a palindrome, has been accused and convicted of a crime, despite his protests that he is innocent. He is given the choice of where he will serve his time. Stanley elects to be sent to Camp Green Lake, a sort of boot camp. When he arrives, Stanley is puzzled by the routine. Each day, Stanley and his fellow detainees are sent to the dried-out lake bed and made to dig deep holes. Stanley begins to wonder just what the warden is looking for in all of these holes. Surely there is more to this than meets the eye?

15.52 Sarrantino, Al, editor. **999: New Stories of Horror and Suspense.** Avon, 1999. 664 pp. ISBN 0380977400. Fiction.

The well-known and the unknown are represented in these twenty-nine never-before-published stories. In one story, vampires have taken over Europe and have targeted the United States as their next conquest. Will there be enough stakes and holy water to conquer such an invasion? William Peter Blatty, whose novel *The Exorcist* made many of us squirm and shudder, offers a new story for this collection. He is joined by Stephen King, Joyce Carol Oates, and others who delight in seeing if they can raise goose bumps on our arms. Be sure to read this book when there is plenty of daylight left!

15.53 Savage, Tom. **The Inheritance.** Dutton, 1998. 278 pp. ISBN 0525944230. Fiction.

Overnight, Holly Smith goes from being a normal twenty-four-year-old to an heiress, due to the death of a great aunt she has never met. Holly, whose real surname is Randall, arrives at her magnificent Connecticut estate to find her Uncle John and his greedy wife in residence. The town and its citizens know Holly's secrets, snubbing her because her birth mother committed a murder many years ago. Holly makes many valiant attempts to discover the skeletons in her closet, only to determine she is a target for murder. Mysterious characters and surprising events await Holly and the reader as some of her lifelong dreams, for better or worse, come true.

15.54 Sikes, Shelley. **For Mike.** Bantam Doubleday Dell, 1998. 197 pp. ISBN 0385323379. Fiction.

Jeff's best friend, Mike, may have disappeared, but he's been haunting Jeff's dreams every night. When Jeff's dad brings home the news that Mike's body has been found, Jeff immediately suspects their friend Kirby, who has been a part of these dreams. Adding to Jeff's suspicion is the necklace that Kirby has begun wearing—the same necklace that Mike used to wear all the time. What Jeff finds at Mike's grave one night challenges his ability to accept the death of his best friend.

15.55 Snicket, Lemony. **The Reptile Room: A Series of Unfortunate Events, Book the Second.** Illustrated by Brett Helquist. HarperTrophy / HarperCollins, 1999. 190 pp. ISBN 0064407675. Fiction.

Author Lemony Snicket warns readers that this tale "begins with the Baudelaire orphans traveling along this most displeasing road, and that from this moment on, the story only gets worse." In a series of misadventures, Violet, Klaus, and Sunny escape from their evil guardian, Count Olaf, and seek haven with Uncle Monty, a fun-loving herpetologist who houses his collection in "the Reptile Room." Here they are introduced to the Dissonant Toad, the Inky Newt, and the Irascible Python, as well as the Incredibly Deadly Viper. While working with Uncle Monty to prepare for a snake-collecting expedition to Peru, mysterious events transpire. This is a humorous tale of mystery in which Snicket inserts his own commentary on the actions and language of the characters. This is the second book in the Unfortunate Events series. Other titles include, *The Bad Beginning, The Austere Academy,* and *The Miserable Mill.*

15.56 Springer, Nancy. **Secret Star.** Philomel, 1997. 144 pp. ISBN 0399230289. Fiction.

Tess does not remember anything that happened to her before her tenth birthday, but it really doesn't bother her. She lives with her Daddy, who is in a wheel chair, in a cement-block house on the outskirts of town. She does not know her birth father, but the man she calls Daddy has been a real father to her. Things are getting bad for Tess and her Daddy, though, without electricity or running water. Now that their food is running out, Tess wants to quit school and get a job, but Daddy won't let her. One day when she is walking home from school, a young man named Kamo stops her. Kamo believes that he is Tess' half brother because they share the same unusual name. Tess wants nothing to do with this tough-looking stranger, but gradually, Kamo insinuates himself into their household. Soon the two are friends. Tess still firmly believes that Kamo isn't her half brother, but she is drawn to him and decides to help if she can. Perhaps the answer to his problems is in the strange dreams she has been having?

15.57 Springer, Nancy. **Sky Rider.** Morrow, 1999. 117 pp. ISBN 0380976048. Fiction.

Fourteen-year-old Dusty hasn't lived without pain for the past two years—not since her mom died, her dad started drinking, and she survived a wreck that caused a serious back injury. Now she and her dad have decided that they must euthanize her beloved horse, Tazz. The night before Tazz is to be euthanized, a mysterious young man appears, somehow cures the lame horse, and rides him into the night. The next day, Dusty discovers a sixteen-year-old boy was killed on their property in a strange accident. Dusty realizes what she saw the night before was the unsettled spirit of the boy. The spirit has discovered who caused his death, and he has come to take his revenge on Dusty's dad. But Dusty finally comes to understand what cures pain—hers, Tazz's, her dad's, and even the spirit's. She just wonders if she'll have the courage to do what must be done.

15.58 Stevenson, James. **The Unprotected Witness.** Greenwillow, 1997. 170 pp. ISBN 0866151337. Fiction.

In this sequel to *The Bones in the Cliff*, Pete and his friend Rootie are still on the run. After Pete's father is killed, they go to stay with Rootie's grandmother. One day a man comes to the door. He says he is from the Witness Protection Program, and that his follow-up division is checking to make sure that Pete and Rootie are doing all right after the death of Pete's father, who was in the program. Everyone soon forgets about the incident, but strange things begin happening. Pete eventually calls the Witness Protection Program and discovers there is no follow-up division. He discovers that there are listening devices planted all over the house. Soon he finds out that there are people after the treasure that his father was hiding, and they believe Pete and Rootie can lead them to it. These people will stop at nothing to get what they want—not even murder.

15.59 Stine, R. L. **Nightmare Hour.** HarperCollins, 1999. 148 pp. ISBN 0060286881. Fiction.

How would you feel if your mother bought an old country inn, complete with a rather interesting guest who claims he is a werewolf? How would you like to visit a secluded pumpkin patch on Halloween night, where the faces on the pumpkin are a little too familiar? What would you do if you discovered a way to see into the past and the future? Could you escape a ghost who is after your skin? Stine shares ten new and terrifying tales of horror, guaranteed to chill your bones. For the first time, Stine also reveals the stories behind the stories by explaining how they came into being. Keep a flashlight handy, just in case the lights go out while you are reading this riveting collection.

15.60 Vande Velde, Vivian. **Never Trust a Dead Man.** Harcourt, 1999, 194 pp. ISBN 0152018999. Fiction.

Sound advice: never trust a dead man—even during medieval times. It is advice that young Selwyn is about to learn firsthand. In the space of one week, the love of Selwyn's life is betrothed to Farold. When Farold is found stabbed to death with Selwyn's knife, there is no need for a trial. The people of the village take Selwyn to the burial chamber along with Farold. He is to be buried alive for his murderous deed. Selwyn is rescued by an old witch who promises Selwyn help in exchange for Selwyn's service to her. In order to prove his innocence, Selwyn must travel back to his village. Accompanied by Farold, newly resurrected and in the body of a bat, Selwyn sets off to find the real murderer.

15.61 Werlin, Nancy. **The Killer's Cousin.** Delacorte, 1998. 229 pp. ISBN 0385325606. Fiction.

David Yaffe, age seventeen, has just been acquitted of murdering his girlfriend. Anxious for a fresh start, David's parents send him off to complete his senior year of high school. He will stay with his Aunt Julia, Uncle Vic, and his eleven-year-old cousin Lily. The cold receptions he receives from his aunt and uncle, and the mysterious and hostile behavior of Lily, make David's adjustment difficult. His problems are compounded by the fact that he will be living in the apartment where Julia and Vic's daughter, Kathy, committed suicide a few years ago. David soon comes to realize that *he* may be the killer's cousin.

15.62 Zach, Cheryl. **Dear Diary: Secret Admirer.** Berkley, 1999. 184 pp. ISBN 0425171140. Fiction.

Brittany writes in her diary, "Dear Prince Charming, Are you out there, somewhere?" Her steady boyfriend, Nate, just isn't exciting or charming enough for her. Then Brittany meets Randall on the Internet, and he charms the tenth-grade girl with romantic online messages. He even sends her flowers at school. Refusing to listen to the warnings of her friends, Brittany agrees to meet Randall alone in the park. If Nate hadn't arrived in time to help Brittany escape from Randall's sexual advances, she would have been another one of the missing or dead teenagers reported on the evening news. Instead, a now much wiser Brittany presses charges. Together, she and Nate arrive at the courthouse to testify against this Internet stalker.

15.63 Zindel, Paul. **Rats.** Hyperion, 1999. 176 pp. ISBN 078682820X. Fiction.

Here is another chilling story from one of the masters of horror and suspense. The city has been gradually paving over a garbage dump, and the rats that populate this particular landfill have begun to act more and more aggressively. First, they attack a man at the landfill. Now the rats are fleeing the dump, and heading toward the heart of the city. Suddenly, rats are popping up through the plumbing and appearing in sinks, bathtubs, pools, and spas. They are bent on revenge, and there seems to be little anyone can do to stop them.

16 Myths, Legends, Superstitions, and Tales

"The two basic stories of all time are Cinderella and Jack the Giant Killer—the charm of women and the courage of men."

F. Scott Fitzgerald

16.1 Andersen, Hans Christian. **The Little Mermaid and Other Fairy Tales.** Collected by Neil Philip. Illustrated by Isabell Brent. Viking, 1998. 139 pp. ISBN 0670878405. Fiction.

In this collection of seventeen of Andersen's tales, you will find such favorites as "The Emperor's New Clothes," "The Little Mermaid," and "The Steadfast Tin Soldier," and discover new tales like "The Goblin at the Grocer's," "Five Peas from the Same Pod," and "The Flying Trunk." You will also discover more about Andersen—sometimes called the father of modern fantasy—through Neil Philip's fascinating introduction. Philip not only explains how Andersen's boyhood visits to the pauper hospital and asylum in Odense, Denmark, affected his later writings, but also discusses the interesting theory that Andersen was in fact the illegitimate son of King Christian VIII and Countess Elise Ahlefeldt-Laurvig.

16.2 Beneduce, Ann Keay. **Jack and the Beanstalk.** Illustrated by Gennady Spirin. Philomel, 1999. 32 pp. ISBN 03992311188. Fiction.

This magical tale comes alive in this beautiful picture book. This is the story of a poor, hungry boy who trades his family's only cow for some beans that magically sprout into vines. The vines carry him through the clouds to a giant's house, where the boy must outwit the giant three times to recover his family's gold coins, golden-egg laying hen, and magical harp. Details often not included in other variations (the Good Fairy who explains to Jack why the beanstalk grew, an explanation of what really happened to Jack's long dead father, and a history of the Jack tales) make this particular edition a must for anyone who is a fan of folklore—or giants.

16.3 Bryan, Ashley. **African Tales, Uh-Huh.** Atheneum, 1998. 198 pp. ISBN 068982076. Fiction.

Fourteen of Bryan's favorite African folktales are retold and illustrated in this collection, which includes some of the tales he has told in his other books. Tales such as "Hen and Frog," "Why Bush Cow and Elephant Are Bad Friends," and "Why Frog and Snake Never Play Together" teach us about the habits of our animal friends, while teaching us truths about relationships of all kinds. Illustrated with Ashley Bryan's woodcuts, and filled with wonderful rhythms, these stories are designed for reading aloud, especially with drums beating in the background, "Pum-Pum."

16.4 Cadnum, Michael. **In a Dark Wood.** Orchard, 1998. 246 pp. ISBN 0531300714. Fiction.

We know a great deal of Robin Hood, but what of Geoffrey, the Sheriff of Nottingham? Geoffrey is tangled in the dark wood of his own mind as he wrestles with the contradictions in his life. He is married to Lady Eleanor, yet he loves the Abbess. He must punish thieves, yet he abhors the sight of torture and death. Sworn to uphold the laws of the land and to collect taxes for the King, Geoffrey is torn between his loyalty to the throne and his personal feelings as he encounters Robin Hood, the "scourge of the highway." What happens when opposing men meet face to face? Enter the dark wood with Geoffrey as he is captured by Robin Hood's fellows, and learns of life on the other side of the law.

16.5 Collis, Harry. **101 American Superstitions: Understanding Language and Culture through Popular Superstitions.** NTC, 1997. 144 pp. ISBN 0844255998. Fiction.

Don't walk under a ladder. Eat an apple, and then spit the seeds into your palm; turn your palm upside down, and the number of seeds that stick are the number of children you'll have. Put a horseshoe above your door pointing up, so all your good luck will stay. These superstitions and many others are recounted in this book, which not only includes sayings that will make you laugh, but also gives you insight into this country's culture, language, and beliefs.

16.6 Craughwell, Thomas J. **Alligators in the Sewer and 222 Other Urban Legends.** Black Dog / Leventhal, 1999. 280 pp. ISBN 157912061X. Fiction.

Urban legends—those "highly captivating and plausible, but mainly fictional, oral narratives that are widely told as true stories"—usually begin, "A friend of a friend told me that. . . ." Generally passed by word of mouth (or, today, via e-mail), these legends are as much fun to tell as they are to hear. You've probably heard the one about how New York's sewers are filled with alligators, or how the woman from the United States rescued a dirty, hungry, abandoned little Chihuahua puppy while on a day trip to Tijuana, Mexico, only to take him to a vet and discover she had rescued a rat. These tales and over two hundred more are included in this collection. So sit back, read, and be prepared to say, "Ah, I thought that was true!"

16.7 Crossley-Holland, Kevin. **The World of King Arthur and His Court: People, Places, Legend, and Lore.** Illustrated by Peter Malone. Dutton Children's Books, 1998. 125 pp. ISBN 0525461671. Fiction.

Since the twelfth century, when Geoffrey of Monmouth first wrote of the amazing King Arthur, people have been attracted to this part hero, part warrior, and part king. In 1470, William Caxton published Sir Thomas Malory's collection of tales about the king known as Le Morte d'Arthur. Today, people continue to speculate about Arthur, Merlin, and the lore surrounding them both. This book provides answers about Arthur's existence, his famous sword Excalibur, his terrible son Mordred, the Knights of the Round Table, and his relationships with Guinevere and Lancelot. With easy-to-read prose and simple illustrations, this text takes you into King Arthur's world.

16.8 DeSpain, Pleasant. **The Emerald Lizard: Fifteen Latin American Tales to Tell.** Translationed by Mario Lamo-Jimenez. Illustrated by Don Bell. August House, 1999. 183 pp. ISBN 0874835526. Fiction.

While on a trip through Latin America, author Pleasant DeSpain purchases a handwoven *bolsa* (shoulder bag) from an elderly Huichol Indian. DeSpain decides that the *bolsa* will hold the stories he collects on his journeys. Into the bolsa he places the story of an old priest, who holds a wriggling lizard to his heart and transforms the creature into a shining emerald with the power to save a life. He adds the tale of a young man who has been forbidden to speak to his eternal love. He transforms himself into a crocodile, and braves a river whirlpool to be near the woman he loves. These are but a few of the fifteen Latin American folktales, myths, and legends contained in this anthology. Each story is presented both in English and Spanish. In the afterword, DeSpain includes notes about the origin of the tales, as well as information about related stories.

16.9 Donoghue, Emma. **Kissing the Witch: Old Tales in New Skins.** HarperCollins, 1997. ISBN 0060275758. Fiction.

Author Emma Donoghue transforms the tales of childhood and weaves together the stories of Cinderella, Snow White, Hansel and Gretel, and others into a tapestry of interconnected lives and events. New skins are put on old tales as Cinderella chooses the fairy godmother over the prince, Snow White reconsiders her relationship with her stepmother, and Hansel and Gretel come to different conclusions about the woman in the gingerbread house. This collection of tales begins with the words of Cinderella, who says, "I heard a knocking in my skull, and kept running to the door, but there was never anyone there. The days passed like dust brushed from my fingers." The images evoked by the words and ideas in these refashioned fairy tales will compel readers to brush off the dust from their old childhood collections of fairy tales and open the door to new interpretations of these classic stories.

16.10 Galloway, Priscilla. **Snake Dreamer.** Delacorte, 1998. 240 pp. ISBN 038532264X. Fiction.

Snakes haunt the dreams of sixteen-year-old Dusa. In fact, her dreams have become increasingly terrifying over the past few months. She thrashes in her sleep, and is a danger to herself and her mother. The doctors are all puzzled; they can find nothing wrong with Dusa. One night, as Dusa and her mother watch a documentary on television, they learn about the Gordon sisters, two psychologists from Greece who have had success treating Dusa's ailment. Reluctantly, Dusa's mother allows her to travel to Greece with the doctors. Once there, Dusa begins to understand that the Gordons are not what they appear to be, and that they have sinister plans for her.

16.11 Haddix, Margaret Peterson. **Just Ella.** Simon & Schuster, 1999. 185 pp. ISBN 0689821867. Fiction.

Isn't her story supposed to end with, "They lived happily ever after," Ella wonders? It does seem to her that life in the palace is anything by happy as she awaits her marriage to Prince Charming. Ella resents the fact that her behavior is constantly corrected by the parade of tutors and others, who explain how she must behave if she is to become the princess. Even Charm seems less desirable now that their marriage is drawing near. When Ella confesses to Charm that she is no longer in love with him, he orders her imprisoned. Ella just might be able to escape, but to what?

16.12 Irving, Washington. **Rip Van Winkle.** Illustrated by Will Moses. Philomel, 1999. Unpaged. ISBN 0399231528. Fiction.

Rip Van Winkle, a somewhat lazy but highly likable fellow who avoided working despite his wife's nagging, spent most of his time playing with children and visiting with neighbors. One day, while on a long walk in the Catskill Mountains, he encounters a strange fellow who takes him higher and deeper into the mountains. Finally, they come to an area filled with oddly dressed men. Rip serves them from a keg he has been carrying for his companion, and then helps himself to some of the drink. Soon overpowered by the intoxicating drink, he falls asleep, only to awaken twenty years later. Read this delightful illustrated version of the classic legend to learn what happens when Rip returns to his village.

16.13 Jaffe, Nina, and Steve Zeitlin. **The Cow of No Color: Riddle Stories and Justice Tales from around the World.** Illustrated by Whitney Sherman. Henry Holt, 1998. 162 pp. ISBN 0805037365. Fiction.

A wise old king decided it was time to divide his land equally between his two sons. The older son was a great warrior, but very selfish. The younger son was kind and gentle. The king asked the older son to go through the land and decide how it could be divided fairly with his younger brother. Did the king make a wise choice? Another king from Ghana was jealous of a wise woman named Nunyala. "Bring me a cow of no color in three days' time or you will be executed," said the king. Nunyala thought about her dilemma, and sent a message to the king that saved her life. What could she have said? In this collection of stories that revolve around fairness and justice, the authors invite you to solve the dilemma, and to test your answer against the one in the tale.

16.14 Krishnaswami, Uma, reteller. **Shower of Gold: Girls and Women in the Stories of India.** Linnet, 1999. 125 pp. ISBN 0208024840. Fiction.

This collection of eighteen traditional folktales from the Indian subcontinent—which include Hindu mythology and Buddhist tales, fables, and legends based on the lives of real women—feature heroines who are faced with dilemmas that test their inner strength and beliefs. In contrast to most traditional European stories in which the heroine ends up living happily ever after in the castle with the handsome prince, the women in these stories often reap their rewards through spiritual gains and enlightenment. Included are stories of reincarnation, tales of powerful and magical Hindu goddesses, and a Romeo and Juliet story from fifteenth-century India. In her introduction, Krishnaswami describes themes, cultural traditions, and women's roles found in the stories, and she provides informative notes at the end of each tale that give each story's context and source. This multilayered book is a great resource for the folklore of India.

16.15 Napoli, Donna Jo. **Crazy Jack.** Delacorte, 1999. 135 pp. ISBN 0385326270. Fiction.

How would you react if the young man you have known and loved since you were both children suddenly started doing crazy things? Things like planting magic seeds, and then claiming he could climb the stalks of his giant plants and enter a magical kingdom? Flora, the young woman who has been promised to Jack since childhood, begins to fear the young man she once thought she loved. Who could possibly believe the incredible tales of treasure and danger Jack spins? Perhaps Flora should find someone else to marry. This retelling of the traditional story of "Jack and the Beanstalk" gives an interesting alternative to the story we all know and love from childhood.

16.16 Napoli, Donna Jo. **Sirena.** Scholastic, 1998. 210 pp. ISBN 0590383884. Fiction.

Sirena, like her sister sirens, must be loved by a mortal man in order to ensure her own immortality. The sirens use their haunting songs to lure unsuspecting sailors to their deaths, however, and Sirena does not want to cause injury to another person. She isolates herself from the rest of the sirens, believing that a life of solitude is her destiny. When a shipwrecked sailor lies dying on a nearby shore, Sirena feels compelled to save him, but at what cost to them both?

16.17 Napoli, Donna Jo, and Richard Tchen. **Spinners.** Dutton, 1999. 197 pp. ISBN 0525460659. Fiction.

Long ago, two spinners lived in the same village. They fell in love, and planned to be married. In an effort to prove his worth to his fiancée's father, one spinner makes a fatal error that causes him to be crippled. He is abandoned by the one he loves, as well as by the rest of the people in the community, who find his deformity repulsive. He flees his village and searches for acceptance across the kingdom. When he comes to the rescue of a young woman trapped in a room full of straw, the old spinner believes his search for happiness may be over. This retelling of the childhood tale of Rumplestiltskin is full of romance and magic.

16.18 Olson, Arielle North, and Howard Schwartz, retellers. **Ask the Bones: Scary Stories from around the World.** Illustrated by David Linn. Viking, 1999. 145 pp. ISBN 0670875813. Fiction.

When the sun goes down, all over the world human imaginations give way to the mysterious, the unexplainable, and the supernatural. Do you believe in witches who eat foolish people that come to their houses, or in hideous skeletons that appear in the night with long bony fingers ready to close around your throat? These ghastly and ghostly folktales from around the world include pirate spirits that take grisly revenge on those who hunt for their buried treasure, a young man who discovers his aunt is really a serpent, and a druggist whose possession of a pickled mermaid wreaks havoc and destruction on the town of Charleston. If you dare to read these stories after dark, just remember to check in the closet and under your bed. You never know what might be lurking there.

16.19 Philip, Neil. **Myths and Legends: The World's Most Enduring Myths and Legends Explored and Explained.** Dorling Kindersley, 1999. 128 pp. ISBN 0789441179. Fiction.

The gods and goddesses of Olympus remain a topic of interest thousands of years after their stories were first told. Epic poems about heroes of the distant past still resonate for today's readers.

How did these stories come into being? Why are we still fascinated by Zeus, Hera, Psyche, and the other immortals? Are there still lessons to be learned from the adventures of Gilgamesh and Odysseus? Central to every culture, myths and legends reveal much about the people who created the stories.

16.20 Press, Petra. **Great Heroes of Mythology**. Metro, 1997. 176 pp. ISBN 1567994334. Nonfiction.

Read about the heroes of Greek, Egyptian, Middle Eastern, Scandinavian, African, North and South American, Chinese, Indian, and Australian mythology. As you read these thrilling tales from around the world, you'll quickly see the common elements—heroes' quests that involve dangerous travels, and deathly fights against seemingly unbeatable enemies. Travel to Africa to meet Anansi, to Greece to find Theseus, to China to encounter Eyebrows Twelve Inches Apart, and home to North America to read of The Invisible Being Gloscap. Arranged by country of origin, the stories in this book offer you a global perspective on the cultures and beliefs of civilizations throughout the world. Illustrations representing each country and an index of heroes make this book particularly attractive and instructive.

16.21 Scieszka, Jon. **Squids Will Be Squids: Fresh Morals, Beastly Fables.** Illustrated by Lane Smith. Viking, 1998. ISBN 067088135X. Fiction.

Open this book and prepare to laugh as you read the Aesop-like fables that Scieszka and Smith have created. Following the classic Aesop fable design—brief tales in which animals or elements of nature face conflicts and learn a moral—these two modern fabulists offer a new twist with adages such as, "You should always tell the truth. But if your mom is out having the hair taken off her lip, you might want to forget a few of the details," and "There are plenty of things to say to calm a hopping mad grasshopper mom. 'I don't know' is not one of them."

16.22 Sogabe, Aki, reteller. **Aesop's Fox.** Illustrated by Aki Sogabe. Browndeer / Harcourt Brace, 1999. Unpaged. ISBN 0152016716. Fiction.

This illustrated storybook tells the classic story of the fox who spends a day learning many lessons as he searches for food.

Beginning with the rooster that he first catches through flattery and then loses through trickery, Fox learns to "think before you speak," to "never believe in flattery," that "the best don't need to boast," and that "no matter how hard you try, you can't hide from bravery." The paper-cut illustrations help bring Aesop's wisdom-filled fable to life. Readers will enjoy hunting for objects from other Aesop's fables in these intricate illustrations.

16.23 Tomlinson, Theresa. **Child of May.** Orchard, 1998. 120 pp. ISBN 0531301184. Fiction.

In this sequel to *The Forestwife,* Magda becomes fed up with her life in Barnsdale Forest, where she lives with Marian, the Forest-wife who practices the healing arts on the forest folk. Magda, trained in archery and fighting, longs to go adventuring with her father John and the "Hooded One." She gets her chance when the Sheriff of Nottingham orders his evil squire to imprison Lady Matilda and her daughter after the daughter refuses to marry the man the Sheriff chooses for her. Along with Robert (Robin Hood), her father (Little John), and their outlaw band, Magda sets out to save the two women from a certain death. When an unexpected turn of events puts Magda at the forefront of the rescue, her skill as an archer is put to the test.

16.24 Vinge, Joan D. **The Random House Book of Greek Myths.** Illustrated by Oren Sherman. Random House, 1999. 152 pp. ISBN 0679823778. Fiction.

This easy-to-read book of Greek mythology offers a wonderful look at the major myths of this ancient civilization. The first part of the book introduces readers to the major Greek gods, while the second part is filled with myths such as "Perseus and Medusa," "Daedalus and Icarus," "Pandora's Jar," "The Great Flood," and "Eros and Psyche." You'll enjoy these timeless stories of drama, conflict, love, and adventure, as well as the beautiful illustrations by Sherman.

16.25 Wilkinson, Philip. **Illustrated Dictionary of Mythology.** Dorling Kindersley, 1998. 128 pp. ISBN 078943413X. Nonfiction.

This comprehensive guide to mythology is divided into nine sections, with each section focusing on the myths of a particular civilization or region of the world. The book covers Western Asia,

Ancient Egypt, India, China and Japan, the Classical World, Northern and Eastern Europe, the Americas, Africa, and Australasia and Oceania, and allows readers to discover similar myths across cultures, including creation myths, fire myths, and fall of humans myths. Learn about the Sphinx, see pictures of Hindu gods and heroes, or read about the tasks of the Finnish Hercules Lemminkainen. Photographs of ancient artifacts and drawings of ancient mythological characters make this book as fascinating to look at as it is to read.

16.26 Wood, Nancy, editor. **The Serpent's Tongue: Prose, Poetry, and Art of the New Mexico Pueblos.** Dutton, 1997. 230 pp. ISBN 0525455140. Fiction.

This important anthology chronicles more than five hundred years of one of North America's oldest and most enduring native cultures: the Pueblo. The collection includes more than one hundred selections—ranging from poetry to historical narratives—written by noted Native American authors and artists such as Simon J. Ortiz, Leslie Marmon Silko, and Pablita Velarde. The literary selections are enhanced by seventy-five works of art that together show us the life, ceremonies, symbols, and cultural legacy of this ancient civilization of the Southwest. Whether reading the tale of how the Old Coyote outwitted himself, looking at a stunning photograph of Tsle-ka (Douglas Spruce Leaf), or reading the recipe for Taos Beaver Tail Roast ("Broil tails over hot fire . . . until rough hide peels off easily."), you'll find yourself moved by the lives of the Pueblo.

17 Physical and Mental Health

"Reading is to the mind what exercise is to the body. It is wholesome and bracing for the mind to have its faculties kept on the stretch."

Augustus Hare

17.1 Altman, Linda Jacobs. **Plague and Pestilence: A History of Infectious Diseases.** Enslow, 1998. 128 pp. ISBN 0894909576. Nonfiction.

From the Black Death to the Ebola virus, the human population has been decimated by epidemics that spread before the disease itself was understood or identified. The introduction of germs and viruses into populations that have never been exposed to them can have devastating effects. This book chronicles how diseases have come to be more readily identified, and what modern science can do to prevent future epidemics.

17.2 Clayton, Lawrence. **Alcohol Drug Dangers.** Enslow, 1999. 64 pp. ISBN 0766011593. Nonfiction.

Alcohol is one of the few legal nonmedicinal drugs in the United States, making it an easy substance for teens to abuse. Unfortunately, alcohol adversely affects many human organs. People who abuse alcohol can suffer liver or heart muscle damage, and may develop digestive problems. An estimated three million teens abuse alcohol. This book will give you plenty of reasons to avoid using this dangerous drug.

17.3 Clayton, Lawrence. **Diet Pill Drug Dangers.** Enslow, 1999. 64 pp. ISBN 0766011585. Nonfiction.

Teens face magazine ads, television shows, movies, and billboards everyday that show them society's ideal of beauty. One thing they see time and time again is that being thin is part of being beautiful. In an effort to become like that thin model in the magazines or television ads, more and more preteens and teens are turning to diet pills. This straightforward and very informative book talks about the dangers of diet pills, as well as eating disorders such as bulimia, anorexia, and compulsive overeating.

Comments from girls who have used diet pills or who suffer from eating disorders, as well as warning signs that indicate an eating or drug problem, make this book valuable reading for teens.

17.4 Curran, Christine Perdan. **Sexually Transmitted Diseases.** Enslow, 1998. 128 pp. ISBN 0766010503. Nonfiction.

There are more than twenty documented sexually transmitted diseases, yet most Americans cannot name a single one. Young adults fifteen to twenty-four years of age are at highest risk to contract gonorrhea, which can cause serious complications if not treated. One of the biggest problems with all sexually transmitted diseases is that no one likes to talk about them, and many affected individuals never seek treatment. This useful book includes a question-and-answer section, glossary, and addresses and telephone numbers to write or call for more information. This book is one of the books in the Diseases and People series. Other titles include *AIDS, Allergies, Anorexia and Bulimia, Asthma, Chickenpox and Shingles, Common Cold and Flu, Depression, Diabetes, Epilepsy, Heart Disease, Hepatitis, Lyme Disease, Measles and Rubella, Mononucleosis, Rabies, Sickle Cell Anemia,* and *Tuberculosis.*

17.5 Dominic, Andie. **Needles.** Scribner, 1998. 224 pp. ISBN 0684842327. Nonfiction.

Needles have been a part of Andie's life for as long as she can recall. Her older sister Denise, who has diabetes, uses needles to inject herself with insulin daily. Andie, fascinated by the syringes and needles, creates elaborate childhood games about needles and diabetes. The games become frightfully real when, at age nine, Andie is herself diagnosed with juvenile onset diabetes. Now it is a necessity for Andie to handle needles daily. She watches as her older sister's reckless lifestyle leads to her death at age thirty-three. Now Andie fears that the same fate awaits her. This nonfiction account of how diabetes affects one family is as compelling as it is informative.

17.6 Farrell, Jeanett. **Invisible Enemies: Stories of Infectious Disease.** Farrar, Straus and Giroux, 1998. 240 pp. ISBN 0374336377. Nonfiction.

Included in this book are nonfiction accounts of seven diseases that have altered human history: smallpox, leprosy, plague, tuberculosis, malaria, cholera, and AIDS. Rich stories, gruesome details, firsthand accounts, and archival documents help to demonstrate how medical discoveries helped to fight dangerous microbes and develop cures. Biology and history combine to inform the reader about past and present public health concerns. The chapter on AIDS provides information about causes and prevention.

17.7 Ferber, Elizabeth. **Diabetes.** Millbrook, 1996. 96 pp. ISBN 1562946552. Nonfiction.

This book is specifically written for teens with diabetes. The book is easy to read, and contains information about the disease in general as well as information about support groups and organizations for those with diabetes. A bibliography, glossary, and index also are included.

17.8 Giblin, James Cross. **When Plague Strikes: The Black Death, Smallpox, AIDS.** HarperTrophy / HarperCollins, 1997. 212 pp. ISBN 0064461955. Nonfiction.

The three deadliest epidemics in human history are the Black Death, smallpox, and AIDS. The Black Death—also known as the bubonic plague—ravaged the human population along the coast of the Black Sea in early 1347. Smallpox was probably a common disease among people as early as 1500 B.C.E. AIDS first surfaced in Zaire, Africa, sometime in the mid-1970s. Centuries apart, these diseases had similar social, political, and cultural ramifications. Read about the history of these epidemics in this fascinating book that not only informs you about the diseases themselves, but also teaches you about facing life in the midst of death.

17.9 Jukes, Mavis. **It's a Girl Thing: How to Stay Healthy, Safe, and in Charge.** Knopf, 1996. 136 pp. ISBN 0679873929. Nonfiction.

This frank explanation of the changes that occur in the female body during puberty should answer any and all questions you might be too embarrassed to ask anyone else. Eating right, taking proper care of your body, and making intelligent choices are all important. This sometimes humorous and always helpful book discusses what to eat, how to care for your skin, and how to stay healthy. And, boys, don't feel left out. Jukes provides information on the changes occurring in your life as well!

17.10 Kolata, Gina Bari. **Flu: The Story of the Great Influenza Pandemic of 1918 and the Search for the Virus That Caused It.** Farrar, Straus and Giroux, 1999. 330 pp. ISBN 0374157065. Nonfiction.

In 1918 and 1919, an influenza virus swept the world, killing over forty million people. This pandemic, which occurred right after World War I, killed more people than the war. What gave this virus its potency? How did it spread so far so quickly? What might a similar virus do today? Pulling from news reports, letters, and interviews, Kolata reconstructs what happened during that one-year period when the influenza virus ruled the world.

17.11 LeVert, Marianne. **AIDS: A Handbook for the Future.** Millbrook, 1996. 160 pages. ISBN 1562946609. Nonfiction.

This handbook provides an overview of AIDS, including the history of the disease, how the AIDS virus works in the body, how HIV is transmitted, how to reduce the risk of infection, the specific threat AIDS poses to teens, and the available testing and treatment options. A glossary, list of sources for more information, and index make this a useful volume.

17.12 Lindsay, Jeanne Warren. **Your Baby's First Year: A Guide for Teenage Parents.** Morning Glory, 1998. 220 pp. ISBN 1885356331. Nonfiction.

This book offers valuable information on caring for an infant, specifically targeted at teen parents, in an easy-to-read format. Issues such as multigenerational living, education, and others are covered as well. This book is part of the Teen Parenting series, which includes other books on discipline and dealing with toddlers.

17.13 Majure, Janet. **AIDS.** Enslow, 1998. 128 pp. ISBN 0766011828. Nonfiction.

Acquired immune deficiency syndrome or AIDS is a disease that kills an estimated 250,000 people per year. Teens are the second-fastest growing group of people in the United States infected with the AIDS virus, yet only a small portion of those exposed to the disease know they are infected. AIDS is a highly preventable disease. The more information you have about AIDS and HIV (the virus that causes AIDS), the better prepared you will be to avoid becoming infected. This thought-provoking book includes interviews with people whose lives have been affected by HIV and

AIDS, the history of the disease, and AIDS treatment and prevention. Part of a series titled Diseases and People, which includes books on epilepsy, anorexia, and sexually transmitted diseases.

17.14 McFarlane, Stewart. **The Complete Book of T'ai Chi.** Dorling Kindersley, 1997. 120 pp. ISBN 0789414767. Nonfiction.

This volume has it all, from the basic movements of t'ai chi to the benefits its followers claim. A general introduction to each sequence of movements is presented, accompanied by stop motion photographs and diagrams that will assist the beginner in learning how to make each movement properly.

17.15 Miller, Brandon Marie. **Just What the Doctor Ordered: The History of American Medicine.** Lerner, 1997. 88 pp. ISBN 082251737X. Nonfiction.

At one time in the United States, a simple cut on the hand could lead to a deadly infection, and being a hospital patient might have proven more dangerous than using herbal remedies to cure serious disease. The invention and discovery of antiseptic methods of caring for the ill, the development of antibiotics to treat common illnesses, and the blending of traditional knowledge with modern science has led to a much healthier population. From poultices to prescriptions, this book discusses how American medicine has developed and continues to evolve.

17.16 Monroe, Judy. **Antidepressants.** Enslow, 1997. 128 pp. ISBN 0894908480. Nonfiction.

This book goes beyond merely explaining the history and types of various drugs used to combat depression. It focuses on young people dealing with their own depressions, and examines some of the causes of depression as well. Far from being a state that a person can "snap out of," depression is a serious disorder that can be successfully treated. This book is part of the Drug Library series.

17.17 Monroe, Judy. **Inhalant Drug Dangers.** Enslow, 1999. 64 pp. ISBN 0766011534. Nonfiction.

The national Inhalant Prevention Coalition labels inhalant abuse the "silent epidemic." Inhalants are easily accessible, they act quickly, and—most importantly—their use is difficult to detect. One of every ten teens in the United States reports current or past use of inhalants. This short and easy-to-read book includes the personal stories of teens who have abused inhalants; interviews with abusers, parents, doctors, and others who work with substance abusers; and plenty of statistics about this growing problem. Other books in the Drug Dangers series discuss crack and cocaine, diet pills, steroids, speed and methamphetamines, and marijuana.

17.18   Moragne, Wendy. **Allergies.** Twenty First Century, 1999. 128 pp. ISBN 0761313591. Nonfiction.

Does your skin ooze? Do you get stomach pains after eating corn? Do you feel dizzy after being stung by an insect? If so, you may be one of the forty million Americans suffering from some type of allergy. But just what is an allergy and how can it be treated? Read this book for in-depth answers to the health issues that surround allergies. Learn what allergies are, what they aren't, what types of allergies (skin, food, drug, insect, plant, mold, etc.) exist, and—most importantly—how to live with them.

17.19   Quant, Mary. **Classic Make-Up and Beauty.** Photographs by Maureen Barrymore and Dave King. Dorling Kindersley, 1998. 120 pp. ISBN 0789432943. Nonfiction.

Lavish photographs and illustrations show you how to correctly apply makeup. The easy-to-follow steps also include beauty tips from some of the world's most beautiful models. Topics range from selecting the right colors, to caring for feet and hands, to dealing with cellulite.

17.20   Simpson, Carol, and Dwain Simpson. **Coping with Post-Traumatic Stress Disorder.** Rosen, 1997. 129 pp. ISBN 0823920801. Nonfiction.

Many people suffer traumatic experiences in their lives. The first part of this book describes the nature of post-traumatic stress disorder, and provides concrete examples of situations that might cause it. Part two explains treatments for the disorder, and includes suggestions for helping someone you know who is having trouble coping with a life-changing incident. This book is part of the Coping series.

17.21   Sivananda. **Yoga, Mind and Body.** Dorling Kindersley, 1998. 168 pp. ISBN 078943301X. Nonfiction.

What is yoga? Yoga is an integrated system of education for mind, body, and inner spirit. It originated in India thousands of years ago. Today, the universal nature of yoga teachings and practices make it just as popular as it was in the past. Easy-to-follow instructions and clear photographs provide a good introduction to anyone interested in yoga and its basic principles.

17.22 Stoppard, Miriam. **Healthy Weight Loss.** Dorling Kindersley, 1999. 96 pp. ISBN 0789437570. Nonfiction.

If you want to lose weight carefully, then check out this book. From the first chapter (which tells you what you need to know about losing weight before you start dieting) to the last chapter (which tells you how to eat healthy throughout your life), you'll find easy-to-follow suggestions, recipes, low-calorie diets, and exercises. This book is part of the DK Health Care series. Other books in this series include *Every Girl's Life Guide, Healthy Sex,* and *Healthy Pregnancy.*

17.23 Westheimer, Ruth K. **Dr. Ruth Talks to Kids: Where You Come from, How Your Body Changes, and What Sex Is All About.** Illustrated by Diane DeGroat. Aladdin, 1998. 96 pp. ISBN 0689820410. Nonfiction.

When you've got questions about your body and sex, Dr. Ruth has answers. Although this book is brief and simple, it may be just the right source for answers to your questions about your body. Beginning with a discussion on emotions and changing relationships with parents, Dr. Ruth then moves into frank discussions on the physical changes in boys' and girls' bodies that come with puberty, sexual attraction, contraception, and sexually transmitted diseases (STDs).

18 Poetry

"Poetry . . . arouses people and shapes their minds . . .
It is the golden treasury in which our values are preserved."

Nadezhda Mandelstam

18.1 Appelt, Kathi. **Just People and Paper / Pen / Poem: A Young Writer's Way to Begin.** Photographs by Ken Appelt. Absey, 1997. 91 pp. ISBN 1888842075.

This collection of poems examines how it feels to be in a new school, what it is like to find a friend in the most unlikely of places (the library), and how much it can hurt to be misunderstood by your parents. Black-and-white photographs accompany many of the poems, and the final third of the book is given over to exercises designed to help you write your own poetry.

18.2 Berry, James. **Everywhere Faces Everywhere.** Illustrated by Reynold Ruffins. Simon & Schuster, 1997. 96 pp. ISBN 0689809964.

In this collection of forty-six poems, Berry uses a variety of poetic forms—from free verse and haiku to ballad and proverb—to explore the themes of nature, cultural conflict, diversity, and love. These poems feature a multiracial cast of characters with faces that are "plum-blue to nutmeg-brown, melon-gold to peach pale." This distinguished Jamaican writer's poetry draws on both his childhood in the Caribbean and his adulthood in the United Kingdom. His wonderful use of metaphor and simile—rain is "the sea the sky throws" and "love is like roundness of a running wheel over a bumpy road or one simply smooth like steel"—draws the reader into the poems. These poems beg to be read aloud, again and again.

18.3 Bloom, Harold, editor. **The Best of the Best American Poetry, 1988–1997.** Scribner, 1998. 383 pp. ISBN 0684847795.

A celebration of the tenth anniversary of the Best American Poetry series, this collection includes seventy-five poems culled from previous editions. The poems are diverse in style, form, and images, and reflect a new generation of daring poetic voices. The anthology is introduced by critic Harold Bloom, and concludes with excerpts from the introductions to previous volumes in the series. Also included are notes and comments from contributors.

18.4   Bly, Robert, editor. **The Best American Poetry 1999.** Scribner, 1999. 223 pp. ISBN 0684860031.

This eleventh annual volume in the acclaimed series contains seventy-five poems by seventy-five different poets, chosen by guest editor Robert Bly, the current U.S. poet laureate. The work of established poets—such as Denise Levertov and Donald M. Hall—is interspersed with the works of a new generation of poets. The collection also includes contributors' notes, with comments by each poet about his or her poem in the anthology.

18.5   Brown, Fahamisha Patricia. **Performing the Word: African American Poetry as Vernacular Culture.** Rutgers University, 1999. 174 pp. ISBN 0813526329.

This book offers a critical analysis of African American poetry. It moves beyond the works of Gwendolyn Brooks, Rita Dove, and Langston Hughes to include the powerful works of many lesser known Black poets. In addition, the book discusses issues such as the oral nature of, didacticism of, and use of vernacular speech in African American poetry, as well as the way such poetry reflects African American traditions and heritage.

18.6   Carroll, Joyce A., and Eddie E. Wilson. **Poetry after Lunch.** Absey, 1997. 164 pp. ISBN 1888842032.

Anyone with an appetite for poetry will find much to devour in this collection, which is divided into sections that range from Appetizers to Desserts. The themes of the poetry include both the familiar and the strange, and both classic and contemporary writers are represented.

18.7   Cofer, Judith Ortiz. **The Year of Our Revolution: New and Selected Stories and Poems.** Arte Publico, 1998. 128 pp. ISBN 1558852247.

This collection of poems, stories, myths, and essays is mainly about Puerto Rican girls growing up in America, specifically in a New Jersey barrio in the 1960s. Looking closely at the conflicts between Puerto Rican immigrant parents and their American-born children, this volume shows the tensions teens felt with their parents, a theme that teens from all cultures will understand.

18.8   Duffy, Carol Ann, editor. **Stopping for Death: Poems of Death and Loss.** Illustrated by Trisha Rafferty. Henry Holt, 1996. 144 pp. ISBN 0805047174.

Although this book is entirely about one topic—death—the poems in this collection reveal the range of feelings one might have when facing such a painful loss. Eighty poems, arranged alphabetically by poet, discuss a range of emotions from anger and fear to humor. Duffy includes both classic and contemporary poems, from Emily Dickinson's "Because I Could Not Stop for Death" and Dylan Thomas's "Do Not Go Gentle into that Good Night" to Audre Lorde's "Girlfriend."

18.9   Ecclesiastes. **To Every Thing There Is a Season.** Illustrated by Leo and Diane Dillon. Blue Sky / Scholastic, 1998. Unpaged. ISBN 0590478877.

The text of this book is taken from the King James Version of the Bible, Ecclesiastes 3:108 and 1:4. The poet Tennyson called Ecclesiastes "the greatest poem of ancient or modern times." These famous verses—which begin, "To every thing there is a season, / And a time to every purpose under the heaven," and conclude, "One generation passes away, and another generation comes: But the earth abides for ever"—are made more stunning by the artwork of Leo and Diane Dillon. These artists have created sixteen paintings that bring each verse to life. At the end of the book, read how they chose to illustrate each verse, and what each illustration represents.

18.10   Fletcher, Ralph. **Ordinary Things: Poems from a Walk in Early Spring.** Illustrated by Walter Lynn Krudop. Simon & Schuster, 1997. Unpaged. ISBN 0689810350.

Birch trees. A pond. Nests. The "monotonous chant" of frogs. Mailboxes that look like "old people dancing slowly cheek-to-cheek." Such ordinary things are among the topics Fletcher considers in this volume of thirty-three poems. Fletcher says that nature walks remind us to reconsider the ordinary in order to see how unique each thing really is. Walk carefully and look gently, he encourages, for "Each footstep is like a word / as it meets the blank page / followed by a pause / before the next one: / step, step, word . . ." Written in a journal-like fashion, with each poem only twelve to sixteen lines in length, Fletcher's book brings the natural world alive with descriptions that reveal that birds' nests are like "unpicked fruit / in branches bare / of any leaves," and that a garter snake's shedded skin is like "strips of cloudy cellophane / that let light shine through."

18.11 Fletcher, Ralph. **Relatively Speaking: Poems about Family.** Orchard, 1999. 42 pp. ISBN 0531301419.

This collection of poems takes you inside a home with a sixteen-year-old, an eleven-year-old, and a soon-to-be-born sister. Read about reunions and breakups, deaths and births, beach parties and hospital visits. Sneak a look inside the hearts and home of one family with poems such as "My Big Brother," which explains how a younger brother feels when his older brother is "sixteen / obsessed with friends, / girls, cars / lifting weights / and I'm nowhere on that list."

18.12 Glenn, Mel. **Foreign Exchange: A Mystery in Poems.** Morrow Junior Books, 1999. 159 pp. ISBN 0688164722.

Some of the students from Tower High School are participating in a unique exchange program. They will spend a week living with the families of teens who reside in a rural part of the state. Each group of teens has preconceived notions of what to expect from the other. The city kids believe their country counterparts will be hicks; the country kids assume the city kids will be gangsters. What neither group suspects is that one among them may be a killer. When beautiful Kristen is found dead, suspicions turn immediately to Kwame, the last person seen with her.

18.13 Glenn, Mel. **Jump Ball: A Basketball Season in Poems.** Lodestar / Dutton, 1997. 160 pp. ISBN 052567554X.

The Tower High School basketball team has had its best season ever. On the return trip from the championship game, the school bus swerves out of control on an icy road. In a series of poems, readers have the chance to meet the players, their coaches, teachers, parents, and friends. Interspersed are eyewitness accounts of the tragic accident, which will surely end the careers of some of the players. Readers are kept guessing as to who will survive this tragedy.

18.14 Hempel, Amy, and Jim Shepard, editors. **Unleashed: Poems by Writers' Dogs.** Three Rivers, 1999. 175 pp. ISBN 0609803794.

Just when you thought the only writers were human, Hempel and Shepard provide this delightful volume of poems penned (with a little help from their owners) by writers' dogs. These sometimes silly and sometimes poignant poems speak of things that concern dogs the most—playing, eating, the mysteries of life, and their owners! Great dog portraits help make this a treat any dog-lover will enjoy.

18.15 Herrera, Juan Felipe. **Laughing Out Loud, I Fly.** Illustrated by Karen Barbour. HarperCollins, 1998. 48 pp. ISBN 0060276045.

This slender volume offers twenty-two poems in English and Spanish. The rhythms are rollicking, even though some of the poems may seem nonsensical. The illustrations by Karen Barbour form a quiet and light-hearted backdrop for the text.

18.16 Hopkins, Lee Bennett, editor. **Lives: Poems about Famous Americans.** Illustrated by Leslie Staub. HarperCollins, 1999. 32 pp. ISBN 006027767X.

The fourteen poems in this collection highlight the contributions that sixteen important individuals made to this country. Read about Eleanor Roosevelt, Babe Ruth, Langston Hughes, Rosa Parks, John F. Kennedy, Martin Luther King Jr., Neil Armstrong, Thomas Edison, Walt Whitman, Harriet Tubman, Sacagawea, and Abraham Lincoln in poems written by well-known poets such as X. J. Kennedy, Nikki Grimes, Jane Yolen, and Lawrence Schimel. Through these poems, readers will learn about the historical, scientific, cultural, and artistic marks these powerful people made.

18.17 Janeczko, Paul. **How to Write Poetry.** Scholastic, 1999. 117 pp. ISBN 0590100777.

A well-known poet and anthologist shares his tips for writing poetry in this easy-to-read book. Keeping a journal is a good first step, and Janeczko suggests that writers begin by writing short, humorous poems before moving on to longer, more complex types of poetry. There are plenty of examples from some of the best classic and contemporary poets to help readers reach their goal. If you are looking for inspiration, you can turn to the books listed in the Something to Read section of each chapter as well.

18.18 Johnson, Angela. **The Other Side: Shorter Poems.** Orchard, 1998. 44 pp. ISBN 0531301141.

Angela Johnson—known for her novels *Toning the Sweep, Humming Whispers,* and *Songs of Faith,* as well as her illustrated storybooks such as *When I Am Old with You* and *Shoes Like Miss Alice's*—has written a book of poetry that provides a glimpse of her past growing up in Shorter, Alabama. Read about the land, the people, the culture, and the escapades of this talented writer in these poems, which not only tell you about the writer, but offer vivid images of the South.

18.19 Koch, Kenneth. **Making Your Own Days: The Pleasures of Reading and Writing Poetry.** Touchstone, 1998. 317 pp. ISBN 0684824388.

Koch, a poet and teacher, intends his book to "say some clean and interesting things about poetry." These things include the basic elements of poetry, illustrated with ample excerpts from classic and contemporary poems. The second part of the book is an anthology of ninety poems by poets from Homer to Gary Snyder, with a comment from Koch on each poem.

18.20 Meltzer, Milton. **Langston Hughes: An Illustrated Edition.** Illustrated by Stephen Alcorn. Millbrook, 1997. 240 pp. ISBN 0761302050.

Read some of the poems of Langston Hughes, and learn about his life as well, in this compelling biography by Meltzer. America's most renowned African American poet, Langston Hughes speaks to all through his eloquent, simple, and poignant poetry about freedom, the African American experience, and the lives and voices of African American people. This biography covers Hughes' life from 1901, when he was born in a small Missouri town, through his college days, the Harlem Renaissance, and his later life. When he was twenty-four years old, Hughes said, "You have to learn to be yourself, natural and undeceived as to who you are, calmly and surely you." Meltzer provides a look at how Hughes learned to be himself so that he could share with many his gift of words.

18.21 Moyers, Bill. **Fooling with Words: A Celebration of Poets and Their Craft.** Morrow, 1999. 230 pp. ISBN 0688173462.

Every two years, poets gather in Waterloo, New Jersey, for the Geraldine R. Dodge Poetry Festival, where they share their poems with fans from all over the country. Bill Moyers has often reported on the event, known as the "Woodstock of Poetry," through his television specials. In 1998, he not only recorded the poets' performances, but he also interviewed them. Those interviews are presented in this wonderful book, which take us inside the lives of the poets who attend this festival. Through this book, you'll learn more about poets such as Jane Hirschfield, Stanley Kunitz, Mark Doty, and Coleman Barks.

18.22 Nye, Naomi Shihab, editor. **This Same Sky: A Collection of Poems from around the World.** Aladdin Paperbacks, 1996. 224 pp. ISBN 0689806302.

Sixty-eight countries are represented in this volume of poetry, which includes the work of 129 poets. Universal emotions—happiness, loss, fear, anger, jealousy, love, joy—are explored in this multicultural look at the world through poetry. Through this volume, you'll learn more about people from other countries and continents, and discover that, although their voice may be different, the emotions they experience are the same.

18.23 Nye, Naomi Shihab, editor. **The Tree Is Older than You Are: A Bilingual Gathering of Poems and Stories from Mexico with Paintings by Mexican Artists.** Aladdin Paperbacks, 1998. 111 pp. ISBN 0689820879.

This anthology features 102 poems and stories by Mexican writers and artists, including Homero Aridjis, Rosario Castellanos, Rodolfo Morales, Octavio Paz, and Emilio Pacheco. The poems appear first in Spanish and then in English translations. Stories from the Mayan people, artwork interspersed throughout, and notes on artists and poets complete the anthology. These poems and stories, which focus on topics such as animals and nature, give you a close look at Mexican culture.

18.24 Nye, Naomi Shihab, editor. **What Have You Lost?** Photographs by Michael Nye. Greenwillow, 1999. 189 pp. ISBN 0688161847.

In the introduction to this thought-provoking anthology of poems that describe things that are lost, Nye writes, "Losing makes us miserable, startles us awake." Combining some well-known poets (Pat Mora, Lucille Clifton, William Stafford) with relatively unknown poets, Nye provides a collection of poems from around the world that offer poignant reflections on loss. Whether they consider little losses ("Is it in the terminal I left / the brown, rabbit-fur-lined gloves / made in Taiwan") or losses parents feel as they let go of little ones growing up ("He pulls me on, then runs ahead, / fearless, blameless, gone") or the loss that comes from death ("Today I miss you, you / and your big belly, the wake-the-dead snore, / your heart like a tea-cup"), all of the poems pull at your heart and make you appreciate all you've found before those things, too, are lost.

18.25 Philip, Neil, editor. **War and the Pity of War.** Illustrated by Michael McCurdy. Clarion, 1998. 96 pp. ISBN 0395849829.

From ancient times to today, the world has always known war. These poems from around the world describe the courage of soldiers, the horror of battle, the agony of loss, and the sacrifices of people caught in the midst of war. Poets include Walt Whitman, Alfred Lord Tennyson, Herman Melville, A. E. Housman, and William Butler Yeats. Translated poems from Russia, France, Poland, Vietnam, Japan, Africa, Greece, and Saudi Arabia make visible the universal emotions that accompany war. McCurdy's woodcut illustrations add to the somber mood of this book.

18.26 Pinksy, Robert, and Maggie Dietz, editors. **Americans' Favorite Poems.** Norton, 1999. 327 pp. ISBN 0393048209.

Robert Pinsky, the U.S. poet laureate in 1997, invited U.S. citizens to write to him and share their favorite poems. Thousands of people of all ages and from all walks of life responded. They wrote passionately about why poems written by their favorite poets— from Shakespeare and Chaucer to Gwendolyn Brooks and Allen Ginsberg—should be included in this anthology. This project— part of the bicentennial celebration of the Library of Congress and sponsored by the White House Millennium Council—provides a unique look at the people of the United States, their passions and beliefs, and their motivations and inspiration.

18.27 Rosenberg, Liz, editor. **The Invisible Ladder: An Anthology of Contemporary American Poems for Young Readers.** Henry Holt, 1996. 210 pp. ISBN 0805058361.

This poetry anthology not only offers poems by some of the United States' best twentieth century poets, but it also offers a look—quite literally—at the lives of the poets themselves. With photographs of the poets when they were children and comments from them about their work, the editor of this collection creates a link between poet and reader, childhood and adulthood, poetry and prose. The poets' childhood photos are endearing, their adult reflections are insightful, and their poetry is mesmerizing.

18.28 Sones, Sonya. **Stop Pretending: What Happened When My Big Sister Went Crazy.** HarperCollins, 1999. 232 pp. ISBN 0060283874.

This novel in blank verse tells the story of an incredibly confusing time in one teenage girl's life when her older sister has a nervous breakdown on Christmas Eve. It is soon apparent to the family that a stay in a psychiatric hospital is necessary for the mental and emotional health of her big sister. Going to the hospital to visit her sister is frightening; she does not look like the person the young girl has known all of her life. How can her own life be normal again if her sister never recovers? Will the young girl have the same experience as her sister one day?

19 References, Dictionaries, and How-to

"From the time that I can remember having any thoughts about anything, I recall that I had an intense longing to learn to read."

Booker T. Washington

19.1 Ash, Russell. **The Top 10 of Everything 1999.** Dorling Kindersley, 1999. 256 pp. ISBN 0789435233. Nonfiction.

Who has been on the cover of *People* magazine the most? What's the best selling book of all times? What's the most common cause of illness in the world? What is the highest grossing movie of all time? Which movie has the distinction of being the biggest money loser? Which country owns the most vehicles? Which breed of dog is considered to be the least intelligent? Find out answers to these questions and to 993 others (yes, there are one thousand lists in this edition!) as you look through this jam-packed edition of *The Top 10 of Everything.* New lists added for the first time are marked with stars, and anniversary lists tell you what was going on fifty, one hundred, or two hundred years ago. This is part of the best-selling Top 10 of Everything series, which is updated yearly.

19.2 Beyer, Thomas R., Jr. **501 English Verbs.** Barron's Educational Series, 1998. 552 pp. ISBN 0764103040. Nonfiction.

If you aren't sure what the past participle of the verb "lie" would be, or if you can't remember the perfect infinitive for "catch," then this is the book for you. This reference work presents verbs in alphabetical order from *accept* to *zero,* and provides active and passive voices, full conjugations, and sentence examples of phrasal verbs such as *buy off* and *write down.* This book is perfect for all students of English grammar, but may be especially useful for second-language learners.

19.3   Bykofsky, Sheree, and Paul Fargis, editors. **The Big Book of Life's Instructions.** Illustrated by Jessica Wolk-Stanley. Galahad, 1999. 496 pp. ISBN 1578660785.

Learn to tie-dye perfectly. Find out how acupressure works. Get your CD player hooked up properly to the receiver. Plan a great garage sale. Discover how to do these things plus hundreds and hundreds of other everyday tasks in this handy, easy-to-read how-to book.

19.4   Cisnero, Isabel. **Spanish in Three Months.** Dorling Kindersley, 1998. 256 pp. ISBN 0789432287. Nonfiction.

This handy guide begins with the basics of foreign language study, such as grammatical rules, and then progresses to readings and conversations in Spanish. Included is a mini Spanish-English dictionary and pronunciation guides, which use English syllables to represent Spanish sounds. Also available in this series are books for learning French, German, and Russian.

19.5   **DK Illustrated Oxford Dictionary.** Dorling Kindersley and Oxford University, 1998. 1008 pp. ISBN 0789435578. Nonfiction.

Oxford University Press, long known for its production of outstanding dictionaries, teamed up with the equally well-respected publisher of nonfiction texts, Dorling Kindersley, to produce an illustrated dictionary. Drawing both on DK's ability to make complex concepts clear through the stunning use of photographs, drawings, and illustrations and on Oxford's talents at capturing the subtleties of the English language, this collaborative effort has raised the bar considerably on how a home or school dictionary ought to look and read. Open up this illustrated dictionary and you will learn about literally thousands of things, including covalent compounds, ospreys, postimpressionistic art, and zithers. The back of the dictionary includes a reference section with everything from a grammar handbook to a stargazer's chart.

19.6   Flexner, Stuart Berg, and Anne H. Souknanov. **Speaking Freely: A Guided Tour of American English from Plymouth Rock to Silicon Valley.** Oxford University, 1997. 472 pp. ISBN 019510692X. Nonfiction.

Who today doesn't know the phrase "dot com"? If you had said that in 1950, however, listeners would have shaken their heads and wondered what in the world you meant. Although we are certainly living at a time when language seems to change as quickly as new Internet companies pop up, the reality is that each time period in our history has its own language. This fascinating book offers you a look at the history of those languages in this country. Arranged by topics such as Pop Culture, Cyberspace: I Hear America Clicking, To Your Health, Trash and Garbage, and Outspace Space: The Final Frontier, you'll discover where words and phrases originated and how they are used today. Discover who first said, "The devil made me do it," "Just the facts, ma'am," and "Been there, done that," and see photographs of many of the folks who made particular terms and phrases popular.

19.7   Helm, Matthew L., and April Leigh Helm. **Genealogy Online for Dummies.** IDG Books Worldwide, 1999. 308 pp. ISBN 0769505432. Nonfiction.

Family history—it's not just about your grandparents anymore. Now, more than at any other time, more folks are spending time discovering just who that great-great-great-great-grandparent was. If figuring out your roots using the Internet seems like a tangled mess, then this how-to book is for you. Let these authors take you step by step down the Information Superhighway as you read about everything from setting up a family tree or becoming a member of a genealogical society to figuring out how to use census records and learning how GenServe works. A CD that offers many helpful organizational tools is included in the back of the book.

19.8   Lamm, Kathryn. **10,000 Ideas for Term Papers, Projects, Reports and Speeches: Intriguing, Original Research Topics for Every Student's Need.** IDG Books Worldwide, 1998. 440 pp. ISBN 0028625129. Nonfiction.

Keep this book close throughout high school and college. It not only offers you ideas for papers and speeches, but it also gives you models of good writing and advice on how to organize papers. It covers more than 130 categories and tells you how much research is available on each topic. Whether you need a paper for history, English, science, or social studies, this book has suggestions for topics.

19.9 Levine, Michael. **The Kid's Address Book: Over 3,000 Addresses of Celebrities, Athletes, Entertainers, and More . . . Just for Kids!** Perigree / Penguin Putnam, 1999. 356 pp. ISBN 0399525165. Nonfiction.

Have you ever tried to write to your favorite celebrity, but did not know where to send the letter? Would you like to know how to get in touch with Rosie O'Donnell, Jim Carrey, or R. L. Stine? This guide contains mailing addresses, e-mail addresses, and fan club addresses for thousands of people, from folks in the entertainment industry to politicians in the White House and Congress.

19.10 MacMillan, Norma. **The Encyclopedia of Cooking Skills and Techniques.** Barnes & Noble, 1999. ISBN 0760715327. Nonfiction.

From making a basic tomato sauce (two tablespoons of butter, four cups finely chopped tomatoes, one-quarter to one-half teaspoon of sugar) and understanding sweating (a process of steaming that draws out a vegetable's juices) to learning how to make the best-ever German chocolate cupcakes (it's the four ounces of sweet chocolate that makes the difference), this step-by-step cookbook is a must-have for the beginner or expert chef. Over one thousand photos help you learn how to butterfly shrimp, knead bread dough, make gravy, or filet a fish. Over two hundred recipes will teach you the tricks of the trade and help you go from burnt to bravo in no time flat.

19.11 Panati, Charles. **The Browser's Book of Beginnings: Origins of Everything Under, and Including, the Sun.** Penguin, 1998. 448 pp. ISBN 0140276947. Nonfiction.

This book examines interesting firsts. What was the first comic strip? Who first discovered bacteria? Who made the first loaded dice? With photographs, illustrations, and a helpful index, this reference book is a great source for understanding how things began.

19.12 Pascoe, Elaine, and Deborah Kops. **Scholastic Kid's Almanac for the 21st Century.** Illustrated by Bob Italiano and David C. Bell. Scholastic Reference, 1999. 352 pp. ISBN 059030724X. Nonfiction.

Looking for information on space, astronomy, chemistry, or the world's energy supply? Want to know who the top scorers are in basketball, baseball, hockey, or football? Ever wondered what are the five most common jobs in the United States? Interested in the ethnic makeup of U.S. teachers, or want to know what percentage of kids in the United States have access to computers? These questions and hundreds of others are answered in this detailed almanac that's filled with graphs, charts, maps, and diagrams.

19.13 Platt, Richard. **Stephen Biesty's Incredible Everything.** Illustrated by Stephen Biesty. Dorling Kindersley, 1997. 32 pp. ISBN 078942049X. Nonfiction.

From the creators of *Incredible Cross-Sections,* over one thousand intricate drawings reveal how almost everything is manufactured, built, extracted, or crafted. Detailed illustrations in this oversized book show the various processes involved in making everything from paper to cathedrals and the Saturn V rocket.

19.14 **Russian Phrase Book.** Dorling Kindersley, 1998. 126 pp. ISBN 0789435942. Nonfiction.

This pocket-size phrase book will be a big help to any tourist who needs assistance with the Russian language. Arranged by headings such as Driving, Doing Business, Restaurants, Train Travel, Post Offices, and Health, the book provides both single-word and phrasal translations. From asking directions to the local train station or ordering food in a restaurant to obtaining emergency help from the authorities, this slim volume will be a powerful tool for those seeking to learn a new language. Part of the Eyewitness Travel Guides series, which also includes *Portuguese Phrase Book, Greek Phrase Book,* and *Thai Phrase Book.*

19.15 Samoyault, Tiphanie. **Alphabetical Order: How the Alphabet Began.** Viking, 1998. Unpaged. ISBN 0670878081. Nonfiction.

This very brief and simple book shows how written language evolved over centuries. Other forms of communication are also presented, including semaphores, Morse code, Braille, sign language, and nautical flags.

19.16 Tarbell, Shirley. **1001 Math Problems.** Learning Express, 1999. 192 pp. ISBN 1576852008. Nonfiction.

If the SAT is looming and you're worried about the math section, the fast-approaching, end-of-the-semester algebra or geometry test means you need some extra practice, or you just enjoy seeing if you can solve math problems, you'll like *1001 Math Problems.* This practice book covers everything from addition and subtraction to algebra and geometry, and includes those percentage problems, word problems, and fraction problems that seem to cause most students trouble.

19.17 Woodtor, Dee Parmer. **Finding a Place Called Home: A Guide to African-American Genealogy and Historical Identity.** Random House, 1999. 452 pp. ISBN 037540595X. Nonfiction.

This book is your step-by-step guide to finding your African American roots and tracing your family tree. Beginning with your immediate family, you'll learn how to interview family members, use census reports to gain information about your past, find and read slave schedules, and use property deeds and courthouse records to uncover your past. As this book helps you learn your own family's history, you'll also learn about the history of all Africans in the Americas.

20 Religion and Inspiration

"However far the stream flows, it never forgets its source."
Yoruba proverb

20.1 Asher, Sandy. **With All My Heart, with All My Mind.** Simon & Schuster, 1999. 164 pp. ISBN 0689820127. Nonfiction.

The Jewish faith is one of tradition. In today's complicated society, is it possible to maintain one's traditions? Thirteen stories explore what it means to be Jewish. Some of the stories are set in the present day, while others take readers back to the past or explore the future. Regardless of the setting, however, the focus of each story is how each character deals with his or her religious beliefs and convictions.

20.2 Beckett, Wendy. **Sister Wendy's Book of Saints.** Dorling Kindersley, 1998. 96 pp. ISBN 0789423987. Nonfiction.

Well-known art historian and television personality Sister Wendy documents the life of thirty-five saints—including St. Peter, St. John the Baptist, St. Thomas Aquinas, and St. Francis of Assisi—in this illuminating volume that uses images, miniatures, and icons. The author chose images from an exhibit at the Italian state libraries that went on tour in Italy in 1998. Many of these priceless treasures have not been viewed by the public for centuries. Sister Wendy gives readers the chance to view exquisite art while learning about the trials and tribulations of each saint, his or her feast day, and what each is remembered for.

20.3 Bennett, William J., editor. **The Book of Virtues for Young People.** Simon & Schuster, 1997. 370 pp. ISBN 0689816138. Nonfiction.

When George Washington was fourteen years old, he copied into his notebook 110 proper ways to act. Some of his "Rules of Civility" include "Play not the peacock, looking everywhere about you to see if you be well decked, if your shoes fit well, if your stockings fit neatly and clothes handsomely," and "Be not apt to relate news if you know not the truth thereof." Look through this collection to read more of the rules Washington set down for himself, and to find many other stories, poems, and folktales that reveal the virtues of responsibility, courage, loyalty, perseverance, and honesty—virtues that Bennett suggests "anchor us in our culture, our history, and our traditions."

20.4 Bowker, John. **The Complete Bible Handbook: An Illustrated Companion.** Dorling Kindersley, 1998. 544 pp. ISBN 0789435683. Nonfiction.

Well-known scholar John Bowker assembled a multidenominational team of Jewish and Christian experts to create this book, which offers insights into the key figures, events, customs, politics, and teachings of the Bible. Every book of the Bible, including The Apocrypha, is outlined and explained. Over five hundred color illustrations help bring meaning to the stories, and photographs and maps show biblical sites as they are today.

20.5 Bowker, John. **World Religions: The Great Faiths Explored and Explained.** Dorling Kindersley, 1997. 200 pp. ISBN 0789414392. Nonfiction.

This comprehensive volume explains ancient religions, Hinduism, Jainism, Buddhism, Sikhism, Judaism, Christianity, Islam, and Native religions. The book not only explains the practices associated with each faith, but also shows the people, sacred places, and places of worship connected to each religions. See what the inner sanctum of the Ch'ing Manchu Imperial Court looks like; learn why paintings of Guru Nanak, a leader of Sikhism, always show him with half-closed eyes; read about the Ramayan; and view sixteenth century artwork that depicts the Last Supper of Jesus and his disciples. A timeline helps readers compare events and developments of the major religions, maps show where the religions are practiced, and a bibliography points readers to other resources on the subject.

20.6 Canfield, Jack, Mark Victor Hansen, and Kimberly Kirberger, compilers. **Chicken Soup for the Teenage Soul II: 101 More Stories of Life, Love and Learning.** Health Communications, 1998. 351 pp. ISBN 1558746161. Nonfiction.

Teenagers love this book, and it literally flies off the library shelves. Written by their peers, these stories and poems appeal to young adults who are experiencing relationships and other challenges life has to offer. For example. one particularly touching story is written by a young woman whose boyfriend has broken his neck on a trip. Instantly, she begins to think of the things they won't be able to do together while he recovers, but then she realizes that "Two months is a very short time in exchange for a lifetime of living." The writing is not always polished, but the stories are definitely heartfelt and meaningful to teens.

20.7 Crowe, Chris, editor. **From the Outside Looking In: Short Stories for LDS Teenagers.** Bookcraft, 1998. 134 pp. ISBN 1570084122. Fiction.

It's hard enough to be a teenager, but being a member of the Church of Jesus Christ of Latter-Day Saints adds another element. These fifteen stories examine the lives of LDS (Latter-Day Saints) teens who feel peculiar, alienated, and outside the mainstream. You don't have to be an LDS teenager to appreciate these stories or the struggles the characters face.

20.8 Demi. **Buddha Stories.** Illustrated by Demi. Henry Holt, 1997. Unpaged. ISBN 0805048863. Nonfiction.

Centuries ago in China, Buddha told parables to his followers. These stories spread throughout the world, and were adapted by famous storytellers such as Aesop and La Fontaine. This illustrated collection represents ten of Buddha's classic stories. Read about the beautiful parrots who find out that "riches and fame come and go like the wind," the little gray donkey who learns "not to be deceived by a donkey in a lion's skin," and the clever crab who discovers that "if you cheat on the earth, the earth will cheat on you."

20.9 Ecclesiastes. **To Every Thing There Is a Season.** Illustrated by Leo and Diane Dillon. Blue Sky / Scholastic, 1998. Unpaged. ISBN 0590478877. Nonfiction.

The text of this book is taken from the King James Version of the Bible, Ecclesiastes 3:108 and 1:4. The poet Tennyson called Ecclesiastes "the greatest poem of ancient or modern times." These famous verses—which begin "To every thing there is a season, / And a time to every purpose under the heaven," and conclude, "One generation passes away, / And another generation comes: But the earth abides for ever"—are made more stunning by the artwork of Leo and Diane Dillon. These artists have created sixteen paintings that bring each verse to life. At the end of the book, read how they chose to illustrate each verse, and what each illustration represents.

20.10 Housden, Roger. **Sacred Journeys in a Modern World.** Simon & Schuster, 1998. 178 pp. ISBN 0684836998. Nonfiction.

Centuries ago, people went on pilgrimages in search of spiritual enlightenment. At the end of the twentieth century, Roger Housden did the same. While journeying to remote parts of the globe, Housden recorded his experiences on his "walkabouts," and has chronicled them in this book. Whether traveling through the Sahara, across East Africa, through Turkey, or to a monastery in the Sinai, this modern-day pilgrim shows us how he discovered the "world to be a seamless whole." He finds the sacred in both the mundane and the fantastic, and in the expected spiritual shrines as well as the unexpected parts of life. This book not only will let you share one man's journey, but also might set you wondering about the journeys of your own life.

20.11 LaHaye, Tim, and Jerry B. Jenkins. **Nicolae: The Rise of Antichrist.** Tyndale, 1997. 420 pp. ISBN 0842329145. Fiction.

This is the third book in the popular Left Behind series, which began with *Left Behind* and continued with *Tribulation Force.* In the first book, millions of people were left behind after the Rapture, the moment when Christians are swept away, leaving unbelievers on Earth. In the second book, Rayford Steele, his daughter Chloe, her husband Buck, Rayford's new wife Amanda, and their pastor Bruce Barnes, have all become believers, and they suspect they know the identity of the prophecized antichrist. In this third book, the saga continues as those characters attempt to convert unbelievers, while facing death at every turn.

20.12 Magee, Bryan. **The Story of Philosophy.** Dorling Kindersley, 1998. 240 pp. ISBN 078943511X. Nonfiction.

When philosophers ask, "What is freedom?" or "What is time?" or "What is the nature of existence?" they are not just asking for a definition. Instead, they seek a deeper understanding of the meaning behind such concepts as freedom, time, and existence. In this comprehensive and accessible overview of philosophy, readers gain insight into the issues and questions of Western philosophy. Great thinkers such as Plato, John Locke, Jean-Jacques Rousseau, Friedrich Nietzsche, Jean-Paul Sartre, and Michel Foucault are among those included.

20.13 Mulvihill, Margaret. **The Treasury of Saints and Martyrs.** Viking, 1999. 80 pp. ISBN 0670887897. Nonfiction.

The word *saint* comes from the Latin *sanctus,* meaning sacred. The saints of the Christian tradition are exceptional men and women who have performed heroic deeds in the name of their faith. Gathered in this book are the interesting stories of more than fifty saints and martyrs. Some of the stories are from long ago, while others are from the modern era. Beautifully illustrated, this collection is a concise but valuable reference book on Christian saints and martyrs.

20.14 Pickering, David. **Bible Questions and Answers.** Dorling Kindersley, 1997. 29 pp. ISBN 0789418991. Nonfiction.

Ten short chapters present multiple choice questions about the people and events of the Old and New Testaments. Answers are included at the end of the book. A comprehensive index will allow you to locate references to specific people, places, and events of the Bible.

20.15 Richards, Chris, editor. **The Illustrated Encyclopedia of World Religions.** Element, 1997. 256 pp. ISBN 1852309962. Nonfiction.

Learn about the most popular religions from around the world as you read about Hinduism, Judaism, Confucianism, Buddhism, Jainism, Christianity, Islam, Shinto, Sikhism, and Taoism to name only a few. Read about the rituals, leaders, doctrines, and history of each religion, and view photographs of the people who practice those beliefs.

20.16 Rylant, Cynthia. **The Heavenly Village.** Blue Sky / Scholastic, 1999. 96 pp. ISBN 0439040965. Fiction.

Somewhere between Heaven and Earth lies the Heavenly Village. The village is home to those who require a place to rest after death and before moving on to eternal life. Some of its inhabitants died young and need a bit more time. Others left behind unfinished business, and need more time to adjust to their new life with God. God, in his goodness, has created this special place where people can prepare for eternal life at their own pace. These short vignettes tell of some of the residents of this remarkable village.

20.17 Skees, Suzanne. **God among the Shakers: A Search for Stillness and Faith at Sabbathday Lake.** Hyperion, 1998. 270 pp. ISBN 0965004039. Nonfiction.

"I went to the Shakers to look for God, who lately had been absent from my harried, distracted days." Thus begins Suzanne Skees' chronicle of her search for faith, a story that also gives us insight into the little understood religion of the Shakers. Discover what it means to be a Shaker dedicated to the concepts of purity, consistency, and simplicity. Learn about the religion's history and leader, Ann Lees. Find out why some people called early Shakers witches. And learn why the Shakers are only eight in number today.

20.18 Tolan, Stephanie. **Ordinary Miracles.** Morrow Junior Books, 1999. 221 pp. ISBN 068816269X. Fiction.

Mark and Matthew Filkins are identical twins. If Mark is hurt, Matthew feels the pain, too. Because Matthew is the "older" of the twins, he has been the dominant one. But Mark is weary of always following along, and yearns for his own identity. He is given the chance to become more independent when a Nobel Laureate scientist named Dr. Hendrick returns to Mark's hometown to live, and asks Mark to be his assistant. When Dr. Hendrick becomes seriously ill, the strength of Mark's belief in God and the power of miracles is put to the test.

20.19 Wilson, Colin. **The Atlas of Holy Places and Sacred Sites.** Dorling Kindersley, 1996. 192 pp. ISBN 0789410516. Nonfiction.

In the introduction to this intriguing book, Colin Wilson asserts that humans differ from animals in "one peculiar respect: . . . they have always been religious animals." He then explains that as he studied various religious sites, from "barrows and sacred groves to cathedrals and mosques," he found again and again that religion expresses a basic truth about humans. This beautiful book takes readers to the Potala Palace (the traditional home of the Dalai Lama), the House of Nanna (Ur's holiest place), and the Stone Forest of Lake Varna (found along the coast of Bulgaria). As you explore those and hundreds of other sites from around the world, you'll read tales of these mysterious ruins and view their location on handdrawn maps.

21 Rights and Responsibilities

"Equality might be denied, but I knew I was not inferior."
Paul Robeson

21.1 Allison, Anthony. **Hear These Voices: Youth at the Edge of the Millennium.** Dutton Children's Books, 1999. 170 pp. ISBN 0525453539. Nonfiction.

As the millennium approaches, fifteen teenagers describe their lives and their concerns about approaching adulthood. They aren't worried about which Internet provider to use, which car to buy, or which college to attend. Living on the fringe as they do, they worry about having enough food, making enough money, finding a place to sleep, escaping from abuse, getting off drugs, or surviving gang wars. In this book, you'll meet a young woman who faced a life-threatening drug addiction, another woman who works two jobs and is trying to get her GED, a boy with AIDS, two boys who were kicked out of their homes when they were eight and ten, and two boys who live in neighborhoods that have more bullets and bombs than grocery stores and schools. You'll learn about the courage and bravery these young people possess as they confront their desperate situations, and work hard to find a better way to live.

21.2 Ashabranner, Brent. **To Seek a Better World.** Photographs by Paul Conklin. Cobblehill / Dutton, 1997. 88 pp. ISBN 0525652191. Nonfiction.

Since 1980, over 200,000 Haitians desperate for a better life have climbed into small and often unsafe boats, and taken to the sea through the Windward Passage in an attempt to reach southern Florida. Prior to this influx of illegal immigrants, thousands of Haitians came to the United States legally in the 1950s and 1960s to escape the regime of the dictator Francois Duvalier. These tradespeople and professionals quickly became accepted citizens of their new country. Now there are approximately 500,000 Haitians in the United States. Problems surrounding illegal immigration and questions about Haitians in America continue. This interesting book helps you understand who these people are.

21.3 Bolden, Tonya. **And Not Afraid to Dare: The Stories of Ten African-American Women.** Scholastic, 1998. 216 pp. ISBN 0590480804. Nonfiction.

These are the stories of African American women who not only lived through adversity, but triumphed over racism and sexism to reach their goals. Clara "Mother" Hale dedicated her life to caring for AIDS babies. Ellen Craft, dressed as a man, escaped from slavery to help others do the same. Ida Wells wrote poignantly against lynchings, at great risk to her own life. These women, and the others included here, represent the strength and courage many women have shown when they are "determined to be free, to be heard, to succeed."

21.4 Currie, Stephen. **We Have Marched Together: The Working Children's Crusade.** Lerner, 1997. 88 pp. ISBN 0822517337. Nonfiction.

William Hartley, born in 1892, began working full-time in one of Philadelphia's largest textile factories when he was thirteen years old. Gus Misuinas worked at the Tommy Brown Hosiery Factory in that same city for $2.50 each week when he was twelve years old. He worked six days a week from seven o'clock in the morning to six o'clock at night. In 1902, Catherine Hutt began working at a knitting mill when she was twelve years old. She worked from half past six o'clock in the morning until six o'clock at night. These three children represent only a fraction of the children who were forced into labor at the turn of the century, working twelve hours a day for wages that amounted to nothing. *We Have Marched Together* tells of the horror of these children's lives, and of the triumphs they experienced as states began to pass child labor laws. Filled with photographs of children at work, this book gives a chilling look at the spirit of turn-of-the-century children.

21.5 D'Angelo, Laura, and Austin Sarat, editors. **Hate Crimes: Crime, Justice, and Punishment.** 121 pp. Chelsea House, 1999. ISBN 0791042669. Nonfiction.

Hate crimes aren't new. Trials against suspected witches during the seventeenth century, cross burnings by the Ku Klux Klan in the late nineteenth century, and lynchings in the South in the early part of this century are all examples of hate crimes. These acts of violence continue today as people are tortured, robbed, or murdered because of their race, ethnicity, religion, or sexual preference. D'Angelo discusses each of these issues in this informative book that looks at the history of hate crimes and the laws that defend people's rights to think and say whatever they believe. She also discusses when a person's freedom of speech rights end, and a victim's rights begin.

21.6 Finklestein, Norman H. **The Way Things Never Were: The Truth about the "Good Old Days."** Atheneum Books for Young Readers, 1999. 112 pp. ISBN 0689814127. Nonfiction.

Have your parents ever begun a conversation with the phrase, "Back when I was a kid"? If so, this book will help you to learn about those good old days of the 1950s and 1960s, as well as why they were not really the best of times. Photos, factoids, and illustrations provide information about the civil rights movement, the McCarthy era, and other often overlooked events of times past.

21.7 Freedman, Suzanne. *Clay v. United States:* **Muhammad Ali Objects to War.** Enslow, 1997. 112 pp. ISBN 0894908553. Nonfiction.

Famous boxer Muhammad Ali took on a new opponent in 1968 when he refused to comply with the draft notice he received and serve in the Vietnam War. In 1964, Ali had become a member of the Nation of Islam, a religious order of black Muslims. Members of the order are opposed to any war that is not one fought for their god, Allah. Citing religious objections to the war, Ali became a conscientious objector. His position was tested in the court system, and the case was appealed all the way to the Supreme Court. In 1971, the Court ruled in his favor. This book, part of the Landmark Supreme Court Cases series, explains the rulings that worked for and against Ali in this fight. Other books in this series include *The* Dred Scott *Case: Slavery and Citizenship;* Engel v. Vitale: *Separation of Church and State;* Gideon v. Wainwright: *Free Legal Counsel;* Roe v. Wade: *The Abortion Question;* and United States v. Nixon: *Watergate and the President.*

21.8 Goldenstern, Joyce. **American Women Against Violence.** Enslow, 1998. 128 pp. ISBN 0766010252. Nonfiction.

Abigail Adams, wife of President John Adams, wrote to her husband before he was president about the "tyranny" of males toward females. Harriet Beecher Stowe and Sojourner Truth spoke out against the evils of slavery. Susette La Flesche, an Omaha, tried to stop the evictions her people faced. These women were some of the first to speak out against violence, especially the violence women face. In this book, readers will learn about women who have worked hard to stop violence, including Linda Fairstein, an attorney who prosecutes sex offenders; Judy Baca, an artist and educator; Prem Sharma, the founder of a residential shelter for Asian American women; and Dianne Hardy-Garcia, a social worker and director of the gay rights lobby of Texas. These women, all from different time periods, parts of the country, and ethnic backgrounds, share a similar goal: to stop the violence.

21.9   Gottfried, Ted. **Police under Fire.** Twenty First Century 1999. 128 pp. ISBN 0761313133. Nonfiction.

When you see a police officer, what is your first reaction? Do you feel safe and protected, or threatened and in danger? *Police under Fire* investigates the volatile issue of police brutality, and examines the life-and-death situations that police officers face very day. This book analyzes how law enforcement officers react to the day-to-day pressures of this dangerous job. It presents an unbiased look at both good and bad police officers, and comes up with answers to tough questions, such as what to do when the police go to far, as they did in the Rodney King case. This book will not be forgotten soon, as it provides a haunting and poignant portrait of the men and women behind the uniform.

21.10   Hansen, Joyce. **Women of Hope: African Americans Who Made a Difference.** Scholastic, 1998. 32 pp. ISBN 0590939734. Nonfiction.

This stunningly beautiful book profiles the lives of twelve African American women who have made a difference through their words and actions. The black-and-white photographs that accompany each biographical sketch were chosen from a series of posters honoring "Women of Hope." Readers will learn about Ida B. Wells-Barnett, Marian Wright Edelman, Alice Walker, Alexa Canady, Mae C. Jemison, and Ruby Dee. They will also encounter Maya Angelou's a stirring words "You may write me down in history with your bitter, twisted lies, you may trod me in the very dirt but still like dust, I'll rise," and Toni Morrison's observation that "My world did not shrink because I was a black female writer. It just got bigger." This book reminds young people, especially today's young African American women, that "greatness looks like them."

21.11 Hanson, Freya Ottem. **The Second Amendment: The Right to Own Guns.** Enslow, Inc. 1998. 128 pp. ISBN 0894909258. Nonfiction.

Will tougher gun control laws stop violence in the United States? Should guns be banned altogether? Persons opposed to gun control laws say the right to own a gun is guaranteed in the Second Amendment of the U.S. Constitution, which states: "A well-regulated militia being necessary to the security of a free state, the right of the people to keep and bear arms shall not be infringed." But there are many interpretations of this amendment, and its meaning is more controversial today than ever before. Each year in the United States, there are approximately thirty-eight thousand firearm deaths, and more than ten thousand involve youth suicide or murder. This book is one in The Constitution series. Other books consider the First, Second, Fourth, Fifth, Thirteenth, Fifteenth, Eighteenth, Nineteenth, and Twenty-First Amendments to the Constitution.

21.12 King, Dr. Martin Luther, Jr. **I Have a Dream.** Foreword by Coretta Scott King. Illustrated by Coretta Scott King Award–Winning artists. Scholastic, 1997. 39 pp. ISBN 0590205161. Nonfiction.

On August 28, 1963, Dr. Martin Luther King Jr. delivered a speech that has inspired thousands. That famous "I Have a Dream" speech is reprinted here with illustrations by fifteen award-winning artists, including Leo and Diane Dillon, Floyd Cooper, Jerry Pickney, Ashley Bryan, Tom Feelings, and Carol Byard. Comments at the end of the book from each artist make this edition a special tribute to the man who shared with generations to come his dream that "one day this nation will rise up and live out the true meaning of its creed . . . that all men are created equal."

21.13 Kraft, Betsy Harvey. **Sensational Trials of the 20th Century.** Scholastic, 1998. 216 pp. ISBN 059037205X. Nonfiction.

There is a fascination with trials in the United States, and this book fulfills the desire to read about them. It documents eight sensational and important trials from the past one hundred years, starting with the Sacco-Vanzetti trial and ending with the O. J. Simpson trial. The 1919 Sacco-Vanzetti trial reflected the attitudes towards immigrants and radical political beliefs at the time, rather than the guilt or innocence of the two men on trial for murder. Other trials in the book include the Scopes monkey trial, the Lindbergh baby kidnapping trial, the Julius and Ethel Rosenberg spy trial, the *Brown v. Board of Education of Topeka* trial, the Watergate trials, and the John Hinkley Jr. murder trial.

21.14 Kuklin, Susan. **Iqbal Masih and the Crusaders against Child Slavery.** Henry Holt, 1998. Nonfiction.

This true story of Iqbal Masih is the story of children in Pakistan who are turned into slaves as they are forced to work in rug-weaving factories. Iqbal, only twelve years old when he was murdered, had been one of those slaves—chained to a loom for up to twelve hours a day, beaten if he missed tying a knot, beaten again if he was caught daydreaming, and beaten more if he attempted to escape. Once Iqbal was freed from bondage, he began to speak out against child labor, and eventually traveled to the United States to receive the Reebok Human Rights Foundation award. Tragically, in 1995, Iqbal was shot, presumably by the carpet mafia in Pakistan. But Iqbal lives on as people continue to fight in his name for freedom for all children.

21.15 McCall, Nathan. **What's Going On: Personal Essays.** Random House, 1997. 217 pp. ISBN 0679455892. Nonfiction.

Nathan McCall speaks from experience as he dissects controversial issues about race relations in the United States. He offers thought-provoking insights on everything from African American sports supremacy and the effects of violent rap lyrics on today's youth to the obligations of successful African Americans to fellow African Americans and other cultural influences.

21.16 Moren, Isobel V. **Politics American Style: Political Parties in American History.** Twenty First Century, 1999. 144 pp. ISBN 0761312676. Nonfiction.

Do you know the differences between the Compromise of 1850 and the Kansas-Nebraska Act? What current political party was once known as the Whigs? If you aren't sure of the answers, then this is the book for you. This volume provides simple summaries of the important issues, concepts, people, and events related to American politics. Tracing the rise of our two party system, this book makes complex political issues such as the New Deal and Reconstruction easy to understand. The book concludes with an informative look at Ross Perot and the Reform Party. If you need to know the difference between the electoral college and an electoral vote, then you need to read *Politics American Style.*

21.17 Nash, Gary B. **Forbidden Love: The Secret History of Mixed-Race America.** Henry Holt, 1999. 214 pp. ISBN 0805049533. Nonfiction.

"American history is taught in four colors: white, black, red, and yellow. But it was lived in every hue, as for centuries peoples of all colors have shared their lives and dreams in America." Thus begins *Forbidden Love,* which examines one of our country's most enduring problems: interracial relationships. Beginning with the first recorded interracial union in North American history in 1614 (John Rolfe and Pocahontas), and continuing through the centuries when interracial marriages were not only discouraged but were against the law, this book reveals that racially mixed relationships and marriages have persisted in spite of ostracism and laws. Changes in the laws have been slow, and changes in attitudes have been even slower. As late as 1994, an Alabama high school principal threatened to cancel the school prom if any racially mixed couples showed up. This historical perspective of interracial relationships gives readers a glimpse of one aspect of the past while offering insight into the future.

21.18 Stevens, Leonard A. **The Case of *Roe v. Wade.*** Putnam, 1996. 188 pp. ISBN 0399228128. Nonfiction.

The issue of a woman's right to personal privacy, including her right to choose whether or not she may have an abortion, has aroused more anger and been debated more intensely in the twentieth century than almost any other right. The story of *Roe v. Wade* began with a Texas petitioner, Jane Roe, a young Dallas woman who was prohibited by state law from ending an unwanted pregnancy. Wade was a well-known Dallas county district attorney responsible for enforcing the Texas law, first passed in 1854, outlawing abortion. Sarah Weddington, an inexperienced young lawyer, argued the case for Roe. The case ended up in the

Supreme Court, which announced its decision on Monday, January 23, 1973. On that day, abortion in the United States became a matter of personal privacy and personal choice protected by the Constitution.

21.19 Wolf, Robert V., editor. **Capital Punishment: Crime, Justice, and Punishment.** Chelsea House, 1997. ISBN 0791043118. Nonfiction.

Should some criminals face death because of their crimes? This question has confronted the legal system for decades, as lawyers and human rights advocates have continued to debate this controversial issue. In this book, you can explore the history of capital punishment, and look closely at some actual criminal cases, as you read arguments for and against the death penalty. Finally, you can examine the legal rights of those found guilty of a capital crime, and look at the effects of capital punishment on other lawbreakers.

22 Romance and School Stories

"If you're not good company for yourself, you have to work to become the kind of person whose company you enjoy. If you enjoy your own company, there is no loneliness."

Toni Morrison

22.1 Anderson, Laurie Halse. **Speak.** Farrar, Straus and Giroux, 1999. 198 pp. ISBN 0374371520. Fiction.

When Melinda starts her first day as a ninth grader at Merryweather High School, she knows nothing will be like she had hoped. No friends, no clubs, no groups to hang out with at the mall or show or football game. No one. She's the outcast, shunned because she did the unimaginable—called the cops when the drinking at a summer party she was at got out of control. Now isolated from her peers, Melinda has nothing to say about what happened, so she simply stops talking. Her grades suffer, her last lingering friends depart, her parents nag, and still Melinda won't speak. Little by little, though, she relives what happened that August night until the moment she remembers everything, and suddenly knows exactly why she called the police. Now with that memory, Melinda wonders if she'll ever find the courage to speak up and tell someone about what happened that fateful night.

22.2 Bennett, Cherie, and Jeff Gottesfeld. **University Hospital.** Berkley Jam, 1999. 179 pp. ISBN 0425171442. Fiction.

Passions flare! Sirens blare! At Fable Harbor University Hospital, five young men and women learn about the life-and-death world of medicine firsthand, as they shadow the doctors and assist with some of the medical care. The purpose, of course, is to learn whether or not they really want to be part of the medical profession. However, in the process of learning about medicine, they learn that life and love, feelings and emotional heartbreaks, are all part of this profession too. Decisions must be made based upon pure scientific evidence rather than what some might feel is just. And above all the tension and decisions, they learn they must remain calm and cool when someone's life is on the line. This romantic fiction is the first in a new series by Bennet and Gottesfeld.

22.3   Cooney, Caroline B. **Prisoner of Time.** Delacorte, 1998. 208 pp. ISBN 0385322445. Fiction.

The third book in the time travel trilogy by Cooney, this story takes Tod Lockwood from the present day back in time to the nineteenth century. There he meets the beautiful and headstrong Devonny Stratton. Tod brings Devonny back with him to his own time, thinking that is the best solution for her problems. Much as Devonny enjoys the freedom women have in contemporary society, she knows she must travel back to her own time. There she will have to stand on her own two feet and try to solve her problems.

22.4   Craft, Elizabeth. **I'll Have What He's Having.** Archway, 1997. 192 pp. ISBN 0671004468. Fiction.

Natalie, Dylan, Blue, Sam, Tanya, and Jason—these are the teens who work at @café, a great coffee shop in San Francisco with an Internet site that everyone enjoys. Once Dylan finally figures out that he's in love with Natalie, he decides to tell his best friend, Sam. But Sam complicates things when he beats Dylan to the punch, and tells Dylan that he's in love with Natalie. Now Dylan's hot—even hotter than the coffee. For fun, visit the real Web site (http://www.simonsays.com) that is mentioned in this story for giveaways, quizzes, insider secrets, and continuing story lines. Other books in the series include *Love Bytes* and *Make Mine to Go.*

22.5   Crew, Linda. **Long Time Passing.** Delacorte, 1997. 197 pp. ISBN 0385324960. Fiction.

When Kathy Shay, a sophomore at Chintimini High, doesn't make the junior varsity rally squad, she is devastated—for about half a minute. Losing the election is a wake-up call for Kathy, who stops trying to be popular like her twin brother, Kenny, and starts trying to be herself. Soon Kathy auditions for a part in the school production of *The Miracle Worker,* joins the drama group, and discovers a place where she can fit in and be herself. Here Kathy meets the social activist James Holderread. As Kathy and James begin to share their thoughts and dreams, she wonders, How do you know when you've met your true love? Do bells ring? Shouldn't there be a monumental kiss? Against the backdrop of the war in

Vietnam, protest marches, and the civil rights movement, Kathy and James learn what life and love are all about.

22.6   Dessen, Sarah. **Keeping the Moon.** Viking, 1999. 224 pp. ISBN 0670885495. Fiction.

It is bad enough having Kiki Sparks, noted weight loss guru, for a mother. Now Colie Sparks learns that her mother intends to dump her for the summer at her Aunt Mira's house in North Carolina. Although Colie has managed to shed quite a few pounds at her mother's insistence, she is still the insecure, sullen person she was before her weight loss. The prospect of a summer with an eccentric aunt is dismal. But Colie soon makes friends with two waitresses who work with her at the Last Chance Café. She thinks there may also be romance in her future as well once she meets Norman, a gifted young artist. Perhaps the summer won't be quite as dreadful as she feared.

22.7   Draper, Sharon M. **Romiette and Julio.** Simon & Schuster, 1999. 240 pp. ISBN 0689821808. Fiction.

Romiette Capelle and Julio Montague meet in an online chat room. Later they discover that they attend the same school. It is not too long before the two are friends. The Devildogs, a local gang, tell Romiette and Julio that they had better be careful. They do not like the fact that a Black girl is dating a Latino boy. When Romiette and Julio ignore the warnings, they place themselves in grave danger. This modern-day retelling of *Romeo and Juliet* deals with issues of racism and prejudice in contemporary society.

22.8   Haddix, Margaret Peterson. **Just Ella.** Simon & Schuster, 1999. 185 pp. ISBN 0689821867. Fiction.

Isn't her story supposed to end with "They lived happily ever after," wonders Ella? Ella resents the fact that her behavior is constantly corrected by the parade of tutors and others who explain how she must behave if she is to become the princess. Even Prince Charming seems less desirable now that their marriage is drawing near. When Ella confesses to Charm that she is no longer in love with him, he orders her imprisoned. Ella might be able to escape, but escape to what?

22.9 Hamilton, Virginia. **A White Romance.** Harcourt Brace, 1997. 233 pp. ISBN 0152958886. Fiction.

Integration of Black and White students is the aim of Colonel Glenn High School. Bringing the students from two different neighborhoods into one school, however, does not settle racial conflicts, especially when they extend into the students' homes. The situation becomes particularly tense for African American Talley Harbour when her father doesn't approve of her new friendship with Didi, who is blond, rich—and White. Matters become more difficult when Talley falls for David, a friend of Didi's, who draws Talley into the world of drugs and sex. To keep her life in control, Talley must overcome prejudice, face reality, and grow up quickly.

22.10 Hewett, Lorri. **Dancer.** Dutton, 1999. 214 pp. ISBN 0525459685. Fiction.

Sixteen-year-old Stephanie wants to be a ballerina, but like Miss Winnie, the aging African American dancer who mentors her, Stephanie faces the prejudice of not having a face "the color of a freshly peeled apple." Miss Winnie's belief in Stephanie's talent fires the young dancer's passion for ballet, increasing her parents' concern that she will sacrifice going to college for a career in which she may not succeed. Being a scholarship student in the private school where her father is a janitor does not make her social life easy either. Then Vance, Miss Winnie's nephew, dances into Stephanie's life, adding a little spice to her days of studying and recitals.

22.11 Jukes, Mavis. **Cinderella 2000.** Delacorte, 1999. 160 pp. ISBN 0385327110. Fiction.

Ashley Ella Toral has been invited to the most exclusive New Year's Eve party of the millennium. Her stepmother has other plans for Ashley, however—plans that involve taking care of her two stepsisters instead of dancing with Trevor at the country club. Maybe Grammie's arrival will change Ashley's miserable existence. Could Grammie be the fairy godmother who can get Ashley Ella to the dance?

22.12 Klause, Annette Curtis. **Blood and Chocolate.** Bantam, 1997. 264 pp. ISBN 0385323050. Fiction.

Vivian is a beautiful young woman, although she is known as a bit of a loner at her high school. Vivian has a secret side, one she has been unwilling to unveil to her peers. Then she meets and falls in love with Aiden, a handsome young man. Vivian is certain that Aiden can handle the truth about her secret side. He seems sensitive and understanding. However, even Aiden is not ready when Vivian reveals that she is a werewolf.

22.13 Lynch, Chris. **Extreme Elvin.** HarperCollins, 1999. 240 pp. ISBN 0060280409. Fiction.

The main character from *Slot Machine* is back for his first year of high school. Though Elvin has slimmed down some, he still faces some terrific obstacles, not the least of which is an awful case of hemorrhoids. The first dance between Elvin's all-boy school and the all-girl school across town is quickly approaching. Elvin needs some new clothes, a home for the rather ugly puppies his dog has given birth to, and, more importantly, some confidence so that he can ask a girl to dance. Elvin does manage to survive the dance, but there are larger problems looming for him at school.

22.14 McKinley, Robin. **Rose Daughter.** Greenwillow, 1997. 320 pp. ISBN 0688154395. Fiction.

In her earlier work, *Beauty*, McKinley examined and retold the fairy tale "Beauty and the Beast." This new work is not a sequel, but rather a reexamination and exploration of that timeless classic. Beauty, bereaved after the death of her mother, is haunted by the scent of roses. Their lovely fragrance reminds her of the perfume that always seemed to permeate her mother's clothes. When Beauty and her family move to the Rose Cottage, her first task is to try to coax back to life the rose garden that surrounds the cottage. Nightmares begin to invade Beauty's sleep, dreams of a long darkened hallway with a mysterious, and perhaps dangerous, presence at the end. Beauty is not sure what awaits her at the end of the hallway, or even if she wants to discover the identity of the presence. Yet, somehow, she is drawn to this sinister place, and the dangers that may lurk within.

22.15 Napoli, Donna Jo. **Crazy Jack.** Delacorte, 1999. 135 pp. ISBN 0385326270. Fiction.

How would you react if the young man you have known and loved since you were both children suddenly started doing crazy things? Things like planting magic seeds, and then claiming he could climb the stalks of his giant plants and enter into a magical kingdom? Flora, the young woman who has been promised to Jack since childhood, begins to fear the young man she once loved. Who could possibly believe the incredible tales of treasure and danger Jack spins? Perhaps Flora should find someone else to marry. This retelling of the traditional story of "Jack and the Beanstalk" gives an interesting twist to the story we all know and love from childhood.

22.16 Napoli, Donna Jo. **For the Love of Venice.** Delacorte, 1998. 245 pp. ISBN 0385325312. Fiction.

While spending the summer in Venice, seventeen-year-old Percy falls in love with a young Venetian woman. Graziella is part of an underground resistance group trying to save Venice from further commercialization. Percy becomes involved with the resistance group, even though he does not agree with their methods—especially their plans to sabotage his father's flood management project, which employs gates to stop the water from flooding the canals. The resistance group would rather see Venice flood than to host the next EXPO. Just as they are about to sabotage the project's electrical system, a storm causes Venice's electrical system to shut down, allowing the flood waters to rush over the canal banks. The heart overrules political fervor when Christopher, Percy's seven-year-old brother, and the handicapped nephew of one of the resistance fighters are lost in the storm. Setting aside any differences they may have, Percy and Graziella risk their lives to save the two boys.

22.17 Napoli, Donna Jo, and Richard Tchen. **Spinners.** Dutton Children's Books, 1999. 197 pp. ISBN 0525460659. Fiction.

Once upon a time, two spinners lived in the same village. They fell in love, and planned to be married. In an effort to prove his worth to his fiancée's father, one spinner made a fatal error that caused him to be crippled. He was abandoned by the one he loved, and by the rest of the community who found his deformity repulsive. He fled his village, and searched for acceptance across the kingdom. When he came to the rescue of a young woman trapped in a room full of straw, the old spinner believed his search for happiness was over. This retelling of the childhood tale of Rumplestiltskin is full of romance and magic.

22.18 Neenan, Colin. **Live a Little.** Harcourt Brace, 1996. 252 pp. ISBN 0152012427. Fiction.

In this sequel to *In Your Dreams,* we rejoin Hale O'Reilly during the final days of his senior year. Hale is stuck in the middle between his two best friends. Sonny is bemoaning his recent break up with his girlfriend. Zoe seems to be making moves on Sonny. And Hale learns some valuable lessons about being a friend. The bottom line is that life is a lot tougher than it looks.

22.19 Neufeld, John. **Boys Lie.** DK Ink, 1999. 224 pp. ISBN 0789426242. Fiction.

Although Gina is only thirteen, she has developed physically beyond her years. Following an assault at her neighborhood swimming pool, Gina and her mother decide to move to a new place. Perhaps there Gina can put the awful incident behind her. However, on the first day in her new school, Gina sees those same furtive glances from some of the boys. One young man, however, seems to be different. He offers Gina his friendship and his protection. Gina ultimately learns, however, that boys can tell lies to gain her confidence. Has she put her trust in the wrong person? Who can she believe?

22.20 Nodelman, Perry. **Behaving Bradley.** Simon & Schuster Books for Young Readers, 1998. 232 pp. ISBN 0689814666. Fiction.

Bradley Gold is on a mission: to change the proposed Code of Conduct at his high school, which he considers barbarous and disrespectful to students. Little does he know that by taking on this project, he will be taking on bullies, weak-willed student leaders, righteous faculty members, and people with personal agendas. Brad's humor helps him through this difficult period, as he comes face-to-face with his own belief system.

22.21 Roberts, Laura Peyton. **Ghost of a Chance.** Delacorte, 1997. 183 pp. ISBN 0385325088. Fiction.

Sixteen-year-old Melissa Soul is having a few problems. Her parents are getting a divorce, her younger brother is a royal pain, and there is a "For Sale" sign in front of the house she calls home. The only positive thing in her life seems to be her best friend, Chloe, and their upcoming summer vacation. When Melissa meets James, a funny, gorgeous, older guy, she thinks her life just may be on the upswing. However, the situation gets sticky when Melissa realizes that Chloe likes the same guy. What happens when two best friends fall for the same guy—a guy who is, by the way, a ghost?

22.22 Rubinstein, Gillian. **Under the Cat's Eye: A Tale of Morph and Mystery.** Simon & Schuster, 1998. 204 pp. ISBN 0689818009. Fiction.

Jai is sent off to a boarding school where all the students seem to behave strangely. His two newest friends, Hugo and Seal, confide in Jai, telling him that the new headmaster of the school is stealing the souls of his classmates. As the three begin to investigate this mystery, Jai finds he must join forces with a cat and a dog from a parallel world in order to stop the headmaster, and send him back to the evil world from which he came.

22.23 Savage, Tom. **The Inheritance.** Dutton, 1998. 278 pp. ISBN 0525944230. Fiction.

Overnight, Holly Smith goes from being a normal twenty-four-year-old to an heiress, due to the death of a great aunt she has never met. Holly, whose real surname is Randall, reaches her magnificent Connecticut estate to find her uncle John and his greedy wife in residence. The town and its citizens know Holly's secret: her birth mother committed a murder many years ago. Holly makes many valiant attempts to discover the skeletons in her closet, only to determine she is a target for murder. Mysterious characters and surprising events await Holly and the reader, as some of her lifelong dreams, for better or worse, come true.

22.24 Seymour, Tres. **The Revelation of Saint Bruce.** Orchard, 1998. 120 pp. ISBN 0531301095. Fiction.

Bruce's moralistic views are the cause of his nickname, "Saint Bruce." The name sticks, until he betrays his friends' confidence by confirming a teacher's suspicions that the four drank a bottle of whiskey in her classroom when the substitute teacher left them unsupervised. Ostracized by his friends (who are suspended from school for the rest of the semester), and eventually by the entire high school, Bruce's senior year is one of self-examination. Bruce's moral choices will result in thought-provoking classroom debate.

22.25 Shakespeare, William. **Romeo and Juliet.** Retold by Bruce Coville. Illustrated by Dennis Nolan. Dial, 1999. Unpaged. ISBN 0803724624. Fiction.

Coville's rendering of this famous tragedy isn't the first adaptation of *Romeo and Juliet.* As Coville points out in the author's note, Shakespeare's play is, "as best we can tell, the Bard's adaptation of an English translation of a French poem. That poem itself resulted from a series of adaptations of what was originally an Italian folktale." Whatever the original source, the fact remains that *Romeo and Juliet* is a well-loved play enjoyed through the ages by people of all ages. This picture book version gives Shakespeare fans a beautiful account of a timeless love story.

22.26 Stoehr, Shelly. **Wannabe.** Delacorte, 1997. 215 pp. ISBN 0385322232. Fiction.

Furious with her older brother for getting involved with the local mob, Catherine Tavarelli suffers from the same attraction. Brother Mickey is attracted to the money and potential power, and Catherine falls for Joey, the coolest of the bad. But along with her infatuation with Joey come alcohol, drugs, and bigger troubles. In the style of her earlier books (*Crosses* and *Weird on the Outside),* Shelly Stoehr tells another story of hard-shelled, vulnerable teens trying to live life in the fast lane.

22.27 Sweeney, Joyce. **The Spirit Window.** Delacorte, 1998. 243 pp. ISBN 038532510X. Fiction.

Fifteen-year-old Miranda travels with her father and stepmother to visit Grandma Lila. Miranda is entranced by the wildlife that inhabits the marshy land on which her grandmother's estate is located. She is equally enamored of the young Cherokee man who is helping her grandmother care for the land. Miranda is horrified when she learns her father plans to sell the land and the marsh to developers. She decides the time has come to confront her father, and face what is sure to be an angry reaction.

22.28 Thesman, Jean. **The Moonstones.** Viking, 1998. 166 pp. ISBN 0670879592. Fiction.

Jane would rather do anything than go with her mother to Royal Bay and clean out her grandmother's house. It is a small town, and Jane is sure it will be boring. When her Aunt Norma and her cousin Ricki arrive, however, things change radically. Ricki is not only obnoxious, but adventurous. She convinces Jane to sneak out of the house when their mothers go to sleep. The two girls go to the amusement park, the only interesting place in town. Once there they meet some boys. For Jane it is love at first sight when she gazes into Carey's eyes. But Ricki becomes wilder and more hateful because she, too, has her eye on Carey.

22.29 Thomas, Rob. **Green Thumb.** Simon & Schuster, 1999. 192 pp. ISBN 0689817800. Fiction.

Grady Jacobs is a genius. He has won the Science Fair at his school every year, and has just been selected to spend the summer assisting the renowned Dr. Phillip Carter in his rain forest reforestation attempt. Dr. Carter has managed to genetically engineer a tree whose growth is so rapid, it can ease the effects of clear-cutting in the rain forest. What Grady soon discovers, however, is that this miracle of modern science is not all Dr. Carter says it is. The genetically engineered tree poisons the other plants and wildlife of the forest. Dr. Carter will not admit his mistake, and who would ever believe a mere thirteen-year-old?

22.30 Thomas, Rob. **Satellite Down.** Simon & Schuster Books for Young Readers, 1998. 266 pp. ISBN 0689809573. Fiction.

Patrick Sheridan, editor of his Texas high school paper, is an avid journalist who is thrilled when he is tapped to be an anchor on a news show that is broadcast directly to high schools across the country. He is amazed and disturbed when he becomes the show's top-rated personality. Sent to Northern Ireland for a story, he decides to take drastic action to free himself from the media whirlwind, and find out who he really is.

22.31 Thomas, Rob. **Slave Day.** Aladdin, 1998. 246 pp. ISBN 068982193X. Fiction.

Slave Day is a long-standing tradition at Robert E. Lee High School. It is a day when teachers and students offer themselves as "slaves" to the highest bidder. This year, however, things will be different. Keene Davenport, an African American student, questions the continuation of a tradition that is demeaning to many students of color. His letter to the editor of the local newspaper causes a stir, but Slave Day continues as planned. It will be a day that several students, teachers, and parents will not soon forget.

22.32 Trembath, Don. **A Fly Named Alfred.** Orca, 1997. 138 pp. ISBN 1551430835. Fiction.

The anonymous columnist called Alfred is the hit of the high school paper with his witty, right-on-target observations about students and teachers. When he reports on a tough guy parking his convertible in the school bus lanes and then refusing to move, the tough guy in question is determined to find Alfred and punish him. Told from the point of view of the writer of the columns, this funny, fast-paced story does an excellent job of representing high school life.

22.33 Wersba, Barbara. **Whistle Me Home.** Henry Holt, 1997. 108 pp. ISBN 0805048502. Fiction.

Noli believes her junior year in high school will be much more interesting than her sophomore year. She doesn't expect, however, that her relationship with her parents will improve, that she'll lose her very best friend, or that she'll fall in love with the new boy in school. But that's exactly what happens. More importantly, T. J. falls in love with Noli. Or at least she thinks he's in love with her. He says he is. He takes her out, buys her gifts, and tells her she is his soul mate. But little by little, Noli begins to realize that something is missing in their relationship. Discovering what it is means learning the truth about T. J., and then being strong enough to know what to do next.

22.34 Williams, Carol Lynch. **My Angelica.** Delacorte, 1999. 149 pp. ISBN 038532622X. Fiction.

Fifteen-year-old Sage thinks she is going to be a famous romance writer. She writes pages and pages about her heroine, Angelica, which she reads aloud to her best friend, George. George is secretly in love with Sage, and doesn't have the heart to tell her that her writing is terrible, even when Sage decides to enter her latest Angelica saga in the school's writing contest. After numerous attempts to stop Sage, George lets the inevitable happen. Much to his surprise, Sage's "parody of a romance" ties for first place with an anonymously written group of love poems—George's entry in the contest. The ever-optimistic Sage discovers that she does have a talent for writing, even if it is parody, and George "gets his girl."

22.35 Woodson, Jacqueline. **If You Come Softly.** Putnam, 1998. 181 pp. ISBN 0399231129. Fiction.

In this modern-day Romeo and Juliet story, Miah and Ellie fall in love. Their relationship angers some people who do not believe that a White girl should date a Black boy. The two defy their critics, certain that their love can conquer the racism they face. A tragedy proves them wrong.

22.36 Zach, Cheryl. **Dear Diary: Secret Admirer.** Berkley, 1999. 184 pp. ISBN 0425171140. Fiction.

Brittany writes in her diary, "Dear Prince Charming, Are you out there, somewhere?" Her steady boyfriend, Nate, just isn't exciting or charming enough for her. Then Brittany meets Randall on the Internet, and he charms this tenth-grade girl with romantic online messages. He even sends her flowers at school. Refusing to listen to the warnings of her friends, Brittany agrees to meet Randall alone in the park. If Nate hadn't arrived in time to help Brittany escape from Randall's sexual advances, she would have been another one of the missing or dead teenagers reported on the evening news. Instead, a now much wiser Brittany presses charges. Together, she and Nate arrive at the courthouse to testify against this Internet stalker.

23 Science Fiction

"In fiction, truth is the search for truth, nothing is pre-established and knowledge is only what both of us—reader and writer—can imagine."

Carlos Fuentes

23.1 Alten, Steve. **Meg: A Novel of Deep Terror.** Doubleday, 1997. 278 pp. ISBN 0385489056. Fiction.

When Dr. Jonas Taylor, a paleontologist and deep-sea submersible pilot, went on the top-secret dive in the Mariansa Trench, he stumbled upon a Carcharodon, a sixty-foot, twenty-ton prehistoric shark. The Carcharodon has survived since the Ice Age by living seven miles below the ocean's surface, where heat from volcanic vents warm the otherwise frigid water. Although he is called a crackpot by his colleagues, Taylor's predictions about the prehistoric beast's destructive capabilities are about to be proven true.

23.2 Card, Orson Scott. **Ender's Shadow: A Parallel Novel to Ender's Game.** Tor, 1999. 379 pp. ISBN 031286860X. Fiction.

In *Ender's Game,* Card introduced us to the brilliant young Andrew "Ender" Wiggins, who was taken from his family when he was six to train in the Battle School, a space station. There Ender learned the difficult lessons he needed to learn to lead the final invasion in the war against the "Buggers," an alien race seemingly intent on destroying Earth. Now, with *Ender's Shadow,* we return to that same time and place to meet another of these child geniuses, whose talents have brought him to the Battle School. This time the focus is on Bean, Ender's friend and right hand. Like Ender, Bean's natural ability sets him apart. This story of how a small band of children fight to save the world is told from Bean's point of view. Along the way, we learn just why Bean is so brilliant, and what that brilliance means for the rest of his life.

23.3 Card, Orson Scott. **Pastwatch: The Redemption of Christopher Columbus.** Tor, 1997. 416 pp. ISBN 0812508645. Fiction.

He must have seen something. Something like . . . the future. That's the conclusion of the members of Pastwatch, a group of scientists in the future, when they consider how Christopher Columbus convinced his European benefactors that the New World was full of gold. Unlike present-day scientists, however, members of Pastwatch such as Tagiri and Hassan can do more than just study they past—they can actually travel in time and influence the course of history. When the environment of the future deteriorates to the point of doom for the planet, Tagiri and Hassan travel to the time of Columbus, hoping to change the events that led to the meeting of people of the Eastern and Western Hemispheres. Their actions might mean the world they know and all they love in it will cease to exist, but in its place might exist a better world.

23.4   Cart, Michael, editor. **Tomorrowland: 10 Stories about the Future.** Scholastic, 1999. 203 pp. ISBN 0590376780. Fiction.

Two of these imaginative stories are set in the past, a few in the present, and the rest in the future. Ron Koertge, Lois Lowry, Tor Seidler, Katherine Paterson, and others thoughtfully deal with such issues as alienation, responsibility, the environment, and family relationships. You will meet the last dog on earth, encounter the last book in the universe, and be there on the night the world is predicted to end.

23.5   Cooney, Caroline B. **Prisoner of Time.** Delacorte, 1998. 208 pp. ISBN 0385322445. Fiction.

The third book in the time travel trilogy by Cooney, this story takes Tod Lockwood from the present day back in time to the nineteenth century. There he meets the beautiful and headstrong Devonny Stratton. Tod brings Devonny back with him to his own time, thinking that is the best solution for her problems. As much as Devonny enjoys the freedom women have in contemporary society, she knows she must travel back to her own time. There she will have to stand on her own two feet, and try to solve her problems.

23.6   Cooper, Roscoe. **The Diary of Victor Frankenstein.** Illustrated by Timothy Basil Ering. Dorling Kindersley, 1997. Unpaged. ISBN 0789424568. Fiction.

A week before Christmas in 1997, Roscoe Cooper receives an unusual package that contains a letter from his great-great-grandfather, Dr. Ephriam Cooper. The letter is dated 1897, and in it, Dr. Cooper explains how he came upon the contents of a package Roscoe now holds in his hands—the diary of Victor Frankenstein, and the reason Frankenstein demanded that his estate executors keep the diary safe for one hundred years. Now that time has elapsed, and Roscoe holds the diary of the man who created the Frankenstein monster. The diary, reproduced quite authentically here, shows us the thoughts, dreams, and fears of one who dared to play god.

23.7 Crichton, Michael. **Timeline.** Knopf, 1999. 450 pp. ISBN 0679444815. Fiction.

Historians employed by a genius billionaire who runs his own technology company are in for a history lesson when they travel from 1999 to 1357 to save a fellow worker. Moving between the Middle Ages and the dawn of the millennium, Crichton gives readers the ride they've come to expect from him. Sword fights, knights in armor, disease, and damsels in distress—this book has it all. Throw in some science to explain the move across time, and you have a science fiction adventure book that will keep anyone reading.

23.8 Gilmore, Katie. **The Exchange Student.** Houghton Mifflin, 1999. 217 pp. ISBN 0395575117. Fiction.

Daria has enough to do around the house without playing host to an exchange student from another planet. She has more than forty different animals she has been taking care of, animals once in danger of becoming extinct. Thanks to Daria's work with The Ark, an endangered species preservation group, many endangered species are making a comeback. Thankfully the exchange student, Fen, seems to have an easy way around Daria's animal menagerie. He is reticent to speak about the animals from his own home, but is more than willing to help Daria care for her charges. Daria begins to believe that perhaps all is not well on Fen's home planet, and that maybe his visit was prompted by ulterior motives.

23.9 Haddix, Margaret Peterson. **Among the Hidden.** Simon & Schuster, 1998. 160 pp. ISBN 0689817002. Fiction.

Luke is one of the "shadow" children. He is a third son in a time when all families are limited to having only two children, so Luke must remain hidden and out of sight, an easy task as the family lives outside of the city. However, when the land near his house is sold for a new housing development, Luke is confined to the stairs and the attic. One day, as he is looking longingly at the rest of the children in his neighborhood head off to school, Luke notices another shadow child living nearby. How can he get her attention and still remain safe?

23.10 Hamilton, Virginia. **Dustland.** Scholastic, 1998. 214 pp. ISBN 0590362178. Fiction.

The second book in the Justice and Her Brothers series continues the story of Justice, her twin brothers Levi and Thomas, and their friend Dorian. All four possess extrasensory perception, a gift that brings them together in a race to save the future inhabitants of Earth. When his jealousy of Justice's power grows out of control, however, Thomas breaks from the group, and takes Levi along with him. This separation endangers all four as they travel through time, and imperils Earth as well.

23.11 Hamilton, Virginia. **The Gathering.** Scholastic, 1998. 214 pp. ISBN 059032626X. Fiction.

This is the third installment in the Justice and Her Brothers series. In this adventure, Justice, her brothers, and Dorian are reunited. The foursome must use their incredible powers of extrasensory perception to protect future inhabitants of Earth from an evil force. The force, known as Mal, seems impossible to defeat, but Justice, Levi, Thomas, and Dorian must try, or place the people of the future in grave danger.

23.12 Hamilton, Virginia. **Justice and Her Brothers.** Scholastic, 1998. 282 pp. ISBN 0590362143. Fiction.

Justice Douglas and her identical twin brothers, Levi and Thomas, are linked to one another by more than their familial relationship. The three are able to communicate telepathically. Justice soon learns that this remarkable ability must be put to careful use. Moreover, she and her brothers must learn how to operate as a team, a feat made difficult when Thomas threatens to break from their unit and go off on his own.

23.13 Hautman, Pete. **Mr. Was.** Aladdin, 1998. 240 pp. ISBN 0689819145. Fiction.

After his grandfather dies, Jack Lund and his parents move into his grandfather's home. There, in an old house in Memory, Minnesota, Jack discovers a secret door, one that will lead him back fifty years into the past. Jack finds himself face-to-face with his own mother as a child. As his present and past begin to collide, Jack discovers that his actions in the past may have incredible consequences in the future. Now he must do everything he can to prevent his father from murdering his mother.

23.14 Howarth, Lesley. **Maphead: The Return.** Candlewick, 1997. 237 pp. ISBN 0763603449. Fiction.

In this sequel to *Maphead,* a boy from a parallel dimension possesses strange powers to project maps onto his head. Maphead, as he is called, is sent away by his father to seek his destiny. Despite his father's warnings, Maphead joins a human family in Rubytown, and influences them with his powers. His interference with the Stamp family's lives causes major problems that must be corrected, and Maphead learns a valuable lesson about himself and his life.

23.15 Hughes, Monica, editor. **What If . . . ? Amazing Stories.** Tundra, 1998. 199 pp. ISBN 0887764584. Fiction.

What if you were given only one wish? What if you found a magic scepter and used it improperly? What if origami paper animals could come to life? What if Frosty the Snowman wasn't really jolly at all? These are some of the fantastic situations explored by Canadian writers in fourteen thought-provoking stories and two poems assembled by famous science fiction writer Monica Hughes. These stories will amaze and delight you.

23.16 Jones, Terry. **Douglas Adams' Starship Titanic.** Harmony, 1997. 246 pp. ISBN 0609601032. Fiction.

The inhabitants of the planet Blerotin are gathered to watch the launch of the greatest hotel starship ever built. Suddenly, the massive structure disappears. The ship and its creator, Leovinus, along with a Blerotin journalist, have been kidnapped by the ship's computer system. They make a temporary stop on Earth, where Leovinus disembarks. Dan, Nettie, and Lucy climb aboard and are accidentally hijacked. In an attempt to control the sabotaged ship, the Blerotin journalist inadvertently begins a self-destruct sequence. The four hostages must now find a way to diffuse the bomb, repair the ship's computer, fight off hostile attackers, and return to Earth. The sophisticated humor of the adventure makes this book an enjoyable reading experience.

23.17 Koontz, Dean. **Seize the Night.** Bantam, 1999. 401 pp. ISBN 0553106651. Fiction.

When children start disappearing in Moonlight Bay, Christopher Snow, first seen in *Fear Nothing,* knows it will be up to him to find out what is happening because the police can't be trusted. With his dog, Christopher tracks the latest victim and ends up at a supposedly deserted army base on the outskirts of town. Christopher keeps going even after his trusty dog disappears, but soon realizes that he can't do it alone.

23.18 Levitin, Sonia. **The Cure.** Harcourt Brace, 1999. 192 pp. ISBN 0152018271. Fiction.

The year is 2407. In this distant future, all children are born as fraternal twins, emotions are kept carefully under control, and music is not permitted in any form. Gemm, one half of a pair of twins, cannot seem to conform to the rules of this future society. For some reason, he hears music in his head. Music also seems to play a key role in his dreams. The doctors have done all they can to change Gemm's behavior, but to no avail. He is finally given a choice: opt to be recycled, or undertake the cure. Gemm wants to continue with his life, and so selects the cure. Soon, Gemm finds himself traveling back in time to the Middle Ages. It is there he will learn a cruel lesson about the power of music.

23.19 Martin, Les. **The Host (X-Files #8).** HarperTrophy, 1997. 144 pp. ISBN 00644718100. Fiction.

Fans of the popular television show will enjoy reading the continuing adventures of agents Fox Mulder and Dana Scully. As usual, Mulder's ability to unlock the mysteries of the unknown is hindered by the F.B.I. and Mulder's boss, Skinner, who assigns Mulder an insultingly simple case. But is it so simple? Scully's autopsy reveals evidence of white, slimy worms—forcing her and Mulder to investigate further. When they see a hairless, earless creature that may be responsible for the worm-like traces on the body, Mulder and Scully know they have once again gone deep into territory that few could understand and even fewer believe.

23.20 Nix, Garth. **Shade's Children.** HarperCollins, 1997. 288 pp. ISBN 006273240. Fiction.

In the terrible and brutal future, Earth is a place dominated by the Overlords. These cruel rulers have created a system where fourteen-year-olds are used to provide young brains and muscles for warring creatures who fight senseless wars. Countless children try to escape this fate, but few succeed. One of those few, Gold-Eye, is helped by other escapees, who show him the way to an abandoned submarine where children live under the protection of Shade, a computer-generated adult. Shade trades his protection for the reconnaissance knowledge obtained by his "children," and he forces them to travel repeatedly into the Overlord's territory. Shade's willingness to provide these young refugees food and shelter makes his demands seem tolerable—until Gold-Eye and others decide to destroy the Overlords and discover Shade's resistance to their idea. Then their caretaker seems as ruthless as the Overlords.

23.21 Parker, Daniel. **Count Down.** Aladdin Paperbacks / Simon & Schuster, 1999. 132 pp. ISBN 0689818289. Fiction.

The countdown to the millennium is causing fear, anxiety, anguish, and a multitude of prophecies. One prophecy appears to have come true, as a plague has killed all adults on Earth, and it is the teenage survivors who must rally to save mankind. One girl knows how to stop the prophecy from reaching a catastrophic end. She is the final hope, but finds she must destroy herself in order to save humanity. Part of the Count Down series, this book explores concerns some groups have as the millennium approaches.

23.22 Patterson, James. **When the Wind Blows.** Little Brown, 1998. 416 pp. ISBN 0316693324. Fiction.

Frannie O'Neill, a veterinarian, lives a quiet life while trying to come to grips with her husband's murder—quiet, that is, until she meets eleven-year-old Max, who puts her life in turmoil and in danger. Max has been part of a diabolical experiment that has given her unusual powers, including the ability to fly.

23.23 Rubinstein, Gillian. **Under the Cat's Eye: A Tale of Morph and Mystery.** Simon & Schuster, 1998. 204 pp. ISBN 0689818009. Fiction.

Jai is sent off to a boarding school where all the students seem to behave strangely. His two newest friends, Hugo and Seal, confide in Jai, telling him that the new headmaster of the school is stealing the souls of his classmates. As the three begin to investigate this mystery, Jai finds he must join forces with a cat and a dog from a parallel world in order to stop the headmaster, and send him back to the evil world from which he came.

23.24 Sheffield, Charles, and Jerry Pournelle. **Higher Education: A Jupiter Novel.** Tor, 1997. 288 pp. ISBN 0812538900. Fiction.

Life in the future is a mess, with overwhelming unemployment, and schools that produce more punks than scholars. When sixteen-year-old Rick Luban is expelled from school, life looks bleak until he takes the advice of a teacher, and signs on as a trainee with Vanguard Mining, an asteroid mining company that trains recruits in space. The difficult-to-please instructor Turkey Gossage demands compliance and success, and Rick soon finds himself fighting hard for a spot with the mining team. His biggest challenge comes in the form of rescuing the survivors of a mining accident—a challenge Rick isn't sure he can meet.

23.25 Shusterman, Neal. **Downsiders.** Simon & Schuster, 1999. 208 pp. ISBN 0689803753. Fiction.

Lindsay is not happy about her recent move to New York City, but after her parents' divorce, she has no other alternative. Lindsay is surprised to find that there is a secret city beneath New York. Downside is a thriving place, but its existence may be threatened by the construction job her father is supervising. Lindsay and her Downside companion, Talon, must find a way to save the underground civilization.

23.26 Shusterman, Neal. **Mindstorms: Stories to Blow Your Mind.** Tom Doherty, 1996. 115 pp. ISBN 0812551982. Fiction.

Imagine you are on vacation inside a museum in Mexico City. You are supposed to be watching your little brother Jackson, but he wants to play hide-and-seek. While looking for him, there is an earthquake, and when they sift through the rubble, your brother is gone. Mickey is the "Midnight Michelangelo," spray painting beautiful murals on buildings. So far the police haven't been able to catch him. Mickey is getting more and more bold, and his murals are getting stranger and stranger. What were once flowers in the landscape become horrifying alien images. He knows that isn't what he painted the night before. What or who is controlling him? These are just two of the eight short stories in this collection that will make you wonder what is real and what is imagined.

23.27 Sleater, William. **The Beasties.** Dutton, 1997. 198 pp. ISBN 0525455981. Fiction.

There's no reason to take Al seriously when he warns Doug about strange creatures called "beasties" that lurk in the woods near Doug's new home. After all, Al is always saying things that nobody believes. But when Doug sees local folks missing a finger, an ear, or a nose, he begins to wonder. No reason to talk to Colette about it—she's always in a world of her own with her books. As fate would have it, though, Colette and Doug stumble upon the secret of the "beasties" together—and face a decision that could threaten their lives, the lives of their neighbors, and the strange beings that live below the ground.

23.28 Sleator, William. **Rewind.** Dutton, 1999. 120 pp. ISBN 0525461302. Fiction.

Angry with his parents, Peter dashes out of his house and directly into the path of an oncoming car. He floats away from his body into a great white light. In the afterlife, he is told that he will be given a certain amount of time in which he has the opportunity to return to any moment in his former life to try to prevent his death. As Peter rewinds his life again and again, he finds that he knows what will happen before it happens—because he's lived it already. Such knowledge only confuses him as he tries to stay focused on his task of staying alive.

24 Self-Help and Well-Being

"Reading is a privileged pleasure because each of us enjoys it, quite complexly, in ways not replicable by anyone else."

Robert Alter

24.1 Allison, Anthony. **Hear These Voices: Youth at the Edge of the Millennium.** Dutton, 1999. 170 pp. ISBN 0525453539. Nonfiction.

Many teens face obstacles that seem impossible to surmount. The teens whose voices are heard in this book include a young Thai girl sold into prostitution by her father, a Denver teen who has been bounced around from foster home to foster home, and other remarkable teens who got help and managed to survive. Social services, caring adults, and schools all made differences in their lives, making it possible for each of them to begin to plan for her or his future. Black-and-white photographs put a face to each of the very distinctive voices heard in this book.

24.2 Bell, Janet Cheatham, and Lucille Usher Freeman, selectors. **Stretch Your Wings: Famous Black Quotations for Teens.** Little Brown, 1999. 166 pp. ISBN 0316038253. Nonfiction.

"I believe in recognizing every human being as a human being, neither white, black, brown, nor red," Malcolm X once said. Lorraine Hansberry wrote, "The thing that makes you exceptional, if you are at all, is inevitably that which must also make you lonely." This book is filled with over four hundred quotations and anecdotes from some of the African Americans you admire most. Read what Kobe Bryant, Chris Rock, Queen Latifah, Toni Morrison, Muhammad Ali, Michael Jordan, Nelson Mandela, and hundreds of others have to say about life, dreams, and adversity.

24.3 Bennett, William J., editor. **Our Country's Founders: A Book of Advice for Young People.** Simon & Schuster Books for Young Readers, 1998. 304 pp. ISBN 0689821069. Nonfiction.

Bennett includes speeches, poems, letters, and articles by early American patriots as inspiration to young people today. He includes some love letters from John Adams addressed to "Miss Adorable," Abigail Smith, during their courtship. Enjoy letters between George Washington and his son, Ben Franklin's "Advice to a Young Tradesman," and notes from Alexander Hamilton's diary. The book also includes facsimiles of important historical documents, including the Constitution and Declaration of Independence.

24.4   Bennett, William J., editor. **Our Sacred Honor: Words of Advice from the Founders in Stories, Letters, Poems, and Speeches.** Simon & Schuster, 1997. 430 pp. ISBN 068484138X. Nonfiction.

The founders of this country, such as George Washington, Thomas Jefferson, Benjamin Franklin, and John and Abigail Adams, left a legacy that still lives on—their advice to future generations of Americans. Read the advice Thomas Jefferson gave to a friend's young son ("Never put off till tomorrow what you can do today" and "Never spend your money before you have it."). See what Benjamin Franklin had to say about silence, order, sincerity, and cleanliness. Read Patrick Henry's words about patriotism, Abigail Adams's comments on love, George Washington's advice about friendship, and Noah Webster's thoughts on the Bible. Through stories, songs, letters, and speeches, you'll get a glimpse into hearts of the Americans who helped create this nation.

24.5   Canfield, Jack, Mark Victor Hansen, and Kimberly Kirberger, compilers. **Chicken Soup for the Teenage Soul II : 101 More Stories of Life, Love and Learning.** Health Communications, 1998. 351 pp. ISBN 1558746161. Nonfiction.

Teenagers love this book, and it literally flies off the library shelves. Written by peers, these stories and poems appeal to young adults who are experiencing relationships and other challenges life has to offer. For example, one particularly touching story is written by a young lady whose boyfriend has broken his neck on a trip. Instantly, she begins to think of the things they won't be able to do together while he recovers, but then she realizes that "Two months is a very short time in exchange for a lifetime of living." The writing is not always polished, but the stories are definitely heartfelt and meaningful to teens.

24.6   Daldry, Jeremy. **The Teenage Guy's Survival Guide.** Little Brown, 1999. 136 pp. ISBN 0316178241. Nonfiction.

Daldry's subtitle to this book is "the real deal on girls, growing up, and other guy stuff," which summarizes nicely what the book is about. With simple, humorous language and cartoon sketches, Daldry answers lots of the questions teenage guys have—mostly about girls and sex. Filled with practical advice about kissing, peer pressure, drugs, body changes, and sexuality, the funny, warm, and friendly approach of the author makes this book comfortable reading.

24.7   Dee, Catherine, editor. **The Girls' Book of Wisdom.** Little Brown, 1999. 199 pp. ISBN 0316179566. Nonfiction.

Wouldn't it be great if you had collected in one place all the wise things you've ever heard so you could pull out pieces of wisdom whenever you needed them? Well, that's what Catherine Dee has done in this book. It provides sage advice from female scientists, musicians, business executives, writers, athletes, actors, doctors, world leaders, and even moms and daughters, on myriad topics. Divided into forty-five categories, the more than four hundred quotations contained here will help you understand yourself and those around you.

24.8   Drill, Esther, Heather McDonald, and Rebecca Odes. **Deal with It! A Whole New Approach to Your Body, Brain, and Life as a gURL.** Pocket, 1999. 320 pp. ISBN 0671041576. Nonfiction.

Here is the complete guide to the birds and the bees, as well as many other topics of interest to teenage girls. Subjects included range from zits and remedies for combating them, to hair and removing it and siblings and surviving them. Questions, answers, and advice from the many who visit the gURL.com Web site are also included. Want to know how to deal with those "sucky" emotions? Need to get information about health issues? Want to know how drugs affect the body? Those questions and many others are addressed in this wide-ranging guide.

24.9   Estepa, Andrea, and Philip Kay, editors. **Starting with I: Personal Essays by Teenagers.** Persea, 1997. 182 pp. ISBN 089255228X. Nonfiction.

This multi-ethnic, multi-issue collection of essays from *New Youth Connections* presents the hard-earned wisdom acquired by the teenage authors included here. The essays are grouped into six categories: family, race, culture, gender, sexuality, and identity. Edwidge Danticat, a former writer for *New Youth Connections,* writes in the foreword of her need to find her voice, and the need of the young writers in this collection to break their silence and find their voices. Quoting from Wislawa Szymborska's poem, "The Three Oddest Words," Danticat observes, "When I pronounce Silence, / I destroy it." There is no silence in this collection.

24.10 Gaskins, Pearl Fuyo. **What Are You? Voices of Mixed-Race Young People.** Henry Holt, 1999. 192 pp. ISBN 0805059687. Nonfiction.

Gaskins interviewed dozens of mixed-race teens and young adults for this frank and funny examination of what it is like to be multiracial. Often mixed-race people are considered to be outside of the traditional racial boundaries, but these forty-five stories make it clear that traditional boundaries must give way. The stunning diversity of the United States is present in these heartfelt stories of both the positive and negative experiences of being multiracial.

24.11 Hersch, Patricia. **A Tribe Apart: A Journey into the Heart of American Adolescence.** Ballantine, 1999. 391 pp. ISBN 034543594X. Nonfiction.

Eight regular kids—adolescents who are average achievers on academic and social levels—were the focus of this author's three-year study. She watched as these teens tried to figure out relationships, began to establish friendships, and determined what was cool and uncool. Many of these teens had been left alone to figure out their own system of ethics, morals, and values. They had to rely on each other for advice on such profound topics as abuse, dysfunctional parents, and sex.

24.12 Hyde, Margaret O., and Elizabeth H. Forsyth. **The Sexual Abuse of Children and Adolescents.** Millbrook, 1997. 81 pp. ISBN 0761300589. Nonfiction.

With clearly focused chapters and informational boxes interspersed throughout the text, this book works to dispel the myths around sexual abuse. Chapters cover abuser profiles, effects on the targeted child, uncovering the truth, preventing abusive behaviors, and ways to get help. The language is accessible to young people, and the book's completeness makes it a valuable resource.

For a young woman or young man who has suffered such an experience, this book will provide a greater understanding of the emotional and psychological trauma attached to sexual abuse.

24.13 Irwin, Cait. **Conquering the Beast Within: How I Fought Depression and Won . . . and How You Can Too.** Times, 1999. 120 pp. ISBN 0812932471. Nonfiction.

Bit by bit, Cait Irwin found herself consumed by a beast that eventually took over her life. This book chronicles her bout with severe depression, as well as her remarkable emergence from the jaws of the beast. The text is accompanied by Cait's sketches, which add a bit of humor to an otherwise serious and frightening story. The right combination of family support, medication, and help from doctors helped Cait emerge from her darkness. Now she shares her story with others.

24.14 Kalengis, Mary Motley. **Seen and Heard: Teenagers Talk about Their Lives.** Stewart, Tabori and Chang, 1998. 128 pp. ISBN 1556708343. Nonfiction.

From the son of a farmer to a recent immigrant to the United States, this book includes the voices of teens who live their lives quietly in towns across the country. In their own words, we learn about their thoughts, fears, failures, triumphs, and hopes. Photographs of each teen accompany the text.

24.15 Kirberger, Kimberly. **Teen Love: On Relationships.** Health Communications, 1999. 371 pp. ISBN 1558747346. Nonfiction.

Falling in love? Worried about what it means when he doesn't call you back? Don't like her hanging all over you at parties? Feeling sad after the breakup you didn't expect? Not sure why everyone has a girlfriend or a boyfriend except you? If you need answers to any of those questions (or nearly one hundred others) about relationships, then this book is for you. Filled with letters, poems, and essays from real teens about being in love, this book will help you navigate through all the overwhelming feelings that accompany falling in love.

24.16 Kravetz, Stacy. **Girl Boss: Running the Show Like the Big Chicks: Entrepreneurial Skills, Stories, and Encouragement for Modern Girls.** Girl, 1999. 95 pp. ISBN 0965975428. Nonfiction.

Get tips and tricks for starting your own business, being your own boss, and making it big in the business world with this book that offers advice and inspiration for girls and young women. Read about successful women who've started every type of business, from marketing vending machines to video production. Find out how to turn your ideas into winning realities, whether you have a boss's attitude, and whether you've got what it takes to succeed.

24.17 Krizmanic, Judy. **The Teen's Vegetarian Cookbook.** Viking, 1999. 186 pp. ISBN 0670874264. Nonfiction.

Do you prefer vegetables over meat? Are you unsure how to get all the protein you need when steak and chicken aren't part of your diet? Or do you just need a new way to cook your favorite vegetables? Check out this cookbook to find the answers to any of these dilemmas. It's a must for any teenager who wants to eat a meat-free diet. Filled with menus and recipes to use throughout the day, it also provides helpful suggestions from fellow vegetarians on everything from meal planning and eating out to surviving the college dining hall.

24.18 Mastoon, Adam. **The Shared Heart: Portraits and Stories Celebrating Lesbian, Gay, and Bisexual Young People.** Morrow, 1997. 87 pp. ISBN 0688149316. Nonfiction.

Adam Mastoon's sensitive and superb photographs are combined here with powerful personal narratives that give a "human face and a dignified voice" to the lives of forty lesbian, gay, and bisexual young adults. Each story presents a candid and poignant look at the meaning of coming out, including the effects on family and friends, the pain of loneliness, and the struggle for the freedom to be who you are. These are stories of honesty and courage, and they speak to the humanity that binds us all. In the words of Craig, "I am a human being. I have thoughts and feelings, skin and bone. I also have talents, just like everybody."

24.19 Parker, Julia, and Derek Parker. **The Complete Book of Dreams.** Dorling Kindersley, 1998. 208 pp. ISBN 0789432951. Nonfiction.

Dreams may be early warning signs that all is not right in your life, or they can be sources of great joy. Often they are a little of both. This comprehensive book examines various subjects, signs, and symbols that can show up when we are at our most vulnerable. If you want to find out what that crazy dream about Aunt Martha was all about, or confirm that your dream of winning the lottery is a precognition, then this is the book for you.

24.20 Pringle, Laurence. **Drinking.** Morrow Junior Books, 1997. 112 pp. ISBN 0688150446. Nonfiction.

One of the toughest decisions faced by young people today is how to handle the opportunities and pressures to drink alcohol. "Each year several thousand people die of acute alcohol poisoning in the United States alone. At least eight hundred of the victims are high school and college students." Alcohol is a poison and a drug, and its abuse is a prescription for family troubles, poor health, and an early death. Knowing the facts and sources of helpful information can aid you in making good decisions.

24.21 Roberts, Tara, editor. **Am I the Last Virgin? Ten African American Reflections on Sex and Love.** Simon & Schuster, 1997. 112 pp. ISBN 0689804490. Nonfiction.

These ten essays range from the title story about Roberts' determination to take the word *virgin* back to its Latin root, *Virgo,* meaning strength, force and skill, to stories of rape, sexual assault, unwanted pregnancy, AIDS, and loss of self. As ten African American women share their personal stories, you learn how triumph can rise from tragedy. The book also includes an extensive, twenty-five-page Resource Directory that lists hotlines and help centers nationwide.

24.22 Roleff, Tamara L., editor. **Suicide: Opposing Viewpoints.** Greenhaven, 1998. 192 pp. ISBN 1565106644. Nonfiction.

Is suicide an individual right? What are the causes of teen suicide? Should assisted suicide be legal? How can suicide be prevented? These questions are the focus of debate in this volume from the Opposing Viewpoints series, which includes selections from books, journals, newspapers, government documents, and position papers. Each section of the volume considers a different question, and is preceded by an introduction that provides background information on the issue. Often sophisticated in style and tone, the selections get at the heart of the issues addressed.

24.23 Shandler, Sara. **Ophelia Speaks: Adolescent Girls Write about Their Search for Self.** HarperCollins, 1999. 285 pp. ISBN 0060952970. Nonfiction.

What do teens want the most? This book suggests some of the answers. In response to *Reviving Ophelia*, college student Sara Shandler sent thousands of letters to high schools across the United States asking for contributions from teenaged girls about their concerns and cares. In poems, essays, and stories, the young women represented in this volume talk about what they need most in order to succeed in life. Issues include food, race, parents, and religion.

24.24 Sneddon, Pamela Shires. **Brothers and Sisters, Born to Bicker?** Enslow, 1996. 98 pp. ISBN 0894909142. Nonfiction.

Brothers and sisters come in all shapes, sizes, and ages, and can be a mixed blessing. Sneddon examines brother-sister relationships, and explains the seemingly inevitable conflicts that arise from them. Her research is based on personal interviews and question-naires conducted with high school teens. Interesting graphics, role-playing suggestions, and multiple-choice quizzes provide different approaches to understanding such relationships. Topics covered include sibling rivalry, childhood and teenage years, and creating positive relationships.

24.25 Swan-Jackson, Alys. **When Your Parents Split Up: How to Keep Yourself Together.** Price Stern Sloan, 1997. 90 pp. ISBN 0843174617. Nonfiction.

Although surviving your parents' divorce is difficult, it can be done! This guide for teenagers answers questions, and includes firsthand advice from teenagers of divorced parents on the following topics: first reactions, life before the split, who is responsible, why relationships fail, personal feelings, practical changes, you and your parents, facing the world, single parents, stepfamilies, surviving divorce, and where to find support.

24.26 Taulbert, Clifton L. **Eight Habits of the Heart: The Timeless Values That Build Strong Communities—Within Our Homes and Our Lives.** Dial / Viking, 1997. 115 pp. ISBN 0670875457. Nonfiction.

Taulbert identifies the values needed to repair today's fractured communities. His personal stories are filled with warm memories of people and events that helped to create in him a spiritual strength. The important habits include a nurturing attitude, dependability, friendship, brotherhood, and hope. In addition to the stories, there are group exercises to help create a strong community.

24.27 Wolf, Naomi. **Promiscuities: The Secret Struggle for Womanhood.** Random House, 1997. 234 pp. ISBN 067941603X. Nonfiction.

With naked honesty, Wolf relives the coming-of-age and sexual awakening of both she and her contemporaries. She tells the story of what every girl lives through as she begins to discover and explore her own body and experience curiosity about boys' bodies. She also discusses dating, sexual intercourse, love, relationships, and the dangers of irresponsibility. A thorough, comprehensive memoir that describes universal female experiences in our culture.

24.28 Woodtor, Dee Parmer. **Finding a Place Called Home: A Guide to African-American Genealogy and Historical Identity.** Random House, 1999. 452 pp. ISBN 037540595X. Nonfiction.

This book is a step-by-step guide to finding your African American roots and tracing your family tree. Beginning with your immediate family, you'll learn how to interview family members, use census reports to gain information about your past, find and read slave schedules, and use property deeds and courthouse records to uncover your past. You'll also learn about the history of Africans in the Americas.

25 Short Stories

"Good readers make much out of little."
Irving Howe

25.1 Asher, Sandy. **With All My Heart, with All My Mind.** Simon & Schuster, 1999. 164 pp. ISBN 0689820127. Fiction.

The Jewish faith is built on tradition. In today's complicated society, is it possible to maintain one's traditions? Thirteen stories explore what it means to be Jewish. Some of the stories are set in the present day, some take readers back to the past, and others explore the future. Each story focuses on how the central characters deal with their religious beliefs and convictions.

25.2 Blume, Judy, editor. **Places I Never Meant to Be.** Simon & Schuster, 1999. 192 pp. ISBN 0689820348. Fiction.

Twelve writers, all of whom have been targets of censorship attacks for their novels for young adults, each contributed an original short story to this collection. Each author also writes about the chilling effect censorship has had on her or his writing. A thoughtful introduction by Judy Blume recounts her own experiences with censorship, and what she does to battle those who would curtail what you read. Some of the stories are frightening, some are humorous, and all are thought-provoking. Whether you are looking for the story of someone trapped in a basement by a vengeful cheerleader, or someone trapped by a friend's betrayal or a coach's fury, you will find this collection unique and interesting.

25.3 Budhos, Marina. **Remix: Conversations with Immigrant Teenagers.** Henry Holt, 1999. 145 pp. ISBN 0805051139. Nonfiction.

Imagine leaving home for the first time, and finding yourself living in a foreign country. You don't know the language and customs, or have any friends. You may not see anyone from your family for years. What would you do to fit in, to try to learn what it means to be a teenager in the United States? This book takes you inside the lives of twenty immigrant teenagers. These true stories will draw you into the world of young people trying to find their way in U.S. society. Some of them overcome the odds, but others fall through the cracks and join gangs or quit school. Each of these teenagers is looking for the same thing: a way to fit into the way of life in the United States.

25.4   Canfield, Jack, Mark Victor Hansen, and Kimberly Kirberger, compilers. **Chicken Soup for the Teenage Soul II: 101 More Stories of Life, Love and Learning.** Health Communications, 1998. 351 pp. ISBN 1558746161. Nonfiction.

Teenagers love this book, and it literally flies off the library shelves. Written by peers, these stories and poems appeal to young adults who are experiencing relationships and other challenges life has to offer. For example, one particularly touching story is written by a young woman whose boyfriend has broken his neck on a trip. Instantly, she thinks of the things they won't be able to do together while he recovers, but then she realizes that "Two months is a very short time in exchange for a lifetime of living." The writing is not always polished, but the stories are definitely heartfelt and meaningful to teens.

25.5   Cart, Michael, editor. **Tomorrowland: 10 Stories about the Future.** Scholastic, 1999. 203 pp. ISBN 0590376780. Fiction.

Two of the imaginative stories in this collection are set in the past, a few in the present, and the rest in the future. Ron Koertge, Lois Lowry, Tor Seidler, Katherine Paterson, and others thoughtfully deal with such issues as alienation, responsibility, the environment, and family relationships. You will meet the last dog on Earth, encounter the last book in the universe, and be there on the night the world is predicted to end.

25.6   Chan, Gillian. **Glory Days and Other Stories.** Kids Can, 1997. 118 pp. ISBN 1550743813. Fiction.

Drawing on her experiences as a teacher and librarian in Canada, Gillian Chan presents five loosely connected stories about the struggles of a handful of teenagers in one high school. They deal with, among other things, peer pressure, date rape, academic cheating, standing up to parents, and the consequences of their actions. Each character is faced with an important decision, allowing thoughtful readers to consider what they would do in the same situation.

25.7   Conford, Ellen. **Crush.** HarperCollins, 1998. 138 pp. ISBN 0060254149. Fiction.

These eight entertaining, easy-to-read stories about the romantic connections between various high school students as the Valentine's Day Sweetheart Stomp approaches will make you smile. Will Amy and Batso ever be completely compatible? Will nerdy Robert LaMotte ever get a date? Will any of B. J.'s wishes ever come true? And who will Di Callahan end up with if she can't make up her mind about whose invitation to accept?

25.8 Coville, Bruce. **Odder Than Ever.** Harcourt Brace, 1999. 146 pp. ISBN 015201747X. Fiction.

A ghost who bakes biscuits, a Japanese mirror that urges a teenage viewer to exchange places with his image, an unhappy boy who sprouts wings, a princess who smells bad because she's been spending too much time with a goblin, a gay teenager who meets his fairy godfather, the thing that waits under the bed for the right victim—all these bizarre situations and more await you in this engrossing (sometimes gross) and very entertaining collection.

25.9 Cowley, Joy. **The Hitchhikers: Stories from Joy Cowley.** Scholastic, 1997. 196 pp. ISBN 0590739042. Fiction.

These nine magical stories are reminiscent of folktales and legends. Some, like "The Tale of Tarama," are about monstrous creatures, while others, like "Cottage by the Sea," are about contemporary teenagers caught in time warps and dream worlds. All of these tales take place in the author's native New Zealand.

25.10 Crowe, Chris, editor. **From the Outside Looking In: Short Stories for LDS Teenagers.** Bookcraft, 1998. 134 pp. ISBN 1570084122. Fiction.

It's hard enough to be a teenager, but being a member of the Church of Jesus Christ of Latter-Day Saints adds another element. These fifteen stories examine the lives of LDS (Latter-Day Saints) teens who feel peculiar, alienated, and outside the mainstream. You don't have to be an LDS teenager to appreciate these stories or the struggles the characters face.

25.11 Dahl, Roald. **The Umbrella Man and Other Stories.** Viking, 1998. 279 pp. ISBN 0670878545. Fiction.

Have you ever wished for a machine that could write all your term papers for you? No problem. Just contact Adolph Knipe and ask him about The Great Automatic Grammatizor. Punch the right buttons, and you could end up writing your own novel! Have you ever been humiliated by someone and wanted to get revenge? Call on Vengeance is Mine, Inc., and choose the punishment. For five hundred dollars, they will punch your nemesis in the nose once, hard. For twenty-five hundred dollars, they will kidnap him and take away all his clothes except his underpants, shoes, and socks. Then, they will dump him out on the busiest street in town! In thirteen short stories that run the gamut from horror to humor and never fail to surprise, Roald Dahl provides the answers to our dreams.

25.12 Danticat, Edwidge. **Krik? Krak!** Vintage Contemporaries, 1996. 227 pp. ISBN 067976657X. Fiction.

In nine beautifully written but challenging stories, Edwidge Danticat vividly portrays both the pain and the beauty of the lives of contemporary Haitian people, especially the strong women who endure unimaginable horrors in the strife-torn country they love. The Haitian tradition of passing of stories from mother to daughter, generation to generation, is sustained in this collection of stories that takes its title from a Haitian saying, "They ask Krik? We say Krak!"

25.13 Dickinson, Peter. **The Lion Tamer's Daughter and Other Stories.** Delacorte, 1997. 298 pp. ISBN 0385323271. Fiction.

The British characters in these four lengthy stories move between present and past in supernatural ways. For example, in "The Spring," Derek finds a boy much like himself in the depths of a hidden spring, and in "Touch and Go," an adult man describes how as a young man, he met a girl from an earlier time who lived in the same place.

25.14 Donoghue, Emma. **Kissing the Witch: Old Tales in New Skins.** HarperCollins, 1997. ISBN 0060275758. Fiction.

Author Emma Donoghue weaves the stories of Cinderella, Snow White, Hansel and Gretel and others into a tapestry of interconnected lives and events. In this retelling of the classic childhood tales, Cinderella chooses the fairy godmother over the prince, Snow White reconsiders her relationship with her stepmother, and Hansel and Gretel come to different conclusions about the women in the gingerbread house. This collection of tales begins with the words of Cinderella who says, "I heard a knocking in my skull, and kept running to the door, but there was never anyone there. The days passed like dust brushed from my fingers." The images evoked by the words and ideas in these retellings will compel readers to brush the dust from childhood tales, and open the door to new interpretations of the old.

25.15 Duncan, Lois, editor. **Night Terrors: Stories of Shadow and Substance.** Simon & Schuster, 1996. 192 pp. ISBN 0689807244. Fiction.

Here are eleven selections that are "not exactly bedtime stories," written for this collection by some of the top writers in the business. Among them are Joan Aiken, Annette Curtis Klause, Joan Lowery Nixon, Theodore Taylor, and Patricia Windsor. From mysterious visitors and a snake-shaped bracelet that moves to the Bogey Man in the basement, these horror stories were designed to be "more terrifying than nightmares."

25.16 Duncan, Lois, editor. **Trapped! Cages of Mind and Body.** Simon & Schuster, 1998. 228 pp. ISBN 068981335X. Fiction.

A play by Rita Williams-Garcia, along with a series of poems by Lois Lowry and eleven original stories by Rob Thomas, Gary Crew, Joan Bauer, Francesca Lia Block, and others, reveal teenagers trapped in a variety of situations. From a contemporary teenage waitress facing a chaotic morning at the House of Pancakes to young Theseus trapped in a maze with the legendary Minotaur, readers will be eager to find out who escapes and who does not.

25.17 Fraustino, Lisa Rowe, editor. **Dirty Laundry: Stories about Family Secrets.** Viking, 1998. 181 pp. ISBN 0670879118. Fiction.

We all have secrets. These eleven stories about family secrets from authors such as Bruce Coville, Chris Crutcher, M. E. Kerr, Richard Peck, and Rita Williams-Garcia, range from ghost stories to personal memoir. The best of these stories—about plagiarism, abortion, transgender acceptance, child abuse, and mental illness—will stay in your mind for a long time.

25.18 Gallo, Donald R., editor. **No Easy Answers: Short Stories about Teenagers Making Tough Choices.** Delacorte, 1997. 324 pp. ISBN 0385322909. Fiction.

What would you do if you had a photograph that would embarrass a teacher? How would you react if you knew a friend was contemplating suicide? Can you make amends for the mistakes you made in the past? In the stories in this collection, the main characters face just these questions, and they must make difficult decisions. Authors whose works appear in this collection include Virginia Euwer Wolff, M. E. Kerr, and Walter Dean Myers.

25.19 Gallo, Donald R., editor. **Time Capsule: Short Stories about Teenagers throughout the Twentieth Century.** Delacorte, 1999. 222 pp. ISBN 0385326750. Fiction.

Although many teenagers believe no one else has ever faced the problems they face, teens throughout this century have faced problems with parents, siblings, society, and the dangers of their particular time. As the book moves through the decades of the twentieth century, readers have a chance to see teens confront the dangers and decisions in their lives. A bonus in this book are the editor's historical notes that appear before each story.

25.20 Gallo, Donald R., editor. **Ultimate Sports: Short Stories by Outstanding Writers for Young Adults.** Bantam, 1997. 352 pp. ISBN 0440227070. Fiction.

Sixteen stories about all types of sports and athletes are presented in this collection. Authors include Chris Crutcher, Chris Lynch, Robert Lipsyte, and Norma Fox Mazer. From the gridiron of contemporary football to the computer hologames of the future, these stories examine such issues as the nature of loss, the danger of competition, and the sacrifices of those who would be champions. What exactly does it take to be a winner in the world of athletics?

25.21 Hughes, Monica, selector. **What If . . . ? Amazing Stories.** Tundra, 1998. 199 pp. ISBN 0887764584. Fiction.

What if people living at a place called Luna base on the moon were haunted by a Moon Maiden? What if really famous people could be cloned over and over again? What if a person could only view the stars once in a lifetime? What if intricately folded paper birds could suddenly come alive and fly? Science fiction author Monica Hughes asked fantasy and science fiction authors from all over Canada to answer such "what if" questions with tales that pose endless possibilities. The result is a collection of fourteen stories and two poems that range from endangered environments and visits from aliens to stories about young people's self-discovery and critical decision making.

25.22 Mazer, Anne, editor. **A Walk in My World: International Short Stories about Youth.** Persea, 1998. 223 pp. ISBN 0892552379. Fiction.

In these sixteen stories from sophisticated adult perspectives, famous authors from around the world write about childhood experiences in Chile, Egypt, Germany, Ghana, Indonesia, Japan, Norway, Russia, and other nations. No matter what the country and in spite of the differences in cultures, readers will see connections with their own childhoods in each of these stories.

25.23 Mazer, Anne, editor. **Working Days: Short Stories about Teenagers at Work.** Persea, 1997. 207 pp. ISBN 0892552239.

The teenagers in these fifteen stories make discoveries about themselves, as well as about the world of work. Some hold a job so they can buy a special object, such as a baseball glove, a bike, or a car; others need money for college. They make burritos at Taco Bell, tutor, harvest chilies, glue labels on pill bottles, clerk at a motel, and drive an ice-cream truck. While performing their jobs, almost all of them connect with other people in life-enhancing ways.

25.24 Mazer, Harry, editor. **Twelve Shots: Outstanding Short Stories about Guns.** Delacorte, 1997. 229 pp. ISBN 0385322380. Fiction.

These twelve thought-provoking and entertaining stories about guns were written for this collection by some of the country's most notable authors, including Chris Lynch, Richard Peck, and Walter Dean Myers. "The gun lies deep, in the American psyche," Mazer writes. Although the threat of violence exists in several of these stories, which feature young women as well as young men, there are also stories of personal discovery, friendship, and even humor. Don't be put off by the topic.

25.25 Peck, Richard. **A Long Way from Chicago: A Novel in Short Stories.** Dial, 1998. 148 pp. ISBN 0803722907. Fiction.

Subtitled *A Novel in Short Stories,* this humorous book follows the adventures of a young boy and his younger sister during seven consecutive summers spent with their grandmother in a small Illinois town during the Great Depression. Although the characters are preteens in the first stories, older readers shouldn't have a problem with that, because the stories are mostly about larger-than-life Grandma Dowdel and some of the bizarre people in town. Peck's tales are tall, and rich with word play.

25.26 Poe, Edgar Allan. **The Pit and the Pendulum and Other Stories.** Illustrated by James Prunier. Viking, 1999. 158 pp. ISBN 0670887064. Fiction.

Edgar Allan Poe is well known for his dark stories, stories that reach into the haunted and tormented souls of his characters. In this collection are seven of Poe's most popular tales. Each story is accompanied by illustrations, with captions that provide a unique look into information relevant to the story. For both seasoned readers and those new to Poe and his works, this edition brings a new dimension to the stories by bringing to life the historical era in which Poe wrote.

25.27 Potok, Chaim. **Zebra and Other Stories.** Knopf, 1998. 146 pp. ISBN 0679854401. Fiction.

All but one of these six stories—four about females, two about males—focus on teenagers who feel alienated or troubled by a lack of self-confidence, a family secret, the death of a sibling, or the remarriage of a parent. In each story, the young person reaches a mature understanding about life. Each story should generate thoughtful responses from readers.

25.28 Rochman, Hazel, and Darlene Z. McCampbell, selectors. **Leaving Home: Stories.** HarperCollins, 1997. 232 pp. ISBN 0060248734. Fiction.

With excerpts from Amy Tan's *The Joy Luck Club,* Tim O'Brien's *The Things They Carried,* and Sandra Cisneros's *The House on Mango Street,* along with stories by a dozen other writers, including Gary Soto, Judith Ortiz Cofer, and Toni Morrison, this volume explores the feelings people have when they see a new direction for their lives. In some cases, it's physically leaving home that brings a new recognition; in others, it's an insight into another person or oneself.

25.29 Rylant, Cynthia. **The Heavenly Village.** Blue Sky / Scholastic, 1999. 96 pp. ISBN 0439040965. Fiction.

Somewhere between Heaven and Earth lies the Heavenly Village. The village is home to those who require a place to rest after death, and before moving on to eternal life. Some inhabitants died young and need a bit more time to adjust to their new life with God, while others left behind unfinished business and need more time. God has created this special place where people can prepare for eternal life at their own pace. These short vignettes tell the stories of some of the residents of this remarkable village.

25.30 Rylant, Cynthia. **The Van Gogh Cafe.** Apple Signature / Scholastic, 1998. 53 pp. ISBN 0590907174. Fiction.

Miraculous events occur in the Van Gogh Cafe in Flowers, Kansas, perhaps because the cafe was once a theater. Each of the six interconnected stories is full of surprises for the reader, from food that cooks itself and poems that come true to seagulls that eat mail and muffins that magically heal sick kids. The stories in this short book, published in a size appropriate for young children, will appeal to readers of all ages who allow themselves to believe in miracles.

25.31 Shusterman, Neal. **Mindstorms: Stories to Blow Your Mind.** Tom Doherty, 1996. 115 pp. ISBN 0812551982. Fiction.

Imagine you are on vacation inside a museum in Mexico City. You are supposed to be watching your little brother Jackson, but he wants to play hide and seek. While looking for him there is an earthquake, and when they sift through the rubble, your brother is gone. Mickey is the "Midnight Michelangelo," spray-painting beautiful murals on buildings. So far the police haven't been able to catch him. Mickey is getting more and more bold, and his murals are getting stranger and stranger. What were once flowers in the landscape become horrifying alien images. He knows that isn't what he painted the night before. What or who is controlling him? These are just two of the eight strange short stories in this collection that will make you wonder what is real and what is imagined.

25.32 Silvey, Anita, editor. **Help Wanted: Short Stories about Young People Working.** Little Brown, 1997. 174 pp. ISBN 0316791482. Fiction.

Many people get their first jobs as teenagers, and this diverse collection of stories reveals the different reasons why teens work and their varied experiences on the job. Some teens work to buy their own clothes. Some work to help out with the family budget. Common to all of these stories is how work sometimes defines who we are, and how we are often changed by our job experiences. Included is a story about Rayona, Michael Dorris's character from *A Yellow Raft in Blue Water*, who works an unusual shift at a fast food restaurant. Vivian Alcock tells us about Lucy Beck, whose mundane typist job takes a turn when she encounters an extraordinary typewriter. Well-known contributors include Ray Bradbury, Judith Ortiz Cofer, and Gary Soto.

25.33 Singer, Marilyn, compiler and editor. **Stay True: Short Stories for Strong Girls.** Scholastic, 1998. 204 pp. ISBN 0590360310. Fiction.

Eleven strong women writers, including M. E. Kerr, Rita Williams-Garcia, Norma Fox Mazer, and Andrea Davis Pinkney, tell original stories about young women learning about themselves and about life. They deal with personal independence, integrity, abuse, friendships, generational differences, and gender roles.

25.34 Stearns, Michael, editor. **A Wizard's Dozen: Stories of the Fantastic.** Scholastic, 1996. 186 pp. ISBN 0590865420. Fiction.

A wizard is a "wonder maker, a person who injects a jolt of the marvelous into the everyday." In this collection of fantastic stories, wizards of all shapes, sizes, ages, colors, and genders spin tales of the mystical and magical. Here we find Caliph Arenschadd, a wizard who puts curses on everyone, and the Princess Who Kicks Butt, who refuses to marry the Evil Enchanter. Then there is Efrum, a wizard who has a very special set of marbles, with a shooter that looks a lot like an eyeball. Great stories from well-known authors, including Patricia Wrede, Will Shetterly, Bruce Coville, and Jane Yolen, contribute to this collection from which "we learn to understand the differences of others, we learn compassion for those things we cannot fathom, and we learn the importance of a sense of wonder."

25.35 Stine, R. L. **Nightmare Hour.** HarperCollins, 1999. 148 pp. ISBN 0060286881. Fiction.

How would you feel if your mother bought an old country inn, complete with a rather interesting guest who claims he is a werewolf? How would you like to visit a secluded pumpkin patch on

Halloween night, where the faces on the pumpkins are a little too familiar? What would you do if you discovered a way of seeing into the past and the future? Could you escape a ghost who is after your skin? Stine shares ten new terrifying tales of horror guaranteed to chill your bones. For the first time, Stine also reveals the stories behind the stories by explaining how the idea for each story came into being. Keep a flashlight handy just in case the lights go out while you are reading this riveting collection.

25.36 Taylor, Theodore. **Rogue Wave and Other Red-Blooded Sea Stories.** Harcourt Brace, 1997. 184 pp. ISBN 015201408X. Fiction.

Based on his own naval experience and interest in the sea, Theodore Taylor presents eight adventure-filled stories, five of them previously published between 1952 and 1967. Among the best stories are the newly written ones. In "The Butcher," nineteen-year-old Michael attempts to avenge his father's death in the jaws of a great white shark, and in "Rogue Wave," a teenage girl is trapped inside the cabin of an overturned sailboat. Lots of action and information about the sea can be found in this collection.

25.37 Thomas, Rob. **Doing Time: Notes from the Undergrad.** Simon & Schuster, 1997. 184 pp. ISBN 0689809581. Fiction.

The stories in this collection are just as hard-hitting as Thomas's novels, *Rats Saw God* and *Slave Day.* Each story is narrated by a different high school senior performing some kind of community service. While directing a play for at-risk kids, delivering food to poor residents of the town, or working in an adoption ward in a convalescent hospital, each student learns something surprising about the world and about him- or herself. These separate stories are united by a common goal of all the characters.

25.38 Thomas, Rob. **Slave Day.** Aladdin, 1998. 246 pp. ISBN 068982193X. Fiction.

Slave Day is a long-standing tradition at Robert E. Lee High School. It is a day when teachers and students offer themselves as "slaves" to the highest bidder. This year, however, things will be different. Keene Davenport, an African American student, questions the continuation of a tradition that is demeaning to many. His letter to the editor of the local newspaper causes a stir, but

Slave Day continues as planned. It will be a day that several students, teachers, and parents will not soon forget.

25.39 Weiss, M. Jerry, and Helen S. Weiss. **From One Experience to Another: Award-Winning Authors Sharing Real-Life Experiences through Fiction.** Forge, 1997. 224 pp. ISBN 0312862539. Nonfiction.

For anyone who says "I don't have anything to write about," fifteen award-winning authors explain how they used their personal experiences to write the stories included in this collection. Avi writes about getting beaten up by bullies, Nancy Springer writes about painting fantasy landscape scenes on garage doors, Joan Lowery Nixon tells about a boy who sees a man die in the doctor's office, and Joan Bauer gets revenge on the security guard who years ago falsely arrested her for shoplifting. These stories show how writers use life events to help them create the stories that entertain so many.

25.40 Woodson, Jacqueline, editor. **A Way Out of No Way.** Henry Holt, 1996. 173 pp. ISBN 0805045708. Fiction.

Acclaimed novelist Jacqueline Woodson was inspired by the African American writers she discovered as a teenager growing up in Brooklyn, and trying to find a way out of her restricting life. Here she provides a taste of those novels, short stories, and poems by James Baldwin, Ernest J. Gaines, Rosa Guy, Jamaica Kinkaid, Toni Morrison, Toni Cade Bambara, Tim Seibles, Nikki Giovanni, and others.

25.41 Yezierska, Anna. **Hungry Hearts.** Penguin Books / Signet Classic, 1996. 239 pp. ISBN 0141180056. Fiction.

Originally published in 1920, this collection of ten short stories about immigrant Jewish women in New York's tenements has universal appeal. The tales capture every immigrant's feelings of loneliness, as well as his or her hopes and dreams. In one story, a young woman working as a janitor to help her old uncle falls hopelessly in love with a handsome young professor who rents a room in the apartment building. In another, a woman paints the kitchen of her apartment to impress her son, who is returning from the war. When her landlord raises the rent because of the improvements, and she can't pay, she is evicted. The women in these stories toil, struggle alone with children, and seek love.

25.42 Yolen, Jane. **Twelve Impossible Things before Breakfast: Stories.** Harcourt Brace, 1997. 175 pp. ISBN 0152015248. Fiction.

Exercise your imagination with these twelve creative stories by author Jane Yolen. Read about a girl's efforts to keep her mother's blood-sucking ghost in her grave. Follow a girl into Neverland where she meets Peter Pan and the girls he keeps in virtual slavery. Listen to the complaints of a bridge that longs for the return of a troll who used to keep the goats from clomping all over him. And spend the evening with a baby-sitter in a haunted house.

26 Solar System, Astronomy, and Space Travel

"Nothing puzzles me more than time and space, and yet, nothing troubles me less."

Charles Lamb

26.1 Berman, Bob. **Secret of the Night Sky: The Most Amazing Things in the Universe You Can See with the Naked Eye.** Harperperennial, 1996. 336 pp. ISBN 006097687X. Nonfiction.

Don't have a telescope but want to know what's up there? With this book, you'll know what to look for in the nighttime sky throughout the year. You can gaze at the giant red star Betelgeuse, meteor showers, satellites, or the Pleiades. Berman's explanations of what's up there will inspire even the most uninspired stargazers. And once he has you hooked on stargazing, check out the back of the book for advice on purchasing a telescope.

26.2 Burnham, Robert, Alan Dyer, Robert Garfinkle, Martin George, Jeff Kanipe, and David Levy. **Advanced Skywatching.** Time Life, 1997. 288 pp. IBSN 0783549415. Nonfiction.

The authors of this book are a mix of professional and amateur astronomers, who have combined their skills to create this great how-to book on skywatching. The book includes practical advice on choosing skywatching tools, and tips on photographing the nighttime sky. Backyard astronomers will enjoy the Starhopping Guide, which offers "20 telescope tours" through the overwhelming heavens. This book is part of the Nature Company series.

26.3 Dickinson, Terence. **Nightwatch: A Practical Guide to Viewing the Universe.** Illustrated by Victor Costanzo. Firefly, 1998. 172 pp. ISBN 1552093026. Nonfiction.

Are you wondering how to pronounce the names of constellations? Do you want to know how the harvest moon got its name, and why it looks so bright? Do you want to know which telescope to buy, how to find a certain star, or how to use a star chart? If you answered yes to any of these questions, then this is the book for you. This excellent handbook for the beginning astronomer tells you everything you need to know. With star charts that are accurate through the year 2010, this book will answer your questions for a long time.

26.4   Dyson, Marianne J. **Space Station Science: Life in Free Fall.** Photographs by NASA. Illustrated by David Klug. Scholastic Reference, 1999. 128 pp. ISBN 0590058894. Nonfiction.

In this book, former NASA (National Aeronautics and Space Administration) mission controller Marianne Dyson explains all the things that must be done to keep Earth's first International Space Station operational. The space station, made up of modules each about the size of a school bus, will be as tall as a twenty-story building and wider than a football field when complete. This book explains the history of space stations; how basics such as fresh air, water, and power are handled; and what astronauts will do when meteors strike or their muscles begin to atrophy from lack of gravitational resistance. Everyday issues such as using bathrooms, sleeping, and cooking are discussed as well. Photos of space taken by NASA astronauts make this book more than a simple handbook.

26.5   Fradin, Dennis Brindell. **The Planet Hunters: The Search for Other Worlds.** Margaret McElderry, 1997. 148 pp. ISBN 0689813236. Nonfiction.

Did you ever wonder when and how each planet was discovered? Here are the stories behind the discovery of each of the nine planets, and the continuing search for Planet X, our solar system's predicted tenth planet. Meet today's planet hunters, and read the firsthand accounts of their discoveries. Then look at the search for planets outside our solar system that may answer the question, Are we alone in the universe?

26.6   Gibbon, John, and Simon Goodwin. **Empire of the Sun: Planets and Moons of the Solar System.** New York University, 1998. 136 pp. ISBN 0814731171. Nonfiction.

With photographs sent to Earth from the Hubble Space Telescope and the Galileo space probe, this book offers an up-close view of the solar system. These breathtaking full-page photos are accompanied by textual explanations of what you are looking at, including the rings of Jupiter and Saturn, the craters on Venus, and the tail of the Hale-Bopp comet. The book also chronicles the history of space missions from 1973 to 1997, and offers Internet sites worth visiting.

26.7   Kerrod, Robin. **Get a Grip on Astronomy.** Time-Life, 1999. 192 pp. ISBN 0737000473. Nonfiction.

Is the universe open or closed? What is the most distant galaxy we can see from Earth without the aid of a telescope? How many constellations do astronomers today recognize? Get a grip on your knowledge of the stars, galaxies, and planets as you browse through this fact-filled resource. Learn about the mysteries of our night sky, and the astronomers who have observed the sky throughout history.

26.8   Mechler, Gary. **National Audubon Society First Field Guide: Night Sky.** Scholastic, 1999. 159 pp. ISBN 0590640860. Nonfiction.

Did you ever wonder how to tell a supernova from a nebula or black hole? This easy-to-use field guide to the night sky can help you answer that and other questions. Complete with detailed sky maps, you can use this reference guide as a way to understand what you're seeing in the night sky. With explanations and pictures of the moon, planets, stars, constellations, and galaxies, and with over 450 color photographs and descriptions of where to look to see certain things, you'll soon find yourself identifying heavenly objects and natural phenomena such as comets, asteroids, eclipses, and meteors. Additionally, the text includes clear, concise descriptions of astronomy equipment, telescopes, and even astrolabes.

26.9   Mitton, Jacqueline, and Simon Mitton. **Scholastic Encyclopedia of Space.** Scholastic Reference, 1998. 80 pp. ISBN 0590592272. Nonfiction.

This concise reference book about space discusses the universe, the stars, the solar system, skywatching, and space exploration. Read about the Big Bang theory, the birth and death of a star, the planets of our solar system, asteroids and comets, star charts, and missions into space. Filled with stunning photographs from

NASA, this book will allow you to gaze at a twin jet nebula, see the surface of Mercury, and look at comet Hale-Bopp up close. Through sidebars on people who have made a difference in our understanding of space, you'll learn about important scientists such as Wernher von Braun and Edwin Hubble.

26.10 Moore, Patrick, and Wil Tirion. **Cambridge Guide to Stars and Planets.** University of Cambridge, 1997. 256 pp. ISBN 0521585821. Nonfiction.

Need a pocket guide to the constellations, planets, and stars? This comprehensive resource helps you study the night sky easily. The rich text includes an overview of astronomy, as well as detailed charts of the night sky. Also included are tables of dates of when interesting phenomena such as comets, star showers, solar flares, and harvest moons will occur.

26.11 Mullane, R. Mike. **Do Your Ears Pop in Space? and 500 Other Surprising Questions about Space Travel.** Wiley, 1997. 240 pp. IBSN 0471154040. Nonfiction.

More than thirty years after the first astronaut orbited the earth, we remain entranced by the mysteries of space travel. How does a space toilet work? Why does the shuttle orbiter fly upside down? Who names the shuttles? Mike Mullane, a three-time veteran astronaut, has the answers to these and five hundred other commonly asked questions about what it is like in space. The inside scoops about launch and orbit operations, life in space, reentry and landing, and the *Challenger* incident are shared.

26.12 Raeburn, Paul. **Mars: Uncovering the Secrets of the Red Planet.** National Geographic, 1998. 224 pp. ISBN 0792273737. Nonfiction.

This National Geographic Society look at Mars gives you what National Geographic is known so well for—absolutely stunning photographs of the Red Planet. With 125 photographs and a three-dimensional foldout (glasses included), this planet literally leaps off the page at you. As you look at photos, many from the 1997 NASA Pathfinder mission, you'll also read interesting facts about the planet, as Raeburn lays out the history of missions to Mars that all attempted to answer that age-old question: Is there life on Mars?

26.13 Ridpath, Ian. **Stars and Planets: The Visual Guide to the Night Sky Viewed from around the World.** Dorling Kindersley, 1998. 224 pp. ISBN 0789435217. Nonfiction.

If you are tired of looking at the night sky and not knowing what stars you are seeing or what constellations they are a part of, then this book is for you. With hundreds of star charts and photographs, you'll learn to identify stars and constellations. Read on and you'll learn about the planets that also make a journey with Earth around the sun.

26.14 Scagell, Robin. **Space Explained: A Beginner's Guide to the Universe.** Henry Holt, 1996. 69 pp. ISBN 0805048723. Nonfiction.

Why does a comet have a tail? What do the colors of stars tell us about their size? Answers to these questions and others are examined in this beginner's guide to the universe that takes a different approach to explaining our complex and mysterious world. Helpful explanations, clear examples, and vibrant color illustrations provide an in-depth look at our solar system, the stars, and the Milky Way and other galaxies.

26.15 Stott, Carol. **Moon Landing: The Race for the Moon.** Illustrated by Richard Bonson. Dorling Kindersley, 1999. 48 pp. ISBN 0789439581. Nonfiction.

Humans have dreamed of reaching the moon for centuries. Realistic ideas for conquering Earth's gravity have been floating around since the nineteenth century. Robert Goddard's first rocket used liquid fuel as early as 1926. That first launch lasted only seconds and managed a mere forty-one feet in height. It was not long, however, before rockets able to travel great distances were common. This brief look at the history of human attempts to reach the moon includes lots of illustrations and diagrams.

26.16 Stott, Carole. **The New Astronomer.** Dorling Kindersley, 1999. 144 pp. ISBN 0789441756. Nonfiction.

Want to learn what to look for in the night sky and where to look for it? Want advice on selecting and using the latest astronomical instruments? Beginning and experienced skywatchers will treasure this comprehensive guide to the night sky. Using the detailed star charts, you will enjoy navigating around the night sky and locating the major planets and constellations.

26.17 Tirion, Wil, and Roger W. Sinnott. **Sky Atlas 2000.0: Field Edition.** Cambridge University, 1999. 30 pp. ISBN 0521654319. Nonfiction.

This atlas of the sky provides star charts of the northern and southern hemispheres in color and on oversized paper. With transparent overlays and lots of room on the page for your own markings, this chart is more than helpful; it's a requirement for the serious stargazer.

26.18 **Ultimate Visual Dictionary of Science.** Dorling Kindersley, 1998. 448 pp. ISBN 0789435128. Nonfiction.

With over sixteen hundred color photographs and illustrations— each accompanied by explanatory text—this book provides a look at physics, chemistry, human anatomy, astronomy, computer science, and biology. An additional section called Useful Data is very useful indeed, as it contains star charts, two-line biographies of noted scientists, a glossary of scientific terms, data about Earth, information on weights and measures, facts about electronics, and general mathematics data.

26.19 Weissman, Paul R., Lucy-Ann McFadden, and Torrence V. Johnson. **Encyclopedia of the Solar System.** Academic, 1998. 794 pp. ISBN 0122268059. Nonfiction.

Over fifty specialists in solar system science contributed to this one-volume encyclopedia. With this book, you'll find information on everything from asteroids to space voyages. Detailed enough to offer authorities useful information, yet simple enough to give the backyard stargazer help in understanding what's out there, this book is a must for anyone interested in space. Starting with a look at the sun and then moving outward, this book not only helps you understand the solar system, but it also gives you information about the origin of life.

27 Sports and Sports Stories

"I've missed more than nine thousand shots in my career. Twenty-six times I've been trusted to take the game winning shot and missed. I've failed over and over and over again in my life. And that is why I succeed."

Michael Jordan

27.1 Anderson, Dave. **The Story of Basketball.** Morrow, 1997. 144 pp. ISBN 0688143164. Nonfiction.

Basketball is one of the few sports that was invented in the United States for U.S. citizens. Football was derived from England's rugby and soccer, golf came from Scotland, tennis came from France, and hockey from Canada. But basketball—well, that came from Dr. James Naismith of Springfield College in 1891. How much has the game changed from the contest Naismith originally invented? What are some of the most memorable games? Who developed the sky hook, the pivot, or the slam? Anderson discusses all of these issues and many more in his story of the players, teams, coaches, and fans who have all been a part of this sport.

27.2 Anderson, Dave. **The Story of Football.** Beech Tree, 1997. 160 pp. ISBN 0688143156. Nonfiction.

How did the sport of football begin? Who are some of the all-time great players and coaches? Who pioneered the forward pass, the T-formation, the huddle, the man-in-motion, the single and double flanker, or the short punt formation? When did the points for a touchdown change from 4 to 6? Which professional team paid each player $210.23 in 1933 as a bonus for winning what was then the equivalent of the Super Bowl? Answers to these questions and many others are offered in this book, which looks at the history, challenges, successes, and problems of the sport called football.

27.3 Anderson, Dave. **The Story of Golf.** Beech Tree, 1998. 144 pp. ISBN 0688157971. Nonfiction.

The early Romans played a game called *paganica* that used sticks and feather-stuffed leather balls. Although some consider this game the precursor of golf, the first written mention of golf comes from a Scottish document in 1457. There the government tried to "ban the game because its popularity was interfering with practicing archery, a citizen's primary military duty in the wars of that medieval era." But the ban didn't work, and over the next three hundred years, the game grew in popularity in England and Scotland. Players originally used primitive clubs to hit feather-stuffed leather balls across unkempt land and unmowed greens, and the game was first played on twelve holes, then twenty-two. What else has changed since those early games? Where are the great golfing spots of today? What motivates greats like Lee Trevino, Tom Watson, Babe Zaharias, Mickey Wright, Nancy Lopez, Tiger Woods, Arnold Palmer, Jack Nicklaus, and Greg Norman? Read this fascinating history to learn everything about this game, from caddies and tees to championship courses and sand traps.

27.4 Bacho, Peter. **Boxing in Black and White.** Henry Holt, 1999. 122 pp. ISBN 080505779X. Nonfiction.

"Among athletes, professional fighters are among the bravest, the most determined," states the author of this boxing history. He goes on to justify his statement by taking you ringside to some of the most exciting boxing matches in the sport's history, and by offering an up-close look at some of the sport's most famous competitors, including Jack Dempsey, Joe Louis, Muhammad Ali, Joe Frazier, Sugar Ray Robinson, and Jim Gilmore. Black-and-white photographs and suggestions for further reading make this book a winner.

27.5 Barnidge, Tom. **Best Shots: The Greatest NFL Photography of the Century.** Dorling Kindersley, 1999. 160 pp. ISBN 0789446391. Nonfiction.

The forward by NFL great Joe Namath sets the stage for the more than one hundred photographs that follow in this book. Here readers will find both "the thrill of victory," and "the agony of defeat," in photographs of incredible passes, receptions, and tackles. You will go behind the scenes to watch players get psyched for the big game, and sit along the sidelines to witness the scowls of players whose injuries force them to watch the action instead of participating. Whether you are an avid fan, a Monday morning quarterback, or a novice to the game, the photographs included here are sure to get you pumped for next season.

27.6   Breashears, David, Audrey Salkeld, and John Mallory. **Last Climb: The Legendary Everest Expeditions of George Mallory.** National Geographic, 1999. 239 pp. ISBN 0792275381. Nonfiction.

George Mallory and his companions made three expeditions in an effort to reach the summit of Mt. Everest. In May of 1924, the final attempt ended in tragedy. Mallory and his climbing companion disappeared, leaving many to wonder if they had ever managed to reach the pinnacle. Seventy-five years later, the body of George Mallory was discovered. Did his body hold the answers to all of the lingering questions about the ill-fated climb? Using excerpts from Mallory's diaries and letters, the authors create a "you are there" atmosphere that permits us an intimate view of the man who gave his life in pursuit of his dream.

27.7   Buckley, James, Jr. **Football.** Dorling Kindersley, 1999. 64 pp. ISBN 0789447258. Nonfiction.

If you want to know all there is to know about the sport of football, here is a quick and easy-to-read book on the subject. This volume tells the history of the sport, provides information on all of the gear necessary for the big game, and relates interesting facts and figures.

27.8   Carter, Alden R. **Bull Catcher.** Scholastic, 1997. 279 pp. ISBN 0590509586. Fiction.

Neil "Bull" Larsen was born to be a catcher in baseball. As a senior project for his English class, Bull tells his own story, which includes his last four years as a baseball player and high school student. His story is full of plenty of baseball action, but Bull also learns a lot about himself, his family, and his best friends as he deals with the various conflicts of high school life.

27.9   **Chronicles of the Olympics.** Dorling Kindersley, 1998. 330 pp. ISBN 078942312X. Nonfiction.

For a look back at the past one hundred years of Olympic games, pick up this handy reference book. From the first Olympics in 1896 in Athens, Greece, to the recent games in 1996 in Atlanta, Georgia, this book covers the history of the sports and athletes that have made the Olympics the spectacular event it is. Photographs allow readers to see the faces of the Olympic athletes we know best—including Kristi Yamaguchi, Jackie Joyner-Kersee,

Carl Lewis, Andre Agassi, and Greg Louganis—as well as those we know less well. At the end of the book, you'll find a complete list of medal winners in all events for all games through 1996.

27.10 Draper, Sharon M. **Tears of a Tiger.** Aladdin, 1996. 180 pp. ISBN 0689806981. Fiction.

Andy Jackson, captain of Hazelwood High's basketball team, learns the hard way about drinking and driving. While cruising (and drinking) with three teammates after a victory, Andy wrecks the car. Andy and two friends escape, but his best friend is trapped in the wreck and burns to death as the boys watch helplessly. Using newspaper accounts, letters, interview transcripts, and journal entries, this novel details the impact of the wreck on Andy's classmates, and Andy's slide into depression and eventual suicide.

27.11 Egan, Terry, Stan Friedman, and Mike Levine. **The Good Guys of Baseball: Sixteen True Sports Stories.** Simon & Schuster, 1997. 111 pp. ISBN 0689802129. Nonfiction.

Tired of the spoiled bad guys of pro baseball? Then you'll love this book, which offers a collection of short biographies of some of baseball's best good guys, including Ken Griffey Jr., Hideo Nomo, Cal Ripken, Jim Abott, and twelve other big leaguers who play with class. Each story includes one full-page black-and-white photo of the player.

27.12 Garner, Joe. **And the Crowd Goes Wild.** Sourcebook, 1999. 179 pp. ISBN 1570714606. Nonfiction.

The text, photos, and CDs that comprise *And the Crowd Goes Wild* give you a chance to relive all those moments when the crowd has done just that. The two CDs that accompany this book allow you to listen to announcers scream plays; hear Al Michaels shout, "Do you believe in miracles? Yes!"; and hear the college football fans scream wildly when the Bears come back to win in the final seconds of the California vs. Stanford game. You'll see, hear, and read about the exciting moment when Secretariat won the Triple Crown, Lou Gehrig gave his emotional goodbye, and Babe Ruth hit his unforgettable World Series home run in 1932.

27.13 Glenn, Mel. **Jump Ball: A Basketball Season in Poems.** Lodestar / Dutton, 1997. 160 pp. ISBN 052567554X. Fiction.

The Tower High School basketball team has had its best season ever. Tragically, on the return trip from the championship game, the school bus swerves out of control on an icy road. In a series of poems, readers have the chance to meet the players, and their coaches, teachers, parents, and friends. Interspersed are eyewitness accounts of the tragic accident that will surely end the careers of some of the players. Readers are kept guessing as to who will survive this tragedy.

27.14 Goodstein, Madeline. **Sports Science Projects: The Physics of Balls in Motion.** Enslow, 1999. 128 pp. ISBN 0766011747. Nonfiction.

Can't think of a thing to do for your upcoming science fair? Just toss a baseball in the air a few times, hit a tether ball around the pole, or lob a tennis ball over the net. As you watch balls spin, fall, slow down, make arcs, and come to a resting point, you're watching the physics of balls in motion. This book shows you how to turn those observations into fascinating science projects that let you combine your love of sports with the laws of science.

27.15 Halberstam, David. **Playing for Keeps: Michael Jordan and the World That He Made.** Random House, 1999. 426 pp. ISBN 0679415629. Nonfiction.

Halberstam's book focuses on more than the game of basketball or Michael Jordan. He moves beyond those two topics to more elusive issues like wealth, fame, and sports myths. He explains that Jordan not only defines this game, but defines an entire era of basketball playing. He captures the extent of Jordan's talent when he writes, "That there had been even one Michael Jordan seemed in retrospect something of a genetic fluke. . . ."

27.16 Johnson, Scott. **Safe at Second.** Philomel, 1999. 245 pp. ISBN 0399233652. Fiction.

Todd Bannister is not only the pitcher for his high school varsity baseball team, but he's also a great pitcher that college scouts love to watch. Todd's life seems set, and his only decision now is which college to sign with. Then, during a high school game, he throws a pitch that changes everything when the batter's line drive hits Todd's eye. Several days later, after surgery to remove the eye, Todd faces a life he never expected—a life where he isn't the baseball star.

27.17 Junger, Sebastian. **The Perfect Storm: A True Story of Men against the Sea.** Harper, 1998. 301 pp. ISBN 006101351X. Nonfiction.

Meteorologists called it "the storm of the century" or "the perfect storm," while the people out in it called it "perfect hell." The six men aboard the *Andrea Gail* were some of those caught in the storm. Junger uses radio dialogues, eyewitness accounts, and comments from other storm survivors to recreate the terror of the men on the fateful ship as they tried to survive the forceful winds and one hundred-foot waves.

27.18 Kadupski, Charlie, editor. **1999 Official Athletic College Guide: Baseball.** Sport Source, 1999. 340 pp. ISBN 0963114867. Nonfiction.

If you want to play baseball in college or simply want to follow an outstanding team, then you will want to look at this book. It includes academic and athletic information on over fourteen hundred colleges and universities that compete in the National Collegiate Athletic Association (NCAA) Divisions I, II, III; the National Community College Athletic Association (NCCAA); and the National Junior College Athletics Association (NJCAA). Also included is information on recruitment and selection procedures. This is part of the Official Athletic College Guide series.

27.19 Klass, David. **Danger Zone.** Scholastic, 1996. 232 pp. ISBN 0590485911. Fiction.

When invited to join a "Dream Team" for an international basketball tournament in Italy, Jimmy Doyle initially turns down the offer. Maybe his widowed mother will struggle while he's gone, he thinks; and maybe he's not good enough to compete with the best high school players in the world. Jimmy joins the team, and discovers that he is good enough, but he's unsure about how to deal with resentment from his Black teammates, and with the fear of terrorists who threaten to kill players from the United States.

27.20 Krull, Kathleen. **Lives of the Athletes: Thrills, Spills (and What the Neighbors Thought).** Illustrated by Kathryn Hewitt. Harcourt Brace, 1997. 96 pp. ISBN 0052008063. Nonfiction.

This collection features short biographies of twelve world-class athletes, including Babe Ruth, Red Grange, Jim Thorpe, Maurice Richard, Jackie Robinson, Duke Kahanamoku (a swimmer and surfer), Gertrude Ederle (the first woman to swim the English Channel), and Flo Hyman (Olympic volleyball player). Each story is accompanied by a full-color illustration of the athlete, and a brief list of their most important athletic achievements.

27.21　Laughlin, Terry. **Total Immersion: The Revolutionary Way to Swim Better, Faster, and Easier.** Fireside, 1996. 286 pp. ISBN 068481855X. Nonfiction.

A master swimmer and coach plunges you into the deep end of the pool and shows you how to become a better swimmer. Step-by-step instructions on the basic strokes; proper positioning of arms, legs, and head; and breathing techniques make this a must have if you want to swim competitively. Dry land exercises and in-water drills are explained, so that even the novice paddler can get in the swim of things.

27.22　Lee, Marie G. **Necessary Roughness.** HarperCollins, 1996. 228 pp. ISBN 0060251301. Fiction.

When Chan Young Kim moves from L.A. to a small town in Minnesota, the culture shock is worse than he imagined. His twin sister has little trouble fitting in, but she even gets along with their father, a person Chan will never understand. Chan eventually finds a niche at school when he joins the football team—against his father's wishes—but being on the football team can't prepare him for cruel racist treatment, or for the sudden death of his sister.

27.23　Lewman, David. **When I Was Your Age: Remarkable Achievements of Famous Athletes at Every Age from 1 to 100.** Illustrated by Mark Anderson. Triumph, 1997. 186 pp. ISBN 1572431458. Nonfiction.

Many of the most famous athletes in history have faced their tough times and won out over them. If you think you can't do it, read about George "The Babe" Ruth, who was "deemed incorrigible" and sent at age seven to St. Mary's Industrial School for Boys, where he learned to play baseball. Read how African American Jesse Owens won four gold medals at age twenty-two at the Berlin Olympics, making Hitler furious. Read how fifteen-year-old Michael Jordan failed to make his varsity basketball team, and how eighteen-year-old Joe Louis lost his first boxing match in two rounds, and swore he'd never fight again. This fascinating look at famous athletes reminds us that the greatest winners have come from all ages, and have faced as many trials as triumphs.

27.24 Lundy, Derek. **Godforsaken Sea: Racing the World's Most Dangerous Waters.** Algonquin, 1999. 272 pp. ISBN 1565122291. Nonfiction.

The Southern Sea off the coast of Antarctica is known as the Everest of Oceans. Lundy recounts the 1996–1997 Vendee Globe, a sailboat race that began with sixteen entrants. By the end of the race, only six crossed the finish line. One sailor perished in the attempt; others saw their vessels crushed under the enormous waves. One erstwhile sailor even had to perform surgery on himself in the middle of the race. Details about waves reaching the height of tall buildings may be enough to keep you on land. But if you are looking for adventure on the high seas, this is the book for you, matey.

27.25 MacCambridge, Michael, editor. **ESPN SportsCentury.** Hyperion, 1999. 288 pp. ISBN 0786864710. Nonfiction.

This book offers a comprehensive look at sports, athletes, and their achievements during the last century. The book is filled with quotations, photographs, and excerpts of commentary from memorable games. Read about Jack Johnson, Jim Thorpe, Babe Ruth, Joe Louis, Babe Didrikson, Pete Rose, Muhammad Ali, Will Chamberlain, and Bobby Orr. Look at Tiger Woods, Wayne Gretsky, Hank Aaron, and Bart Starr in prize-winning situations. MacCambridge has done an outstanding job of bringing together the images, words, and moments that best capture the drama, glory, and agony of sports.

27.26 McCarver, Tim. **Tim McCarver's Baseball for Brain Surgeons and Other Fans.** Villard, 1998. 344 pp. ISBN 0375500855. Nonfiction.

Former catcher and veteran broadcaster Tim McCarver presents an in-depth examination of the game of baseball. From the cut fastball to the four seamer, the pitches are described in such intricate detail that you should be able to head outside and try them yourself. If batting is more your niche, McCarver describes various stances. He also includes plenty of information for you would-be outfielders, too. The knowledge and expertise of this player and analyst makes the plays, strategies, and tactics of our national pastime come to life.

27.27   Meserole, Mike. **The Ultimate Book of Sports Lists 1998.** Dorling Kindersley, 1997. 224 pp. ISBN 0789421348. Nonfiction.

Being a sports fan means knowing which teams did what during what year. It means knowing why Jack Nicklaus is the most familiar name in golf, how Wayne Gretzky came to be the National Hockey League's all-time leading scorer, which pitchers have had perfect games, and who the Iditarod's most successful sled dog drivers have been. You'll find out those things plus hundreds of other interesting facts in this book, which covers everything from hockey and horse racing to Ty Cobb and Tiger Woods.

27.28   Myers, Walter Dean. **Slam!** Scholastic, 1998. 266 pp. ISBN 0590486683. Fiction.

Greg "Slam" Harris is an exceptional athlete. On the basketball court, his explosive moves combine with his instinctive knack for knowing who is open. At sixteen, he dreams of a career in the NBA. Off the court, however, it is Greg's temper that is explosive. This inability to control his emotions causes trouble at his new school. His grades are slipping, and the teachers are not impressed with anything except his athletic ability. Normally Greg would turn to his best friend, Ice, for advice. That is no longer an option as Greg watches Ice deal drugs. How can Greg take his athletic abilities and use them to deal with the greatest opponent he will ever face: himself?

27.29   Osborn, Kevin. **Scholastic Encyclopedia of Sports in the United States.** Scholastic, 1997. 220 pp. ISBN 059069264X. Nonfiction.

This book chronicles sports, athletes, and important sporting events in the United States from 1770 to the present day. Chapter 1 discusses early sports in our country, including sports played by Native Americans. Chapter 2 talks about the early development of organized and professional sports. Chapter 3 chronicles the important athletes of the early 1900s. Later chapters detail important events and athletes from the 1930s to today. Richly illustrated with photographs, this is a book for sports lovers.

27.30 Rappoport, Ken. **Grant Hill.** Walker, 1996. 117 pp. ISBN 0802784550. Nonfiction.

Rappoport's biography of Detroit Pistons' star forward, Grant Hill, traces Hill's career from his early beginnings as an athlete and basketball player in Reston, Virginia, to his successful rookie year in the NBA. The book includes lots of sports detail from Hill's high school and college days, and lively accounts from some of his most important games. Full-page photographs of Hill from high school player to NBA rookie-of-the-year appear in the center of the book.

27.31 Reidenbaugh, Lowell. **Baseball's Hall of Fame—Cooperstown: Where the Legends Live Forever.** Gramercy, 1999. 385 pp. ISBN 0517194643. Nonfiction.

Baseball began in 1876 with uneven fields, crude equipment, and less-than-great players. But its simple rules and simple equipment quickly made it so popular that it's now known as "America's pastime." Only about one percent of all professional players of the national pastime end up in the Baseball Hall of Fame, located in Cooperstown, New York. This book chronicles the lives of each of the people now found in that prestigious place. Read about Yogi Berra, Hank Aaron, Willie Mays, Babe Ruth, Mike Schmidt, Cy Young, Larry Doby, and all the other baseball greats. Photographs and career records for each of the Hall of Famers makes this book educational as well as entertaining.

27.32 Ritter, John. **Choosing Up Sides.** Philomel, 1998. 166 pp. ISBN 0399231854. Fiction.

Luke's father has told him repeatedly that being left-handed is surely the sign of the devil. Therefore, Luke has had to train himself to perform everyday tasks with his right hand. Occasionally, when he is certain his father will not see him, Luke reverts to using his left hand. It definitely is the stronger hand for pitching a baseball, Luke discovers. But what good will it do him to perfect a pitch when his father will never allow him to play baseball? Luke struggles to choose up sides. He wants to please his father, but cannot deny the thrill he feels when his pitching is on target.

27.33 Savage, Jeff. **A Sure Thing? Sports and Gambling.** Lerner, 1997. 96 pp. ISBN 0822533030. Nonfiction.

Betting on sports is a booming business. "In 1974, $50 million was bet legally on sports in Nevada. In 1990, 16 years later, that figure was $1.9 billion—nearly 40 times as much." To that huge amount of money, add about another one hundred billion dollars that's spent on illegal gambling. It's estimated that about eighty-eight percent of people gamble in some way—bingo games, state lottery tickets, games at carnivals, horse races, dog races, office football pools. If everyone's doing it, can it be harmful? Is there such a thing as a gambling addiction? Should the government be able to decide what type of gambling is legal, and what isn't? How does gambling on sports affect sports? These questions and many others are discussed in this frank look at gambling.

27.34 Schwarzenegger, Arnold. **The New Encyclopedia of Modern Bodybuilding.** Simon & Schuster, 1998. 800 pp. ISBN 0684857219. Nonfiction.

The seven-time Mr. Olympian traded on his physique to go from pumping iron to *The Last Action Hero* and *The Terminator.* Here Arnold shares the secrets of competitive bodybuilding. From the history of the sport to training regimens, there is plenty of advice about diet, nutrition, and other related topics. Handling injuries, the psychology of the sport, and many other areas are addressed in this hefty volume. Maybe you can start by lifting this massive book a few times to get your blood pumping.

27.35 Swirsky, Seth. **Every Pitcher Tells a Story: Letters Gathered by a Devoted Baseball Fan.** Times, 1999. 217 pp. ISBN 081293055X. Nonfiction.

Author Swirsky mailed questions to pitchers from teams of the past and the present. Here are their answers, with many pitchers allowing their words to appear in print for the first time. Current players such as Roger "the Rocket" Clemens and Dave Cone write about their careers. Names from the past are represented as well by letters from Hall of Famers such as Tom Seaver. Photographs show each handwritten letter. The author also includes some handwritten notes from players of the 1920s and 1930s who were not alive to answer his questions. Die-hard baseball fans will want to add this volume to their collection.

27.36 Wallace, Rich. **Wrestling Sturbridge.** Knopf, 1996. 133 pp. ISBN 067987803. Fiction.

What if you were the second best 135-pound wrestler in the state, but the best 135-pound wrestler was your friend and teammate? That's Ben's situation in his senior year, and he doesn't like it; he wants to be state champion as badly as his teammate Al does. Ben realizes that to be at peace, he must give everything he has to challenge Al. It's a memorable season, and Ben gains a deeper understanding of friendship and of himself.

27.37 Weaver, Will. **Hard Ball.** HarperCollins, 1998. 240 pp. ISBN 006447208. Fiction.

Billy Baggs is a gifted baseball player who has suffered more than his share of hardship in life. *Striking Out* and *Farm Team*, two previous novels by Weaver, explored Billy's introduction to the sport he loves: baseball. In this third book featuring Billy, he must finally face up to his longtime nemesis, Archer Kingwood. The confrontation turns violent, and Billy and Archer are told by their coach that in order to remain on the team, the two of them must learn how to get along. Coach Anderson's plan is for the two rivals to spend a week living together twenty-four hours a day. Billy is certain that this plan will be disastrous, and Archer agrees. But what each boy learns about the other may just change their relationship from one of rivalry to one of cooperation.

27.38 Wolff, Virginia Euwer. **Bat 6.** Scholastic, 1998. 226 pp. ISBN 0590897993. Fiction.

This story of the months leading to a softball game is told through the voices of twenty very different girls. This game, the fiftieth annual meeting between teams from two small Oregon towns, is played in 1949, and lingering anti-Japanese sentiment causes problems for Aki, a Japanese American girl, and Shazam, whose father was killed in Pearl Harbor. The game is ruined when Shazam assaults Aki in a play at first base, an act that stuns the girls and changes them forever.

28 Television, Movies, and the Music Industry

"We shall stand or fall by television—of that I am quite sure."

E. B. White

28.1 Day, Nancy. **Advertising: Information or Manipulation?** Enslow, 1999. 128 pp. ISBN 0766011062. Nonfiction.

Every day you are bombarded with ads for a wide array of products. Advertisers know that if they hook you into buying their products today, you will likely remain a loyal customer as an adult. So each day, millions of dollars are spent in an effort to attract you to one brand of jeans, one type of music, one franchise in football. This book takes a critical look at the means advertisers use to lure you to their products. Armed with the information in this book, you just might be able to resist the hard sell, and recognize techniques designed to brainwash you into buying products before it is too late.

28.2 Degnen, Lisa. **Leonardo.** Barnes & Noble, 1998. 96 pp. ISBN 0760710848. Nonfiction.

If you saw the blockbuster movie *Titanic,* then you saw Leonardo DiCaprio in the starring role. If you want to see and learn more about him, take a look at this photobiography of the popular star. Learn how he came to be named Leonardo, read about his childhood growing up in a poor section of Los Angeles, and find out how he went from cut-up to pin-up.

28.3 Finkelstein, Norman H. **With Heroic Truth: The Life of Edward R. Murrow.** Clarion, 1997. 175 pp. ISBN 0395678919. Nonfiction.

A memorial plaque located at the CBS Broadcast Center in New York City indicates the importance of Edward R. Murrow to the field of broadcast journalism in the United States. He is noted for setting the standards for the newly developing industry in the 1950s. His career began in radio, however, in the 1930s and 1940s, a tumultuous time in the United States and overseas. Murrow reported on the war and its atrocities, interviewed celebrities of his time, and dedicated his life to telling the truth to the public.

28.4 Furman, Elina, and Leah Furman. **Give It to You: The Jordan Knight Story.** Berkley, 1999. 158 pp. ISBN 0425173577. Nonfiction.

This unauthorized biography of the talented Jordan Knight traces his early life back to a working-class Boston neighborhood. With a priest/carpenter for a father and a social worker for a mother, Jordan, the youngest of six children, joined the church choir at an early age, and almost immediately became an unofficial star. Jordan's break dancing for money in his early teens became a necessity after his father abandoned his family. Enjoy the story of how Jordan is transformed from a typical fourteen-year-old high school kid into an international superstar with New Kids on the Block at age nineteen, and learn about his life since superstardom.

28.5 Gelman, Morrie, and Gene Accas. **The Best in Television: 50 Years of Emmys.** General, 1998. 256 pp. ISBN 1575440423. Nonfiction.

The award of excellence for television programs is called the Emmy. First given in 1949 when television viewing was still a novelty, the award established that television wasn't just about entertainment, but was also about honoring those whose work went beyond the ordinary. As you read about the programs and stars who have won this coveted award, you'll find yourself reading about the history of an industry that has helped shape culture in the United States.

28.6 Gourley, Catherine. **Media Wizards: A Behind-the-Scenes Look at Media Manipulations.** Twenty First Century, 1999. 128 pp. ISBN 0761309675. Nonfiction.

Have you ever wondered why you buy Mountain Dew instead of another soft drink? Or cringe at the realistic operating room scenes on *ER?* Or wondered if the fillings in your teeth may be poisoning you with radiation after watching a report on *60 Minutes?* If you have, then you will definitely want to read *Media Wizards,* which takes a hard-hitting, behind-the-scenes look at how the media manipulate us. This book makes an excellent starting point for researching how popular culture affects us, how news reports alter our sense of reality, and how advertising works its magic on consumers.

28.7 Hamilton, Jake. **Special Effects in Films and Television.** Dorling Kindersley, 1998. 64 pp. ISBN 078942813X. Nonfiction.

James Bond never breaks a sweat while tackling seemingly impossible tasks. Jim Carrey's face folds into incredible positions once he dons *The Mask.* How do they create those wonderful special effects? From miniatures to make-up, from underwater to outer space, and from fire to blizzards, the many techniques used by the folks in the special effects laboratories are explained.

28.8 Haskins, Jim. **Spike Lee: By Any Means Necessary.** Walker, 1997. 160 pp. ISBN 0802784941. Nonfiction.

Award-winning filmmaker Spike Lee is known to be controversial and combative. There is no denying that he is extremely creative as well. Haskins documents Lee's life, noting the importance of education and family in his development as one of the leading filmmakers in the United States. A discussion of Lee's films by movie critics is also included.

28.9 Kamen, Gloria. **Hidden Music: The Life of Fanny Mendelssohn.** Atheneum, 1996. 82 pp. ISBN 068931714X. Nonfiction.

This slim biography offers insights into the life of Fanny Mendelssohn. As a young girl, she sat side-by-side with her brother Felix as the two composed music. Fanny's father, however, told her that a woman's place was not in the music business. Instead, Fanny was forced to turn her attention to running the household. Although she did continue to compose and perform, she was never able to achieve the freedom enjoyed by the men of her era. Only today are some of her contributions to music coming to light. An interesting epilogue presents information on how much the music world has changed since Fanny's time.

28.10 Krohn, Katherine E. **Marilyn Monroe: Norma Jeane's Dream.** Lerner, 1997. 128 pp. ISBN 0822549301. Nonfiction.

One of the most celebrated movie stars of her time was also one of the most unhappy. Abandoned by her mother, Norma Jeane Mortensen spent some of her youth in an orphanage. It was there that she began to dream about leaving her past behind and creating a glamorous future for herself. Her dreams became reality as she went on to become a model and then an actress. Although her film career took off in the 1950s, Marilyn Monroe took her own life in 1962 at the age of thirty-six.

28.11 Littlesugar, Amy. **Shake Rag: From the Life of Elvis Presley.** Illustrated by Floyd Cooper. Philomel, 1998. Unpaged. ISBN 039923005X. Fiction.

This fictionalized account of an event in Elvis Presley's boyhood offers an explanation of how he came to appreciate gospel music. Littlesugar's account tries to counteract some of the rumors that surround this talented but controversial music star's life. This simple picture book will be of interest to those wanting to know more about the King's life. Historical notes about Elvis's first recording contract and a bibliography of other books about Presley offer the serious student of music additional information.

29 Transportation: From Cars and Trains to Rockets and Planes

"Bypasses are devices that allow some people to dash from point A to point B very fast while other people dash from point B to point A very fast."

Douglas Adams

29.1 Ballantine, Richard, and Richard Grant. **Ultimate Bicycle Book.** Dorling Kindersley, 1998. 192 pp. ISBN 0789422522. Nonfiction.

If biking as a sport or recreation is something you are into, you'll want to read this book. Learn about the history of bicycles in the first section of the book. There you'll discover that the first bicycle with pedals was built in 1839, but that Leonardo da Vinci sketched a machine in 1490 that looks a lot like a bike, and a French inventor made a Celerifere—a machine with two in-line wheels that were connected by a beam and propelled by foot power—in the 1700s. Throughout the remainder of the book, read about types of bicycles (street recumbent, Ecocar, tandem, touring, and racing, to name a few), and care and maintenance of all types of bikes. With excellent photographs, you'll learn all you ever wanted to know about choosing a bike, changing a tire, entering a race, or tightening your brakes.

29.2 Bonds, Ray, editor. **The Story of Aviation: A Concise History of Flight.** Barnes & Noble, 1997. 144 pp. ISBN 0760707537. Nonfiction.

On December 17, 1903, Orville Wright made history when he took to the air for all of twelve seconds in the "first sustained, powered, and manned flight by a heavier-than-air machine." Now, less than one hundred years later, millions of people travel daily across oceans and continents in airplanes. Learn about these fascinating machines in this detailed history of aviation. Read about civil aviation, air safety, airships, competing airlines, fighter planes, and space flight, while looking at photographs of the planes and people who are a part of this important history.

29.3 Carroll, John. **Classic Pickups Made in America from 1910 to the Present.** Photographs by Garry Stuart. Barnes & Noble, 1999. 144 pp. ISBN 0760715319. Nonfiction.

The pickup truck—as American as apple pie—helped shaped this country as it became the mainstay of the farmer in the United States. This book not only chronicles the truck's history decade by decade, but it also provides hundreds of photographs of both the classic models and the models of today. As you enjoy this close-up look at pickups, you'll also be picking up a lot of history about this country's development.

29.4 Chaikin, Andrew L. **A Man on the Moon: The Voyages of the Apollo Astronauts.** Penguin, 1998. 704 pp. ISBN 0140272011. Nonfiction.

This incredible book was the basis for the HBO miniseries *From the Earth to the Moon.* In this history, Chaikin meticulously interviews Apollo astronauts and goes into the NASA files to create a detailed picture of what the race to the moon was all about, and what being an astronaut headed to the moon felt like. Chaikin captures the excitement and drama of the successful Apollo missions, and the tension the world experienced as the crippled Apollo 13 came back to Earth. He reminds readers of the funny events (Alan Shepard trying to play golf in space) and forces readers to consider the space program against the backdrop of the Vietnam War. This is essential reading for anyone interested in the history of the space program.

29.5 Englehart, Steve. **Countdown to Flight.** Excel, 1999. 101 pp. ISBN 1583484035. Nonfiction.

Today we take for granted the fact that we can hop aboard a plane and travel across the country or around the world in a matter of hours. Travel was not always so easy. It took five years of work and testing to accomplish what humans have always dreamed of doing: flying. At the sandy dunes of Kitty Hawk, North Carolina, Wilbur and Orville Wright's creation took flight for twelve seconds, and forever changed human travel. Here is how it was done.

29.6 Harland, David M. **Exploring the Moon: The Apollo Expeditions.** Springer Verlag, 1999. 468 pp. ISBN 1852330996. Nonfiction.

Here's the up-close, detailed information on what happened during the Apollo missions. Starting with the first lunar orbits and moving on to the landings, this book uses transcripts of conversations between the astronauts and mission control to provide an authentic look at what these missions really accomplished. Rarely seen panoramic photographs complete this interesting history of the Apollo missions. This book is part of the Springer-Praxis Series in Space Science and Technology.

29.7   Levinson, Nancy Smiler. **She's Been Working on the Railroad.** Photographs by Shirley Burman. Lodestar, 1997. 104 pp. ISBN 0525675450. Nonfiction.

By the end of the nineteenth century, trains streaked across 200,000 miles of track that crisscrossed America. These railroads were owned, built, and run by men—or at least that's how it seems at first glance. But a closer look reveals that women also played a part in the railroad industry. These women were generally not accepted or welcomed by their male colleagues, but their contributions were important. Read about Ella Campbell, whose telegraphic skills kept two trains from a head-on collision; Mary Pennington, who designed refrigerated railroad cars; and Sarah Clark Kidder, who became one of the first women to head a railroad company. Look at the discrimination women encountered and the progress they made as they proved that they too could work on the railroads.

29.8   Miller, Ron. **The History of Rockets.** Franklin Watts, 1999. 128 pp. ISBN 0531114309. Nonfiction.

Did you know that rockets were first invented in ancient Greece over twenty-three hundred years ago? This work traces the history of rockets, from their use as weapons of war to their use in space exploration. The dreamers of rocket design as well as the "rocket riders" come to life in this fascinating account.

29.9   Stott, Carol. **Fly the Space Shuttle.** Dorling Kindersley, 1997. 32 pp. ISBN 078942021X. Nonfiction.

Four modules take you step-by-step through the training required to pilot the space shuttle. In the first module, you will learn about life in space, as well as the mechanics of the vehicle used in the flight. Subsequent modules train you to operate the controls, plan the launch, and dock with the space station.

29.10 Uys, Erroll Lincoln. **Riding the Rails: Teenagers on the Move during the Great Depression.** TV, 1999. 288 pp. ISBN 1575000377. Nonfiction.

During the Great Depression, hundreds of thousands of teens across the country left home, hopped a freight train, and started riding the rails. Some left in search of jobs, to help keep their families afloat during the financial crisis. Others left in search of adventure, only to find that life riding the rails was dangerous. Uys collected letters from thousands of teens who lived lives on the road. They tell of the physical dangers they encountered, as well as the kindness of strangers who shared food, clothes, and whatever else they had. Walker Evans, Dorothea Lange, and others recount the hopes and the hardships of these teens in this book, which includes vintage photographs.

29.11 Wagner, Rob Leicester. **Hot Rods.** Photographs by Randy Lorentzen. Metro, 1999. 120 pp. ISBN 1567998224. Nonfiction.

Hot rods have been around almost as long as cars themselves. Take a look at the factory designed cars and the tinkered-with hot rod versions of the same vehicles in this photographic history of cars and hot rods. From the 1934 Vicky and the 1951 Ford Woodie to the 1955 Chevy sedan and the 1969 Camaro Z28, this book will show you all the ways people have fired up, souped up, and jazzed up their cars. Lots of photographs and easy-to-read text provide a solid history of both hot rods and the automobile industry in general.

29.12 Willson, Quentin. **Classic American Cars.** Dorling Kindersley, 1997. 192 pp. ISBN 078942083X. Nonfiction.

Sixty of the most stylish cars of all time are presented in this collection for car buffs of all ages. Interesting facts about the history of the model, the creator of the particular line of cars, and the special features of each automobile accompany glossy full-color photographs of the vehicles. Classic cars never go out of style!

29.13 Wilson, Hugo. **Classic Motorcycles: Harley-Davidson.** Dorling Kindersley, 1998. 44 pp. ISBN 0789435063. Nonfiction.

Each book in this series begins with an overview of a particular classic motorcycle, and includes a timeline that shows important milestones in its development. This general information is then followed by a two-page spread on each of the important models in the motorcycle's history. Glossy photographs are accompanied by detail about the bike's body, motor, and accessories. Other titles in this series feature bikes by Honda, BMW, and Triumph.

29.14 Wilson, Hugo. **Motorcycle Owner's Manual: A Practical Guide to Keeping Your Motorcycle in Top Condition.** Dorling Kindersley, 1997. 112 pp. ISBN 0789416158. Nonfiction.

Clear, concise directions offer authoritative help for those who wish to maximize the performance of their motorcycles without expensive mechanic bills. Step-by-step color photographs elaborate the simple, easy-to-follow text. Topics range from routine cleaning to more complex service and repairs. A glossary offers definitions of the more technical terms.

30 Trivia and Fun Facts

"The sum of it all is: read what you like, because you like it, seeking no other reason and no other profit than the experience of reading."

Holbrook Jackson

30.1 Agee, Jon. **Sit on a Potato Pan, Otis! More Palindromes.** Farrar, Straus and Giroux, 1999. Unpaged. ISBN 0374318085. Nonfiction.

Palindromes are phrases or sentences that read the same both forward and backward. As the title of this collection indicates, the phrases and sentences do not necessarily need to make sense. This collection contains humorous pencil sketches provided by the author, and challenges readers to create their own palindromes.

30.2 Ash, Russell. **Incredible Comparisons.** Dorling Kindersley, 1996. 64 pp. ISBN 0789410095. Nonfiction.

A blue whale can reach the length of eighteen adult humans laying head to toe. Even the blue whale, however, would be dwarfed by the diplodocus of ancient times. The largest tooth in an elephant's mouth can measure as much as twelve inches, and weigh more than nine pounds. Human teeth, on the other hand, grow to an average size of one and a half inches and weigh only ounces. These and other amazing facts are contained in this fascinating look at size, strength, and weight. Topics include mountains, buildings, and disasters.

30.3 Ash, Russell. **The World in One Day.** Dorling Kindersley, 1997. 32 pp. ISBN 0789420287. Nonfiction.

Every day, five million crayons are produced by the Crayola Company, more than three hundred thousand people are born, and sixteen and a half million people celebrate a birthday. These are just a few of the astonishing facts in this book about things that occur every day on our planet. This is a book you might enjoy while munching on one of the seven million pizzas sold each day in the United States.

30.4 Asimov, Isaac, editor. **Isaac Asimov's Book of Facts: 3,000 of the Most Interesting, Entertaining, Fascinating, Unbelievable,**

Unusual and Fascinating Facts. Outlet, 1997. 512 pp. ISBN 0517065037. Nonfiction.

Who was the first president born in a hospital? How do Eskimos keep their food from freezing? How did Europeans in the Middle Ages discipline their animals? Find out answers to these three questions and 2,997 more in this amazing book by one of America's best-known science writers, Isaac Asimov.

30.5 Betz, Adrienne. **Scholastic Treasury of Quotations for Children.** Scholastic, 1998. 254 pp. ISBN 0590271466. Nonfiction.

Sometimes the words of someone else can best express our feelings. If you are searching for just the right words to convince someone of your argument, to remind someone to be more polite, or to express your feelings succinctly, this treasury of quotations is sure to come in handy. The people whose words are cited include the famous, the infamous, and the everyday.

30.6 Burleigh, Robert. **Who Said That? Famous Americans Speak.** Illustrated by David Catrow. Henry Holt, 1997. 45 pp. ISBN 0805043942. Nonfiction.

Who said, "I have never been lost; but I was bewildered once for three days"? What about, "I swing big and I live big"? If you guessed Daniel Boone and Babe Ruth, then you may not need this book. Whether from the playing fields or the field of politics, the words of the famous Americans in this book have enriched our collective lives. In the words of the immortal Louie Armstrong, "Man, if you have to ask, you'll never know."

30.7 **Guinness 2000 Book of Records: Millennium Edition.** Guinness Records, 1999. 288 pp. ISBN 1892051001. Nonfiction.

This millennium edition of the *Guiness Book of Records* brings together all the current record-holders for everything you could imagine. You'll find the tallest, fastest, strangest, biggest, smallest, corniest, funniest, scariest, and weirdest in this newest edition.

30.8 Johnson, Sylvia A. **Tomatoes, Potatoes, Corn, and Beans: How the Foods of the Americas Changed Eating around the World.** Atheneum Books for Young Readers, 1997. 127 pp. ISBN 0689801416. Nonfiction.

Did you know that sweet potatoes were first grown in the warmer regions of the Americas like the Caribbean? When Columbus brought them to Spain, the Spanish called them *patatas*. English-speaking people changed it to potatoes. What we know as white potatoes grew only in the Andes before they were taken to Europe, where they became a staple for the Irish people. This book surveys many other foods that first grew in the Americas, and then spread elsewhere. The book is illustrated with archival prints from Native American sources and European plant books.

30.9 Kranes, Marsha, Fred Worth, and Steve Tamerius. **5087 Trivia Questions and Answers.** Black Dog / Leventhal, 1999. 752 pp. ISBN 1579120865. Nonfiction.

Want to win at Trivial Pursuit? Interested in those little facts that most people don't know? If you answered yes to either of these questions, then this book is for you. Arranged by topics such as The Cinema, The World, Language, War, and Space, this book is fun to read. Find out little-known facts about famous people (Which president got speeding tickets from Washington, D.C., police?), as well as interesting information that is just about totally useless (How many grooves are there on a quarter?).

30.10 Lang, Stephen. **The Big Book of American Trivia.** Tyndale, 1997. 390 pp. ISBN 0842304711. Nonfiction.

Over three thousand questions and answers about everything that's American—including politics, food, television, music stars, movie stars, religion, states, fashion, school—can be found in this book of trivia. You'll find it hard to put down once you start reading, because the facts are interesting and the question-and-answer format keeps you guessing.

30.11 Lauber, Patricia. **What You Never Knew about Fingers, Forks, and Chopsticks.** Illustrated by John Manders. Simon & Schuster, 1999. Unpaged. ISBN 0689804792. Nonfiction.

"Don't eat with your fingers," children hear parents say all the time. But at one time, eating with your fingers was not only acceptable, but it was also the only way to eat. In the Middle Ages, you'd expect to find in a book of manners instructions on how to wipe greasy fingers on a tablecloth! So when did eating utensils become a part of the dining habit? This historical account of forks and knives gives you a look at how people from long ago got food from the table to their mouths.

30.12   Marzollo, Jean. **I Spy Treasure Hunt: A Book of Picture Riddles.** Photographs by Walter Wick. Scholastic, 1999. 36 pp. ISBN 0439042245. Nonfiction.

Pick up this newest "I Spy" book and have fun searching for a myriad of things, including "a cat, a horse, and a lock, / a trapdoor, a nest, a reel, and a clock," or "an arrowhead, two turtles, a dog, / antlers, a pinecone, a feather, and a frog." When you've finished the hunts, turn to the last page of the book for an explanation of how the lavish sets for this book were made, and how you can create your own "I Spy" riddles.

30.13   Mooney, Julie. **The World of Ripley's Believe It or Not.** Black Dog / Leventhal, 1999. 160 pp. ISBN 1579120881. Nonfiction.

For more than eighty years, people have turned to the books in the Ripley's Believe It or Not series when they wanted to see the truly unbelievable. Robert Ripley established the tradition of seeking out the incredible, and the editors of the Ripley series continue that tradition today. Whether showing us a person who can stuff his mouth with numerous tennis balls and golf balls and still whistle a tune, or the strong-jawed man who could lift two tables and six chairs with his teeth, this book introduces people and animals doing the strangest of things.

30.14   Murphy, Pat, Ellen Klages, Pearl Tesler, Linda Shore, and the Exploratorium. **The Brain Explorer: Puzzles, Riddles, Illusions, and Other Mental Adventures.** Owl / Henry Holt, 1999. 144 pp. ISBN 0805045384. Nonfiction.

The brain is an intricate organ whose functions can be something of a mystery. This book explains how the brain works, and then provides interesting experiments that you can use to test your own brainpower. Want help remembering your locker combination? Maybe you have lost an important piece of paper and need to find it soon? This book is crammed with tips to help sharpen your thinking skills.

30.15   O'Neill, Jaime. **We're History: The 20th Century Survivor's Final Exam.** Fireside, 1998. 384 pp. ISBN 0684829223. Nonfiction.

You've lived through at least a part of the twentieth century, and you've probably studied the history of the rest of the century in school. You've watched the movies, heard the music, worn the clothes, driven the cars, eaten the food, and seen the art of this century—or at least the end of this century. Now you can test your knowledge of this century with this ultimate trivia book. Questions are grouped by topics (Rhymes of Our Times, First Things First, and Morbid Fascinations to mention a few) and answers are provided at the ends of chapters. See if you know when the skateboard was invented, what Mussolini's first name was, who the two wild and crazy guys were from *Saturday Night Live,* or what happened in Cooperstown, New York, in 1936. Be careful as you read this book, however; you'll find yourself learning more history than you ever thought you wanted to know!

30.16 Platt, Richard. **Stephen Biesty's Incredible Everything.** Illustrated by Stephen Biesty. Dorling Kindersley, 1997. 32 pp. ISBN 078942049X. Nonfiction.

Making gunpowder without incinerating yourself is quite a tricky task. Turning a tree into paper involves a complex process as well. To find out how things are made—things as simple as a bar of chocolate and the holes in your morning doughnuts or as complicated as the family car and the lunar-landing vehicles—all you have to do is turn the pages of this remarkably detailed book.

30.17 Reynolds, David West. *Star Wars Episode I* **Incredible Cross-Sections.** Illustrated by Hans Jenssen and Richard Chasemore. Dorling Kindersley, 1999. 32 pp. ISBN 078943962X. Nonfiction.

Created in cooperation with Lucasfilms, this book provides detailed cutaway illustrations of some of the ships used in the filming of the *Star Wars: Episode I* movie. The inner workings of the droid starfighter, the weapons aboard the armored fighting vehicles, and much more are presented in painstaking detail. Cross sections of the ships and their components provide an inside look at their intricacies. For those of you who loved the movie, this book is a must-read.

30.18 Reynolds, David West. *Star Wars* **Incredible Cross-Sections: The Ultimate Guide to** *Star Wars* **Vehicles and Spacecraft.** Dorling Kindersley, 1998. 32 pp. ISBN 0789434806. Nonfiction.

Die-hard fans of the movie will find it difficult to resist this in-depth look at the cruisers and battleships that soared across the galaxy. Look inside the vehicle Darth Vader piloted, see the interior workings of Hans Solo's Millennium Falcon, and take a look at the infamous Death Star that threatened to put an end to the Empire.

30.19 Segaloff, Nat. **The Everything Trivia Book.** Adams Media, 1999. 308 pp. ISBN 1580621430. Nonfiction.

From little-known secrets and absolutely weird facts to bits of information from long ago, this trivia book is fun, informative, and sure to make you smarter about things no one else knows. From commercial jingles, political slogans, and inside facts about politicians and movie stars to comic book heroes and fast food delights, this book has fascinating historical tidbits that will help you better understand our culture.

30.20 Wardlaw, Lee. **Bubblemania: The Chewy History of Bubble Gum.** Illustrated by Sandra Forrest. Aladdin, 1997. 144 pp. ISBN 0689817193. Nonfiction.

Stuck on gum? Wonder why bubble gum is pink? Get the facts about this chewy, gooey stuff from Lee Wardlaw, who became a champion bubble blower at the age of seven, and who now gives tips for blowing a world-record-sized bubble. Included in this colorful book are a history of bubble gum and the current five hundred million dollar industry, a gum recipe, bubble bloopers and blunders, and how to unstick yourself from some sticky gum-induced situations.

30.21 Young, Karen Romano. **Guinness Record Breakers.** Guinness Media, 1997. 64 pp. ISBN 0965238334. Nonfiction.

The greatest, the shortest, the deepest, and the hottest—records for these and other categories are revealed in this collection. From the strange (the longest and biggest chicken dance ever held) and the more commonplace (the best-selling doll) to the incredible (the most people playing a game of Twister at one time), there is much in this slim book to delight and entertain you and your friends.

31 UFOs and Other Unexplained Phenomena

"The fairest thing we can experience is the mysterious. It is the fundamental emotion which stands at the cradle of true art and true science."

Albert Einstein

31.1   Bell, Art, and Brad Steiger. **The Source.** Paper Chase, 1999. 267 pp. ISBN 1879706504. Nonfiction.

Ghosts. UFOs. Aliens. Mysteries of ancient civilizations. All these topics and many more are explored by nighttime radio talk-show host Art Bell and bestselling author Brad Steiger in this fascinating book about unexplained phenomena. So whether you want to know about alien abductions, wonder about those strange crop circles you've seen in photos, or just want to read about some things that no one can quite explain, this book is for you.

31.2   Brown, Courtney. **Cosmic Explorers.** Dutton, 1999. 260 pp. ISBN 0525944303. Nonfiction.

In this follow-up to *Cosmic Voyage,* in which Brown suggested that two extraterrestrial civilizations exist, the author takes his research further. Now using scientific remote viewing (SRV), Brown makes a case that extraterrestrial life not only exists, but is closer than most would ever want to think.

31.3   Carlson, H. G. **Mysteries of the Unexplained.** Contemporary, 1997. 192 pp. ISBN 0809234971. Nonfiction.

If seeing is believing, then some folks believe in some pretty strange things. Every year, hundreds of people report seeing things that cause others to raise their eyebrows and say, "Oh really?" This book takes a look at some of those unexplained events as it explores topics such as aliens, UFOs, ghosts, and mythical beasts. Read about psychics, extrasensory perception (ESP), ships and planes that have vanished without a trace, and mysterious places like Atlantis and the pyramids. Photographs and first-person accounts add interest and information to this text, which offers insights into many of the mysteries of this world.

31.4 Corso, Philip J., with William J. Birnes. **The Day after Roswell.** Pocket, 1998. 371 pp. ISBN 067101756X. Nonfiction.

In 1947, something crashed into the desert near Roswell, New Mexico. Some people said it was an alien spacecraft. Other people—especially government people—said it certainly was not. Now, at the turn of the millennium, retired Colonel Philip J. Corso, a member of President Eisenhower's National Security Council and the former head of the Foreign Technology Desk at the U.S. Army's Research and Development department, has written this book that supposedly sets the record straight. It explains that an alien spacecraft not only crashed near Roswell, but that what was found led to today's use of fiber optics, lasers, and integrated circuit chips. Corso writes convincingly about the crash, what was found, and the cover-up. Whether you believe him or not, the book is still an interesting read.

31.5 Fradin, Dennis Brindell. **Is There Life on Mars?** Margaret McElderry, 1999. 130 pp. ISBN 0689820488. Nonfiction.

The Red Planet has always fascinated human beings. Some people have been convinced that there is life on Mars because of the "canals" astronomers saw through their telescopes. Fradin explores the history of speculation and research about life on Mars, and the legends about Martians that have circulated. He summarizes current knowledge about the planet, and the missions planned for future exploration.

31.6 Gutsch, William. **1001 Things Everyone Should Know about the Universe.** Doubleday, 1998. 353 pp. ISBN 038548223X. Nonfiction.

Are we alone in the universe? The search for extraterrestrial life is one of many space phenomena discussed in this entertaining, comprehensive overview of space. This resource consists of 1001 "mini essays" that explore the mysteries of the universe, as well as provide basic knowledge about our solar system, black holes, galaxies, supernovas, and other fascinating subjects.

31.7 Hausdorf, Hartwig. **The Chinese Roswell.** New Paradigm, 1998. 275 pp. ISBN 189213800X. Nonfiction.

Anyone even somewhat interested in UFOs and aliens might want to look at this book. Hartwig journeyed to the Far East to find answers about extraterrestrials. While there, he found answers to many Eastern mysteries, including the puzzling stone disks of Bayan Kara Ula that some believe are connected to an alien landing over twelve thousand years ago.

31.8 Kettelkamp, Larry. **ETs and UFOs: Are They Real?** Morrow Junior Books, 1996. 86 pp. ISBN 0688128688. Nonfiction.

Investigate the reported kidnapping of two teenage camp counselors in Vermont by "a group of goggle-eyed, web-fingered beings." Here are the photographic evidence and eyewitness drawings of more than a dozen UFO sightings and personal reports of alien abductions. The thought-provoking evidence is presented, and now it's up to you to decide: Are we alone in the universe?

31.9 Lemesurier, Peter. **Decoding the Great Pyramid.** Barnes & Noble, 1999. 255 pp. ISBN 0760719624. Nonfiction.

For over forty centuries, the Great Pyramid has generated controversy as people wonder if it was built for some purpose other than a royal tomb. This grand structure invites lots of speculation when you consider that it was built over four thousand years ago, with stones weighing over seventy tons and so carefully positioned that their joints are less than a fiftieth of an inch in thickness. Curious coincidences, such as the fact that the Great Pyramid is built exactly to correspond to the earth's four cardinal points and is at the exact center of the geometrical quadrant formed by the Nile Delta, make this great wonder even more curious. This book attempts to look at all the mysteries that surround the Great Pyramid, and give an up-close look at its structure and the myths that surround it.

31.10 Marrs, Jim. **Alien Agenda: Investigating the Extraterrestrial Presence Among Us.** HarperCollins, 1998. 656 pp. ISBN 0061096865. Nonfiction.

Read this book and you'll find yourself looking up at a dark sky just a little more frequently. Marrs skillfully sets the groundwork for convincing readers that UFOs and aliens do exist. He begins by describing his own UFO sighting, and then discusses his involvement in writing newspaper stories about other sightings. Finally, he talks about his belief that the government has conspired to keep secret all that they know about UFOs. The book is filled with data from fifty years of UFO sightings, and carefully builds a case that the author hopes will prove not only that aliens exist, but also that they've been here and the government knows it.

31.11 Neff, Fred. **Mysterious Persons in History: Baffling Cases of Unsolved Mysteries.** Runestone, 1997. 112 pp. ISBN 0822539322. Nonfiction.

Why did Lizzie Borden kill her parents? What was the real identity of the killer known as The Black Dahlia? Was Napoleon Bonaparte murdered? Why were police unable to find and stop Jack the Ripper? These questions and many more are answered in this fascinating look at real-life crimes, some of which remain unsolved decades later. An annotated bibliography is included for anyone who wishes to explore these mysteries in more detail.

32 War and the Holocaust

"I am tired—my heart is sick and sad. From where the sun now stands I will fight no more forever."

Chief Joseph

"Perhaps some day someone will explain how, on the level of man, Auschwitz was possible; but on the level of God, it will forever remain the most disturbing of mysteries."

Elie Wiesel

32.1 Alonso, Karen. *Korematsu v. United States:* **Japanese-American Internment Camps.** Enslow, 1998. 128 pp. ISBN 0894909665. Nonfiction.

This book, part of the Landmark Supreme Court Cases series, examines the case of Fred Korematsu, a Japanese American who was put into an internment camp during World War II. He later sued the U.S. government for damages incurred because of his imprisonment. On December 18, 1944, the U.S. Supreme Court ruled against Korematsu. Almost forty years later, that case was overturned as the Court ruled that the government had withheld information and lied to the Justice Department. This fascinating case brings to light the issue of the imprisonment Japanese Americans faced during World War II.

32.2 Beller, Susan Provost. **Never Were Men So Brave: The Irish Brigade during the Civil War.** Simon & Schuster / Margaret McElderry, 1998. 98 pp. ISBN 0689814062. Nonfiction.

The Irish Brigade, comprised of Irish immigrants new to the United States, was one of the famous fighting units of the Civil War. On September 17, 1862, during the bloody Battle of Antietam, 535 members of the Irish Brigade were killed or wounded. *Never Were Men So Brave* chronicles the history of the Irish immigrants who fought in this brigade, and introduces readers to Thomas Francis Meagher, who created the Irish Brigade to help defend the Union these immigrants had so recently embraced as their home.

32.3 Bitton-Jackson, Livia. **My Bridges of Hope: Searching for Life and Love after Auschwitz.** Simon & Schuster, 1999. 272 pp. ISBN 0689820267. Nonfiction.

In this sequel to *I Have Lived a Thousand Years,* the author describes her life after liberation from the concentration camp in 1945. At age fourteen, Livia returns to her Czech village along with her mother and brother. They hope to gain passage to the United States and a new life. However, there are interminable delays in getting permission to travel. As they wait, Livia and her mother help smuggle Jews out of Czechoslovakia and into Israel. Eventually, Livia and her mother escape to the United States, arriving in New York in 1954.

32.4 Boyle, David. **World War II: A Photographic History.** Barnes & Noble, 1998. 600 pp. ISBN 076061116. Nonfiction.

From the icy seas of the Arctic Circle and the jungles of the South Pacific to the sands of the Sahara and the mountains of Russia, this book chronicles the turbulent events of the Second World War between the years 1939 and 1945. With over nine hundred photographs, this book shows not only the destruction of this terrible war, but the anguish, fear, loneliness, and bravery of soldiers and civilians. See Churchill standing in a throng of people celebrating VE Day, gaze into the eyes of concentration camp inmates as they learn of their liberation, look at Chinese troops using elephants for transportation, and see photographs of the destruction in Nagasaki and Hiroshima in the days after the atomic bombs were dropped. A table of contents that divides the war into major events, a well-written introduction that explains events leading up to the war, and an index that takes readers to particular text references make this book essential reading for anyone studying World War II.

32.5 Byers, Ann. **The Holocaust Overview.** Enslow, 1998. 128 pp. ISBN 0766010627. Nonfiction.

This first book in the Holocaust Remembered series gives an overview of the horrors that Hitler planned for the Jews once he gained power. Anti-Semitism was not new with Hitler, but when he gained political power he was able to make it national policy. His four-part plan to eliminate the Jews included exclusion, expulsion, enclosure, and extermination. This book explains each of these policies, and some of the early legislation against Jews that were prompted by Hitler's plan.

32.6 Clinton, Catherine. **Scholastic Encyclopedia of the Civil War.** Scholastic Reference, 1999. 112 pp. ISBN 0590372270. Nonfiction.

This easy-to-read look at the United States during the Civil War begins with the 1820 Missouri Compromise and concludes with the end of Reconstruction in 1877. Photographs, maps, side boxes that give battle highlights, and inserts on individuals such as Johnnie Clem—the nine-year-old boy who ran away from home to become a Union army drummer boy—make this account appealing and interesting. Important documents like Lincoln's Gettysburg Address are included, as well as eyewitness accounts of moments in the war from slaves, women, children, and soldiers. This reference book reads like a novel you won't want to put down.

32.7 Cox, Clinton. **Come All You Brave Soldiers.** Scholastic, 1999. 182 pp. ISBN 0385322240. Nonfiction.

Many African Americans served valiantly in the Revolutionary War. Ironically, after the war was over, most of them were returned to lives of servitude. This fascinating book chronicles the involvement of African Americans in the war for American independence, an independence in which these brave soldiers were not to share.

32.8 Dudley, William, editor. **The Vietnam War: Opposing Viewpoints.** Greenhaven, 1998. 248 pp. ISBN 1565107004. Nonfiction.

Following a format that the Opposing Viewpoint series has used successfully in other books, this book presents pro and con arguments on six issues related to the Vietnam War. Issues discussed in this book include reasons for initial involvement in the war, the United States' continued presence in Vietnam, the bombing of Hanoi, draft evaders, and media coverage of the war. The views of John F. Kennedy, Ho Chi Minh, David Hotham, Lyndon B. Johnson, William C. Westmoreland, Richard M. Nixon, Henry Kissinger, and George Moss are included. This book is an important source for anyone studying the Vietnam War.

32.9 Ferrie, Richard. **The World Turned Upside Down: George Washington and the Battle of Yorktown.** Holiday House, 1999. 168 pp. ISBN 0823414027. Nonfiction.

On October 19, 1781, the British Army surrendered to the Continental Army, which was under the command of General George Washington. With that surrender secured, a new nation was born and the history of the world changed forever. But how did a ragtag army with little equipment, less training, and no confidence manage to win the Battle of Yorktown? This book explains the events leading up to that decisive battle, and describes the people involved. Interesting appendices take a look at the battleships, weapons, and uniforms of the Revolutionary War.

32.10 Fraser, Mary Ann. **Vicksburg: The Battle That Won the Civil War.** Henry Holt, 1999. 104 pp. ISBN 0805061061. Nonfiction.

Only seven months into the Civil War, President Lincoln told federal officers that "Vicksburg is the key. The war can never be brought to a close until that key is in our pocket." What made Vicksburg such an important key? Was Lincoln correct in his assessment? Why did the North have a difficult time taking this one city? What did General Ulysses S. Grant finally understand he would have to do to overpower that Southern stronghold? Fraser uses primary-source material, period illustrations, and diagrams and maps to answer these and many other questions, and to recreate the battle many historians believe was the decisive battle of the Civil War.

32.11 Green, Carl R., and William R. Sanford. **Union Generals of the Civil War.** Enslow, 1998. 112 pp. ISBN 0766010287. Nonfiction.

By the time the Civil War ended, 620,000 Americans had died. This book offers a look at ten notable Union generals who were a part of that bloody war. A companion title in the Collective Biographies series, *Confederate Generals of the Civil War,* tells about the generals of the South. This book begins with a chart that compares facts about the North and South (everything from population and miles of railroad tracks to numbers of soldiers and warships) and a concise timeline of major events of the war. Then the author presents a brief biography of Union generals, including Ulysses S. Grant, Winfield Hancock, Joseph Hooker, George Meade, and Philip Sheridan.

32.12 Haskins, Jim. **Black, Blue and Gray: African Americans in the Civil War.** Simon & Schuster, 1998. 154 pp. ISBN 0689806558. Nonfiction.

Although many Northern Whites called the Civil War a "white man's war," and continually asserted that the war was not about slavery, in the eyes of the four and a half million African Americans—some slaves, some free—it was most certainly about slavery. Why did free African Americans have a hard time joining the army to fight for the Union? What finally allowed African Americans to join in the war? Under what conditions did they fight, and who were the African American leaders on the battlefield? Haskin uses excerpts from letters and government documents to bring authenticity to this account of the Civil War.

32.13 Knapp, Ron. **American Generals of World War II.** Enslow, 1998. 128 pp. ISBN 0766010244. Nonfiction.

Almost every nation in the world was involved in World War II. It was fought on three continents—Asia, Europe, and Africa—and caused the death of approximately thirty-five million soldiers and civilians. The United States' active involvement in this war began when Japan bombed Pearl Harbor on December 7, 1941. Quickly Germany and Italy joined with Japan in declaring war against the United States. The Allies—Great Britain, the United States, and the Soviet Union—united in war against the Axis Powers. Read about the great U.S. generals who fought hard to defeat the armies of Adolf Hitler, Hideki Tojo, and Benito Mussolini—generals such as Omar Bradley, Dwight Eisenhower, Douglas MacArthur, George Marshall, George Patton, and Joseph Stilwell.

32.14 Kuhn, Betsy. **Angels of Mercy: The Army Nurses of World War II.** Atheneum Books for Young Readers, 1999. 114 pp. ISBN 0689820445. Nonfiction.

More than fifty-nine thousand women signed up to serve in the Army Nurse Corps during World War II. They faced great danger and tremendous hardship as they worked to save men injured in battles far from home. Some were taken hostage and held for years; others suffered under crude living conditions. These heroic women brought more than healing to the tent hospitals; they brought cheer and courage. A monument in Washington, D.C., honors those women who served to defend our country in a variety of capacities.

32.15 Leapman, Michael. **Witnesses to War: Eight True Life Stories of Nazi Persecution.** Viking, 1998. 128 pp. ISBN 0670873861. Nonfiction.

Millions of children living in Europe in the 1930s faced the most terrifying experiences of their youth as they watched the Nazi forces march into town, round up those suspected of being Jewish, and arrest them. Thousands of the inhabitants of the concentration camps were children. Many of them perished due to the harsh living conditions of the camps. Here is the story of eight extraordinary young men and women who suffered at the hands of the Nazis. Most readers will be familiar with at least one of the stories, that of the young girl named Anne Frank, who spent two years living in the cramped quarters of an attic annex with her family before being caught and sent to Bergen-Belsen where she died.

32.16 Lobel, Anita. **No Pretty Pictures: A Child of War.** Greenwillow, 1998. 208 pp. ISBN 0688159354. Nonfiction.

Noted children's book illustrator Anita Lobel recalls her childhood in Krakow during the Nazi occupation of World War II. For five years, Anita and her younger brother were forced to flee their homeland, and they survived only through the kindness of others. This firsthand account of what it was like to be a child during this dark period of history makes the time come alive for readers today, more than fifty years after the war. Despite all of the hardship she faced, Lobel reports that her life "has been good. I want more."

32.17 Marrin, Albert. **Commander in Chief Abraham Lincoln and the Civil War.** Dutton, 1997. 246 pp. ISBN 0525458220. Nonfiction.

On February 8, 1861, representatives from seven Southern states met in Montgomery, Alabama, to secede from the United States and form the Confederate States of America. Just three days later, Abraham Lincoln, president-elect of the United States, boarded a train from Springfield, Illinois, bound for Washington, D.C. On the same day, Jefferson Davis left his plantation in Mississippi for his inauguration as president of the Confederacy. Two months later, the "great American tragedy," the Civil War, "exploded across the land." In this book, Albert Marrin has created an informative and authentic narrative by weaving together contemporary historical accounts, Lincoln's own words, and original illustrations and photographs to "bring our greatest president to life by placing him in the context of his own personal background and the larger circumstances of our country's greatest conflict."

32.18 Novac, Ana. **The Beautiful Days of My Youth: My Six Months in Auschwitz and Plaszow.** Translated by George L. Newman. Henry Holt, 1997. 160 pp. ISBN 0805050183. Nonfiction.

When she was sent to a concentration camp as a fourteen-year-old during World War II, Ana Novac kept her sanity by writing about her experiences on scraps of paper she tore up and hid in her shoe. Her observations of her companions give insight into the people who encountered daily horrors with her. Her story is a record of one girl's triumph over evil.

32.19 Opdyke, Irene Gut, with Jennifer Armstrong. **In My Hands: Memories of a Holocaust Rescuer.** Knopf, 1999. 276 pp. ISBN 0679891811. Nonfiction.

Irene Gutowna, a Polish nursing student, was seventeen years old when World War II began. Six years later, feeling like she was "a million years old," she recalls living through tragic times: separation from her family, rape, forced labor, and gripping fear as she viewed cruel acts by German and Russian soldiers. She became a German major's housekeeper and while there, hid twelve Jews in the major's villa. When the major discovered them, Irene became his mistress in order to protect them. Later, after helping them escape, she too escaped and joined the Polish Resistance. Her tale of bravery and hope in a time of despair is a poignant and powerful addition to Holocaust literature.

32.20 Phillips, David. **Maps of the Civil War: The Roads They Took.** Barnes & Noble, 1999. 160 pp. ISBN 0760718709. Nonfiction.

This photohistory provides many perspectives on the Civil War using maps of the routes armies took to a particular battle field, descriptions of the battles themselves, and the events leading up to them, and photographs and drawings of the people and the places that were part of the war. Fascinating background histories and tactical analyses of the military strategies make this book helpful for studying the Civil War, as well as interesting for anyone who wants to know more about this bloody home-front war.

32.21 Strangis, Joel. **Lewis Hayden and the War against Slavery.** Linnet, 1999. 167 pp. ISBN 020802430. Nonfiction.

The time: pre–Civil War days. The place: Boston, Massachusetts. The man: Lewis Hayden. The problem: Hayden is an escaped slave. In this well-researched novel about Lewis Hayden, author Joel Strangis portrays a strong and sensitive man committed to freedom for himself, his family, and his people. Hayden survived the search by federal marshals and became an influential force in the Boston African American community, raising money for John Brown's raid on Harper's Ferry and supplying information for the Underground Railroad. Based on original documents, letters, and testimonials, this is a moving biography of an important antislavery hero and African American leader.

32.22 Wassiljewa, Tatjana. **Hostage to War: A True Story.** Scholastic, 1997. 244 pp. ISBN 0590134469. Nonfiction.

In June 1941, Germany declared war on Russia, and Tatjana Wassiljewa's carefree childhood was gone forever. In this true story based on her diary entries, Tatjana tells about surviving German bomb attacks and suffering near starvation, only to become one of seven million captive laborers from Eastern Europe who were forced to work on German farms and factories to support the German war effort. This story of survival and the resilience of the human spirit, told from the perspective of a Russian civilian prisoner of war during World War II, will inspire readers of all ages.

32.23 **World War II Extra: An Around-the-World Newspaper History from the Treaty of Versailles to the Nuremberg Trials.** Castle, 1999. 326 pp. ISBN 0785811362. Nonfiction.

Original newspapers from around the world are used to tell the story of World War II. Beginning with the Saturday, June 28, 1919, *Los Angeles Express* headline "Treaty Signed; War Ends" and ending with the Tuesday, October 1, 1946, *New York Daily Mirror* headline that announced "Goering to Die!" this book gives readers the headlines, news, and photographs that made this war real to people throughout the world. Included are newspapers from the United States, Great Britain, Japan, Germany, Italy, and France. This outstanding historical account of World War II comes from Eric C. Caren, who provided the original newspapers from his private collection.

33 Writers and Writing

"Reading maketh a full man, conference a ready man, and writing an exact man."

Francis Bacon

33.1 Ada, Alma Flor. **Under the Royal Palms: A Childhood in Cuba.** Atheneum Books for Young Readers, 1998. 87 pp. ISBN 0689806310. Nonfiction.

Alma Flor Ada, author of books such as *The Gold Coin, My Name Is Maria Isabel,* and *The Malachite Palace,* continues the story of her life, which she began in the autobiography *Where the Flame Trees Bloom.* Wonderful childhood photos and rich stories give readers an inside glance at the life of this popular author. Whether telling of how she and her grandmother would attempt to count the bats that lived above the porch as they flew out to feed on the fruit of the backyard—"sweet mangoes, guavas, soft and delicious nisperos"—or telling the poignant story of her uncle's work with children with leprosy, Alma Flor Ada hopes that the stories she tells here will "help you see the richness all around you . . . and the richness within you."

33.2 Block, Francesca Lia, and Hillary Carlip. **Zine Scene: The Do It Yourself Guide to Zines.** Girl, 1998. 120 pp. ISBN 0965975436. Nonfiction.

If you're not sure what a zine is, or know what it is but are not sure how to write one, then this how-to book is for you. Block and Carlip introduce you to several zinesters (people who write zines), and give you all the info you need to get started writing your own.

33.3 Dyer, Daniel. **Jack London: A Biography.** Scholastic, 1997. 228 pp. ISBN 0590222163. Nonfiction.

The author of classics such as *Call of the Wild* and *White Fang,* Jack London left school at age eleven and worked at a variety of jobs before returning at age nineteen to complete his education. He set out with countless others who were seeking their fortune in the Klondike Gold Rush. Although he did not strike it rich in the gold mines, he did find material that would later make its way into his adventure and survival stories. This biography follows the action-packed life of one of the most noted authors in the United States.

33.4   Garland, Sherry. **Writing for Young Adults.** Writer's Digest, 1998. 214 pp. ISBN 0898798574. Nonfiction.

This comprehensive book provides beginning authors with essential information about writing for the young adult book market. From learning how to generate story lines, figuring out trends in publishing, and writing powerful hooks (yes, you can go beyond "It was a dark and stormy night"!) to understanding how to write effective dialogue and knowing which publisher to send manuscripts to, this handbook by an award-winning author of young adult books will be helpful to anyone who wants to be a better writer.

33.5   Graham, Paula W. **Speaking of Journals.** Boyds Mills, 1999. 226 pp. ISBN 1563977419. Nonfiction.

Jack Gantos began keeping a journal in second grade. Naomi Shihab Nye has several journals going simultaneously. Kathleen Krull is addicted to them. More than twenty-five authors discuss the importance of writing in a journal, recording ideas and snippets of conversations that might later be included in one of their books. Photographs of each of the authors, many as young children, are included with each interview. Sample pages from the journals are included as well.

33.6   Horning, Kathleen T. **From Cover to Cover: Evaluating and Reviewing Children's Books.** HarperCollins, 1997. 230 pp. ISBN 0060245190. Nonfiction.

What makes a children's book good? Is there a set of standards that can be applied to all books? Are there different standards for different types of books? The information in this book can assist those who want to learn how to evaluate a book and write a review. Beginning with an introduction to the world of children's book publishing, the book carefully explains the evolution of an idea into a book and the process of making the book. Other chapters describe the various genres in the field, and how to write reviews that go beyond personal response to encompass analysis.

33.7 Jaffe, Nina. **A Voice of the People: The Life and Work of Harold Courlander.** Henry Holt, 1997. 177 pp. ISBN 0805034447. Nonfiction.

In order to enjoy a tale from another country today, you only have to pluck one from the library bookshelf. That was not always the case. Before a tale from another country can be enjoyed in America, someone must travel to other lands, locate the stories that are a part of the culture, and then translate those stories for you. That is exactly what Harold Courlander spent his life doing. An inveterate traveler, Courlander spent time in Haiti, Cuba, and an array of other countries, bringing traditional stories from these countries back to the United States, where future generations of readers could enjoy them.

33.8 Jones, Patrick. **What's So Scary about R. L. Stine?** Scarecrow, 1998. 249 pp. ISBN 0810834685. Nonfiction.

What do horror books and joke books have in common? How did the attic of a three-story house affect a little boy named Robert Lawrence? Why do some folks call R. L. Stine "extremely destructive," while others call him "a youth advocate"? Are his Fear Street books something to be feared? This highly interesting look at R. L. Stine and the books he's written gives us insight into the man, the books, the genre, and the reasons why some people love to hate the author, while others just love him.

33.9 Kerr, M. E. **Blood on the Forehead: What I Know about Writing.** HarperCollins, 1998. 262 pp. ISBN 0064462072. Nonfiction.

"Writing is easy: all you do is sit staring at a blank sheet of paper until the drops of blood form on your forehead." So begins the advice of author M. E. Kerr, who sold her first novel, planned on a poster board, when she was twenty-three years old. Kerr compares preparing to write a short story to packing for a "trip to a nearby town," and writing a novel to taking "a trip to another country." She suggests that future writers "Read a lot," "Write the kind of novel you like to read," and "Recognize how brave you are. Respect yourself and reward yourself." Kerr illustrates her comments with examples, short stories, and excerpts from novels she has published. With entertaining and insightful advice, Kerr gives would-be writers an insider's look at the writing and publishing process.

33.10 Meltzer, Milton. **Carl Sandburg: A Biography.** Twenty-First Century, 1999. 144 pp. ISBN 0761313648. Nonfiction.

Raised in poverty, Carl Sandburg grew up to become a beloved American poet. In this biography, Meltzer writes about Sandburg's early life, when he did everything from selling ice cream and harvesting ice off a frozen lake to making pottery and washing bottles in order to earn money. Later he spent years as a journalist and wrote about such social issues as labor problems and racial tensions. Eventually he began writing the poems that we now know so well. Throughout the book, you'll find black-and-white photographs that chronicle the poet's life, comments from Sandburg himself, bits and pieces of his poems, and interesting commentary from Meltzer. You'll finish the book with insights into this great poet, and a desire to read a collection of Sandburg's poems.

33.11 Meltzer, Milton. **Langston Hughes: An Illustrated Edition.** Illustrated by Stephen Alcorn. Millbrook, 1997. 240 pp. ISBN 0761302050. Nonfiction.

One of America's preeminent poets and authors comes to life in this biography. Meltzer was a contemporary of Langston Hughes; the two collaborated on two books prior to Hughes' death in 1967. It is his intimate knowledge of Hughes that gives us the rare opportunity to meet a brilliant thinker, writer, and humanitarian.

33.12 Neimark, Anne E. **Myth Maker: J. R. R. Tolkien.** Harcourt Brace, 1996. 128 pp. ISBN 0152988475. Nonfiction.

John Ronald Reuel Tolkien was a noted linguist and scholar who lived his life surrounded by the magical characters that inhabited his books for children and young adults. *The Hobbit* and the books in the Lord of the Rings trilogy were his creations, and they continue to find new audiences nearly fifty years after their initial publication. Born in South Africa, Tolkien experienced much hardship as a young man. Despite his humble beginnings, he managed to win scholarships that permitted him to study at Oxford. His life as a writer of fantasy gave him great pleasure. "Fantasy," he wrote, "remains a human right." Meet the man behind Gandalf, Bilbo Baggins, and Gollum.

33.13 Rinaldi, Ann. **Hang a Thousand Trees with Ribbons: The Story of Phillis Wheatley.** Gulliver / Harcourt Brace, 1996. 352 pp. ISBN 0152008764. Nonfiction.

Phillis Wheatley was kidnapped from her native Senegal and brought to the United States in 1761 as a slave. Her owners soon realized that she was a bright girl with a flair for writing. They tried in vain to find a publisher who would print her remarkable poems, but no one was interested in the work of an African American woman. This biography lovingly tells the story of how Phillis Wheatley finally came to be the first African American poet ever to be published in the United States. More than two hundred years later, her poems are still the subject of study in English classes across the nation.

33.14 Stanley, Diane, and Peter Vennema. **Bard of Avon: The Story of William Shakespeare.** Illustrated by Diane Stanley. Mulberry, 1998. Unpaged. ISBN 0688162940. Nonfiction.

This photobiography of William Shakespeare combines meticulous research with exquisite artwork to create a dramatic account of this master of drama. Stanley and Vennema painstakingly studied the life of this famous man, a difficult task since he did not keep a diary and none of his personal letters survived. Working as historians, the writers used his plays, poems, business transactions, court papers, and will to recreate the life he led. An interesting postscript points out that if you have "seen better days," or were "tongue tied," or "suspected foul play" because someone was "dead as a doornail," you are quoting Shakespeare!

Appendix A: Award-Winning Books

The following awards and recognitions are helpful resources for locating excellent books. We have included major awards for poetry, fiction, drama, and nonfiction for young readers, presented from 1997 to 2000, as well as descriptions of other useful booklists.

Jane Addams Award

The Jane Addams Award, established in 1953, is given annually to the book for young people that most effectively promotes peace, social justice, world community, or equality of the sexes and races. It is given by the Women's International League for Peace and Freedom, and the Jane Addams Peace Association.

1997   Bartoletti, Susan Campbell. *Growing Up in Coal Country.* Houghton Mifflin.

1998   Nye, Naomi Shihab. *Habibi.* Simon & Schuster.

1999   Wolff, Virginia Euwer. *Bat 6.* Scholastic.

Hans Christian Andersen Award

Sometimes called the "Little Nobel," this award was established in 1956. This international award is presented every other year to an author and to an illustrator for his or her body of work. An international committee selects winners from those nominated by their respective countries.

1998   Katherine Paterson

2000   Ana Maria Machado

The ALAN Award

Each year, NCTE's Assembly on Literature for Adolescents (ALAN) presents an award to an outstanding individual in the field of adolescent literature.

1997   Mildred Taylor

1998   S. E. Hinton

1999   Robert Lipsyte

Mildred L. Batchelder Award

Presented annually (unless no book is deemed worthy) to a U.S. publisher, the Batchelder Award honors the most outstanding translated book for children. The committee may also designate up to four other titles as Honor Books. Established in 1968, it is given by the Association for Library Service to Children of the American Library Association.

1997   Farrar, Straus and Giroux: *The Friends,* by Kazumi Yumoto. Translated from the Japanese by Cathy Hirano.

1998   Henry Holt: *The Robber and Me,* by Josef Holub. Translated from the German by Elizabeth D. Crawford.

Honor Books

Scholastic: *Hostage to War: A True Story,* by Tatjana Wasslijewa. Translated from the German by Anna Trenter.

Viking Books: *Nero Corleone: A Cat's Story,* by Elke Heidenreich. Translated from the German by Doris Orgel.

1999   Dial: *Thanks to My Mother,* by Schoschana Rabinovici. Translated from the Hebrew by James Skofield.

Honor Book

Viking: *Secret Letters from 0 to 10,* by Susie Morgenstern. Translated from the French by Gill Rosner.

2000   Walker: *The Baboon King,* by Anton Quintana. Translated from the Dutch by John Nieuwenhuizen.

Honor Books

Farrar, Straus and Giroux: *Collector of Moments,* by Quint Buchholz. Translated from the German by Peter F. Neumeyer.

Front Street: *Asphalt Angels,* by Ineke Holtwijk. Translated from the Dutch by Wanda Boeke.

R. & S.: *Vendela in Venice,* by Christina Bjork. Translated from the Swedish by Inga-Karin Eriksson.

Pura Belpré Award

This award, established in 1996, is presented every two years to a Latino/Latina author and a Latino/Latina illustrator whose work best portrays and celebrates Latino culture. It is cosponsored by the American Library Association and the National Association to Promote Library Services to the Spanish Speaking (REFORMA). The awards for authors are included here.

1998   Martinez, Victor. *Parrot in the Oven: Mi Vida.* HarperCollins.

Honor Books

Alarcón, Francisco X. *Laughing Tomatoes and Other Spring Poems.* Children's Book Press.

Martinez, Floyd. *Spirits of the High Mesa.* Arte Público Press.

2000   Ada, Alma Flor. *Under the Royal Palms: A Childhood in Cuba.* Atheneum.

Honor Books

Alarcón, Francisco X. *From the Bellybutton of the Moon and Other Summer Poems.* Children's Book Press.

Herrera, Juan Felipe. *Laughing Out Loud I Fly: Poems in English and in Spanish.* HarperCollins.

Booklist's Top of the List

The "Top of the List," initiated in 1991, represents selections of the very best books from *Booklist*'s "Editor's Choice" annual list. The complete list may be found in *Booklist* each January 15.

1997   **Youth Fiction**

Fine, Anne. *The Tulip Touch.* Little Brown.

Youth Nonfiction

Wick, Walter. *A Drop of Water: A Book of Science and Wonder.* Scholastic.

1998   **Youth Fiction**

Paulsen, Gary. *Soldier's Heart.* Delacorte.

Youth Nonfiction

Lobel, Anita. *No Pretty Pictures: A Child of War.* Greenwillow.

1999   **Youth Fiction**

Almond, David. *Skellig.* Delacorte.

Youth Nonfiction

Cowley, Joy. *Red-Eyed Tree Frog.* Scholastic.

Boston Globe–Horn Book Award

Given annually since 1967 by the *Boston Globe* and *Horn Book Magazine*, these awards are conferred in three categories: outstanding fiction or poetry, outstanding nonfiction, and outstanding picture book.

1997   **Fiction and Poetry Award**

Yumoto, Kazumi. *The Friends.* Farrar, Straus and Giroux.

Fiction and Poetry Honor Awards

Giff, Patricia Reilly. *Lily's Crossing.* Delacorte.

Myers, Walter Dean. *Harlem.* Scholastic.

Nonfiction Award

Wick, Walter. *A Drop of Water: A Book of Science and Wonder.* Scholastic.

Nonfiction Honor Awards

Adler, David A. *Lou Gehrig: The Luckiest Man.* Harcourt Brace.

Stanley, Diane. *Leonardo da Vinci.* Morrow.

1998 **Fiction and Poetry Award**

Jiminez, Francisco. *The Circuit: Stories from the Life of an Immigrant Child.* Houghton Mifflin.

Fiction and Poetry Honor Awards

Conly, Jane Leslie. *While No One Was Watching.* Henry Holt.

Holt, Kimberly Willis. *My Louisiana Sky.* Henry Holt.

Nonfiction Award

Tillage, Leon Walter. *Leon's Story.* Farrar, Straus and Giroux.

Nonfiction Honor Awards

Freedman, Russell. *Martha Graham: A Dancer's Life.* Clarion.

Greenberg, Jan, and Sandra Jordan. *Chuck Close Up Close.* Dorling Kindersley.

1999 **Fiction and Poetry Award**

Sachar, Louis. *Holes.* Farrar, Straus and Giroux.

Fiction and Poetry Honor Awards

Horvath, Polly. *The Trolls.* Farrar, Straus and Giroux.

Myers, Walter Dean. *Monster.* HarperCollins.

Nonfiction Award

Jenkins, Steve. *The Top of the World: Climbing Mount Everest.* Houghton Mifflin.

Nonfiction Honor Awards

Armstrong, Jennifer. *Shipwreck at the Bottom of the World: The Extraordinary True Story of Shackleton and the* Endurance. Crown.

Andrew Carnegie Medal

This medal, first given in 1937 to commemorate the centenary of the birth of Andrew Carnegie, is awarded annually by the British Library

Association to an outstanding children's book written in English and first published in the United Kingdom.

1997   Bowler, Tim. *River Boy.* Margaret McElderry.

1998   Almond, David. *Skellig.* Delacorte.

1999   Chambers, Aidan. *Postcards from No Man's Land.* Bodley Head.

Christopher Award

Presented each February by the Christophers, this award is given to books that affirm the highest values of the human spirit. The award for Books for Young People was first presented in 1970. The winners for books written for readers aged twelve and up are presented here.

1997   Calvert, Patricia. *Glennis, Before and After.* Atheneum.

  Kuklin, Susan. *Irrepressible Spirit: Conversations with Human Rights Activists.* Philomel.

1998   Albon, Mitch. *Tuesdays with Morrie.* Doubleday.

  Bitton-Jackson, Livia. *I Have Lived a Thousand Years.* Simon & Schuster.

1999   Alexander, Caroline. *The* Endurance: *Shackleton's Legendary Antarctic Expedition.* Knopf.

  Hill, Donna. *Shipwreck Season.* Houghton Mifflin.

  Sachar, Louis. *Holes.* Farrar, Straus and Giroux.

Margaret A. Edwards Award

Established in 1988, this award recognizes the lifetime achievement of a young adult literature author. The award is sponsored by *School Library Journal* and is administered by the Young Adult Library Services Association (YALSA) of the American Library Association.

1997   Gary Paulsen

1998   Madeleine L'Engle

1999   Anne McCaffrey

2000   Chris Crutcher

Golden Kite Award

The Golden Kite Award is presented by the Society of Children's Book Writers and Illustrators, making it the only award presented to authors and illustrators by their colleagues in the field. Awards are given for fiction, nonfiction, picture-book text, and illustration. Included here are the winners and honor winners for fiction and nonfiction.

1997 **Fiction**

Napoli, Donna Jo. *Stones in Water.* Dutton.

Fiction Honor

Fleischman, Paul. *Seedfolks.* HarperCollins.

Nonfiction

Schulman, Arlene. *Carmine's Story: A Book about a Boy Living with AIDS.* Lerner Publications.

Nonfiction Honor

Finklestein, Norman H. *With Heroic Truth: The Life of Edward R. Murrow.* Clarion.

1998 **Fiction**

Bauer, Joan. *Rules of the Road.* Putnam.

Fiction Honor

Fleischman, Paul. *Whirligig.* Henry Holt.

Nonfiction

Freedman, Russell. *Martha Graham: A Dancer's Life.* Clarion.

Nonfiction Honor

Partridge, Elizabeth. *Restless Spirit: The Life and Work of Dorothea Lange.* Viking.

1999 **Fiction**

Anderson, Laurie Halse. *Speak.* Farrar, Straus and Giroux.

Fiction Honor

Curtis, Christopher Paul. *Bud, Not Buddy,* by Delacorte.

Nonfiction

Dyson, Marianne J. *Space Station Science: Life in Free Fall.* Scholastic.

Nonfiction Honor

Kimmel, Elizabeth Cody. *Ice Story: Shackleton's Lost Expedition.* Clarion.

International Reading Association Children's Books Award

Given annually since 1975, this award honors the first or second book by an author from any country who shows unusual promise.

1999 Ritter, John H. *Choosing Up Sides.* Philomel.

2000 Curtis, Christopher Paul. *Bud, Not Buddy.* Delacorte.

Coretta Scott King Award

Established in 1967, this award is designed to commemorate the life and work of Dr. Martin Luther King Jr., and Mrs. Coretta Scott King for her courage and determination in working for peace and brotherhood. It is presented to an African American author and to an African American illustrator each year for an outstanding book. The awards for authors are given here.

1997 Myers, Walter Dean. *Slam!* Scholastic.

Honor Book

McKissack, Patricia, and Fredrick McKissack. *Rebels against Slavery: American Slave Revolts.* Scholastic.

1998 Draper, Sharon. *Forged by Fire.* Atheneum.

Honor Books

Hansen, Joyce. *I Thought My Soul Would Rise and Fly: The Diary of Patsy, a Freed Girl.* Scholastic.

Haskins, James. *Bayard Rustin: Behind the Scenes of the Civil Rights Movement.* Hyperion.

1999 Johnson, Angela. *Heaven.* Simon & Schuster.

Honor Books

Grimes, Nikki. *Jazmin's Notebook.* Dial.

Hansen, Joyce, and Gary McGowan. *Breaking Ground, Breaking Silence: The Story of New York's African Burial Ground.* Holt.

Johnson, Angela. *The Other Side: Shorter Poems.* Orchard.

2000 Curtis, Christopher Paul. *Bud, Not Buddy.* Delacorte.

Honor Books

English, Karen. *Francie.* Farrar, Straus and Giroux.

McKissack, Patricia, and Fredrick McKissack. *Black Hands, White Sails: The Story of African-American Whalers.* Scholastic.

Myers, Walter Dean. *Monster.* HarperCollins.

National Book Award for Young People's Literature

Beginning in 1996, the National Book Awards, administered by the National Book Foundation, have included a category for Young People's Literature, with an emphasis on literary merit.

1997 Sachar, Louis. *Holes.* Farrar, Straus and Giroux.

Finalists

Cameron, Ann. *The Secret Life of Amanda K. Woods.* Farrar, Straus and Giroux.

Gantos, Jack. *Joey Pigza Swallowed the Key.* Farrar, Straus and Giroux.

Lobel, Anita. *No Pretty Pictures: A Child of War.* Greenwillow.

Peck, Richard. *A Long Way from Chicago.* Dial.

1998 Holt, Kimberly Willis. *When Zachary Beaver Came to Town.* Henry Holt.

Finalists

Anderson, Laurie Halse. *Speak.* Farrar, Straus and Giroux.

Erdrich, Louise. *The Birchbark House.* Hyperion.

Horvath, Polly. *The Trolls.* Farrar, Straus, and Giroux.

Myers, Walter Dean. *Monster.* HarperCollins.

NCTE Award for Excellence in Poetry for Children

Established in 1977, this award is presented every three years to a living American poet for an aggregate body of work for children aged three to thirteen.

1997   Eloise Greenfield

NCTE Orbis Pictus Award for Outstanding Nonfiction for Children

This award commemorates John Comenius's book, *Orbis Pictus: The World in Pictures*, published in 1657, and historically considered to be the first book actually intended for children. The selection committee chooses one outstanding nonfiction book each year on the basis of accuracy, organization, design, writing style, and usefulness for classroom teaching.

1997   Stanley, Diane. *Leonardo da Vinci.* Morrow.

Honor Books

Blumberg, Rhoda. *Full Steam Ahead: The Race to Build a Transcontinental Railroad.* National Geographic.

Freedman, Russell. *The Life and Death of Crazy Horse.* Holiday House.

Osborne, Mary Pope. *One World, Many Religions: The Ways We Worship.* Knopf.

1998   Pringle, Laurence. *An Extraordinary Life: The Story of a Monarch Butterfly.* Orchard.

Honor Books

Dorros, Arthur. *A Tree Is Growing.* Scholastic.

Giblin, James Cross. *Charles A. Lindbergh: A Human Hero.* Clarion.

Hampton, Wilborn. *Kennedy Assassinated! The World Mourns: A Reporter's Story.* Candlewick.

Wick, Walter. *A Drop of Water: A Book of Science and Wonder.* Scholastic.

1999   Armstrong, Jennifer. *Shipwreck at the Bottom of the World: The Extraordinary True Story of Shackleton and the* Endurance. Crown.

Honor Books

Burleigh, Robert. *Black Whiteness: Admiral Byrd Alone in the Antarctic.* Simon & Schuster.

Holmes, Thom. *Fossil Feud: The Rivalry of the First American Dinosaur Hunters.* Julian Messner.

Jenkins, Steve. *Hottest, Coldest, Highest, Deepest.* Houghton Mifflin.

Lobel, Anita. *No Pretty Pictures: A Child of War.* Greenwillow.

John Newbery Medal

The Newbery Medal and honor book designations have been given annually since 1922 to the most distinguished contributions to children's literature published in the United States during the preceding year. The award is given by the Association for Library Service to Children of the American Library Association.

1997   Konigsburg, E. L. *The View from Saturday.* Atheneum.

Honor Books

Farmer, Nancy. *A Girl Named Disaster.* Orchard.

McGraw, Eloise. *Moorchild.* Simon & Schuster.

Turner, Megan Whalen. *The Thief.* Greenwillow.

White, Ruth. *Belle Prater's Boy.* Farrar, Straus and Giroux.

1998   Hesse, Karen. *Out of the Dust.* Scholastic.

Honor Books

Giff, Patricia Reilly. *Lily's Crossing.* Delacorte.

Levine, Gail Carson. *Ella Enchanted.* HarperCollins.

Spinelli, Jerry. *Wringer.* HarperCollins.

1999   Sachar, Louis. *Holes.* Farrar, Straus and Giroux.

Honor Book

Peck, Richard. *Long Way from Chicago.* Dial.

2000   Curtis, Christopher Paul. *Bud, Not Buddy.* Delacorte.

Honor Books

Couloumbus, Audrey. *Getting Near to Baby.* Putnam.

dePaola, Tomie. *26 Fairmount Avenue.* Putnam.

Holm, Jennifer L. *Our Only May Amelia.* HarperCollins.

Scott O'Dell Award for Historical Fiction

Established in 1981, the Scott O'Dell Award is given to a distinguished work of historical fiction for children or young adults. The author must be a citizen or resident of the United States, the work must be written in English and published in the United States, and the story must be set in North, South, or Central America. The award is given annually (if a worthy book has been published) by the Advisory Committee of the Bulletin of the Center for Children's Books.

1997 Paterson, Katherine. *Jip: His Story.* Lodestar.

1998 Hesse, Karen. *Out of the Dust.* Scholastic.

1999 Robinet, Henriette Gillem. *Forty Acres and Maybe a Mule.* Atheneum.

The Phoenix Award

Established in 1985, this award is presented annually to a book originally published twenty years ago that did not receive an award at the time of its publication.

1997 Cormier, Robert. *I Am the Cheese.* Delacorte.

1998 Walsh, Jill Paton. *A Chance Child.* Econo-Clad.

1999 Konigsburg, E. L. *Throwing Shadows.* MacMillan.

Edgar Allan Poe/Mystery Writers of America Award for Juvenile Mystery

The Mystery Writers of America have given awards for the best juvenile mysteries every year since 1961. Each winner receives an "Edgar," a ceramic bust of Edgar Allan Poe, who was one of the originators of the mystery story.

1997 Roberts, Willo Davis. *Twisted Summer.* Atheneum.

Nominees

Glenn, Mel. *Who Killed Mr. Chippendale?* Lodestar/Dutton.

Hautman, Pete. *Mr. Was.* Simon & Schuster.

Hayes, Daniel. *Flyers.* Simon & Schuster.

McGregor, Rob. *Hawk Moon.* Simon & Schuster.

1998   Hobbs, Will. *Ghost Canoe*. Morrow.

Nominees

Bloor, Edward. *Tangerine*. Harcourt Brace.

Levitin, Sonia. *Yesterday's Child*. Simon & Schuster.

Qualey, Marsha. *Thin Ice*. Delacorte.

Singer, Marilyn. *Deal with a Ghost*. Henry Holt.

1999   Werlin, Nancy. *The Killer's Cousin*. Delacorte.

Nominees

Bacon, Katharine Jay. *Finn*. Simon & Schuster.

Hobbs, Will. *The Maze*. Morrow.

Reiss, Kathryn. *Paperquake*. Harcourt Brace.

Sykes, Shelley. *For Mike*. Delacorte.

2000   Vande Velde, Vivian. *Never Trust a Dead Man*. HarperCollins.

Nominees

Anderson, Laurie Halse. *Speak*. Farrar, Straus and Giroux.

Cameron, Vicki. *That Kind of Money*. Indigo.

Hoobler, Dorothy, and Thomas Hoobler. *The Ghost in the Tokaido Inn*. Delacorte.

Myers, Walter Dean. *Monster*. HarperCollins.

Michael L. Printz Award

Established in 1999, the Michael L. Printz Award is presented by the Young Adult Library Services Association (YALSA) of the American Library Association. It recognizes the most outstanding contribution to literature for young adults.

2000   Myers, Walter Dean. *Monster*. HarperCollins.

Honor Books

Almond, David. *Skellig*. Delacorte.

Anderson, Laurie Halse. *Speak*. Farrar, Straus and Giroux.

Wittlinger, Ellen. *Hard Love*. Simon & Schuster.

Laura Ingalls Wilder Award

Presented by the Association for Library Services to Children of the American Library Association, the award is given every three years to an author or illustrator whose work has made a substantial and lasting contribution to literature for children.

1998   Russell Freedman

Booklists

In addition to recognizing selected titles with awards, several organizations issue annual lists of recommended books. Although such lists are too lengthy to include in this volume, below we include descriptions of the booklists that might be of interest to readers of *Books for You*, and indicate how to obtain these booklists. Many of these lists can be accessed through Web sites. See appendix B for further information.

Descriptions of other awards, prizes, and lists can be found at the front of recent editions of *Children's Books in Print*, an annual publication of R. R. Bowker; at the Children's Book Awards Web site maintained by David K. Brown at the University of Calgary, Alberta, located at http://www.ucalgary.ca/~dkbrown/awards.html; or at the Database of Award-Winning Children's Literature Web site maintained by Lisa R. Bartle, located at http://www2.wcoil.com/~ellerbee/childlit.html.

American Library Association Notable Children's Books

The Notable Children's Book Committee of the Association for Library Service to Children, a division of the American Library Association (ALA), selects notable books each year on the basis of literary quality, originality of text and illustrations, design, format, value and interest of subject matter to children, and likelihood of acceptance by children. The complete list of Notable Children's Books appears yearly in the March 15 issue of *Booklist*, an ALA journal.

American Library Association Best Books for Young Adults

Each year, the Young Adult Library Services Association of the American Library Association chooses the fiction and nonfiction titles that best satisfy the criteria of good literary quality and popular appeal to young adult readers. The complete list is published in the April 1 issue of *Booklist*. You may also receive a copy of the list by sending a self-addressed stamped business-size envelope to YALSA, 50 E. Huron Street, Chicago, Illinois 60611.

American Library Association Quick Picks for Young Adults

The ALA's Young Adult Library Services Association also publishes a list each year of books with high appeal to young adult readers who, for whatever reason, do not like to read. The complete list is published each year in the April 1 issue of Booklist, or you may receive a copy by sending a self-addressed stamped business envelope to YALSA, 50 E. Huron Street, Chicago, Illinois 60611.

International Reading Association

Each year, the International Reading Association asks children, young adults, and teachers to vote on a list of books recommended by recognized sources such as *Booklist, Horn Book,* and the *Journal of Reading.* The complete list of Children's Choices appears yearly in the November issue of *The Reading Teacher,* the Young Adults' Choices appear in the November issue of the *Journal of Reading,* and the Teachers' Choices appear in the November issue of *The Reading Teacher.* Single copies of any of the lists may be obtained for one dollar (U.S.) from The International Reading Association, Order Department, 800 Barksdale Road, P.O. Box 8139, Newark, Delaware 19714-8139.

Notable Children's Trade Books in the Field of Social Studies

A Book Review Committee appointed by the National Council for the Social Studies, in cooperation with the Children's Book Council, each year selects books published in the United States that (1) are written primarily for students in grades K–8, (2) emphasize human relations, (3) represent a diversity of groups and are sensitive to a broad range of cultural experiences, (4) present an original theme or a fresh slant on a traditional topic, (5) are easily readable and of high literary quality, and (6) have a pleasing format and, when appropriate, illustrations that enrich the text. The complete list of these notable books appears yearly in the April/May issue of *Social Education,* the journal of the National Council for the Social Studies. Single copies of the list may be obtained at no charge by sending a self-addressed six-by-nine-inch envelope with sufficient postage for three ounces to the Children's Book Council, 568 Broadway, Suite 404, New York, New York 10012.

Outstanding Science Trade Books for Children

Each year, a book review panel appointed by the National Science Teachers Association and assembled in cooperation with the Children's Book Council selects a list of outstanding books for young readers that present substantial science content in a clear, accurate, and up-to-date manner. Each book is also evaluated on its freedom from gender, ethnic, and socioeconomic bias, and on the quality of its presentation of material. The complete list of outstanding science books is published each spring in the March issue of *Science and Children.*

School Library Journal's Best Books of the Year

The Book Review Editors of *School Library Journal* annually choose the best among the thousands of new children's books submitted to the journal for review during the preceding year. Books are selected on the basis of strong story line, clear presentation, high-quality illustration, and probable appeal to young readers. The complete list is published each year in the December issue of the journal.

Appendix B: URLs for Young Adult Literature Award and Booklist Web Sites

http://www.ala.org/yalsa/booklists/index.html
> Includes links to Best Books for Young Adults, ALEX, and Quick-Picks Lists

http://www.ala.org/yalsa/booklists/2000alextxt.html
> ALEX Awards Web site

http://www.ala.org/yalsa/booklists/2000bestbooks.html
> Best Books for Young Adults Web site

http://www.ala.org/yalsa/booklists/2000quickpicks.html
> Quick Picks for Young Adults Web site

http://www.ala.org/yalsa/printz/index.html
> Michael Printz Award for Young Adult Literature

http://www.ala.org/alsc/
> Links to Newbery, Notables, and other awards

http://www.ala.org/alsc/newbery.html
> Newbery Award Web site

http://www.ala.org/alsc/belpre.html
> Pura Belpre Award Web site

http://www.ala.org/alsc/nbook00.html
> Notable Books Web site

http://www.ala.org/yalsa/awards/winners.html
> Margaret A. Edwards Award Web site

http://www.ncte.org
> National Council of Teachers of English Web site

http://www.reading.org
> International Reading Association Web site

http://www.ala.org/alaorg/oif/top100bannedbooks.html
> Top 100 Banned Books for the 1990s Web site

Appendix C: Multicultural Titles

The following titles offer readers a look at various cultures, races, and ethnic groups. Following the author and title is the chapter title, and then an indication of the culture, race, or ethnic group represented in the book. When the book addresses a broad world view or many cultures, races, or ethnic groups, no specific group is listed.

Abelove, Joan. *Go and Come Back.* Friendships, Choices, and Transitions. Peru.

Ada, Alma Flor. *Under the Royal Palms: A Childhood in Cuba.* Writers and Writing. Cuba.

Aker, Don. *Stranger at Bay.* Family Relationships. Nova Scotia.

Allison, Anthony. *Hear These Voices: Youth at the Edge of the Millennium.* Self-Help and Well-Being.

Alonso, Karen. Korematsu v. United States: *Japanese-American Internment Camps.* War and the Holocaust. Japanese American.

Altman, Linda Jacobs. *Plague and Pestilence: A History of Infectious Diseases.* Physical and Mental Health.

Andersen, Hans Christian. *The Little Mermaid and Other Fairy Tales.* Myths, Legends, Superstitions, and Tales.

Anderson, Dave. *The Story of Basketball.* Sports and Sports Stories.

Anderson, Dave. *The Story of Football.* Sports and Sports Stories.

Anderson, Dave. *The Story of Golf.* Sports and Sports Stories.

Armstrong, Jennifer. *Shipwreck at the Bottom of the World: The Extraordinary True Story of Shackleton and the* Endurance. Adventure and Survival. Antarctica.

Ashabranner, Brent. *To Seek a Better World.* Rights and Responsibilities. Haiti, Haitian American.

Asher, Sandy. *With All My Heart, with All My Mind.* Religion and Inspiration. Jewish.

Asion, Mick, and Tim Taylor. *The Atlas of Archeology.* Geography and Archeology.

Bacho, Peter. *Boxing in Black and White.* Sports and Sports Stories. African American.

Baer, Edith. *Walk the Dark Streets.* Historical Fiction. Jewish, Germany.

Barrett, Tracy. *Anna of Byzantium.* Historical Fiction. Byzantine Empire.

Beckett, Wendy. *Sister Wendy's Book of Saints.* Religion and Inspiration.

Bell, Janet Cheatham, and Lucille Usher Freeman. *Stretch Your Wings: Famous Black Quotations for Teens.* Self-Help and Well-Being. African American.

Bell, William. *Zack.* Family Relationships. African American, Jewish.

Beller, Susan Provost. *Never Were Men So Brave: The Irish Brigade during the Civil War.* War and the Holocaust. Irish American.

Bernard, Bruce. *Century: One Hundred Years of Human Progress, Regression, and Hope.* Arts and Architecture.

Berry, James. *Everywhere Faces Everywhere.* Poetry.

Betz, Adrienne. *Scholastic Treasury of Quotations for Children.* Trivia and Fun Facts.

Bitton-Jackson, Livia. *My Bridges of Hope: Searching for Life and Love after Auschwitz.* War and the Holocaust. Czechoslovakia, Jewish.

Blackwood, Gary. *The Shakespeare Stealer.* Historical Fiction. England.

Bolden, Tonya. *And Not Afraid to Dare: The Stories of Ten African-American Women.* Autobiography and Biography. African American.

Booth, Martin. *War Dog.* Historical Fiction. England.

Bowker, John. *The Complete Bible Handbook.* Religion and Inspiration. Israel, Egypt.

Bowker, John. *World Religions: The Great Faiths Explored and Explained.*

Boyle, David. *World War II: A Photographic History.* War and the Holocaust. German, Chinese, Japanese, Russian, Jewish.

Bridges, Ruby. *Through My Eyes.* Autobiography and Biography. African American.

Brown, Fahamisha Patricia. *Performing the Word: African American Poetry as Vernacular Culture.* Poetry. African American.

Brown, Lester R. *State of the World 1999: The Millennium Edition.* Environment and Ecology.

Bruchac, Joseph. *The Arrow Over the Door.* Historical Fiction. Quaker, Native American.

Bryan, Ashley. *African Tales, Uh-Huh.* Myths, Legends, Superstitions, and Tales. Africa.

Budhos, Marina. *Remix: Conversations with Immigrant Teenagers.* Short Stories.

Buettner, Dan. *Africatrek: A Journey by Bicycle through Africa.* Adventure and Survival. Africa.

Burgess, Melvin. *Smack.* Friendships, Choices, and Transitions. England.

Burleigh, Robert. *Who Said That? Famous Americans Speak.* Trivia and Fun Facts.

Byers, Ann. *The Holocaust Overview.* War and the Holocaust. Jewish.

Cadnum, Michael. *In a Dark Wood.* Historical Fiction. England.

Carbone, Elise. *Stealing Freedom.* Historical Fiction. African American.

Carter, Alden R. *Crescent Moon.* Family Relationships. Native American.

Chronicles of the Olympics. Sports and Sports Stories.

Clark, Joanne, and Chrisanne Beckner. *100 African Americans Who Shaped American History.* History. African American.

Clinton, Catherine. *Scholastic Encyclopedia of the Civil War.* War and the Holocaust. African American.

Cofer, Judith Ortiz. *The Year of Our Revolution: New and Selected Stories and Poems.* Poetry. Puerto Rican American.

Colbert, David. *Eyewitness to America.* History. Native American, African American, Hispanic, Latino.

Coleman, Loren, and Jerome Clark. *Cryptozoology A to Z: The Encyclopedia of Loch Monsters, Sasquatch, Chupacabras, and Other Authentic Mysteries of Nature.* Animals, Pets, and the Natural World. England, South America, North America.

Collis, Harry. *101 American Superstitions: Understanding Language and Culture through Popular Superstitions.* Myths, Legends, Superstitions, and Tales. Native American, African American, Appalachian.

Cooper, Susan. *King of Shadows.* Historical Fiction. England.

Cormier, Robert. *Heroes.* Historical Fiction. France.

Cox, Clinton. *Come All You Brave Soldiers.* War and the Holocaust. African American.

Cox, Clinton. *Fiery Vision: The Life and Death of John Brown.* Autobiography and Biography. African American.

Craughwell, Thomas J. *Alligators in the Sewers and 222 Other Urban Legends.* Myths, Legends, Superstitions, and Tales.

Crook, Connie Brummel. *Nellie's Quest.* Historical Fiction. Canada.

Crossley-Holland, Kevin. *The World of King Arthur and His Court: People, Places, Legend and Lore.* Myths, Legends, Superstitions, and Tales. England.

Crowe, Chris. *From the Outside Looking In: Short Stories for LDS Teenagers.* Religion. Mormon.

Cruz, Barbara C. *Jose Clemente Orozco: Mexican Artist.* Arts and Architecture. Mexico.

Cumming, Robert. *Great Artists.* Arts and Architecture.

Curry, Jane Louise. *Dark Shade.* Historical Fiction. Lenape Nation.

Curtis, Christopher Paul. *Bud, Not Buddy.* Historical Fiction. African American.

Dalkey, Kara. *The Heavenward Path.* Fantasy. Japan.

Danticat, Edwidge. *Krik? Krak!* Family Relationships. Haiti and Haitian American.

DeAngelis, Therese. *Native Americans and the Spanish.* History. Native American.

Dee, Catherine. *The Girls' Book of Wisdom.* Self Help and Well-Being.

Degens, T. *Freya on the Wall.* Historical Fiction. Germany.

Demi. *Buddha.* Religion and Inspiration. China.

DeSpain, Pleasant. *The Emerald Lizard: Fifteen Latin American Tales to Tell.* Myths, Legends, Superstitions, and Tales. Latin American.

Dickinson, Peter. *The Lion Tamer's Daughter and Other Stories.* Fantasy. England.

Dramer, Kim. *Native Americans and Black Americans.* History. African American, Native American.

Draper, Sharon. *Forged by Fire.* Family Relationships. African American.

Draper, Sharon. *Romiette and Julio.* Romance and School Stories. African American. Hispanic/Latino.

Draper, Sharon. *Tears of a Tiger.* Sports and Sports Stories. African American.

Dudley, William. *Asian Americans: Opposing Viewpoints.* History. Asian American.

Dudley, William. *The Vietnam War: Opposing Viewpoints.* War and the Holocaust. North Vietnam, South Vietnam.

Duncan, Dayton. *People of the West.* History. Native American.

Durbin, William. *The Broken Blade.* Adventure and Survival. Canada.

Durbin, William. *Wintering.* Adventure and Survival. Canada.

Easley, Maryann. *I Am the Ice Worm.* Adventure and Survival. Alaska.

Egan, Terry, Stan Friedman, and Mike Levine. *The Good Guys of Baseball: Sixteen True Sports Stories.* Sports and Sports Stories. African American.

Ellison, Suzanne Pierson. *Best of Enemies.* Historical Fiction. Navajo.

English, Karen. *Francie.* Historical Fiction. African American.

Estepa, Andrea, and Philip Kay. *Starting with I: Personal Essays by Teenagers.* Self Help and Well-Being. African American, Hispanic/Latino.

Farrell, Jeanett. *Invisible Enemies: Stories of Infectious Disease.* Physical and Mental Health. Europe, China, Africa.

Fletcher, Susan. *Shadow Spinner.* Historical Fiction. Iran.

Forrester, Sandra. *My Home Is over Jordan.* Historical Fiction. African American.

Freedman, Suzanne. Clay v. United States: *Muhammad Ali Objects to War.* Rights and Responsibilities. African American.

Galloway, Priscilla. *Snake Dreamer.* Fantasy. Greece.

Garden, Nancy. *Dove and Sword: A Novel of Joan of Arc*. Historical Fiction. France.

Garland, Sherry. *The Last Rainmaker*. Family Relationships. Native American.

Gaskins, Pearl Fuyo. *What Are You? Voices of Mixed-Race Young People*. Self Help and Well-Being. African American, Asian American, Hispanic/Latino, Mexican American.

George, Jean Craighead. *Julie's Wolf Pack*. Adventure and Survival. Native American.

Gerstein, Mordicai. *Victor: A Novel Based on the Life of the Savage of Aveyron*. Adventure and Survival. France.

Giblin, James Cross. *When Plague Strikes: The Black Death, Smallpox, AIDS*. Physical and Mental Health. Europe

Giovanni, Nikki, editor. *Grand Fathers: Reminiscences, Poems, Recipes, and Photos of the Keepers of Our Traditions*. Autobiography and Biography. African American.

Glenn, Mel. *Foreign Exchange: A Mystery in Poems*. Mysteries, Intrigue, Suspense, and Horror.

Glenn, Mel. *Jump Ball: A Basketball Season in Poems*. Poetry.

Goldenstern, Joyce. *American Women Against Violence*. Rights and Responsibilities. African American, Asian American, Hispanic/Latino.

Goodnough, David. *Simon Bolivar: South American Liberator*. Autobiography and Biography. South America.

Graham, Paula W. *Speaking of Journals*. Writers and Writing.

Grove, Vicki. *Starplace*. Friendships, Choices, and Transitions. African American.

Halberstam, David. *Playing for Keeps: Michael Jordan and the World That He Made*. Sports and Sports Stories. African American.

Hamilton, Virginia. *Dustland*. Science Fiction. African American.

Hamilton, Virginia. *The Gathering*. Science Fiction. African American.

Hamilton, Virginia. *Justice and Her Brothers*. Science Fiction. African American.

Hamilton, Virginia. *A White Romance*. Romance and School Stories. African American.

Hansen, Joyce. *Women of Hope: African Americans Who Made a Difference*. Rights and Responsibilities. African American.

Haskins, Jim. *Black, Blue and Gray: African Americans in the Civil War*. War and the Holocaust. African American.

Haskins, Jim. *The Geography of Hope: Black Exodus from the South after Reconstruction*. History. African American.

Haskins, Jim. *Separate but Not Equal: The Dream and the Struggle.* History. African American.

Haskins, Jim. *Spike Lee: By Any Means Necessary.* Television, Movies, and the Music Industry. African American.

Haywood, John. *Historical Atlas of the Ancient World.* Geography and Archeology.

Herrera, Juan Felipe. *Laughing Out Loud, I Fly.* Poetry. Latino/Hispanic.

Hertsgaard, Mark. *Earth Odyssey: Around the World in Search of Our Environmental Future.* Environment and Ecology.

Hewett, Lorri. *Dancer.* Romance and School Stories. African American.

Hightower, Paul. *Galileo: Astronomer and Physicist.* Autobiography and Biography. Italy.

Hill, David. *Take It Easy.* Adventure and Survival. New Zealand.

Hobbs, Will. *Far North.* Adventure and Survival. Native American.

Hobbs, Will. *Ghost Canoe.* Adventure and Survival. Native American.

Hobbs, Will. *Jason's Gold.* Adventure and Survival. Canada.

Holm, Jennifer L. *Our Only May Amelia.* Historical Fiction. Finnish American.

Hoobler, Dorothy, and Thomas Hoobler. *The Ghost in the Tokaido Inn.* Historical Fiction. Japan.

Hopkins, Lee Bennett. *Lives: Poems about Famous Americans.* Poetry.

Housden, Roger. *Sacred Journeys in a Modern World.* Religion and Inspiration.

Houston, Gloria. *Bright Freedom's Song: A Story of the Underground Railroad.* Historical Fiction. African American.

Hurley, Joanna. *Mother Teresa, 1910–1997: A Pictorial Biography.* Autobiography and Biography. India.

Hurmence, Belinda. *Slavery Time When I Was Chillun.* History. African American.

Jaffe, Nina. *A Voice of the People: The Life and Work of Harold Courlander.* Writers and Writing. Haitian, Cuban, South American.

Jaffe, Nina, and Steve Zeitlin. *The Cow of No Color: Riddle Stories and Justice Tales from around the World.* Myths, Legends, Superstitions, and Tales.

Jeffrey, Laura S. *Barbara Jordan: Congresswoman, Lawyer, Educator.* Autobiography and Biography. African American.

Jiang, Ji-Li. *Red Scarf Girl: A Memoir of the Cultural Revolution.* Autobiography and Biography. China.

Johnson, Angela. *Heaven.* Family Relationships. African American.

Johnson, Angela. *The Other Side: Shorter Poems.* Poetry. African American.

Johnson, Sylvia A. *Tomatoes, Potatoes, Corn, and Beans: How the Foods of the Americas Changed Eating around the World.* History. Native American, South American, Europe.

Jones, Charlotte Foltz. *Yukon Gold: The Story of the Klondike Gold Rush.* History. Canada.

Jordan, Sheryl. *The Raging Quiet.* Historical Fiction. African American.

Kalengis, Mary Motley. *Seen and Heard: Teenagers Talk about Their Lives.* Self Help and Well-Being.

Kaniut, Larry. *Danger Stalks the Land: Alaskan Tales of Death and Survival.* Adventure and Survival. Alaska.

Katz, Welwyn Wilton. *Out of the Dark.* Historical Fiction. Newfoundland.

Katz, William Loren. *Black Pioneers: An Untold Story.* History. African American.

Katz, William Loren. *Breaking the Chains: African-American Slave Resistance.* History. African American.

Kimmel, Elizabeth Cody. *In the Stone Circle.* Historical Fiction. Wales.

King, Dr. Martin Luther, Jr. *I Have a Dream.* Rights and Responsibilities. African American.

King, Stephen. *Bag of Bones.* Mysteries, Intrigue, Suspense, and Horror. African American.

Klass, David. *Danger Zone.* Sports and Sports Stories. African American.

Kolata, Gina Bari. *Flu: The Story of the Great Influenza Pandemic of 1918 and the Search for the Virus That Caused It.* Physical and Mental Health.

Kort, Michael G. *Yitzhak Rabin: Israel's Soldier Statesman.* Autobiography and Biography. Israel.

Koslow, Philip. *Building a New World: Africans in America.* History. African American.

Krishnaswami, Uma. *Shower of Gold: Girls and Women in the Stories of India.* Myths, Legends, Superstitions, and Tales. India.

Krull, Kathleen. *They Saw the Future: Oracles, Psychics, Scientists, Great Thinkers, and Pretty Good Guessers.* History.

Kuklin, Susan. *Iqbal Masih and the Crusaders against Child Slavery.* Rights and Responsibilities. Pakistan.

Laird, Christa. *But Can the Phoenix Sing?* Historical Fiction. Poland, Jewish.

Lawrence, Iain. *The Smugglers.* Adventure and Survival. England.

Lawrence, Iain. *The Wreckers.* Historical Fiction. England.

Leapman, Michael. *Witnesses to War: Eight True Life Stories of Nazi Persecution.* War and the Holocaust. Jewish.

Lee, Marie. *Necessary Roughness.* Sports and Sports Stories. Asian American.

Lee, Marie. *Night of the Chupacabras.* Mysteries, Intrigue, Suspense, and Horror. Mexico.

Lemesurier, Peter. *Decoding the Great Pyramid.* UFOs and Other Unexplained Phenomena. Egypt.

Lester, Julius. *Pharaoh's Daughter.* Historical Fiction. Egypt.

LeVert, Marianne. *AIDS: A Handbook for the Future.* Physical and Mental Health.

Levine, Michael. *The Kid's Address Book: Over 3,000 Addresses of Celebrities, Athletes, Entertainers, and More . . . Just for Kids.* References, Dictionaries, and How-to.

Levitin, Sonia. *The Cure.* Science Fiction. Jewish.

Lindon, Edmund. *Great Britain and the United States: Rivals and Partners.* History. England.

Litwin, Laura Baskes. *Benjamin Banneker: Astronomer and Mathematician.* Autobiography and Biography. African American.

Lobel, Anita. *No Pretty Pictures: A Child of War.* War and the Holocaust. Jewish.

Lyons, Mary E. *The Poison Place.* Historical Fiction. African American.

MacCambridge, Michael. *ESPN SportsCentury.* Sports and Sports Stories. African American.

Macy, Sue. *Winning Ways: A Photobiography of American Women in Sports.* Autobiography and Biography.

Magee, Bryan. *The Story of Philosophy.* Religion and Inspiration.

Mah, Adeline Yen. *Chinese Cinderella: The True Story of an Unwanted Daughter.* Autobiography and Biography. China.

Majure, Janet. *AIDS.* Physical and Mental Health.

Marchetta, Melina. *Looking for Alibrandi.* Family Relationships. Australia.

Marsden, John. *The Dead of Night.* Adventure and Survival. Australia.

Marsden, John. *A Killing Frost.* Adventure and Survival. Australia.

Mastoon, Adam. *The Shared Heart: Portraits and Stories Celebrating Lesbian, Gay, and Bisexual Young People.* Self Help and Well-Being. African American, Hispanic/Latino, Asian American.

Matas, Carol. *After the War.* Historical Fiction. Jewish.

Matas, Carol. *The Garden.* Historical Fiction. Israel, Jewish.

Matas, Carol. *Greater than Angels.* Historical Fiction. France, Jewish.

Matcheck, Diane. *The Sacrifice.* Historical Fiction. Pawnee.

Mazer, Anne. *A Walk in My World: International Short Stories about Youth.* Short Stories.

Mazer, Norma Fox. *Good Night, Maman.* Historical Fiction. Jewish, Jewish American.

McCall, Nathan. *What's Going On: Personal Essays.* Rights and Responsibilities. African American.

McCaughrean, Geraldine. *The Pirate's Son.* Adventure and Survival. Madagascar.

McFarlane, Stewart. *The Complete Book of T'ai Chi.* Physical and Mental Health. Asia.

McGuigan, Mary Ann. *Where You Belong.* Friendships, Choices, and Transitions. African American.

McKissack, Patricia C., and Fredrick L. McKissack. *Black Hands, White Sails: The Story of African-American Whalers.* History. African American.

McLaren, Clemence. *Inside the Walls of Troy: A Novel of the Women Who Lived the Trojan War.* Historical Fiction. Greece.

Meltzer, Milton. *Langston Hughes: An Illustrated Edition.* Writers and Writing. African American.

Meltzer, Milton. *Witches and Witch Hunts: A History of Persecution.* History.

Menicak, Stephen. *The Muffin Child.* Historical Fiction. Balkans.

Meyer, Carolyn. *Mary, Bloody Mary.* Historical Fiction. England.

Miklowitz, Gloria. *Masada: The Last Fortress.* Historical Fiction. Israel, Jewish.

Monceaux, Morgan, and Ruth Katcher. *My Heroes, My People: African Americans and Native Americans in the West.* Autobiography and Biography. African American, Native American.

Morpugo, Michael. *Joan of Arc of Domremy.* Historical Fiction. France.

Muller, Melissa. *Anne Frank: The Biography.* Autobiography and Biography. Jewish.

Mulvihill. Margaret. *The Treasury of Saints and Martyrs.* Religion and Inspiration.

Myers, Walter Dean. *Amistad: A Long Road to Freedom.* History. African American.

Myers, Walter Dean. *At Her Majesty's Request: An African Princess in Victorian England.* Autobiography and Biography. Africa, England.

Myers, Walter Dean. *Monster.* Friendships, Choices, and Transitions. African American.

Myers, Walter Dean. *One More River to Cross: An African American Photo Album.* History. African American.

Myers, Walter Dean. *Slam!* Sports and Sports Stories. African American.

Naidoo, Beverly. *No Turning Back: A Novel of South Africa.* Friendships, Choices, and Transitions. South Africa.

Namioka, Lensey. *Ties That Bind: Ties That Break.* Historical Fiction. Chinese.

Napoli, Donna Jo. *For the Love of Venice.* Romance and School Stories. Italy.

Nappo, Salvatore. *Pompeii: A Guide to the Ancient City.* History. Italy.

Nash, Gary B. *Forbidden Love: The Secret History of Mixed-Race America.* Rights and Responsibilities. African American, Native American.

Neimark, Anne E. *Myth Maker: J.R.R. Tolkien.* Writers and Writing. England.

Newth, Mette. *The Dark Light.* Historical Fiction. Norway.

Nolan, Han. *A Face in Every Window.* Family Relationships. African American.

Novac, Ana. *The Beautiful Days of My Youth: My Six Months in Auschwitz and Plaszow.* War and the Holocaust. Jewish.

Nye, Naomi Shihab. *This Same Sky: A Collection of Poems from around the World.* Poetry.

Nye, Naomi Shihab. *The Tree Is Older Than You Are: A Bilingual Gathering of Poems and Stories from Mexico with Paintings by Mexican Artists.* Poetry. Mexico, Latino, Latino American.

O'Reilly, James, Larry Habegger, and Sean O'Reilly. *Danger: True Stories of Trouble and Survival.* Adventure and Survival.

Olson, Arielle North, and Howard Schwartz. *Ask the Bones: Scary Stories from Around the World.* Myths, Legends, Superstitions, and Tales.

Opdyke, Irene Gut. *In My Hands: Memories of a Holocaust Rescuer.* War and the Holocaust. Jewish.

Osborn, Kevin. *Scholastic Encyclopedia of Sports in the United States.* Sports and Sports Stories. Native American, African American.

Osborne, Mary Pope. *Standing in the Light: The Captive Diary of Catherine Carey Logan.* Historical Fiction. Lenape Nation.

Palmer, Douglas. *Atlas of the Prehistoric World.* Geography and Archeology.

Pandell, Karen. *Journey through the Northern Rainforest.* Environment and Ecology.

Pascoe, Elaine, and Deborah Kops. *Scholastic Kid's Almanac for the 21st Century.* References, Dictionaries, and How-to.

Patrick, Denise Lewis. *The Longest Ride.* Historical Fiction. African American.

Paulsen, Gary. *Sarney: A Life Remembered.* Historical Fiction. African American.

Pfitsch, Patricia Curtis. *The Deeper Song.* Historical Fiction. Jewish.

Philip, Neil. *In a Sacred Manner I Live: Native American Wisdom.* History. Native American.

Philip, Neil. *Myths and Legends: The World's Most Enduring Myths and Legends Explored and Explained.* Myths, Legends, Superstitions, and Tales.

Pickering, David. *Bible Questions and Answers.* Religion and Inspiration.

Pinsky, Robert, and Maggie Dietz. *Americans' Favorite Poems.* Poetry.

Platt, Richard. *Disaster!* Adventure and Survival.

Portuguese Phrase Book. References, Dictionaries, and How-to. Portugal.

Press, Petra. *Great Heroes of Mythology.* Myths, Legends, Superstitions, and Tales.

Rappoport, Ken. *Grant Hill.* Sports and Sports Stories. African American.

Reidenbaugh, Lowell. *Baseball's Hall of Fame—Cooperstown: Where the Legends Live Forever.* Sports and Sports Stories. African American.

Richards. Chris. *The Illustrated Encyclopedia of World Religions.* Religion and Inspiration.

Rinaldi, Ann. *Hang a Thousand Trees with Ribbons: The Story of Phillis Wheatley.* Writers and Writing. Africa, African American.

Rinaldi, Ann. *Mine Eyes Have Seen.* Historical Fiction. African American.

Rinaldi, Ann. *The Second Bend in the River.* Historical Fiction. Native American.

Roberts, Tara. *Am I the Last Virgin? Ten African American Reflections on Sex and Love.* Self-Help and Well-Being. African American.

Rochman, Hazel, and Darlene Z. McCampbell. *Leaving Home: Stories.* Short Stories. African American, Hispanic/Latino, Asian American.

Russian Phrase Book. References, Dictionaries, and How-to. Russia.

Salisbury, Graham. *Shark Bait.* Family Relationships. Hawaii, Chinese.

Sayre, April Pulley. *Africa.* Geography and Archeology. Africa.

Schama, Simon. *Rembrandt's Eyes.* Arts and Architecture. Europe.

Shahan, Sherry. *Frozen Stiff.* Adventure and Survival. Alaska.

Shakespeare, William. *Macbeth.* Historical Fiction. Scotland.

Shandler, Sara. *Ophelia Speaks: Adolescent Girls Write about Their Search for Help.* Self-Help and Well-Being.

Siliotti, Alberto. *Guide to the Valley of the Kings.* Arts and Architecture. Egypt.

Silvey, Anita. *Help Wanted: Short Stories about Young People Working.* Short Stories. Hispanic/Latino.

Sivananda. *Yoga, Mind and Body.* Physical and Mental Health.

Skees, Suzanne. *God among the Shakers: A Search for Stillness and Faith at Sabbathday Lake.* Religion and Inspiration. Amish.

Skurzynski, Gloria. *Spider's Voice.* Historical Fiction. France.

Spangenburg, Ray, and Diane K. Moser. *The American Indian Experience.* History. Native American.

Stanley, Diane. *A Time Apart.* Family Relationships. England.

Stanley, Diane, and Peter Vennema. *Bard of Avon: The Story of William Shakespeare.* Writers and Writing. England.

Stanley, Jerry. *Digger: The Tragic Fate of the California Indians from the Missions to the Gold Rush.* History. Native American.

Strangis, Joel. *Lewis Hayden and the War against Slavery.* War and the Holocaust. African American.

Sutcliff, Rosemary. *Sword Song.* Historical Fiction. British Isles.

Sweeney, Joyce. *The Spirit Window.* Romance and School Stories. Native American (Cherokee).

Talbert, Marc. *Heart of a Jaguar.* Historical Fiction. Mayan.

Taylor, Michael. *Cave Passages: Roaming the Underground Wilderness.* Adventure and Survival.

Tessendorf, K. C. *Over the Edge: Flying with the Arctic Heroes.* Adventure and Survival. Arctic.

Thomas, Rob. *Green Thumb.* Adventure and Survival. South America.

Thomas, Rob. *Satellite Down.* Friendships, Choices, and Transitions. Ireland.

Thomas, Rob. *Slave Day.* Romance and School Stories. African American.

Todras, Ellen H. *Angelina Grimke: Voice of Abolition.* Autobiography and Biography. African American.

Tomlinson, Theresa. *Child of May.* Myths, Legends, Superstitions, and Tales. England.

Turner, Glennette Tilley. *Follow in Their Footsteps: Biographies of Ten Outstanding African Americans with Skits about Each One to Act Out.* Autobiography and Biography. African American.

Vanasse, Deb. *Out of the Wilderness.* Adventure and Survival. Alaska.

Vinge, Joan D. *The Random House Book of Greek Myths.* Myths, Legends, Superstitions, and Tales. Greece.

Wassiljewa, Tatjana. *Hostage to War: A True Story.* War and the Holocaust. Jewish.

Watts, Irene N. *Good-bye Marianne.* Historical Fiction. Germany.

Westall, Robert. *Time of Fire.* Historical Fiction. England.

Wharton, William. *A Midnight Clear.* Historical Fiction. France.

Wilkinson, Philip. *Illustrated Dictionary of Mythology.* Myths, Legends, Superstitions, and Tales. Greece, Egypt, Native American, China, South America.

Willis, Clint. *Climb: Stories of Survival from Rock, Snow, and Ice.* Adventure and Survival.

Wilson, Budge. *Sharla.* Family Relationships. Canada.

Wilson, Colin. *The Atlas of Holy Places and Sacred Sites.* Religion and Inspiration.

Wilson, Erlene B. *The 100 Best Colleges for African-American Students.* Colleges. African American.

Winter, Kathryn. *Katarina.* Historical Fiction. Jewish, Jewish American, Czechoslovakia.

Wolff, Virginia Euwer. *Bat 6.* Sports and Sports Stories. Japanese American.

Wood, Nancy. *The Serpent's Tongue: Prose, Poetry, and Art of the New Mexico Pueblos.* Myths, Legends, Superstitions, and Tales. Native American (Pueblo Nation).

Woodson, Jacqueline. *If You Come Softly.* Romance and School Stories. African American.

Woodson, Jacqueline. *A Way Out of No Way.* Short Stories. African American.

Woodtor, Dee Parmer. *Finding a Place Called Home: A Guide to African-American Genealogy and Historical Identity.* References, Dictionaries, and How-to. African American.

World Reference Atlas. Geography.

World War II Extra: An Around-the-World Newspaper History from the Treaty of Versailles to the Nuremberg Trials. War and the Holocaust. Europe, Russia, Japan, Jewish.

Wyeth, Sharon Dennis. *Once on This River.* Historical Fiction. Madagascar.

Yamanaka, Lois-Ann. *Name Me Nobody.* Friendships, Choices, and Transitions. Hawaii.

Yezierska, Anna. *Hungry Hearts.* Short Stories. Jewish American.

Appendix D:
Books for You:
A History of the Booklist

The end of this millennium also marks the end of the publication of the print edition of the NCTE senior high booklist *Books for You*. As the booklist moves to an online format, this transition gives us good reason to reflect on the history of a booklist that began almost in tandem with the founding of the Council.

Predecessors of *Books for You*

1913

Although the first Committee on Senior High School Booklists wasn't formed until 1943, NCTE began publishing booklists for senior high school students in 1913, a mere two years after the official founding of NCTE. The first published booklist, "A List of Books for Home Reading of High-School Pupils," was "intended to aid teachers in recommending books for home reading." Prepared by the Committee Upon Home Reading, this sixteen-page, stapled document cost ten cents or "sixty cents a dozen." This booklist—simply a list of books that included only the author's last name and the title of the book—began with a Principles of Selection statement that explained that the included titles

> differ as widely as the needs of the individual students. Some are intended to awaken a taste for reading in those who have never read for pleasure. Others are to bridge the gap between trash and good literature. Others are to open new fields of interest to tastes already forming or developed beyond the average. Still others are to stimulate thought, to inspire a worthy view of life, to arouse ambition. Some are intended merely as models for the student's own writing. Each has been recommended that it may be helpful in at least one respect. (p. 3)

Books in this list were separated into the following categories: Fiction, Drama, Poetry, Biography, History and Mythology, Speeches, Travel and Adventure, Essays, and Works Not Otherwise Classified. Fiction titles carried the designation (M) for "books suitable chiefly for pupils of the fourth year" and (Y) for "books suitable chiefly for students of the first year." The Committee concluded their comments with a recommendation that the list be revised every four years so that it will "meet the altering needs of young people in a changing world."

This first booklist, although different in many ways from the *Books for You* booklist, established at least two traditions that have always been present in the NCTE booklists. First, the books included are primarily for student enjoyment. Although helping students with coursework has always been a secondary goal, encouraging reading for enjoyment has long been the primary goal. Second, books of all types are included to fit "the needs of individual students." This commitment to offering a range of books to meet the needs and interests of many students—to the point of including books that some would censor—is seen repeatedly throughout the history of *Books for You*. Richard Alm, chair of the *Books for You* booklist committee in 1964, perhaps stated this most clearly in his preface to the book when he wrote:

> Books included in this revision have been selected with care, to give wide representation of current literature as well as the literature of our heritage. It is the firm belief of the members of this Committee that to remove a title from a list or to keep a title off a list because someone, somewhere has objected, or might object, to it would been an abdication of our role. (p. xiv)

This statement reminds us that NCTE exists in no small measure to extend an appreciation of all types of literature far beyond the classroom walls.

Despite this shared mission, however, several differences between the 1913 booklist and the subsequent *Books for You* booklists are evident. First, the lists prior to 1945 were nothing more than lists of authors and titles that were each discussed and voted upon by the entire committee (see Figure 1 for a list of 1913 committee members). The chair of the committee noted that "the list does not represent a majority vote, although no book favored by a majority fails to appear. On the other hand, many books appear that have not a clear majority; a minority is proportionately represented" (p. 4). This practice of voting on each title has not been continued by current booklist committees. However, it is unclear when this practice of voting on—or at least discussing—each title stopped. Even today, we can see in the American Library Association's (ALA) many booklists—including the *Best Books for Young Adults* list—an ongoing commitment to creating a booklist built from consensus. That list, which is compiled using a process of nomination and discussion, mirrors the early NCTE booklist process.

Herbert Bates, Manual Training High School, Brooklyn, New York, Chair of the Committee

Laura Benedict, High School, Burlington, Iowa

Emma J. Breck, Oakland High School, Oakland, California

M. Ella Morgan, Central High School, Washington, D.C.

O. B. Sperlin, Stadium High School, Tacoma, Washington

*Allan Abbott, Teachers College, Columbia University

*Percy H. Boynton, University of Chicago

*Ida Menenhall, Public Library, Utica, New York

*Jesse B. Davis, Central High School, Grand Rapids, Michigan

*Allisik Gaw, University of Southern California

*Mary E. Hall, Girls' High School, Brooklyn, New York

*Alfred M. Hitchcock, Public High School, Hartford, Connecticut

*Added in September 1913, to assist the original committee in the work of revision

Figure 1. Members of the 1913 Committee Upon Home Reading.

Second, beginning with the 1945 inaugural edition of *Books for You,* annotations of books have appeared after the bibliographic information. These annotations were very brief (generally one sentence) until the 1976 edition. It appears that as the topics and themes discussed in books for adolescents began to reflect current societal issues and concerns, more information about the books was offered in each annotation.

Third, although it is designed to recommend books for students, this first booklist places the teacher in the pivotal position of connecting students to books. The introduction to the 1913 booklist contains the admonition that the

> list should not be put without comment into the hands of the pupils. The books are suited to many needs and it is essential that each pupil shall get the books that fits his case. From this list, as from a pharmacopoeia where the cure for one would be poison to another, the teacher must prescribe the right medicine. To do this he must know the needs of his pupils and the qualities of the books. (p. 4)

The burden to select the appropriate books for students shifts from the teacher to the student with the appearance of *Books for You.* That shift, apparent even in the title of the booklist, is made abundantly clear in the preface of the 1976 edition when committee chair Ken Donelson writes to students, "You are therefore warned that some books included here may offend, irritate, or anger you" (p. 3). This "reader beware" approach is not evident in the 1913–1940 booklists, which continue to remind teachers that it is their job to know which books would be "poison" to which students.

1923–1940

The 1913 list remained unchanged until 1923, when the committee's name changed to the Committee on Recreational Reading/Home Reading. This committee, chaired by Herbert Bates, was charged with creating a booklist "for home reading for high school and junior high school." In 1930, Max Herzberg (who later became the director of publications for NCTE) and Stella Stewart (who later became president of NCTE) were named co-chairs of the committee, and were charged to revise the 1923 list. Herzberg and Stewart continued co-chairing this committee through the 1934, 1937, and 1940 revisions of the booklist. Each booklist continued to be published as a sixteen-page stapled booklet that simply listed authors and titles of books, with no annotations of any length.

In addition to this booklist, NCTE published another booklist in 1943 titled "Victory Corps Reading List, Containing Books, Mainly Recently, On Issues of the War, Preparation for Military Service, and Activities on the Homefront." Max Herzberg also chaired this committee.

Books for You

The Committee on Recreational Reading/Home Reading continued functioning until April 28, 1943, when Angela Broening made a motion during an NCTE Executive Committee meeting "that a Committee on Senior High School Booklists be appointed." After discussion, it was decided that the committee would include three members from the Council and two members from the American Library Association. This official connection with ALA continued until the 1970s. The committee was "directed to investigate the field of reading lists in the senior high school and to recommend a plan to both organizations."

Months later, during the November 1943 Executive Committee board meeting, Mark Neville, Bertha Handlan, and Simon Certner were named to this committee as the Council delegates, while Mildred Batchelder was named the ALA consultant. (Many recognize Batchelder's name from the ALA Mildred L. Batchelder Award, which honors the publisher of the most outstanding translated book for children. Established in 1968, this award is presented annually. Recent recipients of the Batchelder award are listed in appendix A of this volume.)

As this first Senior High Booklist Committee began choosing books for the *Books for You* booklist, discussion at times must have centered on whether or not this committee was to consider books for junior high students. Indeed, by the February 1944 Executive Committee meeting, the minutes reflect such a discussion. John DeBoer moved that the committee "be instructed to make junior high school as well as senior high school lists." That motion carried. At the same time, the committee was instructed to "consider whether these should be separate lists or a single one."

1945: The First Edition

In November 1945, the first edition of *Books for You: A High-School Reading List* was published. This six-by-nine inch saddle-stitched booklist sold for thirty cents each, or twenty-two cents if ten or more were bought at one time. With 154 pages and eleven chapters, this booklist not only offered more titles than the previous booklists, but also arranged them by thematic categories and offered brief annotations for each title. Figure 2 offers a look at some typical entries from this first edition. Some chapter titles included "This Is Our America," "The Individual and His Environment" (which included a subcategory called "Etiquette"), "Understanding Nature," and "The Search for the Good Life." For a complete list of committee members and a look at the table of contents for this first edition of *Books for You*, see Figures 3 and 4 (pages 361–363).

This inaugural edition began with an introduction from the chair of the committee (who in later editions is called the editor), a tradition that has continued with all subsequent editions. Titled "What Makes a Book Interesting," this one-page introduction by Mark Neville makes it clear that *Books for You* is intended to be inclusive rather than exclusive by explaining that the books selected

> represent experiences as emotional as lyric poetry and as practical as scientific investigation. They discuss problems as romantic as falling in love and as necessary as choosing a career. They portray the significance of social problems and the spirituality of a good life. They carry us to the adventurous jungle, and they direct our play on the football field. They show us the meaning of courage in the heat of battle, and they indicate the seriousness of maintaining the values underlying our form of government. Books then are like men. We can't know them all, but among them we find our friends.

From "Upheaval and Reconstruction"

Clarke, George Herbert (Ed.) *New Treasury of War Poetry; Poems of the Second World War* (10, 11, 12)

> More than a hundred and fifty poems dealing with many aspects of the Second World War topically arranged.

Hope, Bob. *I Never Left Home* (9–12)

> Bob Hope pays a tribute to the boys he saw fighting World War II.

From "Other Lands and Other Peoples"

Matsui, Haru. *Restless Wave* (9–12)

> The delightful autobiography of an educated Japanese woman who, in spite of opposition from her family, sought a new life in the United States.

Waln, Nora. *Reaching for the Stars* (9–12)

> "I am writing of life as I found it in my four years among Germans, with no bitterness and no malice but a sincere attempt at interpretation," explains Mrs. Waln.

From "Progress of Science"

Hart, Alan L. *These Mysterious Rays* (10, 11, 12)

> The fascinating story of the multiple uses to which X-rays are put in the service of modern medicine.

Figure 2. Samples of entries found in the 1945 edition of *Books for You.* Note the limited bibliographic information, which included author and title only. Numbers after titles indicate for which grade level(s) the book is recommended.

Mark Neville, chair
Mildred Batchelder (ALA consultant)
Simon Certner
Margaret Greer
Bertha Handlan
Max Herzber (consultant to committee)
Blanch Rutledge
Dorothea Western

Figure 3. Committee members of the first committee of booklists for junior and senior high schools.

TABLE OF CONTENTS

Figure 4. Table of contents from the 1945 inaugural edition of *Books for You.*

It quickly became apparent that this new booklist would be a bestseller; during the February 1946 NCTE Executive Committee board meeting, a report from Robert G. Pooley, director of publications, explained that the first edition of *Books for You* sold out soon after publication. Max Herzberg (consultant to the booklist committee) moved that *Books for You* go immediately into a second printing of 60,000 copies. That motion carried.

Figure 4 *(Cont.)*

1951–1976 Editions

After that first edition, *Books for You* continued to grow in popularity among both teachers and librarians. Figure 5 on pages 365 and 366 lists dates of publication and chairs of the committee from 1945 to 2001. In 1950, the Executive Committee approved the formation of a separate junior high booklist committee. Until this point, the Senior High Committee had been responsible for creating both *Books for You* and *Your Reading* (the junior high booklist). Now, these two books would be created by two separate committees.

The 1951 edition of *Books for You* not only retained the same chair (Mark Neville), similar chapter divisions, and a similar length, but began with basically the same introduction, now titled "To the Student." Interestingly, while serving as chair of the committee, Neville was also the president of NCTE. The title on the cover of the book was shortened to *Books for You: A Reading List for Teen-Agers.* This title continued for several years. By the 1956 edition, Max Herzberg—the man who served as chair of the earliest booklist committees and as consultant to Neville's first two *Books for You* committees—had been named the director of publications for NCTE.

Supplements to editions appeared between the 1951 and 1956 editions, the 1956 and 1959 editions, and the 1959 and 1964 editions. These supplements were sixteen-page inserts that offered more titles and were given away free of charge.

The 1956 edition, created by the committee chaired by G. Robert Carlsen, offered a departure in format. Now titled *Books for You: A List for Leisure Reading for Use by Students in Senior High School,* the book included a significant change in the table of contents. In this edition, Carlsen titled every chapter "I Read. . . ," followed by tags such as "To Laugh" or "To Look in a Mirror" or "To Know Adults" or "To Test Values." Without a doubt, this table of contents reflected ideas seen in many of Carlsen's articles on young adult literature and the developmental nature of young adults and their reading interests. He expanded the introduction from one brief page to more than three pages of dense text, and offered advice on everything from why to read ("Books provide one of the handiest ways to open the doors of life") to what to do after reading ("Ask questions . . . that cut across many, many books . . . [such as] 'What causes arguments, disagreements, misunderstandings, or actual fights between people?'").

Carlsen opens each chapter with a brief paragraph describing the contents of the chapter. He begins the chapter called "I Read: To Look in a Mirror" with the following:

> Certainly there is no greater pleasure in reading than finding a character who has the problems and feelings that we have. We feel a warm glow of kinship whenever this happens in a book. It is good for us to have this experience, for we come to understand ourselves a little more clearly. We know then that we are not the

Date	Chair/Editor	Title of booklist
1945	Mark Neville	*Books for You: A High-School Reading List Arranged by Themes and Types*
1951	Mark Neville	*Books for You: A List for Leisure Reading for Use by Students in Senior High School*
1952	Mark Neville	(Supplement) "Supplementary List of Recent Books, 1951–52"
1956	G. Robert Carlsen	*Books for You: A List for Leisure Reading for Use by Students in Senior High School*
1958	G. Robert Carlsen	(Supplement) "1958 Supplement to *Books for You*"
1959	Anthony Tovatt	*Books for You: A List for Leisure Reading for Use by Students in Senior High School*
1961	Anthony Tovatt	(Supplement) "1961–1962 Supplement to *Books for You*"
1964	Richard S. Alm	*Books for You: A Reading List for Senior High School Students*
1971	Jean A. Wilson	*Books for You: A Reading List for Senior High School Students*
1976	Kenneth Donelson	*Books for You: A Booklist for Senior High Students*
1982	Robert C. Small	*Books for You: A Booklist for Senior High Students*
1985	Donald R. Gallo	*Books for You: A Booklist for Senior High Students*
1988	Richard F. Abrahamson Betty Carter	*Books for You: A Booklist for Senior High Students*

Figure 5. List of *Books for You* chairs/editors and dates of publication of revised booklists.

Figure 5 *(Cont.)*

1992	Shirley Wurth	*Books for You: A Booklist for Senior High Students*
1995	Leila Christenbury	*Books for You: An Annotated Booklist for Senior High Students*
1997	Lois Stover Stephanie F. Zenker	*Books for You: An Annotated Booklist for Senior High Students*
2001	Kylene Beers Teri S. Lesesne	*Books for You: An Annotated Booklist for Senior High Students*

only person who worries about whether he is a coward, or who is concerned about his physical appearance, or who feels left out at a dance. These books are all centered in the lives of young adults between the ages of sixteen and twenty. There are also a handful of factual books giving authoritative information about how to get along with others. (p. 13)

These chapter introductions were continued in the 1959 edition (although they were much shorter), and then were stopped. The 1995 Stover and Zenker edition and this current edition both pay homage to Carlsen by beginning each chapter with a brief quotation from someone of note to set the stage for books included in that chapter.

In addition to chapter introductions, Carlsen placed at the beginning of each chapter a "menu" to help readers create reading plans. He explained that the menus "offer a small taste of books that have something in common. The subjects range all the way from a menu of the world's great novels to a menu of cars, engines, and hot rods" (p. 4). He hoped these menus would offer readers ideas about, if not a sequence for, approaching particular categories of books.

Another format change appeared in the bibliographic information offered for each book. Until 1956, that information had included only author, title, and a suggested grade level. With the 1956 edition, author, title, publisher, and publication date appeared. Books "mature in content and style" were marked with an asterisk (*), and NF (for nonfiction) appeared at the end of the bibliographic entry for each nonfiction book. Grade-level designations disappeared. Although annotations were still very brief ("Debra tries her hand at sculpture—parakeets, dogs, and cats—and earns enough money to care for her needs" [p. 21]), the focus clearly became the needs and interests of teens. A chapter on humor was added, and a chapter on science fiction appeared for the first time. Information at the end of the book was expanded from a single title-author index to separate indexes for author and title and a list of addresses for publishers. With only 129 pages of annotations, this booklist was clearly not the longest; however, without a doubt, this edition of *Books for You* carried the mark of the man who would dedicate his life to writing about the power of young adult literature and the reading interests of teens.

The 1959 edition was compiled by a committee chaired by Anthony Tovatt, and included ALA member Margaret A. Edwards. Remembered now through the Margaret A. Edwards Award, which is given for lifetime achievement in young adult literature, Edwards brought her considerable expertise and stature to this book that was fast becoming one of the most important publications from NCTE (for a list of current Edwards Award recipients, see appendix A in this volume). This edition included paperback books, and the addresses of paperback book publishers were added to the backmatter. Although Carlsen's innovative table of contents disappears, it's interesting to note that the chapter titled "Careers to Consider" includes a subcategory called "A Woman's Place." Carlsen's lengthy chapter introductions, designed to guide students through the books included in the chapter, are replaced with shorter introductions that focus less on readers and more on books. For instance, the chapter titled "Society's Problems" begins:

> How is it that people can be poverty stricken in a land that has food to store? How can we preach freedom when many of our people are denied equality because of race or creed? Why is it that man periodically gets embroiled in a war that nobody wants? Here are stories that are centered in the lives of people enmeshed in some of the varying problems of our times. (p. 68)

The format of *Books for You* changed again in 1964 when the book was published as a smaller, pocket-size paperback. This pocket-size format continued through the 1976 edition. Along with the smaller size came a shorter title: *Books for You: A Reading List for Senior High School Students.* The 1964 edition saw additional changes, such as the inclusion of short stories and books about race relations and desegregation. This edition continued the practice of using an asterisk to indicate books with mature content, and also used a small dagger to indicate "a book of marked literary quality." One of the longest lists, with over two thousand titles, this edition contained titles from previous editions as well as about nine hundred new titles.

The 1971 edition offered more books that included "serious issues" such as racism, prejudice, alcoholism, and the difficulties of growing up. This edition, created by the committee chaired by Jean Wilson, appears to be the final edition in which an ALA member was required to serve on the committee. However, the connection with ALA certainly continued, as evidenced by the number of committee members who are librarians, as well as by Betty Carter's co-chairing of the 1988 committee. Carter is a long-time and respected member of ALA who has served on numerous ALA booklist committees. Additionally, Michael Cart, a former president of the ALA Young Adult Literature Youth Services Association, wrote the foreword to the current edition.

The 1976 edition, newly titled *Books for You: A Booklist for Senior High Students,* is mislabeled the "6th edition" instead of the 7th edition, and thereby created a bit of confusion. This edition was definitely representative of the times, as seen in chapter titles such as "I Am Woman," "Ethnic Experiences," "Popular Culture," and "Mass Media." The "Our Religions" chapter was no longer based exclusively on Christianity, but included selections from other world religions. This edition confronted censorship head-on when Kenneth Donelson wrote in his "Introduction to the Student":

> We have indicated in the annotations of some books that they have explicit sexual scenes or some language which may be offensive to some readers; but modern literature is frank and realistic, so you should be warned that we may not have spelled out all the problems you or your friends may see in a book. A few teachers and librarians suggested that we note certain controversial books with statements like "This book is antifeminist" or "Some readers may object to the racism implied." Yet almost every book could be objected to by someone for some reason. . . . To leave out a book simply because of a hypothetical objection to it was not a convincing argument to us. You are therefore warned that some books included here may offend, irritate, or anger you. But books that please and books that disturb may serve equally valid purposes by making you think or by challenging your beliefs. A book, almost by definition, is subversive: it can alter what you believe to be true by testing ideas or theory you have too easily accepted. (p. 3)

1982–2001 Editions

The 1982 edition not only changed the size of *Books for You,* from a pocket-size paperback to a larger trade-size paperback, but it also narrowed the scope of what is published in *Books for You.* Until that time, all books in print were considered for inclusion in each edition. In fact, the preface to the 1964 edition noted that the committee not only "retained all the titles still in print which seemed to us suitable for the list" but that "titles, and in some instances, annotations, have remained the same, from one edition to another" (p. xii). This practice of carrying forward book titles stopped with the 1982 edition. From that point on, the booklist committee considered only titles published since the previous edition.

Also beginning with this edition, the table of contents became an alphabetical listing of topics or genres, annotations became longer, and artwork that occasionally appeared throughout the pages of *Books for You* disappeared. In this and all subsequent editions, it became the norm rather than the exception for readers to find books about previously taboo subjects such as sex, homosexuality, teenage pregnancy and abortion, drugs and alcohol, low self-esteem and self-image, divorce, abuse, rape, anorexia, violence, horror, witchcraft and the occult. Books now considered classics in young adult literature, such as *I Am the Cheese, The Chocolate War, Go Ask Alice,* and *Jacob Have I Loved,* appeared in this edition.

The 1985 edition reflected the societal changes in science and technology with the inclusion of chapters on computers and space exploration, in addition to the ever-present "Science" chapter. Books focusing on the tough issues teens face continued to be included as evidenced by chapters titled "Death and Suicide," "Drugs and Alcohol," and "Sexuality." The chapter titled "Holocaust" included autobiographical accounts of the Holocaust. This edition also included a section of "Easy Reading," which appeared in some other editions and was a precursor to a new booklist called *High Interest—Easy Reading.*

Abrahamson and Carter's 1988 edition included a chapter on diaries, journals, and oral histories. In addition, a chapter titled "Your Health and Your Body" included books that deal with the most serious health development of the twentieth century: AIDS.

The 1992 edition changed the indexing system so that each annotation is numbered within each chapter. This tracking system allows a reader to look up a topic such as *divorce* in the index, and find the exact annotation to consult rather than just a page number.

The 1995 edition changed the title again, this time to *Books for You: An Annotated Booklist for Senior High.* Furthermore, the trim size of the book was increased, a foreword written by a trade book author was added, and the number of indexes was expanded to three: author, title, and subject. The 1997 edition retained each of these changes, expanded the appendixes to include multicultural and world literature titles, and began each chapter with a brief quotation. The current edition follows closely the format of the previous two editions.

Final Words

On a personal note, to have served as editor of this edition of *Books for You* with co-editor Teri Lesesne, who long ago passed the boundary of colleague and became a close friend, has been a real highlight in my connection with the National Council of Teachers of English. As a committee member for the 1988 edition of *Books for You,* and as co-editor of the 1996 edition of *Your Reading,* my professional life has long been intertwined with the NCTE booklists. My reading has been shaped not only by the books included in the many editions of the NCTE booklists, but also by the work of the editors of *Books for You.* This booklist has not only endured, but has remained a highlight for the Council, largely because of the work of committee members and previous editors who gave their best to this booklist and to young adult literature, teachers, and students. The roll call of editors is impressive: Herzberg, Neville, Carlsen, Tovatt, Alm, Wilson, Donelson, Small, Gallo, Abrahamson and Carter, Wurth, Christenbury, and Stover and Zenker. From each of them, we've learned much about readers, about books, and about connecting the two. Many thanks to those former editors and their committees, and best of luck to the future editors and their committee members, who will most certainly continue the goal of helping teachers and librarians find books they can confidently hand to students while saying, "These look like some books for you."

Kylene Beers, co-editor
14th edition
Books for You

Note: Many thanks to Cheri Cameron, librarian/archivist for the National Council of Teachers of English. Cheri answered questions, found references to Books for You *in decades-old executive committee minutes, located those first booklists, faxed me copy after copy after copy of anything I needed, checked my interpretations of facts and dates, and generally acted as a cross between a super sleuth and a head engineer in the construction of this history. Without her help, this account would be nothing other than an idea I mentioned one day in passing to Pete Feely.*

Author Index

Subject Index

Haiti, 13.1, 21.2
Haitians and Haitian Americans, 8.19,
    13.1, 21.2, 25.12
Hale, Clara "Mother," 4.3
Haley, Alex, 4.37
Hall of Fame, Baseball, 27.31
Hall, Donald, 18.4
Halloween, 15.13, 15.20
Handbooks and manuals, 1.44, 2.1,
    2.8–2.10, 2.17, 26.3, 26.17, 29.14
Harlem Renaissance, 18.20
Harley-Davidson, 29.13
Harper's Ferry, 4.5, 12.72, 32.21
Harvest, 30.3
Hate crimes, 21.5, 21.8
Hatfield-McCoy feud, 12.71
Haunted houses, 9.53, 12.40, 15.41, 25.42
Havel, Vaclav, 7.11
Hawaii, 8.54, 10.53, 10.62
Hayden, Lewis, 32.21
Health, emotional, 10.29
Health, physical, 17.1, 17.3, 17.4, 17.6,
    17.9–17.11, 17.13–17.15, 17.18, 17.21,
    17.22, 24.8, 24.17, 24.20
Hearing impairment and deafness, 12.61,
    21.19
Heaven, 20.16, 25.29
Helen of Troy, 12.54
Henry VIII, 12.56
Hermits, 1.2
Heroes and heroines, 16.20, 16.25
Heroin, 10.10
Hidden treasure, 15.51, 15.58
High school, 10.51, 12.14, 22.24 (*see also*
    School)
Hiking, 1.17, 1.28, 1.36, 1.44, 15.31
Hill, Grant, 27.30
Hinckley, John, 21.13
Hinduism, 16.14, 20.5, 20.15
Hispanic Americans and Latino
    Americans, 4.11, 10.19, 18.23, 22.7
Historical documents, 32.6
History, 1.10, 1.41, 3.2, 3.10, 3.13, 3.15, 7.3,
    7.19, 13.1–13.40, 16.19
History, African American, 13.5, 13.8,
    13.16, 13.17, 13.18, 13.20, 13.21, 13.23,
    13.27, 13.32, 19.17, 24.28
History, British, 12.56
History, French, 12.26
History, Irish, 32.2
History, Jewish, 12.46
History, sports, 27.1, 27.2, 27.12, 27.25,
    27.27, 27.29
History, state, 13.3

History, U.S., 4.2, 4.5, 4.17, 10.23, 12.48, 12.59,
    13.1–13.6, 13.8–13.13, 13.16–13.23,
    13.26, 13.27, 13.30, 13.32, 13.34–13.36,
    13.38, 13.40, 17.15, 19.6, 21.6, 21.16,
    24.3, 24.4, 25.19, 29.3, 29.5, 29.10, 30.10,
    30.15, 30.19, 32.1, 32.2, 32.6–32.9, 32.20
History, world, 11.10, 13.15, 13.29, 20.5,
    20.15, 20.19, 27.3, 30.8, 30.15, 32.4
History of television, 28.5
Hitchhiking, 15.40
Hitler, Adolf, 32.4, 32.5, 32.23
Holiday celebrations, 8.16, 15.13, 15.20 (*see
    also* Parties and celebrations)
Hollerith, Herman, 6.17
Hollywood, 10.7, 10.34, 10.59
Holmes, Sherlock, 15.44
Holocaust, 4.27, 12.2, 12.43, 12.49, 12.51,
    12.53, 12.84, 13.28, 32.3, 32.4, 32.5,
    32.15, 32.16, 32.19
Home schooling, 9.2, 15.1
Homelessness, 8.37, 10.22, 10.46, 21.1
Homophobia, 21.5, 21.8
Homosexuality, 8.31, 8.36, 9.7, 10.5, 10.21,
    10.33, 10.62, 16.9, 22.33, 24.18, 24.21,
    25.8, 25.14
Honesty, 10.35, 22.24
Hood, Robin, 12.9, 16.4, 16.23
Hopper, Grace, 6.17
Horror and suspense, 1.29, 9.53, 15.3, 15.4,
    15.21, 15.24, 15.30, 15.32, 15.33, 15.47,
    15.52, 15.59, 15.63, 16.18, 23.1, 23.17,
    25.9, 25.11, 25.15, 25.16, 25.26, 25.35,
    25.42, 33.8
Horses, 1.3, 2.6, 8.66, 15.57
Hospitals, 12.62, 17.15, 22.2
Hot rods, 29.11
Houses and homes, 3.1
Housman, A. E., 18.25
How-to books, 1.36, 1.44, 3.3, 3.4, 3.14,
    3.19, 6.5, 6.10, 6.14, 6.18, 6.19, 7.18,
    14.1, 14.3, 14.8, 14.10, 17.12, 18.1,
    18.17, 19.3, 19.7, 19.8, 19.10, 24.28, 26.1,
    26.2, 27.14, 27.21, 27.26, 27.34, 29.14,
    33.2, 33.4, 33.9
HTML (*see* Hypertext Markup Language)
Hubble Space Telescope, 26.6
Hubble, Edwin, 26.9
Hughes, Langston, 18.20, 33.11
Human rights, 4.12, 21.4, 21.10, 21.14
Humor, 2.5, 9.27, 9.44–9.46, 9.48, 10.3, 10.12,
    10.52, 12.17, 12.29, 15.55, 16.11, 16.21,
    18.14, 18.15, 22.6, 22.11, 22.13, 22.18,
    22.20, 22.29, 22.30–22.32, 22.34, 23.16,
    25.7, 25.8, 25.25, 25.37, 25.38, 27.8

National Football League (NFL), 27.7
National Socialist Party (Nazi Party), 12.2,
    12.51, 12.81, 32.5, 32.15
Native Americans, 1.11, 1.13, 1.19, 1.20,
    4.26, 8.10, 8.23, 9.51, 12.7, 12.21, 12.52,
    12.64, 12.65, 12.73, 13.7, 13.8, 13.10,
    13.36, 13.38, 13.39, 16.26, 18.16, 22.27,
    27.29, 30.8
Natural resources, 7.10
Nature, 1.30, 1.36, 1.39, 1.44, 1.46, 2.13,
    2.16, 3.4, 7.2, 7.12, 7.13, 7.15, 7.17,
    10.63, 12.73, 18.2, 18.10, 18.23, 22.27
Nature, laws of, 14.4
Navigation, 11.9
Nazis (*see* National Socialist Party)
Neighborhoods, 10.19
Neglect (*see* Abandonment and neglect;
    Child abuse)
Nevada, 12.44, 15.3
New Deal, 13.34
New Kids on the Block, 28.4
New Mexico, 16.26
New Testament, 20.14
New York, 10.43, 12.7, 23.25
New Zealand, 1.17
Newfoundland, 12.39
Newspapers, 22.32, 32.23
Nicklaus, Jack, 27.3
Nietzsche, Friedrich, 20.12
Nixon, Richard, 21.7
Nobile, Umberto, 1.48
Norman, Greg, 27.3
North America, 11.4
North Pole, 1.48
Northwest Territories, 1.19
Norway, 12.62
Novac, Ana, 32.18
Nuclear power, 7.6
Nurses, 32.14
Nurturing (*see* Caring and nurturing)
Nutrition, 17.3, 17.9, 17.18, 17.22, 24.17

Obesity, 8.20, 8.28, 22.6, 22.13
Obsession, 10.15
Obsessive-compulsive behavior, 10.27, 10.58
Ocean, 2.3 (*see also* Water, bodies of)
O'Grady, Scott, 4.30
Ohio, 12.73
Ojibwe people, 1.11
Oklahoma, 8.37, 12.31
Old Testament, 20.14
Olympics, 27.9, 27.20

Oppression, 25.12
Oral histories, 13.18
Oregon, 12.14
Orozco, Jose Clemente, 3.5
Orphan Trains, 12.63
Orphans, 1.21, 12.17, 12.52, 12.55, 12.59,
    12.69
Outer space, 26.2, 26.4–26.12, 26.14, 26.16,
    31.6 (*see also* Astronomers and astron-
    omy; Planets; Solar system; Star
    charts; Stargazing)

Painting, 3.5, 3.6, 3.8, 3.14, 3.17
Pakistan, 21.14
Paleontologists, 23.1
Paleontology, 2.14, 11.5
Palindromes, 30.1
Palmer, Arnold, 27.3
Pandemics (*see* Epidemics and
    pandemics)
Paranormal activities, 31.3
Parent-child relationships, 8.1, 8.32, 10.2,
    12.34, 17.23, 18.1, 24.23
Parenting, 17.12
Parents, 10.51, 12.30, 24.25, 25.6
Parties and celebrations, 15.7 (*see also*
    Holiday celebrations)
Pawnee nation, 12.52
Peale, Charles Willson, 12.48
Peer pressure, 10.24, 20.7, 22.24, 24.6,
    24.20, 25.6, 25.10
Peer relationships, 1.23
Penguins, 2.12
Pennsylvania, 12.16
Persecution, 12.55, 12.81, 13.39, 32.15
Perseverance (*see* Determination and
    inner strength)
Personal narratives (*see* Narratives,
    personal)
Peru, 10.1
Pets and companion animals, 2.1, 2.8–2.10,
    2.17, 18.14
Pfetzer, Mark, 1.40, 4.32
Pharmacology, 7.17
Philanthropy, 4.19
Philosophy and philosophers, 20.12
Photography, 2.12, 3.2, 3.4, 3.7, 3.10, 3.12,
    3.15, 7.12
Photohistory, 27.5
Physical abuse, 8.22, 8.26, 8.36, 8.42, 8.51,
    10.50, 10.55, 15.9, 15.22, 15.29, 21.1,
    25.33

Title Index

Editors

Kylene Beers is a veteran middle school teacher who has turned her commitment to helping struggling readers into the major focus of her research, writing, speaking, and teaching. Now an assistant clinical professor at the University of Houston, she continues to spend much of her time in classrooms collaborating with teachers on developing strategies for helping students become skilled and engaged readers of literary and informational texts. Beers is editor of *Voices from the Middle*, co-editor of the widely read professional text *Into Focus: Understanding and Creating Middle School Readers*, and former co-editor of the NCTE middle school/junior high booklist, *Your Reading*. Beers serves on the review boards for NCTE's *English Journal* and *The ALAN Review*. She frequently presents at state and national conferences.

Teri S. Lesesne is an associate professor in the department of library science at Sam Houston State University where she teaches classes in children's and young adult literature at the graduate and undergraduate levels. A former middle school English teacher, department chair, and gifted education coordinator, Teri has been teaching at the university for eleven years. She coordinates an annual young adult literature conference each fall that draws teachers and librarians from across the state to meet noted authors and experts in the field of YA literature. Teri is past president of the Texas Council of Teachers of English and the Greater Houston Area Reading Council. She is president-elect of the Assembly on Literature for Adolescents of the National Council of Teachers of English (ALAN). She has also served on the committees to revise prior editions of *Books for You* and *Your Reading*.

In her spare time, Teri reads and spends time with her granddaughters. She is a licensed motorcyclist and enjoys riding the back roads of Texas. She is much in demand as a speaker for children, teachers, and librarians. Last year she spoke to more than five thousand children and several hundred teachers about the power of books and reading.

This book was typeset in Palatino and Helvetica by Precision Graphics.
Typefaces used on the cover were University Roman and Palatino.
The book was printed on 50 lb. White Williamsburg by Versa Press.